HIDDEN LAWS

ROBINSON WOODWARD-BURNS

Hidden Laws

How State Constitutions
Stabilize American Politics

Yale
UNIVERSITY PRESS
NEW HAVEN & LONDON

Published with assistance from the foundation established in memory of William McKean Brown.

Copyright © 2021 by Robinson Woodward-Burns.
All rights reserved. This book may not be reproduced, in whole or in part, including illustrations, in any form (beyond that copying permitted by Sections 107 and 108 of the U.S. Copyright Law and except by reviewers for the public press), without written permission from the publishers.

Yale University Press books may be purchased in quantity for educational, business, or promotional use. For information, please e-mail sales.press@yale.edu (U.S. office) or sales@yaleup.co.uk (U.K. office).

Set in Times Roman type by Integrated Publishing Solutions, Grand Rapids, Michigan.
Printed in the United States of America.

Library of Congress Control Number: 2020945831
ISBN 978-0-300-24869-2 (paper: alk. paper)

A catalogue record for this book is available from the British Library.

10 9 8 7 6 5 4 3 2 1

To Mom and Dad

CONTENTS

Acknowledgments   ix

1 Rethinking American Constitutional Development   1

2 First Conventions, 1760–1791   24

3 Antebellum Consensus, 1792–1849   47

4 State Reconstruction, 1850–1877   66

5 Progressive Experimentation, 1878–1931   90

6 Welfare States, 1932–1979   145

7 Contemporary Constitutionalism, 1980–2020   179

Appendices   195
Notes   221
Bibliography   295
Index   331

ACKNOWLEDGMENTS

I HAVE ACCUMULATED MANY DEBTS IN writing this book. First is to Rogers Smith, my dissertation advisor at the University of Pennsylvania. Rogers shepherded the project from proposal to dissertation to manuscript to publication. His advice was always swift and sage. Mark Graber mentored me at the University of Maryland, joined my committee at Penn, and guided my understanding of American constitutional law. Anne Norton also shaped the project, first with a seminar on radical democracy and then as a committee member. Jeff Green too shaped the book by encouraging my work on American political thought.

A few other scholars and friends gave the manuscript careful readings. I am grateful for thorough review and comments from David Bateman, Thomas Bell, William Blake, John Dinan, Connor Ewing, Anthony Grasso, Anthony Ives, Stephan Stohler, Alan Tarr, Brianne Wolf, Joanna Wuest, and Charles Zug. Useful discussions on the manuscript and the discipline came from Penn colleagues Ellen Donnelly, Alex Garlick, Danielle Hanley, Juman Kim, Greg Koutnik, James Morone, Nate Shils, Tim Weaver, and Elspeth Wilson. I also benefited from advice from Sean Beienberg, Nolan Bennett, Josh Braver, Paul Herron, Carol Nackenoff, Julie Novkov, Carole Sargent, Peter Wissoker, and Emily Zackin.

I am thankful for support from my Howard colleagues. Niambi Carter, Kwame Dixon, Keneshia Grant, Daryl Harris, Ron Hira, Keesha Middlemass, and Rick Seltzer gave thoughtful guidance on the manuscript and the publication process. Conversations with Howard graduate students advanced the project, as did start-up and summer research grants from the university. Comments from panels and talks at the University of Maryland School of Law, Georgetown

University Department of Government, and the annual meetings of the American Political Science Association and Western Political Science Association also honed my argument.

I would like to thank William Frucht at Yale University Press for his guidance and advice. I am also indebted to Karen Olson for her assistance in preparing the manuscript for publication, Joyce Ippolito for her work on production, Andrew Katz for his thorough, excellent copy editing, Bob Land for proofreading, and Enid Zafran for indexing the manuscript. Thoughtful comments from two anonymous reviewers helped me clarify my theory and tighten my arguments.

Finally, I would like to thank my parents. This book belongs to them.

HIDDEN LAWS

1
Rethinking American Constitutional Development

> *The question of the relation of the States to the Federal Government is the cardinal question of our constitutional system. At every turn of our national development we have been brought face to face with it, and no definition either of statesmen or of judges has ever quieted or decided it.*
> —Woodrow Wilson, Constitutional Government in the United States, *1908*

WE MISUNDERSTAND AMERICAN CONSTITUTIONAL development. Most accounts of American constitutionalism focus on national political institutions, not on state constitutionalism. This book argues that state constitutional reform guides national constitutional development. In ignoring state constitutional politics, we risk misinterpreting national politics.

This is a bold claim. It can be demonstrated by considering the federal Constitution's longevity. The United States boasts the world's first and oldest national constitution. Stability defines the document. Americans have ratified only 27 of the 11,969 proposed amendments, never convened to replace the Constitution, and rarely significantly reinterpret the document. Comparatively stable, the federal Constitution undergirds American political institutions. In contrast, Americans have called 411 state constitutional revision assemblies, ratified 144 constitutions, held 255 state constitutional conventions, proposed 11,635 amendments to the current state constitutions, ratified 7,695, and repeatedly reinterpreted these documents.[1] What explains this difference?

I argue that state constitutional revision often resolves national constitutional controversies, preventing national reform. Shifting controversy to the states destabilizes the states while stabilizing national political development.

Liberal constitutions entail a contradiction. They durably entrench rules against reform while also authorizing the people to reform these rules. These two aims, promising both stability and flexibility, are opposed. In the American context, new, growing, and excluded groups may attempt national constitutional reform but rarely draw enough support to clear federal amendment supermajority requirements, to strong-arm or oust entrenched judicial elites, or to force widespread popular constitutional reinterpretation.[2] Further, the extraordinary consensus required for a national amendment or for significant reinterpretation means that each major reform is a compromise, functional but imperfect, deferring controversy. This gap between evolving civic aspirations and entrenched legal realties plagues all constitutions but perhaps none more than the U.S. Constitution, which both promises and impedes active democratic legitimization. Thwarted reformers can instead gradually reinterpret and rework existing clauses, pitting clauses and doctrines against each other, exacerbating controversy. Unable to adapt by amendment, the federal Constitution is turned against itself. The Constitution's extreme inflexibility threatens the document's survival. How has the Constitution survived?

This book details how this pressure, mediated through a process I call *conflict decentralization*, yields constitutional reform. A few brief clauses in the federal Constitution create overlapping, concurrent powers shared by the state and federal governments.[3] This brevity grants elites and reformers broad interpretive leeway to construct and often enlarge the overlap, strategically channeling national reform pressure and power to the states, stabilizing and guiding national political development.

I theorize that this logic of conflict decentralization follows a pattern. Constitutional controversy can emerge at the national or state level. This can force reform at the national or state level, yielding four possible paths: preemption, devolution, elevation, and obviation. Within each path, federal involvement can be active or passive, yielding alternative subpaths (table 1).

Preemption occurs when national controversy yields national reform. This happens through exclusion or supersession. Federal exclusion of state law is passive. In cases of exclusion, the federal government maintains powers already expressly denied to the states, yielding solely national reform. This includes, for example, congressional power to make war, treaties, and post offices. But the

Table 1. Patterns in Federal Constitutional Development

Path	Pressure	Reform	Process	Example
Preemption	National	National	National exclusion of states	Treaty-making
			National supersession of states	Interstate commerce
Devolution	National	State	National deference to states	Balanced-budget amendments
			National dictation to states	National voting age minimums
Elevation	State	National	State convergence and national imitation	Female suffrage
			State divergence and national intervention	Slavery
Obviation	State	State	State preclusion and national inaction	Jeffersonian franchise expansion
			State circumvention and national inaction	Jim Crow laws

Constitution lists few exclusive federal powers, leaving all other matters subject to construction as shared, concurrent powers. Federal supersession of state law is active. In cases of supersession, federal actors—often judges—initiate change, invoking the Constitution, often through the Supremacy or Commerce Clauses, to preempt contradictory concurrent state lawmaking, yielding only federal reform. For example, federal judges have forbidden state laws conflicting with congressional interstate commerce regulations.[4]

Devolution occurs when national controversy yields state reform. Devolution happens through deference or dictation. Federal deference to state law is passive. In cases of deference, national actors leave national controversies to the states, forcing state reform. States have broad constitutional powers to regulate voting under the Elections Clause, to design "republican" governments under the Guarantee Clause, and to secure health, safety, morals, and general welfare under the Tenth Amendment, which also allows the states all powers not delegated to the federal government or forbidden to the states. Fiscal reform followed a process of deference in the late twentieth century—after federal balanced-budget amendments failed in Congress, reformers pushed the states to ratify similar state amendments. Federal dictation of state law is active. In cases of dictation, national actors force the states to address national concerns. Congress has made states affirm each other's laws under the Privileges and Immunities and Full Faith and Credit Clauses and directed state labor, citizenship, suffrage, and liquor laws under the Thirteenth, Fourteenth, Fifteenth, Eighteenth, Nineteenth, Twenty-Fourth, and Twenty-Sixth Amendments. For example, Congress passed the Twenty-Sixth Amendment to forbid states from disenfranchising citizens eighteen or older. Devolution of conflict is therefore not the same as devolution of authority—in cases of deference, the national government pushes both reform and constitutional authority on the states, while in cases of dictation, it pushes reform on the states without ceding ultimate authority.[5]

National actors use devolution strategically. Reformers blocked by the high barriers to Article V amendment or by federal judges may push for reform among the states, which have lower bars to constitutional amendment and often elect their judges. Political maneuvering and agenda setting are also at work. Constitutional and civic controversies can internally divide national parties and empower marginal coalitions and actors. In response, presidents and congressional leadership can retrench their power by gagging divisive, cross-cutting constitutional issues in Congress, leaving them to the states.[6] Proactive federal judges may dictate or defer issues to the state courts and constitutions to preempt confrontation with a hostile Congress or to avoid thorny or protracted legal battles. Paradoxically, national institutions exercise power by limiting themselves, narrowing the scope of national conflict, and venting conflict, by pushing divisive issues on the states.[7]

Elevation occurs when state constitutional controversy yields national reform. Elevation happens through convergence or divergence. Federal response to state convergence is passive and reactive. In cases of convergence, states unite around one or several constitutional policies, which federal actors then adopt. For example, after most states enfranchised women, it became electorally risky for congressional incumbents representing these franchise states, and thus relying on the female vote, to resist a federal female suffrage amendment. Federal response to state divergence is active. In cases of divergence, conflicting state constitutional law forces federal actors to impose a uniform national standard. For example, discordant state-level slavery regulation forced the Supreme Court and Congress to enact national slave law in the 1850s. Through convergence and divergence, the states act, in Justice Louis Brandeis's words, as laboratories of democracy, attempting "novel social and economic experiments."[8]

Obviation occurs when state constitutional controversy yields state reform. Obviation happens through preclusion or circumvention. Federal response to state preclusion is passive. In cases of preclusion, states address and resolve state-level constitutional conflict, preventing that issue from pressuring federal actors. Attempting widespread state constitutional revision can exhaust or fracture a nascent reform movement across states or alternately can appease reformers, preventing reform issues from affecting national institutions. For example, in the Jeffersonian era, state constitutional framers repealed the taxpaying and property qualifications that disenfranchised workingmen, placating reformers, who never took their constitutional grievances to members of Congress. And diverse, seemingly parochial state constitutional provisions can create a national patchwork that lets mobile residents, litigants, or reformers pick a state that satisfies their aims, forestalling petitions to the national government. Preclusion is akin to the dog that did not bark, describing the nationally salient constitutional controversies that rarely appear in congressional or federal court records but are present in state debates. Federal response to state circumvention is active, if limited. In cases of circumvention, states address and regulate an issue, with the federal government considering but refusing similar reform, leaving the states to continue revision. For example, as Southern states constitutionally entrenched racial discrimination, Congress considered but ultimately rejected intervention, letting states finish constitutionalizing Jim Crow. Like deference, here the federal government leaves matters to the states, but in cases of circumvention, these constitutional matters begin and end at the state level.

These four paths—preemption, devolution, elevation, and obviation—are ideal types. In practice, these paths may occur partially or completely, often over several cycles, as state reform may prompt failed national reform, renewing attempts at state reform. Reformers also blend paths. By framing a controversy as a concurrent powers matter, reformers can attempt change at the national level, state level, or both. Reformers may seek a congressional amendment or federal court decision to dictate policy against recalcitrant states but will face high Article V federal amendment barriers, divided Congresses, and gradualist judges. Reformers may instead circumvent Congress for laxer state constitutional amendment and convention processes and elected state courts but may find that these state reforms cannot bind national actors.[9] Reformers therefore usually attempt both national and state reform, opportunistically following the path of least resistance between national and state venues. Reformers may first redraft and reinterpret state constitutions, looking for early, easy victories before launching a larger, tougher national campaign. Or reformers may begin nationally but, if blocked by Article V, federal judges, or national elites and parties, may then look to the states. Or reformers may work simultaneously at both levels.

While there are incentives for reformers to attempt both state and national reform, the most common outcome is state reform without national reform. State constitutions have the flexibility the federal Constitution lacks—all states impose lower amendment thresholds and, with smaller legislatures, can better coordinate to propose revision by amendment, convention, or commission. In nearly all states, amendment ratification requires only a simple majority of voters. Consequently, two-thirds of attempted amendments to standing state constitutions have passed.[10] Failing amendment, in most states a simple majority of voters can let a convention or commission draft a new document, and fourteen states require these votes at least every twenty years. Eight states do not fully describe the procedure for calling a convention, and historically this underspecification was even more common, allowing frequent, extralegal popular conventions. Half of state constitution-making bodies have drafted and ratified new documents.[11]

This flexibility keeps state constitutions in constant flux. Easy revision lets state legislators pass partisan pork-barrel provisions, and so all state constitutions are longer than the federal one, on average quadruple the length.[12] This overspecificity limits state judges' interpretive leeway, further increasing reliance on constitutional amendment and replacement, relatively narrowing, though not eliminating, state-level judicial review.[13] And the public, to the extent it is aware that state constitutions exist, views these long, flexible documents as if they were ordinary statutes and so has few qualms with amendment or replacement. This channels state constitutionalism in a feedback loop, with frequent revision increasing state constitutional length and decreasing public veneration, incentivizing voters and lawmakers to further reform. The process, self-reinforcing and difficult to reverse, exemplifies path dependence, yielding hundreds of proposed state constitutions and thousands of amendments.[14] State constitutional revision is therefore a steady, constant, quiet background process in American politics, the heretofore largely unnoticed channel for most American constitutional development. Most paths to American constitutional reform pass through

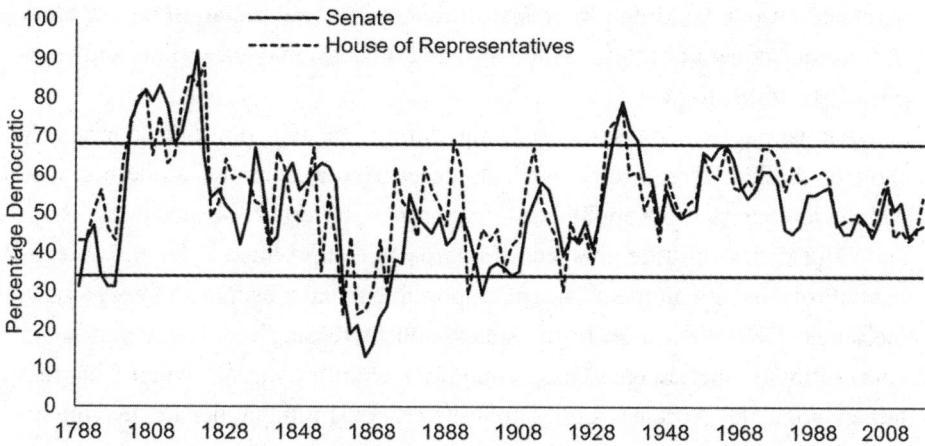

Fig. 1. Congressional party division, 1788–2020. Horizontal lines indicate thresholds for Article V passage. Pre-1828 data indicate percentage Democratic-Republican.

the states, whether through devolution, elevation, or obviation, guiding and stabilizing national constitutionalism. These three common paths are therefore the main concerns for this book.

This theory of conflict decentralization has a few implications for understanding American political development. First, a cyclical pattern emerges in the logic of conflict decentralization. The balance of congressional parties follows punctuated equilibrium, with long stretches of relative party parity interrupted by rare realignments granting one party fleeting bicameral Article V supermajorities (figure 1). Under one-party bicameral supermajorities, Congress can more easily pass Article V amendments and statutes to actively dictate a uniform constitutional policy across divergent states. This occurred during Reconstruction and the New Deal and the Great Society. Under party parity, Congress struggles to pass Article V amendments, deferring reform to the states, which may then converge. This occurred in the long Jacksonian, Progressive, and Reagan eras. Party realignment therefore guides conflict decentralization, with long periods of congressional parity, passivity, and deference to states and occasional state convergence, interrupted by momentary congressional unity and active dictation against divergent state laws. Reformers seeking amendment should and often do look first to the states during party parity and to Congress during party unity. This recurrent cycling between eras of deference and convergence on one hand and moments of divergence and dictation on the other occupy subsequent chapters, which also detail occasional exceptions and complications in this logic.

What happens when parties settle into durable, sustained parity, consistently short of Article V requirements? This describes the sclerotic modern era, in which Democrats and Republicans trade narrow, bitterly contested congressional majorities, with little prospect of interparty compromise or federal amendment. Proposed amendments, nearly impossible to pass, become token, partisan measures. Reformers look to the states, and increasingly only the states, for constitutional amendment. These conditions entail obviation, when Congress largely abdicates Article V duties and serious constitutional debate, leaving reformers to begin and end meaningful amendment campaigns at the state level.

This cyclical logic may also affect issue realignment in congressional parties. Writing in the desegregation era, V. O. Key asserted the states largely responded to national party realignments, trailing federal reform, especially in the South and especially on race.[15] Subsequent scholars attributed national party realignment not to state reform but rather to shifts in national ideologies, issue cleavages, and presidential regimes.[16] I posit that state constitutional reform can also nudge national parties to revise their platforms. Specifically, Article V and gradualist federal courts frustrate reform movements, incentivizing state reform and bottling reform pressure at the state level, where it builds until it clears discrete Article V barriers to amendment ratification, forcing amendment petitions to Congress, sometimes shifting congressional and national party platforms and membership toward convergence with the states. For example, suffragettes, rebuffed by Congress and the Supreme Court, built state chapters, won widespread state constitutional reform, and tactically pressured national parties for amendment. This pattern of convergence may explain the gradual "pressure buildup" that realignment scholars observe but, per David Mayhew, struggle to explain. Partisan and constitutional realignment may work in tandem.[17]

Second, scholars who neglect state constitutionalism risk mischaracterizing the development of national institutions. Imagine, for the sake of simplicity, that American constitutionalism is reduced to the federal courts and state constitutions, with national pressure emerging, filtering through both the federal courts and state constitutions and yielding national stability or instability (figure 2).

National outcomes attributed to the federal courts may instead be caused by

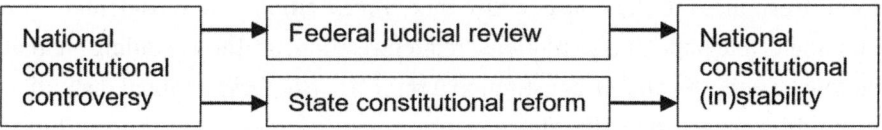

Fig. 2. The courts and states in national constitutional reform.

state constitutional reform. Scholars have praised the Supreme Court's 1966 *Harper v. Virginia Board of Elections* decision for echoing the 1964 Twenty-Fourth Amendment and outlawing the poll tax nationwide; however, by the time the Court, which had long upheld poll taxes, finally overruled the tax in *Harper,* all but four states had already statutorily or constitutionally outlawed the poll tax. State constitutional reformers, not federal judges, did the initial hard work.[18] National outcomes may change *after* judicial review but not solely *because of* judicial review. Ignoring state constitutionalism risks misattributing the influence of the states to the federal courts and thus mischaracterizing, however slightly, the role of the courts. In neglecting state constitutionalism, we not only have misunderstood a part of the American constitutional system but also risk misunderstanding the whole.

We may better understand federal judicial development by considering intersections with state constitutionalism. Consider the long-standing, central debate over whether unelected federal judges defy democratic majorities. Mark Tushnet and Larry Kramer voice this concern, while Robert Dahl and Mark Graber object that federal judges often support majoritarian positions established by Congress or the president. But in studying only the cases that receive certiorari, scholars in both camps may miss how the Court quietly denies certiorari to defer issues to the states.[19] Judges push reform on the states, whether acting as impartial arbiters deferring political questions to the states or as partisan tacticians preempting interbranch conflict by forcing thorny issues on the states.[20] Federal judges in the United States are therefore neither uniformly majoritarian nor uniformly countermajoritarian but rather are tactically deferential, pushing controversies to the states, which then may or may not reach a position consistent with national majorities. If the states do unite on a majority position, then federal judges may expressly imitate this—a case of convergence. This judicial imitation can defuse interbranch conflict.[21] Put differently, the United States' strong federal courts have helped obviate constitutional reform by Article V amendment but have often done so in ways that rely on state constitutional reform. Responses to the court-centric model may emphasize presidential, congressional, and popular constitutional reinterpretation, usefully detailing alternate national routes to national constitutional reform.[22] But these national institutions similarly defer reform to the states. In observing deference to state constitutionalism, we can better understand the development of these national institutions.

Third, reading federal amendments alongside parallel state amendments may change how we interpret these federal amendments. For example, the Fifteenth Amendment, forbidding disenfranchisement by race, is nearly textually identical to the Twenty-Fourth Amendment, forbidding disenfranchisement by poll tax. Congress framed both amendments to address state-level racial disenfranchisement. Yet these amendments functioned differently. Congress passed the Fifteenth Amendment to override noncompliant states, particularly in the South, which threatened to impose racial disenfranchisement schemes—a case of federal dictation. Conversely, by the ratification of the Twenty-Fourth Amendment, nearly all had already statutorily or constitutionally repealed their poll tax clauses—in this case, the Congress affirmed and nationalized a policy initiated by the states, an example of convergence.[23]

Finally, state constitutional reform makes national politics less dysfunctional. This book explains how Americans gradually abandoned the blunt tool of state nullification in favor of the subtler mechanism of venting pressure through ongoing state reform, letting state framers address, interpret, and resolve national constitutional issues. This state constitutional experimentation relaxes the old normative tension between constitutional inflexibility and popular sovereignty. The federal Constitution claims popular authorization but imposes high barriers to amendment, deferring or delaying democratic reform. Yet Americans regularly revise their state constitutions by amendment, convention, commission, and extralegal popular reform. Ongoing state constitutional revision makes American constitutionalism more legitimate. The national Constitution raises barriers to political action, but state constitutional flexibility invites reform and empowers reformers. Constitutions are not always constraints.

Lest these claims seem polemical, I do not deny the importance of national actors or of mainstream scholarly accounts, nor do I claim that all cases of national constitutional change involve the states. Rather, I suggest that state constitutional revision resolves most national conflict, quietly and consistently shaping the choices of national actors. To understand American political development, one must look to the states.

Canonical Explanations of American Constitutional Development

Consider mainstream accounts of American constitutional development. Many scholars neglect the state constitutions for the federal one. Scholars emphasize the Constitution's longevity and stability, credited to its high barriers to amendment. The document is notoriously difficult to amend. Article V requires that a proposed constitutional amendment clear either two-thirds of both houses of Congress or a convention called by two-thirds of states and then three-fourths of states' ratifying conventions or legislatures. The Supreme Court has upheld congressional provisions limiting this process to seven years.[24] All proposals to formally amend Article V—there have been hundreds—have themselves failed to clear these supermajority requirements, which grow even tougher with contemporary congressional and state legislative polarization.

Generations of scholars have therefore attributed the Constitution's stability to these Article V supermajority requirements. In 1888, the British Lord Bryce blamed the document's inflexibility on "the inherent disputatiousness and perversity (what the Americans call 'cussedness') of bodies of men. It is difficult to get two-thirds of two assemblies (the Houses of Congress) and three-fourths of thirty-eight commonwealths . . . to agree to the same proposition." In 1902, the progressive political scientist John William Burgess agreed that the Constitution's great "error lies in the artificially excessive majorities required in the production of constitutional changes."[25] Writing in 1929, Michael Musmanno reiterated this conclusion, as did Lester B. Orfield in 1942, Charles Leedham in 1964, Clement Vose in 1972, and Alan Grimes in 1978. Recently, Michael Kammen, Bruce Ackerman, and Robert Dahl have reaffirmed this Article V story. Sanford Levinson concludes, "Article V constitutes what may be the most important bars of our constitutional iron cage. . . . [It] has made it next to impossible to achieve such adaptation where amendment is thought to be necessary."[26]

But Article V alone cannot explain the Constitution's endurance. Some supermajorities that cleared Article V still failed to pass new amendments.[27] Additionally, Zachary Elkins, Tom Ginsburg, and James Melton find that inflexible national constitutions often cannot adapt to survive unexpected crises and that the United States has the world's least flexible national constitution. They therefore conclude that "Article V is neither necessary nor sufficient to explain constitutional change" in the United States.[28] To take the point further, if durable constitutions bend but do not break, then Article V's inflexibility makes the U.S. Constitution's stability all the more puzzling. Why, then, has the U.S. Constitution endured *despite* Article V?

We might instead attribute the Constitution's longevity to the broader coalition politics of constitutional reform. Presidents can ally with Congress, the states, and the public to push a proposed amendment past Article V. Since such harmony is rare, constitutional development might follow punctuated equilibrium, with long stretches of constitutional stability interrupted by moments of one-party control and systemic political and constitutional change. V. O. Key, Walter Dean Burnham, and James Sundquist establish this story of periodic partisan realignment, which Stephen Skowronek attributes partly to the leadership of skilled, reconstructive presidents and Bruce Ackerman, Larry Kramer, and Sidney Milkis and Daniel Tichenor trace to mass social movements. Thanks to the United States' Madisonian system of institutional power sharing and compromise, constitutional reform occurs glacially, with rare new amendments accreting on the old, reflecting bargaining between parties, presidents, Congress, and the people themselves.[29]

Constitutional reform occurs not only through amendment but also through reinterpretation. The Supreme Court has a special and often exclusive role in constitutional reinterpretation, preserving existing constitutional meanings. Per Robert Dahl, presidents and Congress appoint like-minded federal judges, which requires fewer congressional votes than does an amendment. Since partisan realignments in the White House and Congress are rare, so too are major realignments of the Court and constitutional interpretation. As Ran Hirschl puts it, these elites appoint judges "to entrench or 'lock in' their policy preferences against growing influence of 'peripheral' groups and interests," partly by slowing or dismissing appeals, narrowing their docket to preempt immediate constitutional reform. The Constitution's exceptional brevity and vagueness allow judges interpretive leeway to preserve or legitimize the status quo, reworking the Constitution through gradual common law reinterpretation, obviating formal amendment or replacement. Some theorists have therefore generalized that briefer national constitutions with judicial review will last longer.[30] Further, reformist judges lack enforcement powers, may have their jurisdiction narrowed by Congress, and may see powerful presidents or Congresses themselves seize the power of constitutional interpretation.[31]

Some scholars, including Larry Kramer, have instead looked beyond courts and political institutions to constitutional reinterpretation by the broader public. In this narrative, citizens circumvent the Article V amendment process and the federal courts to unilaterally reinterpret and even block enforcement of repugnant constitutional provisions, reforming the Constitution in practice. These extralegal protests rise only in moments of revolution or exception, since ordinary Americans usually venerate the Constitution.[32] Michael Kammen proposes that this public veneration has carried the Constitution through its toughest trials, arguing that "veneration has often become most intense as part of the process whereby controversies are resolved and issues reconciled." Robert Dahl and Sandy Levinson add that veneration allows the brief Constitution to age nearly unamended, further increasing veneration.[33] This feedback loop has preserved the document with little change.[34]

Yet these explanations, focusing on constitutional brevity, veneration, and gradual reinterpretation, raise more questions than they answer. On average, judicial review has little effect on the longevity of national constitutions. Moreover, detailed national constitutions tend to last longer.[35] If anything, these comparative findings suggest that the U.S. Constitution should be short-lived. The Constitution's longevity is still not fully explained.

In short, scholars explain American constitutional development, and relative stability, through Article V, through glacial partisan and institutional realignment, Supreme Court gradualism, and popular veneration. But in many countries, these factors instead are associated with national constitutional breakdown. Further, each account focuses mainly or exclusively on the national Constitution and branches.[36] I argue that they therefore cannot adequately explain American constitutional development.

Most scholars ignore the state constitutions. Progressive-era political scientists chronicled state constitutional change, but despite the recent return to historical institutionalism and American political development, the hundreds of dauntingly long, seemingly obscure state constitutions have deterred many scholars in political science, history, and law.[37] "The problem," the *New York Times* concluded, is that "the study of state law is considered parochial. Of even more vital interest to professors anxious to make a name for themselves, national reputations have generally been thought to come only by studying 'national law.'"[38] Scholars of American constitutionalism and political development have disregarded the state documents for the briefer, more stable and august federal one and thus have misunderstood both.

This is indeed a problem. Almost all American constitutional reform happens at the state level. Of the 7,722 amendments made to the standing fifty-one American constitutions, 99.6 percent have been state constitutional amendments. Similarly, the states have proposed drafting at least 290 constitutions and held 255 conventions, compared to the single federal Constitution and Convention. About 95 percent of American litigation is filed in state courts.[39] More importantly, states have special, often exclusive, prerogative to regulate positive rights, elections, grassroots initiatives and referenda, municipal law, and broad police powers. And, with uniformly lower barriers to constitutional revision, the states can experiment and reform law more easily than can gradualist, gridlocked national institutions. In focusing on the national Constitution, mainstream scholars miss almost all American constitutional reform and exaggerate the stability of American constitutionalism and politics generally.

A sparse but growing literature emphasizes state constitutionalism. Historians and lawyers chronicle particular eras,[40] regions,[41] intellectual traditions,[42] and rights and policy issues[43] but sometimes shy from systematically explaining constitutional development and duration.[44] More recently, political scientists have adeptly and usefully chronicled state constitutional conventions and amendments;[45] regulation of rights, family and marriage law, and prohibition;[46] and Western and Southern constitutional framing.[47] A few works carefully trace the full arc of state constitutional development,[48] and others speculate that the federal Constitution opens space for state experimentation.[49] Still, the field is new, and state constitutions remain understudied.

Observing Conflict Decentralization

The central claim of this book is that through conflict decentralization, state constitutional reform guides and stabilizes national constitutional development. Constitutional reform takes many shapes. Reform, whether state or national, includes constitutional amendment and replacement, judicial review, and executive, legislative, and popular reinterpretation. Frequent, unprecedented, or fundamental reform can qualify as instability. Identifying destabilizing reform therefore requires case studies, as this section explains.[50]

I observe national constitutional reform as amendment, judicial review, and executive, legislative, and popular reinterpretation. Amendments are easier to observe. Since Article V requires amendments be submitted to Congress, I use the congressional record to build a data set of all 11,969 federal amendments proposed from 1788 to 2020. As Michael Kammen notes, knowledge of these amendment proposals, "of their stimuli, and of the controversies they generated, is woefully limited." Recent accounts of these amendments rely on case studies or on inexact, speculative overviews. Darren Latham, for example, posits that amendment content has shifted from sweeping structural revisions to narrower partisan proposals but admits that his claims about the unratified amendments are "speculative" and "may seem far too superficial" given that "too much data remains inaccessible or un-obtained thus far." John R. Vile, David Strauss, and Aziz Huq each propose a similar shift in amendment content but stop short of a conclusive claim, which "demands the application of econometric tools to large-n samples."[51]

This book fills that scholarly gap, coding and analyzing the nearly twelve thousand proposed amendments. I derive this data from an incomplete National Archives and Records Administration (NARA) data set. The NARA data set uses six congressional publications to collect amendment-level data on amendments' introduction date, resolution type, resolution number, chamber, committee, sponsor, sponsor state, and content description. I correct systematic errors in the NARA data and use the congressional record to hand code missing amendments and update the data to 2020. I code amendments by topic by identifying common policy-relevant terms across all amendment descriptions, then using conditional text string matching to identify individual amendments containing these terms. Since amendment descriptions often contain multiple policy-relevant terms, a single amendment can match for multiple topics, though almost all amendments (11,359) match for four topics or fewer. Using 98 topic variables, I code 11,648 of the 11,969 amendments by subject. This is probably the first systematic analysis of these amendments.[52]

Congressional amendment proposals vary over time. Figures 3 and 4 elaborate this. Members of Congress consistently engage some topics, like congressional, executive, and judicial powers, selection, terms, and removal, though these structures and powers topics predominated in the antebellum years, when members addressed periodic sectional and electoral controversies, leaving citizenship, voting, and policy matters to the states. Reconstruction and Progressive-era members proposed amendments reforming citizenship, suffrage, election, morality, marriage, education, and prohibition law. New Dealers intervened in labor and commerce, and by the mid-twentieth century, members of Congress

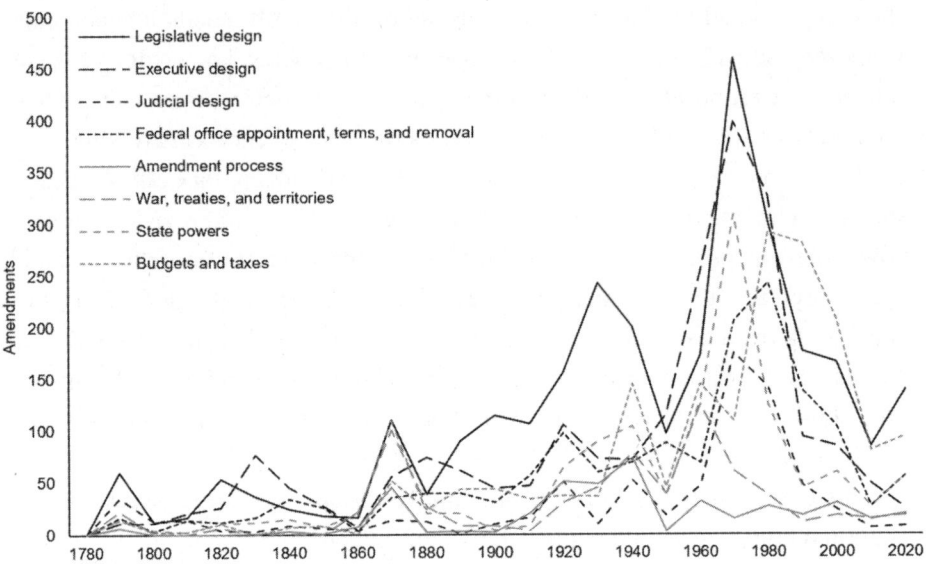

Fig. 3. Proposed federal structures and powers amendments, 1780–2020.

(often conservative) proposed amendments (often symbolic) to lower taxes, balance budgets, and reverse progressive Warren and Burger Court decisions on voting rights, legislative apportionment, busing, prayer, abortion, and flag burning. In sum, Congress has shifted from narrowly tailored structural reform amendments to broader rights, citizenship, and policy concerns. Subsequent chapters explore Congress's amendment behavior in greater detail by era.

But this aggregate amendment data cannot alone demonstrate national constitutional reform and instability. Amendment counts are only a rough approximation of national constitutional instability. Not all amendments are equally important. A single amendment could radically change a constitution's central commitments, while a slew of amendments on a topic could be inflated by duplicate amendments and not actually indicate meaningful change.[53] Significant reform targets a constitution's core normative provisions.[54] One might then give more weight to proposals amending these core commitments. But the United States' constitutional commitments are disputed, have contradictory interpretations, can inhere in multiple clauses, and can exist outside of the Constitution's text altogether, with their meanings varying by context and era.[55] Further, destabilizing reform also occurs outside Article V amendment, through judicial, congressional, presidential, and public constitutional reinterpretation.

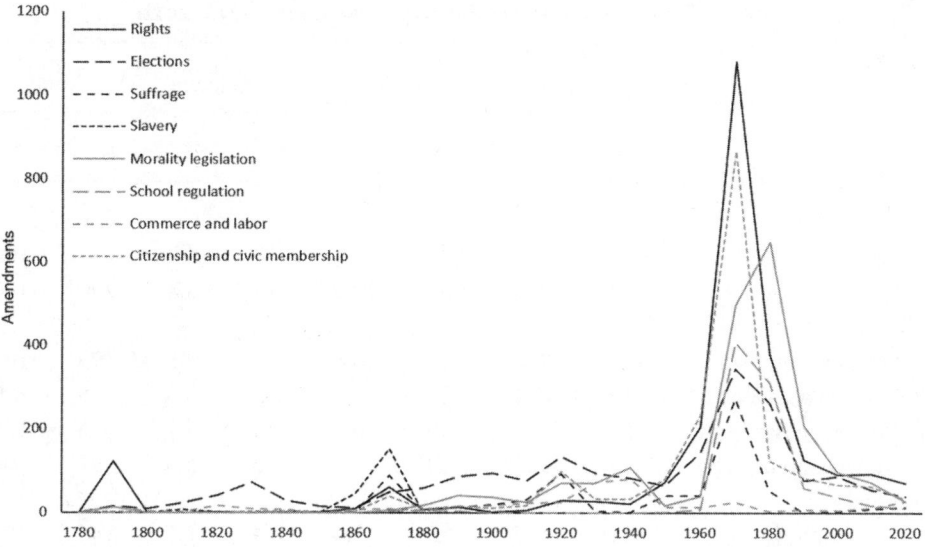

Fig. 4. Proposed federal rights and citizenship amendments, 1780–2020.

Therefore, this book additionally refers to federal judicial review and congressional, executive, and press records to observe attempted constitutional reform and reinterpretation.

State constitutional revision occurs through constitutional replacement, amendment, and reinterpretation. States have called hundreds of assemblies to propose and ratify new constitutions. To identify these state constitutional revision assemblies, I merge five sources' lists of constitutional revision bodies, checking each against the others and against my own hand coding of assemblies listed in the Council of State Governments' annual *Book of the States* report. To catch any observations not included in these sources and to verify and expand information on each observation, I also code every reference to every state constitutional assembly in every volume of the Oxford Commentaries on the State Constitutions of the United States, an up-to-date reference series on the constitutional history of each state.[56] As needed, I confirm information through secondary sources and convention, commission, legislative, and newspaper reports. This data set includes 411 state constitutional revision bodies, including 290 assemblies authorized to draft new constitutions, with data on these assemblies' duration, type, scope, ratification process, and ratification outcome (table 2).[57] I extract state-level amendment data from the *Book of the States*.[58]

These state-level replacement and amendment data confirm scholars' intuitions

Table 2. State Constitutional Revision Assemblies, 1776–2020

	Convention		Commission		Legislature		Total	
	No.	%	No.	%	No.	%	No.	%
Limited								
Yes	33	27.2	81	66.9	7	5.7	121	100
No	222	76.5	58	20.0	10	3.4	290	100
Vote								
Vote, passage	141	70.8	53	26.6	5	2.5	199	100
Vote, no passage	36	55.3	27	41.5	2	3.0	65	100
No vote, passage	52	92.8	0	0	4	7.1	56	100
No vote, no passage	26	28.5	59	64.8	6	6.5	91	100
Ratified								
Constitution	135	93.7	5	3.4	4	2.7	144	100
Amendment(s)	43	44.7	48	50.0	5	5.2	96	100
No ratification	77	45.0	86	50.2	8	4.6	171	100
Total	255	62.0	139	33.8	17	4.1	411	100

that in the twentieth century, piecemeal amendment, often by limited commission or convention, largely replaced wholesale replacement by convention. For a list of all state constitutional revision assemblies, see appendix A.[59]

Simple counts of state constitutional amendment and replacement proposals cannot alone demonstrate state constitutional instability. State framers may radically change their constitutions through a single revision or may propose and ratify many insignificant revisions. As a California judge explained, "Our revision/amendment analysis has a dual aspect, requiring us to examine both the quantitative and qualitative effects of the measure on our constitutional scheme. Substantial changes in either could amount to revision." Qualitative observation is also tricky. State framers and judges, like their federal counterparts, assert that state constitutional identity inheres in core clauses, so one might study these specific clauses for significant change.[60] But these core provisions are themselves disputed and are drafted, revised, and reinterpreted by diverse actors, including state convention delegates, commission members, judges, legislators, governors, extralegal mobs and committees, and voters in referenda and initiatives. Distinct regional and historical patterns also emerge, as framers in nearly every nineteenth-century convention borrowed from compendia of state constitutions, relying mainly on the newest and nearest documents. The method and significance of reform varies significantly by era and region, reaffirming the need for historically situated case studies.[61]

To test the book's thesis, I compare these measures of state and federal reform. Chapters proceed by era. For each era, I offer case studies on the three to five most common topics among proposed federal amendments, confirming the salience of these topics against federal judicial, congressional, executive, and press records.[62] I then observe whether the states amend, replace, or reinterpret their constitutions on these same national topics. Finally, I see whether this reform affects national conflict and reform on these issues. These national outcomes can be observed in federal amendment proposals, court decisions, and congressional, executive, and press records. If I do not find this evidence, then we can safely reject the book's claims.

I conclude this section with a brief observation on the relationship between federal and state constitutional reform. My claims about devolution and elevation suggest that attempts at federal and state constitutional reform are associated. Specifically, I expect a positive association between biennial counts of proposed federal amendments and proposed state amendments and proposed state constitutional replacement. Consistent with this expectation, I find a strong positive correlation between proposed federal amendments and proposed state amendments (0.67) and state constitutional replacement (0.64).[63] Figure 5 elaborates this association. Proposals for federal and state constitutional amendment and replacement increase in tandem after the 1787 Constitutional Convention, again during and after the Civil War, and once more during the civil rights movement of the 1960s. This observation cannot test the book's claims but does suggest a consistent, strong association between proposed federal and state constitutional reform.[64]

This book unpacks the relationship between proposed federal and state constitutional reform across different eras and issues. Chapter 2 shows how Revolutionary-era state constitutional framing resolved national debates over legislative sovereignty, frontier regulation, and slavery. In May 1776, the Continental Congress split over proposed resolutions for independence and instead asked the states to declare independence by drafting new constitutions. The chapter's second section describes how state framers, recalling Parliamentary tyranny, im-

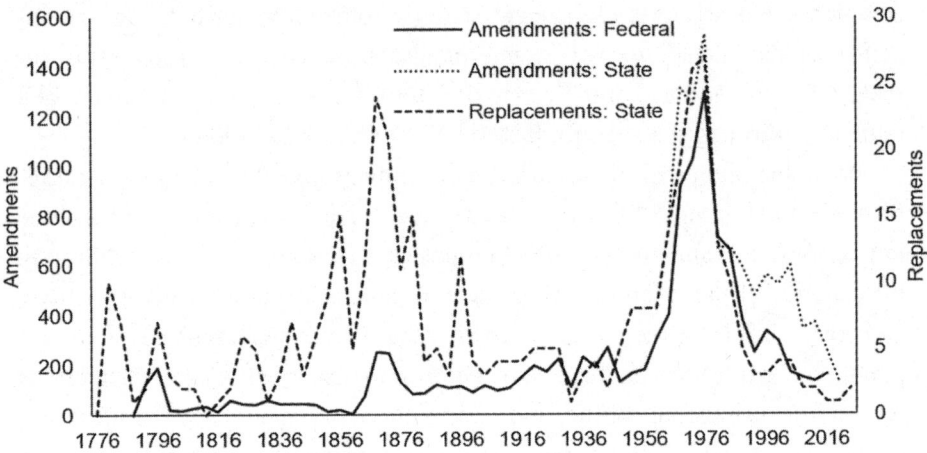

Fig. 5. Proposed federal and state constitutional amendment and replacement, 1776–2020.

itated Virginia's bicameral legislature checked by an independent executive and judiciary. Many states equitably reapportioned their legislatures to better represent and appease rebellious western frontier counties and began regulating slavery, with gradual abolition in Northern and Mid-Atlantic states and entrenched slavery in Southern states. By the 1787 Philadelphia convention, as the final section explains, a national consensus emerged around the Virginia Constitution's bicameral model, which federal framers adopted on the Convention's second day with little debate or controversy. Federal delegates also deferred to state constitutional apportionment and slave law, confronting the divisive slavery question only as it affected national concerns like taxation, representation, and trade. The framing was completed with the Bill of Rights, which easily passed thanks partly to its close imitation of existing state bills.

As chapter 3 shows, federal deference to the antebellum states effectively preempted, delayed, or resolved the era's main national controversies over banking, elections, and slavery. At the turn of the nineteenth century, congressmen proposed hundreds of amendments to charter a national bank and to reform presidential and congressional elections, while white workingmen began rallying locally for suffrage expansion. Jeffersonian congressmen eventually cleared the supermajority requirements needed for a national amendment, but as the chapter's second section explains, by the early 1810s, the states had already revised their constitutions to charter state banks, expand the franchise to most adult white males, and allow popular election of congressmen and presidential electors. Congress subsequently proposed fewer amendments on electoral reform. In the chapter's third section, I show that banking remained contentious until Andrew Jackson assumed the presidency and cowed Chief Justice John Marshall into recognizing state banking power. Jackson then vetoed rechartering the National Bank and distributed federal surplus funds to the states, which passed hundreds of additional constitutional provisions establishing and regulating banks, while Congress abandoned national bank amendments. Jackson also made the federal post impound abolitionist mail, with Congress blocking antislavery petitions, keeping slave law a state-level concern. Only two federal amendments passed in this era, while the states proposed fifty-six new constitutions, ratifying thirty-four constitutions and many additional state amendments.

In chapter 4, I argue that state constitutionalism exacerbated and then resolved national constitutional controversies over slavery and Black citizenship. While Congress's 1850 Compromise and 1854 Kansas-Nebraska Act opened the West to slavery, Westerners did not recognize slavery under their proposed state constitutions. Further, Northerners revised their laws and constitutions to protect fugitive enslaved people, prompting Southern secession. Alongside the Supreme Court's *Dred Scott* decision and Lincoln's 1860 election, this sudden divergence in state-level slave law sparked the Civil War. Second, I show how Lincoln and Congress first tested Reconstruction policies by prompting constitutional revision in conquered Southern states. Third, this experimentation culminated with postwar Reconstruction, as Congress called state conventions that abolished slavery, granted freed Blacks citizenship and equal protection of the laws, disenfranchised ex-Confederates, and used their police-power prerogatives to expand labor, welfare, and education rights. Rather than pushing Reconstruction through a new national constitution or a host of amendments, Congress carefully imitated these state constitutions, passing only three amendments, which allied state legislators quickly ratified. The state documents expounded, enforced, and buttressed the untested national Reconstruction Amendments, stabilizing national politics. Even as Congress and Lincoln expanded their powers, dictating state policy, they imitated state constitutionalism, a case of convergent constitution-making.

Chapter 5 demonstrates how Progressive-era members of Congress, federal judges, and presidents deferred national disputes over income taxation, elections and voting, labor rights, and prohibition to the states and how state-level organizing and experimentation converged on solutions that Congress and the federal courts then imitated. Progressive-era reform movements often looked first to the states. Reformers, thwarted by a conservative Senate and Supreme Court, implemented the income tax and direct election of senators through state constitutional and statutory reform, easing the passage of the Sixteenth and Seventeenth Amendments, which encouraged additional, complementary state reform. Similarly, as the National Woman Suffrage Association (NWSA) failed to achieve a national franchise amendment, the American Woman Suffrage Association (AWSA) pushed for state-by-state franchise expansion. As the campaign succeeded, the AWSA and NWSA merged in 1890 and campaigned for state reform as a means to a national amendment, urging women enfranchised at the state level to oust hostile congressional incumbents. By 1918, members of Congress from both parties urged national reform, passing the Nineteenth Amendment, which the states, already supporting the female vote, quickly ratified. Similarly, the chapter recounts how populists and progressives in the state legislatures and constitutional conventions began entrenching labor rights rejected by the conservative Congress and Supreme Court. When the 1924 Child Labor Amendment fell short of ratification, the states added this and other labor rights to their constitutions. The chapter's last section also addresses prohibition. While the states had long successfully and stably regulated liquor laws to suit diverse local needs, an insurgent national temperance campaign culminated in prohibition through the Eighteenth Amendment. State nonenforcement encouraged repeal under the Twenty-First Amendment, subsequently keeping the issue off the national agenda.

Chapter 6 recounts how state constitutional reform resolved national controversies over labor, pension, voting, and gender rights during the New Deal and Great Society years. This era, like Reconstruction, saw federal dictation of state policy coincide with federal imitation of state policy. Before and during the Depression, state framers enlarged constitutional and statutory labor and pension protections, pushing state judges to develop doctrinal justifications for these new tax-funded programs. When the Supreme Court rejected Franklin Delano Roosevelt's analogous federal programs, Roosevelt threatened to restructure the Court. Justice Louis Brandeis helped frame the Roosevelt administration's cooperative, "second" New Deal, imitating, affirming, and funding these state programs. Adopting state pension law doctrine, the Court upheld these new federal programs, prompting renewed state constitutional labor and pension protections, cementing the new, collaborative welfare order and cooling interbranch tensions. And through the 1940s and 1950s, federal courts, Congress, and the Department of Justice attacked states' white-primary, literacy-test, poll tax, and legislative-malapportionment practices. Some reforms, like white-primary and literacy-test repeal, came primarily through federal intervention against noncompliant states, a case of dictation. But New Deal state legislators and civil rights reformers repealed state constitutional poll tax provisions by amendment, almost always without federal help. State-level repeal of the poll tax eased federal repeal of the tax through the Voting Act, Twenty-Fourth Amendment, and *Harper* decision. Similarly, when the Supreme Court urged racially equitable state legislative reapportionment, new state legislators quickly rebuilt their constitutions to entrench the Court's aims, preempting a potentially disastrous second national constitutional convention in 1967. Finally, after the Equal Rights Amendment failed ratification in the 1970s, state legislators and judges amended and reinterpreted their constitutions to entrench similar gender-equality clauses, discouraging national reform.

Chapter 7 concludes the work in two parts. The first part recalls how Congress in the 1980s and 1990s proposed constitutional amendments for a balanced budget, tax limits, an item veto, and legislative term limits. While a divided Congress did not pass any of these measures, nearly every state passed balanced-budget, tax, item-veto, or term-limit provisions in these years, venting popular pressure for fiscal reform, a case of federal deference to state constitutionalism. The final section considers the nature and democratic advantages of ongoing state constitutional reform. The question is an old one. As Woodrow Wilson concluded, "the relation of the states to the federal government . . . is a question of growth, and every successive stage of our political and economic development gives it a new aspect, makes it a new question."[65] This book explains the relationship.

2

First Conventions, 1760–1791

It has been frequently remarked that it seems to have been reserved to the people of this country, by their conduct and example, to decide the important question, whether societies of men are really capable or not of establishing good government from reflection and choice, or whether they are forever destined to depend for their political constitutions on accident and force.
—Alexander Hamilton, Federalist 1, *1787*

THE FIRST AMERICAN CONSTITUTIONS were short-lived. Between the Revolution and the ratification of the Bill of Rights, Americans proposed twenty-three new state constitutions and ratified eighteen, creating the first American states. These states then convened the Continental Congress in 1774, which drafted the Articles of Confederation in 1781 and called the federal convention in 1787, framing a new Constitution and Congress, which proposed hundreds of amendments and passed ten by 1791. This was the most intense period of federal amendment in American history.[1]

The drafting and survival of the national Constitution was not a matter of "accident and force." State constitutional drafting, failure, and adaptation answered national questions on legislative sovereignty and design, slavery and franchise law, and the enumeration of rights. This state constitutional experimentation guided the framing of the federal Constitution.

On May 15, 1776, the Continental Congress asked colonists to design new governments. Weeks later, Pennsylvania's Provincial Conference, preparing for the state's first constitutional convention, reminded colonists, "Divine Providence is about to grant you a Favor which few People have ever enjoyed before, the Privilege of choosing Deputies to form a Government under which you are to live." The sentiment echoed across the states. Carter Braxton told delegates to the first Virginia convention to proceed with "all the candor and deliberation due to its importance."[2] State framers worked gradually and thoughtfully, sampling from English Whig, unicameralist Saxon, Roman republican, and Greek confederation plans. Massachusetts's exacting framers, adopting the Whig design, took four years and several tries to draft their first constitution, a widely imitated model that is now the world's oldest constitution in continuous use. In addressing national controversies over legislative sovereignty and design; the regulation of slavery, suffrage, and the frontier; and the enumeration of rights, state framers preempted or curtailed these debates at the federal convention. John Dickinson saw as much, reminding convention delegates that previous state constitutional "experience must be [the delegates'] only guide."[3] Imitating state constitutional design, federal delegates therefore proceeded "from reflection and choice," able, in delegate James Wilson's words, to decide "leisurely and peaceably, upon the form of government by which they will bind themselves and their posterity."[4]

This chapter proceeds chronologically in three parts, first introducing colonial debates over Parliamentary sovereignty, slavery, and frontier and suffrage law. Second, the chapter shows how in 1776 the Second Continental Congress deferred the divisive legislative sovereignty question to the state legislatures and constitutional conventions, which were smaller, more united, and better able to address the issue. Through the 1780s, state framers coalesced around Massachusetts's and Virginia's plan to check the legislature through bicameralism and gubernatorial and judicial restraints, while tailoring franchise and slave law to local demands. Delegates to the 1787 federal convention, many of them former state framers, also imitated Massachusetts's and Virginia's design and bowed to state slave and franchise law. Since the nation cycled through several constitutions and legislatures in these years, establishing the national Constitution only at the era's end, this chapter cannot test the claim that conflict decentralization resolved national disputes and stabilized the national Constitution. However, this chapter shows that state framers narrowed and quieted national debates over legislative sovereignty and design, slavery, and the franchise, aiding the drafting and ratification of the national Constitution and stabilizing national constitutionalism.

Conflict and Revolution

In 1606, James I chartered the Virginia Company to settle the Chesapeake. Colonists landed at Jamestown the following year, settling the eastern seaboard. On wresting control of the Delaware from the Dutch in 1667, the English Crown claimed much of the Atlantic coast, which it split into separately chartered colonies, progenitors of the modern states. Proprietary charters exclusively and durably empowered a few of the Crown's allies, disenfranchising Jews, Catholics, Blacks, and Native Americans, who might serve an authority besides the Protestant Crown, and excluding servants, women, slaves, and transients and the poor, who had little landed property or material clout in their community. Periodic unrest over disenfranchisement swelled into full revolt in 1686 when James II revoked colonial sovereignty, calming only when William and Mary restored the colonies' authority and when the deferential Prime Minister Robert Walpole in 1721 began, in Edmund Burke's words, a "wise and salutary neglect," letting the colonies each take their "own way to perfection."[5]

But the mid-eighteenth century brought graver controversies over legislative sovereignty and frontier and slave law. Slavery underpinned colonial economies both Northern and Southern. Southern colonies shifted from white servant labor to Black slave labor and increasingly legally distinguished Black people from free whites and Native Americans. In the North, Black slaves, though only 5 percent of the region's population, farmed Connecticut and Rhode Island plantations, worked half of New York City homes, and supplied sugar and human property to New England seaports. To protect these industries across generations, colonial legislators attached slave status to Black physiology, making slavery hereditary.[6]

Abolitionists began attacking these laws. Britons did not rely solely on domestic chattel slavery, spurring abolitionist petitions and pamphlet campaigns. The British Granville Sharp canvassed Philadelphia and corresponded with Benjamin Rush, an abolitionist professor at the College of Philadelphia, where in 1768, students publicly debated the morality and legality of slavery. The Philadelphia clergyman John Woolman preached against slavery in Virginia, where slaves soon celebrated Lord Mansfield's antislavery *Somerset* decision of 1772 and Governor John Murray, Lord Dunmore's 1775 proclamation freeing loyalist slaves and indentured servants. With the war's opening, Rhode Island liberated slaves joining the Continental Army, while revolutionary pamphleteers attacked chattel slavery and monarchy as dual affronts to freedom.[7]

Frontier colonists also defied the Crown and their legislatures. Through charter privileges, primogeniture, entail, and intermarriage, landholding dynasties dominated mid-Atlantic proprietary colonies and Southern plantation colonies. In the smaller New England colonies, grand estates were few, but so were the chances to own land and gain accompanying voting rights and political power, forcing families to split and overwork their plots. In Chebacco, Massachusetts, for example, nearly half of all sons failed to inherit land. For these white men, and particularly for immigrants, land and accompanying political rights lay across the Appalachians, so families streamed west.[8]

Frontiersmen rallied against disenfranchisement and legislative malapportionment. White settlers asserted that Appalachian Native Americans neglected the land and so abdicated their right to it, petitioning their legislatures to appoint and salary militias to attack and displace local tribes. But old, inflexible colonial charters and apportionment laws, particularly in Pennsylvania and the Carolinas, concentrated legislative seats in wealthy eastern counties, which refused to finance western militias, forts, and infrastructure projects. When Pennsylvania's eastern legislators reaffirmed the 1701 charter's malapportionment scheme, frontiersmen marched twice on the Assembly, but they earned only token reforms.[9] Pennsylvania's charters also deeded land to a few families, who leased it to tenant farmers, disenfranchised under the charter's landholding requirements for suffrage. Frontiersmen and Philadelphia workingmen, unable to clear the fifty pounds in property needed to vote, mobbed polling places at least five times between 1739 and 1755, casting multiple illegal ballots, clubbing and stoning wealthy voters, and attacking constables sent by the legislature.[10] With the conclusion of the French and Indian War in 1763, the Crown granted the newly captured Ohio River Valley to French Catholics and outlawed trans-Appalachian migration, further frustrating Protestant settlers and overriding land claims by Massachusetts, Connecticut, and Virginia.[11]

Then came the last and worst crisis for British rule. In 1765, Prime Minister George Grenville levied the Stamp Act tax to recoup expenses from the French and Indian War. The new tariff reversed decades of lax tax collection, requiring payment in pounds sterling, which few colonists carried, and fell on notarized purchases as big as a plantation or as small as a pair of dice, hitting colonists of all classes. Americans rich and poor rioted, pilloried tax and customs officials, boycotted British goods, and refused to pay the tax.[12]

Many American pamphleteers claimed that a legislative tax was legitimate only if it was passed by the representatives of those who were taxed. Since colonists lacked specific delegates to the House of Commons, these writers attacked the Stamp Act as an overextension of Parliamentary authority. In response, Grenville's deputy, Thomas Whately, concocted the idea of virtual representation, claiming that all members of Parliament represented all of Britain and its colonies. Colonial pamphleteers did not buy it. In an October 1765 pamphlet, the Marylander Daniel Dulany derided Whately's scheme as "a cob-web spread to catch the unwary, and intangle the weak." Two months after the Stamp Act, Patrick Henry proposed several insurrectionary resolutions to Virginia's House of Burgesses, which soon affirmed that laws of "internal Polity and Taxation" required the consent of the colonial legislatures. Massachusetts, Rhode Island, Connecticut, New York, Pennsylvania, Maryland, and South Carolina followed suit. In October, nine colonies dispatched delegates to the Stamp Act Congress in New York, which recognized Virginia's resolutions, now extending colonists' exclusive legislative power past taxation to all matters of "internal policy."[13]

Traditional modes of conflict resolution faltered. Colonists had long rallied and mobbed to win legal and charter reform from the Crown, Parliament, and colonial lawmakers.[14] As before, Americans answered the Stamp Act by mobbing to harass tax officials and collectors, to free those who had been imprisoned under the statute, and to depose loyalist legislators and governors. In an era of plural governors, proprietors, and trustees and, later, of rotating executive councils, it was normal for executive power to belong to a plural, ad hoc group.[15] And as hoped, a cowed Parliament repealed the act and ousted Grenville.

But Parliament also claimed authority over America "in all cases whatsoever" under the Declaratory Act. Levying heavy taxes on colonial tea merchants while exempting the failing British East India Company, Parliament sparked renewed colonial riots in 1773. This time, Parliament did not retreat. The 1774 Coercive Acts enforced the tea tax by blockading Boston's port, closing the Massachusetts government, stationing British troops in unoccupied buildings, and extraditing the acts' violators to Britain for trial. Unable to win reform by mobbing, pamphleteers like Daniel Dulany, John Dickinson, and Patrick Henry urged revolt, drawing on natural law, English common law, the colonial charters, and their own English ancestry.[16]

The courts aggravated these controversies. In *Paxton's Case* of 1761, the Boston attorney James Otis attacked Parliament's tax acts but was rebuffed by Massachusetts Chief Justice Thomas Hutchinson, who upheld the acts and the broad search writs used to enforce them against smuggling. The decisions sparked charges of nepotism, inflamed when George III appointed new sycophant loyalist judges and forced customs cases into special Crown-controlled Vice-Admiralty Courts, meeting resistance in New Jersey, North Carolina, and Massachusetts. Frustrated Bostonians ransacked Hutchinson's home and that of the customs officer Andrew Oliver, while Rhode Islanders shelled the customs ship *St. John* and burned the Royal Navy's schooner *Gaspee*.[17] Courts also deepened divisions over slavery and the franchise. Emboldened by the era's liberalizing spirit, several Massachusetts slaves successfully sued for freedom under the 1691 Massachusetts charter's promise of "liberties and Immunities," while wary Southern legislators statutorily curtailed slaves' grounds for freedom suits. *Somerset* widened the gap, as Northern judges cited the decision to protect runaways' habeas corpus rights against return and Southerners embraced the decision's support of Virginia's positive proslavery law. Colonial judges, often the scions of wealthy families, proved similarly hostile to the petitions of frontiersmen, small farmers, and the working poor. For example, in 1766, New York's Justice Robert Livingston, a planter, sentenced the rebel tenant farmer William Prendergast to be publicly mutilated alive and then drawn and quartered. When Daniel Nimham, a sachem of the Wappinger tribe, sued the same Hudson Valley planter families to reclaim his ancestral lands, the New York Council, staffed by judges from these families, dismissed his case, sentenced him guilty of high misdemeanors, and jailed his lawyer. Colonists began circumventing the courts, in Massachusetts assembling in Cambridge to write a new state constitution appointing new judges and requiring writs with "a special designation of the persons or objects of search, arrest, or seizure."[18]

Colonists began forming sovereign governments. Through 1775, colonial mobs and militias ousted loyalist judges, legislators, and governors, so that by 1776, only Connecticut's patriot Governor Jonathan Trumbull kept his seat. Temporary congresses, conventions, and correspondence committees claimed control of many colonies but lacked express authority to govern and fend off

British troops. In response, New Jersey, Maryland, and North Carolina answered by convening permanent legislatures and courts, and Georgia created a new governorship. Virginia, New Hampshire, South Carolina, and Massachusetts appealed to the First Continental Congress, newly assembled in Philadelphia, for advice on drafting entirely new state constitutions. As militiamen reinforced the heights at Bunker Hill on June 9, Congress told Massachusetts to modify and reinstate its abrogated 1691 charter and by year's end allowed New Hampshire, South Carolina, and Virginia to draft state constitutions. These first conventions met under duress, declaring independence and drafting provisional wartime constitutions. New Hampshire's and South Carolina's expressly temporary constitutions rebranded their colonial legislature as the state legislature but failed to clarify their lawmaking authority relative to Parliament, appealing for reconciliation with Britain.[19]

The Continental Congress also avoided outright confrontation over Parliament's sovereignty. Pennsylvania's John Dickinson and New York's James Duane rallied Congress's conciliatory, middle-state delegates to quash John Adams's proposals repudiating Parliamentary sovereignty and declaring state sovereignty. The Second Congress, hamstrung by unanimity requirements and wartime organizing, also repeatedly defeated votes to declare independence. Adams soon realized that middle-state "delegates here, and other persons from various parts are unanimously very sanguine that if Boston and the Massachusetts [sic] can possibly steer a middle course . . . the exertions of the colonies will procure a total change of measures and full redress" for the colonists. New England and Southern state governments, already under invasion, increasingly sought to declare independence. These state legislatures, smaller and more homogeneous than the deadlocked Congress, could more quickly and easily pass resolutions repudiating Parliamentary sovereignty.[20]

Adams saw this. Increasingly preoccupied with Bostonians' hardship under British blockade, he hatched a plan to circumvent Congress's Dickinson-Duane faction by deferring to the state legislatures to declare independence. Late one evening in January 1776, he met with George Wythe, an elder Virginian congressman and jurist, to discuss the coming state constitutional conventions. Nearly forty years later, Adams recalled the meeting in detail. Wythe, he wrote, agreed "upon the necessity of independence, . . . observing that the greatest obstacle in the way of a declaration of it was the difficulty of agreeing upon a government" in Congress. "I replied," Adams remembered, "that each colony should form a government for itself, as a free and independent State." An impressed Wythe asked, "What plan would you institute or advise for any of the States?" Unsure, Adams deferred the question, later drafting a model state constitution in a letter to Wythe. From this, he penned a pamphlet, *Thoughts on Government*, which he sent to the Virginia and New Jersey conventions.[21]

But in early May 1776, only these two states, joined by New Hampshire and South Carolina, had called conventions. Adams now sought a congressional resolution to coax the remaining states to independence. Again, he ran aground against the moderate New York faction, the "greatest obstacle in the way of a declaration." Seconded by Richard Henry Lee, on May 10, Adams introduced to the Committee of the Whole a new resolution, only a single sentence long, calling on the colonies' revolutionary committees and assemblies to declare independence by drafting new governments. The short, seemingly innocuous resolution passed. Assembling a private subcommittee with Lee and Edward Rutledge, Adams added a strategically vague and brief preamble to the resolution declaring that "the exercise of every kind of authority under the crown should be totally suppressed." After two days of heated debate, the resolutions narrowly passed on the morning of May 15, with one to two abstentions, six or seven colonies voting in support and four against, including Duane's New York delegation. A defeated Duane, now realizing Adams's maneuvers in the private subcommittee, attacked Adams, calling his resolution "a Machine for the fabrication of independence." Adams happily agreed.[22]

The May resolutions' brevity let the state conventions address legislative design, slavery, the frontier, and every other constitutional matter without congressional oversight. New Jersey immediately answered the call with a convention on May 26, drafting a constitution and declaration of independence. And Pennsylvania's Provincial Conference, meeting from June 18 to 25, soon declared itself sovereign and called a constitutional convention.[23]

In early 1776, little was clear. The first untested, provisional state constitutions alone could not stabilize the emerging national order, the survival of which also depended on Continental armies at Trenton, Saratoga, and Yorktown. Yet for their brevity and novelty, these documents were the first to expressly list and limit the powers of government. Later state framers would hammer this raw form into a more durable instrument to hand to their federal counterparts.[24]

In addressing the legislative sovereignty debate, the states nudged congressional delegates toward independence. On June 7, 1776, Richard Henry Lee, backed by Adams and Wythe, asked Congress to follow Virginia in formally declaring the states sovereign. Four days later, a united Congress delegated the Declaration's drafting to Thomas Jefferson, John Adams, Benjamin Franklin, Roger Sherman, and Robert R. Livingston, dubbed "the Committee of Five."[25]

Jefferson and Adams consulted state constitutions while writing the Declaration. Charged as committee chair with penning a first draft, Jefferson copied heavily from his draft Virginia Constitution's preamble,[26] which the Virginia convention later adopted into the final state constitution.[27] Adams then revised Jefferson's draft Declaration while conferring with Virginia and New Jersey framers and recording New Hampshire's, South Carolina's, and Maryland's independence resolutions in his diary.[28] The Committee of Five and the state convention delegates mailed each other, read the same pamphlets, and faced the same hardships under British rule. Consequently, the national Declaration of Independence closely resembled those printed in the four existing state constitutions.[29] All but five of the Declaration's provisions appeared in some form in a prior state constitution.[30] After Congress's Declaration, seven state constitutional conventions followed, imitating the national Declaration.[31] Through collaboration, state and national framers together met the challenge of declaring independence.

The Declaration's meaning also changes when read with the state constitutions. Consider the Declaration's infamous silence on slavery. Jefferson's first draft of the Declaration condemned George III, who had "prostituted his Negative for Suppressing every legislative Attempt to prohibit or to restrain an execrable Commerce" in slaves.[32] When the Committee of the Whole debated Jefferson's draft on July 2 and 3, Georgians and South Carolinians and Northerners representing slave merchants rejected the clause,[33] and the Committee of Five cut the provision. Generations of scholars have mourned this deletion.[34]

But Jefferson's redacted clause, drawn from a provision he penned for the Virginia Constitution of 1776,[35] defended the state legislatures' constitutional right to control the slave trade. These nonimportation laws let white plantation owners hold a monopoly on slave labor and limit and control the growth of rebellious slave populations.[36] Virginia legislators proposed at least nineteen slave tariffs between 1699 and 1772 and, with independence, passed a 1778 nonimportation act and a 1793 act prohibiting immigration by free Black people.[37] Similarly, Delaware's 1776 constitutional convention simultaneously declared the state's independence from the Crown and right to abolish the royal slave trade but maintained slavery in Delaware.[38] Jefferson's redacted clause, like its author, was hostile to Blacks' liberty. The clause loftily proclaimed freedom for Black slaves but protected states' rights to control and move Black people.[39] Jefferson's redacted clause indirectly affirmed slavery. Accordingly, the Declaration cannot be understood only through the Committee of Five's notes or scrapped provisions but must be read as a response to state statutory and constitutional experimentation.

Legislative Design, the Franchise, and Slavery

Prompted by Adams's May resolutions, state constitutional framers addressed the era's main constitutional controversies, reapportioning legislative seats and voting power to frontiersmen and the urban poor, clarifying slavery's status, and limiting legislative sovereignty. The latter was perhaps their main concern. Framers imposed several checks on the legislature, most notably, transferring sovereignty from the legislature to the people and their representatives in constitutional convention, with all but two states calling conventions or special legislative sessions to draft their first constitutions. These meetings, checked by public election and oversight, assuaged colonists' anxieties over legislative detachment.[40]

Pennsylvanians pioneered the process. Within hours of Adams's May 15 instructions, Philadelphians circumvented their loyalist legislature, calling a preliminary meeting to organize a constitutional convention. On May 20, four thousand Philadelphians rallied in the rain to cheer a reading of their resolution. Two days later, William Bradford, a Philadelphia militiaman and printer of the *Pennsylvania Journal,* republished the resolution with this dialogue: "Q. Who ought to form a new Constitution? A. The people. Q. Should the officers of the old constitution be entrusted with the power of the making of a new one when it becomes necessary? A. No. Bodies of men have the same selfish attachments as individuals, and they will be claiming powers and prerogatives inconsistent with the liberties of the people." Underlying Bradford's dialogue was the English Whig assumption that legislators, elected by county, represented their constituents' parochial interests, while convention delegates, elected by general ballot, sought the common good. Convention delegates would therefore "regard not the person of the rich, nor despise the state of the poor," and at the "moment the constitution is framed, [would] descend into the common paths of life."

Only a fleeting emergency could unite the people to elect such a special convention. Here was born the great dilemma in liberal constitutionalism, for popular sovereignty, though legally unlimited, was limited temporally. Bradford's dialogue appeared in at least one other Philadelphia paper, while an anonymous four-page pamphlet, *The Alarm,* also called for a special election for convention delegates. On June 18, Pennsylvanians assembled at Carpenter's Hall as a Provincial Conference, charged with organizing the election of convention delegates, who would then frame a "new government in this province, on the authority of the people only."[41]

This populism was not merely rhetorical. The Provincial Conference let all free males over twenty-one with a year of residency elect convention delegates, bumping the proportion of enfranchised freemen from 50 to 90 percent. The convention met in late summer, framing, printing, and distributing four hundred copies of the draft constitution. Pennsylvanians debated the document in town meetings, newspapers, and pamphlets for a month—the first review of this sort in America—and sent edits to the convention, which incorporated the revisions into the final draft approved on September 27. Before dissolving, the convention prohibited the legislature from amending the Constitution, trusting constitutional review to a Council of Censors, chosen septennially from the people's representatives. "Demophilius," a popular pseudonymous pamphleteer, praised this measure for keeping sovereignty solely in "*the hands of* THE PEOPLE." "Here we see a regular process," Thomas Paine added, "a Government issuing out of a Constitution, formed by the people in their original character, and that Constitution serving not only as an authority, but as a law of control to the Government." Sovereignty lay in the people's Constitution, not the legislature.[42]

Imitating Pennsylvania, other states used oaths and prohibitions on dual officeholding to exclude legislators from their conventions. Delaware legislators scheduled convention delegate elections on the advice of the Pennsylvania framer Thomas McKean, and provincial congresses in New York, New Jersey, Maryland, and North Carolina forbade delegates from legislating. Likewise, when South Carolina's legislature attempted to frame a new constitution, Governor John Rutledge resigned in protest, and his replacement refused to take office. Convention delegates, many of them small farmers, backcountry lawyers, printers, merchants, and shopkeepers, checked legislators with open legislative sessions, publication and public review of proposed bills, frequent elections, a broad franchise, and bills of rights. Delaware, New Jersey, Georgia, and Vermont framers expressly forbade the legislature from amending the constitution, and eleven states declared a popular right to revolt and convention.[43]

Massachusetts, which took the brunt of Parliament's Coercive Acts, went furthest in restraining legislative sovereignty. In 1776, twenty-three town meetings rebuffed the revolutionary legislature's bid to draft a new constitution, and two years later, voters across the state resoundingly rejected a constitution drafted by a specially elected legislative session. The legislature capitulated in June 1779, calling a constitutional convention "with the sole purpose of framing a constitution," which voters soon approved. Massachusetts's framers subsequently forbade legislators from constitutional revision, providing instead for constitutional replacement by popular referenda.[44]

Beyond stripping legislative sovereignty, early framers placed institutional checks on their state legislatures, first in Pennsylvania, through open elections, and later in Virginia and Massachusetts, through bicameralism and separation of powers. Pennsylvanians, among the first to design a state legislature, checked their unicameral legislature with a broad, equitably apportioned franchise and frequent elections. Unlike the eastern-dominated loyalist Assembly, Pennsylvania's patriot Provincial Convention of 1775 and Provincial Conference of 1776 allocated seats to western counties, which in turn granted each county equal representation at the later constitutional convention. This stacked the convention with a supermajority of westerners and urban radicals committed to a broad franchise and to abolishing the legislature's aristocratic upper house.[45] Joining forces with John Dickinson's populists, this faction easily overwhelmed the constitutional convention's conservative bicameralist minority.[46]

The Pennsylvania Constitution of 1776 was a radical document. The document abandoned property requirements for voting and officeholding among adult male taxpayers, creating, in the historian Gary B. Nash's words, "the most liberal franchise known in the Western world to that date." The constitution subjected legislators to annual direct election, strict term limits, public debate and review of laws, loyalty pledges, and constitutional review and impeachment by the popularly elected Council of Censors.[47] An Executive Council of nine, embedded within the legislature, appointed judges serving at the legislature's pleasure. The constitution also granted the working poor a host of relief measures. A redacted bill of rights provision held, "an enormous proportion of property vested in a few individuals is dangerous to the rights, and destructive of the common happiness, of mankind; and therefore every free state hath a right by its laws to discourage the possession of such property."⁴⁸ Finally, after public meetings, petitioning, and pamphleting, convention delegates redrafted two-thirds of the document's provisions, evenly apportioning the legislature by taxable population, penning a bill of rights, and letting voters pick executive councilmen.⁴⁹

Five states imitated Pennsylvania's plan. The radical Pennsylvania delegates Timothy Matlack, James Cannon, and Thomas Young sent their constitution to Vermont and Georgia, recommending that these framers embed the people's "supreme constituent power" in similar constitutions.⁵⁰ On July 8, 1777, Vermont ratified a constitution almost identical to Pennsylvania's, including a unicameral legislature, universal manhood suffrage, abolition of slavery, a limited executive, and regular public review of the constitution. The Georgia convention, meeting by night in a tavern, followed Pennsylvania in establishing a unicameral legislature, secret balloting, and electing nearly all civil officers annually. Maryland instituted a bicameral legislature but took Pennsylvania's public constitutional review and regular elections, while North Carolina borrowed from Pennsylvania's bill of rights, as did the Delaware framer Thomas McKean, who had served in the Pennsylvania convention.⁵¹

Philadelphia's democratic, egalitarian spirit unnerved John Adams. Serving in the Continental Congress, he witnessed the Pennsylvania convention and the appearance of "a phenomenon in Philadelphia—a disastrous meteor": "I mean Thomas Paine." Paine, an Englishman and former privateer with only a grade-school education, had run "about picking up what information he could concerning [colonists'] affairs, and finding the great question was concerning independence, he gleaned from those he saw the common-place arguments," sketching a plan for independence and a model state government "flowing from simple ignorance, and a mere desire to please the democratic party, in Philadelphia." Paine found a correspondent and ally in Timothy Matlack, a brewer expelled from the Society of Friends for horseracing, cockfighting, and the occasional jail stint, who incorporated Paine's populism into the Pennsylvania Constitution. Unnerved at the runaway success and influence of *Common Sense*, Adams concluded, "I dreaded the effect so popular [a] pamphlet might have among the people, and determined to do all in my power to counteract the effect of it."⁵²

In April 1776, Adams replied with a defense of English Whig bicameralism and separation of powers. He first sent the pamphlet, titled *Thoughts on Gov-*

ernment, to his old Virginia planter allies George Wythe and Patrick Henry in anticipation of their state's coming constitutional convention, one of the first, and an expected counterexample to Pennsylvania's. The patrician Richard Henry Lee and Carter Braxton printed additional tracts defending an aristocratic upper house, for, as Robert Williams writes, "What was at stake was how new state governments would be structured and which groups in society would have the dominant policy-making role under the new governments."[53] Virginians instituted a bicameral legislature that would appoint a governor and Privy Council and life-tenured judges, with a prohibition on plural officeholding to ensure separation of powers. Framers maintained malapportionment toward eastern counties and the colonial suffrage requirement of fifty acres of land, which "tended to perpetuate the old oligarchy of rich Tidewater planters," according to Alan Nevins.[54]

With Virginia's ratification, Adams sent his pamphlet to New York, North Carolina, and South Carolina, each of which imitated parts of his plan. In each state, wealthy landholders sought an upper house as a counterweight so that bicameralism emerged as the compromise, with South Carolina's William Henry Drayton thumbing the scales by suggesting that state senators be appointed for life from the state's wealthiest families. As the Revolution's egalitarian zeal cooled, John Adams returned triumphant to Massachusetts to lead the state's 1780 convention, imposing his scheme for bicameralism, a tenured judiciary, and a novel gubernatorial veto as a hedge against legislative tyranny. Four years later, New Hampshire replaced its constitution to match Adams's conservative Whig design.[55]

Even Pennsylvanians turned against their powerful state legislature. Recalling Parliamentary despotism, the polemicist pamphleteer "Associator" in 1777 derided the Pennsylvania Constitution as a plan "full of whimsies—a government with only one legislative branch, which has never yet failed to end in tyranny." Conservatives called for a new constitution with a strong executive and a bicameral legislature to represent society's natural division into upper and lower classes, pulling Pennsylvania toward the nation's more conservative, Whig consensus. In 1790, Pennsylvanians scrapped their old constitution for a tripartite, bicameral scheme. Pennsylvania's new constitution was, in Tocqueville's words, "the final consecration of the principle of the division of legislative power; henceforth the need to share legislative activity between several bodies has been regarded as a demonstrated truth."[56]

State judges used constitutional review to further constrain the legislature and affirm their independence. Virginia's state Court of Appeals moved first in *Commonwealth v. Caton* (1782), claiming exclusive review powers and rebuffing the legislature's council of revision. Similarly, in *Rutgers v. Waddington* (1784), judges on the Mayor's Court of New York City voided the legislature's Trespass Act of 1783 for violating the state constitution's seizure prohibitions. And in *Trevett v. Weeden* (1786), Rhode Island Supreme Court judges overturned a statute stripping several merchants' constitutional rights to appeal and jury trial. North Carolina's *Bayard v. Singleton* (1787) was perhaps the decisive case, in which James Iredell stated that sovereignty lay not in the legislature but in the people and their constitution. By the late 1780s, judiciaries in five states had asserted a right to judicial review, buttressing Adams's now dominant model. By the late 1780s, the states settled on a bicameral, separation-of-powers design.[57]

Conservative, Whig pamphlets aided the adoption of property requirements in every state. Wary of growing rural rabble-rousing, planters at Maryland's 1776 convention defeated a proposed inclusive franchise measure, restricting the franchise to the wealthiest half of property owners and reducing the frequency of elections. Populist agitation at New York's 1776 convention halved freehold qualifications—in New York City, nearly all freemen could vote—but in Duchess and Westchester Counties, the seats of the state's landholding Hudson River dynasties, restrictions were tighter and, in some rural counties, excluding two-thirds of freemen. By Jefferson's count, Virginia's 1776 constitution disenfranchised most freemen. The Carolinas and Georgia disenfranchised a quarter to half of freemen, varying by location. Overall, property qualifications disenfranchised a quarter to half of free American males, depending on the state or locality. The rising Whig consensus harmonized state framers around property requirements that might be expanded or contracted to address local demands.[58]

Finally, state constitutional framing assuaged white Southerners' abolition anxieties by tailoring slave law to regional economic demand. In New England, this meant expanding liberty and due process immediately; in the Mid-Atlantic, gradually; and in the South, withdrawing these rights. *Somerset,* which affirmed local authority to regulate slavery, was now read to support each of these approaches without forbidding any of them. Many New England due process clauses promised liberty to all persons, spurring at least eighteen freedom suits in Massachusetts, including *Commonwealth v. Jennison* (1783), the first judicial abolition of slavery in America.[59] Vermont judges and New Hampshire legislators similarly extended due process protections to immediately free slave petitioners, so that by 1800, New Hampshire counted only eight slaves. In contrast, Connecticut and Rhode Island, lacking due process clauses and depending on plantation labor, only gradually manumitted slaves.[60]

Mid-Atlantic states, relying on some plantation labor, deferred abolition. In 1780, Pennsylvania passed America's first statute for gradual emancipation, which New Jersey imitated five years later. New York framers expressly refused a proposed abolition clause, letting their legislature pass gradual abolition laws in 1781, 1788, and 1799, joined by Maryland and Delaware. Since these laws freed slaves' children only after decades of service, Pennsylvania and New York only fully abolished slavery in the 1840s.[61]

Southern states retrenched slavery. The Carolinas' constitutions reserved due process protections to freemen, preempting slaves' freedom suits and petitions. South Carolina's legislature bound the cause of revolution and liberty to protecting slavery, promising "one grown negro" to every patriot militiaman and "three large and one small negro" to every officer. Though Virginia slaves lacked constitutional due process rights, state courts took Blacks' and Native Americans' freedom suits until the legislature passed at least four statutes limiting appeal. In *Hudgins v. Wrights* (1806), George Wythe capitulated by stripping Black Virginians' due process rights, and later that year, the legislature amended a 1786 manumission statute to require freed Black residents leave the state.[62]

Rooting slave law in local positive law, judges and legislators precluded nationalizing slavery or abolition on universalistic natural rights grounds. Since many Northern states refused due process to Southern runaway slaves, most disputes over slavery in this period were intrastate, not interstate, limiting the scope of national conflict. Finally, Northern opponents of the international slave trade found allies in Southern planters seeking a monopoly on the domestic slave trade, so that by 1787, eleven of thirteen states heavily taxed or outright abolished the trade, an unexpected bisectional accord. Shifting sovereignty from Parliament to the state constitutions not only relieved Revolutionary-era anxieties but also let legislators and judges interpret these documents to address local economic and political needs, quieting national controversies over legislative apportionment, the franchise, and slavery.[63]

However, the era's antilegislative consensus hobbled America's first national legislature. Imitating Patrick Henry's Stamp Act resolutions, Revolutionary framers in at least seven states claimed sovereignty over broad "internal Police" powers, to the exclusion not only of Parliament but also of the Continental Congress and the Articles of Confederation's Congress. Equal sovereignty let each state veto Confederation Congress bills, inspired frontier republics to badger Congress for recognition, and to the frustration of large states, gave each state equal representation. The very legitimacy of the Articles of Confederation was suspect, as the document had been framed legislatively and not in convention, as had become common practice among the states. After an initial convention in Annapolis, delegates assembled in Philadelphia in 1787 to modify the Articles.[64]

Imitating State Design at the Philadelphia Convention

Delegates to the federal convention copied state constitutional design. Up to half of the fifty-five delegates were former state framers and, by expressly citing state precedent, claimed that they in convention held plenary power to draft an entirely new constitution. Delegates immediately narrowed their aim to imitating the states' proven bicameral, tripartite plan. While Northern and Southern delegations clashed over slavery and large and small state delegations over legislative apportionment, they united by reaffirming the states' diverse slavery and franchise laws. State constitutionalism quietly guided and stabilized the federal convention.[65]

Delegates quickly settled on tripartite government. In the weeks before the convention, James Madison, Gouverneur Morris, and James Wilson, all opponents of the Pennsylvania model, quietly planned a tripartite alternative that Madison and Edmund Randolph proposed on the first day of substantive debate. Following Charles Pinckney's similar plan and John Dickinson's claim that state framing showed that "government must never be lodged in a single body" but rather in "[three or four] great departments," the next day the Committee of the Whole resolved to check the legislature with an independent executive and judiciary.[66]

Framers then split the legislature. Edmund Randolph and George Mason each suggested imitating their bicameral Virginia model, with Madison proposing adopting Virginia's single-member legislative districts. Wilson answered with

New York's multimember district model, prompting delegates to postpone the districting question while unanimously affirming bicameralism on May 31.[67] Two weeks later, small-state delegates backed William Patterson's unicameral proposal, but as John Dickinson noted, these delegates hailed from bicameral states and really "wish[ed] for two branches in the General Legislature," defecting only to extract concessions from large-state delegates. Small-state delegates won equal representation in the upper house on July 16, settling the issue and narrowing debate to the districting question, which was resolved by "abstracting as much as possible from the idea of State Gov[ernments]." Compromise itself was a lesson taken from the state conventions, for as Elbridge Gerry reminded colleagues, "We must make concessions on both sides. Without these[,] the constitutions of the several States would never have been formed."[68]

State experience also guided debates around executive powers and selection. Plural and legislatively appointed executives proved contentious in Virginia, South Carolina, and especially Pennsylvania, where scattered Executive Council officers often failed to assemble. Federal delegates instead borrowed New York's and Massachusetts's unitary veto-equipped executive, selected by an Electoral College akin to Maryland's. But, as in New York, this executive would report yearly to the legislature and was subject to legislative impeachment. Imitating proven state examples let federal framers narrow convention debate to the tamer question of formalizing cabinet positions, with James Wilson and Roger Sherman both rooting their opposed positions in earlier state constitutional design. Per Willi Paul Adams, "The presidential system at the federal level can be ascribed much more to the beliefs of the authors of the first state constitutions" than to any other source.[69]

State framing also guided judicial design. Federal delegates easily copied state plans for joint executive and legislative selection of life-tenured judges. Constitutional review, tested in only five states, found fewer friends at the convention. Delegate William Davie had exercised judicial review in North Carolina's *Bayard v. Singleton* in 1787, as had delegates John Francis Mercer, John Blair, and George Wythe in Virginia's *Commonwealth v. Caton* in 1782, a case that Edmund Randolph argued as Virginia's attorney general. Elbridge Gerry blocked John Randolph's May 29 proposal for constitutional review by a Council of Censors akin to Pennsylvania's and defeated Madison's July 21 proposal for a similar Council of Revision, holding that constitutional review belonged to the judiciary. But Rhode Islanders, New Yorkers, and North Carolinians, including now-delegate Richard Dobbs Spaight, had chastised their judges for overruling elected legislators. Since the states had not settled the issue of constitutional review, neither did federal delegates, leaving the issue with the state judiciaries.[70]

Unlike institutional design questions, slavery and suffrage debates split delegates, who, unable to compromise, deferred to existing state law. On May 31 and June 6, delegates pitched federal suffrage plans, with Madison reminding the convention that "the people have been accustomed to this [suffrage] right in various parts of America, and will never allow it to be abridged": "We must consult their rooted practices if we expect their concurrence in our propositions." The Committee of Detail then rejected a national property-based franchise requirement, and in August, the convention formally affirmed state authority to regulate the time, place, manner, and eligibility for federal elections. As Alexander Keyssar concludes, "By making the franchise in national elections dependent on state suffrage laws, the authors of the Constitution compromised their substantive disagreements to skirt a potentially explosive political problem."[71]

Delegates also left the fractious slavery question to the states. They learned the sensitivity of the issue early. On May 30, Randolph proposed apportioning Congress by "free inhabitants," decreasing Southern seats and prompting Southern delegates to threaten to leave the convention. Madison now realized that "the great division of interests in the U. States . . . did not lie between large & small States: it lay between the Northern & Southern." He then cut Randolph's clause. Unnerved, delegates shied from offering new abolition or proslavery clauses. Connecticut's Oliver Ellsworth and Roger Sherman moved to table abolition debates entirely, citing the sufficiency of Northern-state abolition provisions. Sherman felt that "abolition of slavery seemed to be going on in the U.S. & that the good sense of the several States would probably by degrees compleat it" and that the convention ought to continue "dispatching its business." Abraham Baldwin of Georgia believed the same, while South Carolina's Charles Pinckney posed "serious objections" to overriding Southern law. Divergent state constitutionalism satisfied divergent delegates, defusing the issue.[72]

With the delegates' aims curtailed, they passed few provisions addressing slavery. Returning to the apportionment question on July 12, delegates compromised on James Wilson and Charles Pinckney's infamous three-fifths clause for representation and, later, for taxation, creating Southern majorities in the House and Electoral College. The Fugitive Slave Clause promised return of runaways but failed to deputize federal enforcers, leaving implementation to state officials. And since each of the states had already banned the international slave trade, delegates on August 21 and 22 proposed a matching national ban, backed by both the abolitionist Luther Martin and the slaveholder George Mason, who hoped to prevent slave overpopulation and revolt. Other provisions implicitly protected slavery. Article V prohibited immediately banning the slave trade and required that amendments get Southern support to clear the high supermajority threshold. Constitutional reform of slavery would henceforth be local, to Southern satisfaction. Oliver Ellsworth best captured the convention's sentiment: the "morality and wisdom of slavery are considerations belonging to the states themselves, . . . and the states are the best judges of their particular interest."[73]

Deference did not resolve deeper disagreements. Northern delegates expected the states to abolish slavery nationwide, while South Carolinian and Georgian delegates predicted entrenchment. One section would lose. George Mason waxed prophetic in the convention's last days, warning that slavery brings "the judgment of heaven on a Country. As nations can not be rewarded or punished in the next world they must be in this. By an inevitable chain of causes & effects providence punishes national sins, by national calamities."[74]

Closing the convention, Madison, Mason, Morris, and Gorham, imitating state ratification methods, asked each state to call a special convention to approve the proposed Constitution. Article V left amendment ratification to state legislatures and conventions for the same reason. In *The Federalist,* Madison and Hamilton then demonstrated that their federal proposal complemented the bicameral, tripartite state constitutions, pacifying New Yorkers' ratification anxieties. New Hampshire's convention cast the deciding ninth vote to approve the Constitution on June 21, 1788, with Georgia, Pennsylvania, South Carolina, Delaware, and Vermont soon replacing their constitutions to match the tripartite federal model. Though the Constitution's Guarantee Clause only requires of states "a republican form of government," since 1787, states have almost invariably chosen bicameral, tripartite governments.[75]

The era's final constitutional debate concerned rights protections. By the 1787 convention, eight states enumerated rights in dedicated bills, four in the body of their constitution, and two in their colonial charters, leading delegates, in Rufus King's words, to reject a federal bill redundant to the "express provisions in the State Constitutions." George Mason, a framer of the Virginia bill, proposed combining the state bills into a federal one at the convention's close, but weary delegates unanimously refused, with Roger Sherman reiterating that the "State Declarations of Rights are not repealed by this Constitution; and being in force are sufficient." Proponents of ratification, including Hamilton in *Federalist* 84, repeatedly cited the state bills to preempt national debate.[76]

Skeptical antifederalists threatened to block ratification without a federal bill. Mason's widely read *Objections to the Proposed Federal Constitution* alleged that the federal Supremacy Clause overrode the state bills, and allied Virginia and New York antifederalists called for a second convention. But the moderate Richard Henry Lee instead proposed new rights amendments to the Confederation Congress, which punted the issue to the state ratifying conventions. Pennsylvania's federalist-leaning convention rejected amendment, following James Wilson's claim that listing rights in a federal bill would void nonlisted rights. Conversely, John Hancock appeased Massachusetts's larger antifederalist bloc by proposing additional federal amendments listing individual rights, limiting federal powers, and reserving unlisted powers to the states. By merging the states' bill of rights model with the latter provision reserving nondelegated rights, Hancock answered both Wilson's claim and Mason's Supremacy Clause objection, reconciling Massachusetts federalists and antifederalists. Conventions in New Hampshire, New York, Virginia, North Carolina, and South Carolina imitated Hancock's plan, in New Hampshire almost verbatim, and together proposed 123 additional amendments, many of which duplicated the same rights proposals, including eight amendments reserving nondelegated powers. Other new provisions significantly restricted federal judicial, military, electoral, and taxation power. Madison, serving in the Virginia ratifying convention, shared Wilson's concerns with enumerating rights, which he deemed mere "parchment barriers," but nonetheless grudgingly backed Virginia's amendments to secure ratification.[77]

But by the spring of 1789, Rhode Island and North Carolina still refused ratification, waiting on approval of the proposed amendments, and New York and Rhode Island called for another convention. Congressmen from nine states proposed another 188 amendments in 1789, including 14 amendments reserving nondelegated powers to the states or people. Madison capitulated and compiled a federal bill. But rather than using the congressional and state convention proposals, many of which reduced federal power, he borrowed almost the entire national bill from the state bills, sometimes taking the states' exact phrasing. Antifederalists got explicit rights protections and Hancock's reservation of non-delegated powers, ratified as the Tenth Amendment, but lost the larger fight to constrain the new federal leviathan. As Donald Lutz concludes, Madison used "the state constitutions as his model. The antifederalists had difficulty opposing Madison's use of this model. It was a model of their own making, and it was part of what they were demanding."[78] By imitating the state bills, Madison silenced the national antifederalist opposition on the issue.

With Congress's antifederalist minority outmaneuvered, Madison's proposals cleared both houses of Congress with only slight revisions and, at Sherman's behest, were bundled as a formal bill akin to the state bills. In what David Kyvig calls a "pattern of rapid and uncontested approval," antifederalist state legislators and convention delegates cut their losses and hastily ratified all but two of the proposed twelve amendments. Massachusetts and Virginia cast the final two votes in 1791, ending national debate. The new Congress immediately turned to questions on banking, coinage, and taxation, and rights provisions essentially disappeared from the antebellum rolls of proposed national amendments, as the states used the new Tenth Amendment to seize this legal domain for themselves, muscling out even the Supreme Court on most individual rights issues.[79]

State framing narrowed national debates over legislative, executive, and judicial design and quieted controversy over slavery, suffrage, and rights protection. Most scholars rely on Madison's *Notes,* often reported through Farrand's *Records,* to observe convention bargaining over bicameralism but therefore miss how previous state framing made bicameralism a foregone conclusion. Similarly, many scholars interpret Hamilton and Wilson's strong, unitary executive as repudiating the Articles' lethargic Congress but miss how Hamilton and Wilson drafted their executive to repudiate Pennsylvania's weak, plural Executive Council. In neglecting state convention records and studying only the Philadelphia convention, many scholars misunderstand the convention and national politics in the founding era.[80]

Early Americans better understood the states' stabilizing role. By taking prior framing experience, especially by the states, as the "only guide," in Dickinson's words, delegates bridged their divides and sold the Constitution to a skeptical public. The ploy worked, for a 1796 schoolbook claimed that these framers "had all the examples of former ages and governments before them, their beauties and defects; they sat down in a state of profound peace, and had full leisure to form the most perfect constitution that the nature of things would admit of." So began the public veneration that helped carry the Constitution through the antebellum era.[81]

3
Antebellum Consensus, 1792–1849

> *The confederation of all the American states does not suffer from those disadvantages usual to large conglomerations. . . . Political passions, instead of spreading like a sheet of fire instantaneously over the whole land, break up in conflict with the individual passions of each state.*
> —*Alexis de Tocqueville,* Democracy in America, *1835*

THE ANTEBELLUM YEARS BROUGHT state constitutional instability and federal constitutional stability. States completed the Constitution's framing by ratifying the Bill of Rights in 1791. Between 1792 and the slavery crisis of 1849–50, almost all constitutional change occurred at the state level. The states called fifty-six revision assemblies, empowering forty-nine to draft new documents, ratifying thirty-four constitutions, and proposing and ratifying dozens of amendments. In contrast, Congress passed only 2 of the 511 proposed amendments—the narrow Eleventh and Twelfth Amendments—while the staid Marshall and Taney Courts generally upheld congressional legislation, instead overseeing and directing state lawmaking. Why, then, did antebellum Americans rework their state constitutions while leaving the national Constitution intact?

There are a few familiar explanations for the national Constitution's stability. One might think that high Article V requirements deterred federal amendment. But between 1802 and 1824, Democratic-Republicans cleared Article V thresholds in Congress and the state legislatures. Democrats too held significant bicameral congressional majorities between 1828 and 1840. Yet both parties largely refused federal constitutional amendments. Alternatively, scholars have suggested that constitutional veneration deterred amendment. Jefferson, for example, noted that some people regarded the Constitution "like the ark of the covenant, too sacred to be touched. They ascribe to the men of the preceding age a wisdom more than human, and suppose what they did to be beyond amendment." But jurists like Jefferson, Madison, St. George Tucker, and John Taylor of Caroline derided this "sanctimonious reverence," especially as cyclical slavery crises tarnished the document. Nullificationists, both proslavery, like John C. Calhoun, and antislavery, like William Lloyd Garrison, condemned the Constitution, and Federalists, Democratic-Republicans, and Democrats attempted several conventions and hundreds of amendments.[1] Alternatively, perhaps judicial review or presidential or congressional constitutional reinterpretation obviated Article V amendment. Stephen Skowronek and Keith Whittington, for example, demonstrate that Andrew Jackson's landslide elections empowered him to veto the Second National Bank and forcibly relocate Native Americans without amendment or Supreme Court authorization. Here we are closer to an answer. The Marshall and Taney Courts bowed to Jackson and Congress, often by devolving regulation on the states. As this chapter notes, this devolution, and consequent state constitutional reform, facilitated this deescalation through decentralization of national conflict.[2]

Common explanations of state instability are also incomplete. Westward expansion drove some reform, bringing sixteen new states and constitutions into the Union, but cannot account for widespread Eastern constitutional amendment and replacement. Some states imposed relatively low, simple-majority thresholds for amendment, garnering many amendments and losing veneration and inviting revision. But other states failed to specify amendment procedure, and others set high bars, earning veneration and dissuading reform. Pennsylvania's constitution, according to Thomas Paine, became "the political Bible of the state. Scarcely a family was without it. Every member of the Government had a copy."[3]

More importantly, these state constitutions did not develop in isolation. Nor did the federal Constitution, courts, Congress, or presidency. To fully understand antebellum political development, one must consider the interaction of the state and federal constitutions.

This chapter asserts that conflict decentralization stabilized national politics in the antebellum era. Congressional parties split over banking, election, and slavery law, pushing these fractious issues on the states. In response, states constitutionally chartered banks, expanded popular election and white male suffrage, and affirmed a bisectional compromise entrenching Southern slavery and Northern abolition. Congressmen consequently avoided ratifying or sometimes even proposing amendments on these nationally contentious topics, which federal courts also avoided. These three cases exemplify devolution broadly and deference and preclusion specifically—national actors' delegation of nationally salient issues to state legislatures and conventions destabilized the states and stabilized the Union.

Controversies over banking, slavery, and election law gripped the early republic. Between 1792 and 1849, the most common topics among proposed amendments concerned, in roughly descending order, the powers, terms, and selection of the president and members of Congress, the powers of the states, the regulation of banks and corporations, and the regulation of slavery. Slavery and bank questions also occupied the Supreme Court. This chapter therefore offers case studies on election, finance, and slave law. Table 3 displays the twenty-five most common topics among amendments proposed between 1792 and 1849.

The chapter recounts antebellum processes of conflict decentralization. First, the chapter describes bank charter debates in Congress and the Supreme Court, explaining how Andrew Jackson's distribution of the national surplus to the states encouraged states to constitutionally charter and regulate banks, replacing the previous national banking system and quieting federal amendments on the topic. Second, the chapter shows how Jeffersonian congressmen pushed territorial slavery regulation on the states, with new Northern states constitutionally entrenching abolition and new Southern ones recognizing slavery, accepting congressional instruction and preventing congressional intervention. Finally, Jeffersonian and Jacksonian state constitutional framers expanded popular elections and the adult white male franchise, precluding suffrage and federal election reform amendments. Elections, slavery, and banking controversies, pitting congressmen and judges against each other through the 1790s and 1800s, gradually faded from national agendas due to successful state constitutional reform. State constitutionalism specifically, and not federalism more broadly, defused these controversies, channeling, and stabilizing, national institutional development. One therefore cannot fully understand antebellum American political development without studying the state constitutions.

Table 3. Proposed Federal Amendments by Topic, 1792–1849

Topic	Years topic most often proposed (descending frequency)	Total	Concurrent power
Article I			
Congress	1815, 1836, 1825, 1826, 1822	81	Yes
House of Representatives	1818, 1816, 1826, 1823, 1821	60	Yes
Senate	1808, 1816, 1814, 1810, 1795	27	Yes
Article II			
Executive	1826, 1836, 1841, 1823, 1803	196	Yes
Presidency	1803, 1802, 1830, 1799, 1826	29	Yes
Vice presidency	1802, 1830, 1808, 1803, 1799	5	Yes
Article III			
Federal courts	1793, 1794, 1808, 1800, 1836	47	No
Judicial jurisdiction	1793, 1794, 1805, 1806, 1807	15	No
Federal officeholding			
Term length and limits	1841, 1829, 1836, 1840, 1842	86	Yes
Removal	1808, 1839, 1842, 1836, 1835	25	No
Qualifications	1839, 1842, 1849, 1822, 1840	9	Yes
Elections			
Elections: general issues	1826, 1823, 1818, 1802, 1836	190	Yes
Election by district	1818, 1816, 1825, 1823, 1826	80	Yes
Electoral College	1818, 1816, 1826, 1802, 1813	53	Yes
Election by popular vote	1826, 1825, 1836, 1827, 1834	42	Yes
Taxes and finance			
Commercial regulation	1814, 1832, 1815, 1793, 1822	40	Yes
Taxes: general issues	1815, 1814, 1832, 1793, 1813	17	Yes
Income and direct taxes	1815, 1814, 1793, 1844, 1804	6	Yes
Rights and citizenship			
Race distinctions under law	1832, 1825, 1826, 1824, 1833	7	Yes
Slavery			
Slavery: general issues	1806, 1839, 1805, 1804, 1818	12	Yes
International trade	1806, 1805, 1804, 1803, 1808	8	No
Other			
State powers	1815, 1832, 1793, 1826, 1844	44	Yes
Veto overrides	1842, 1841, 1835, 1838, 1833	12	No
Regulation of DC	1820, 1839, 1818, 1821, 1819	8	No
Legislative apportionment: general issues	1815, 1843, 1814, 1804, 1831	7	Yes

Federal Deference to State Banking Law

Banking posed immediate congressional controversy. The brief Tenth Amendment did not expressly delineate the states' economic powers, leaving Treasury Secretary Alexander Hamilton and the First Congress to centralize power by financing the nation's mounting debt with a federal mint, taxation system, and national bank.[4] But the Constitution did not expressly let Congress charter a bank, prompting Jefferson, Madison, and Edmund Randolph of Virginia to ally with George Clinton and Aaron Burr of New York against the bank bill. New England, Delaware, and South Carolina Federalists together passed the bill, splitting Congress into two competing interregional parties, which together proposed nearly a dozen federal constitutional amendments to legitimize and entrench their position on banking.[5]

Unconstrained by the federal Constitution, states began chartering banks to raise funds. By 1792, Boston, New York, Albany, Philadelphia, and Baltimore all hosted state banks that competed with a National Bank branch, and when Hamilton proposed opening a National Bank office in Virginia, the state legislature promised competing state bank branches in Alexandria and Richmond. States chartered twenty-three more banks by 1800, often through constitutional revision, and with President Jefferson's blessing opened uncounted others, such that by 1811 each state had established at least one bank. Accordingly, each senator represented a state bank threatened by the national one. Through the 1810s and 1820s, congressmen unsuccessfully proposed amendments prohibiting rechartering the National Bank, while states, with smaller legislatures and easier constitutional revision, successfully chartered banks.[6]

Justice Marshall's 1819 *McCulloch* ruling compounded these congressional bank debates. The early Court, deferential to states'-rights congressmen, avoided matters internal to state politics.[7] But banking and economic regulation was a concurrent area subject to federal intervention, letting the Marshall Court strip state contract and commerce powers in a set of contentious decisions. In *McCulloch v. Maryland,* Marshall expanded federal power to charter a national bank while overturning bank regulation in six states, including Maryland's debilitating tax on the local National Bank chapter. When Ohio challenged *McCulloch* by taxing local branches of the National Bank, Marshall overturned the Ohio tax in *Osborn v. Bank of the United States.* Backed by the legislatures of Illinois, Indiana, Maryland, Ohio, Tennessee, and Pennsylvania,

Democratic-Republican Walter Lowrie proposed a national amendment effectively prohibiting chartering of a national bank, and other congressmen proposed at least five other constitutional amendments overriding Marshall's *McCulloch* ruling.[8]

Marshall remained bullish. Not long after, he enlarged federal commerce authority by overruling state regulation in *Gibbons v. Ogden* (1824). Democratic-Republicans attempted to dismantle the Court itself. Previous Jeffersonians had tried unseating and impeaching Federalist judges and now proposed federal amendments and resolutions removing and term limiting justices and requiring the concurrence of seven justices to overturn state law. States passed matching resolutions, signaling their willingness to ratify these amendments. The stability of the Constitution, the powers of the fledgling Court, and the very equality of the branches hung in the balance.[9]

Far from the halls of Congress, state legislators joined the attack. Between 1800 and 1830, the United States doubled in territory and tripled in population, mainly on the frontier. Tennessee's population alone increased sixfold. Western legislators and framers chartered canal, turnpike, and railway projects to draw Eastern settlers and export raw goods like Appalachian coal and Southern cotton. But infrastructure companies built these large projects slowly with little prospect of immediate profit, turning to state and local banks for loans. Frontier farmers too took bank loans, the interest rates for which were set by the distant, elite-run Second Bank headquartered in Philadelphia. After the Second Bank exacerbated inflation and contributed to the default and foreclosure of small farms in 1819, Democratic-Republican state legislators questioned its constitutionality.

These agrarians elected Andrew Jackson to the presidency in 1829. Jackson began dismantling the nation's system of centralized finance, vetoing congressional appropriations bills and the National Bank's rechartering, effectively voiding Marshall's *McCulloch* and *Osborn* rulings, and snubbed Marshall's *Worcester v. Georgia* (1832) decision on states'-rights grounds. Emboldened by Jackson's election, congressmen proposed six amendments limiting federal judges' terms and jurisdiction; Georgia called for a constitutional amendment to distribute a federal surplus raised under the 1833 Tariff; and two years later, John C. Calhoun proposed a pair of amendments to pass the surplus to the states, which the Democratic Congress, short of Article V requirements, did by statute in 1836. Distributing the surplus let the states charter and regulate new banks, reversing Marshall's gains.[10]

Marshall was now in a bind. Jacksonians in the House threatened to curtail federal judges' terms and jurisdiction. But Marshall had been a keen student of interbranch politics since *Marbury*. Avoiding direct confrontation, he instead deferred finance questions to the states. In *Willson v. Black-Bird Creek Marsh Co.* (1829), he affirmed the Delaware legislature's police power to charter a dam that impeded interstate commerce, and in *Barron v. Baltimore* (1833), Marshall asserted that the Bill of Rights did not block Maryland from interfering in the private business of the Baltimore resident John Barron. These deferential decisions deterred federal court-constraining amendments, helping preserve court power. The Marshall Court's rise reflects not only Marshall's clever reasoning in *Marbury,* per Robert McCloskey, and not only the waning of Democratic-Republican executive power, per Keith Whittington, but also the Court's strategic deference to the states.[11]

Upon Marshall's death, Jackson picked Roger B. Taney, architect of the surplus distribution scheme, as chief justice. In his first year, Taney issued a series of decisions dramatically expanding the states' banking and economic powers, continuing this pattern of devolution. In *Mayor of New York v. Miln,* he upheld a New York law regulating interstate commerce and, in *Charles River Bridge v. Warren Bridge,* expanded state legislatures' powers to charter corporations, extending this to bank charters in *Briscoe v. Bank of Commonwealth of Kentucky.* He soon let these state banks operate across state lines, supplanting the old National Bank. The Court, alongside Congress and the White House, now jointly pushed bank regulation on the states, establishing a uniform national policy of devolution.[12]

State legislators set to work. Spurred by the mercantilist desire to protect unprofitable public projects, by the promise of eventual returns on their investments, and by outright corruption, state legislators chartered, incorporated, and funded roads, turnpikes, bridges, canals, and railways. The number of banks in the United States boomed from four hundred to six hundred between 1833 and 1836, and bank liability skyrocketed, particularly in the developing Midwest and South, where bank note issues increased by 100 and 120 percent, respectively.

Financial regulations were lax. After Michigan's 1835 convention, lobbyists swarmed the new legislature, which chartered railroads and banks without personal liability clauses, leaving investors little recourse against financial mismanagement. A clause requiring that the state government make costly internal improvements nearly bankrupted the booming state. In neighboring Ohio, legislators lowered bank reserve requirements, subsidized private infrastructure ventures under the 1837 Loan Act, and granted these companies tax breaks. Corporate tax cuts and increased spending inflated the state's annual deficit to nearly $22 million, which legislators covered with heavy taxes on personal and real property, irritating voters.[13]

Then, in March 1837, a decline in cotton prices bankrupted New Orleans's major cotton firm, Herman Briggs and Company. A panic in New Orleans ensued, leading to the collapse of other local firms and then ones in New York. British lenders, worried that American banks had overextended themselves, called in their loans. This sparked a nationwide panic. In Ohio, bank runs drained the shallow reserves of local banks, which collapsed. Newly insolvent banks lacked capital to lend to existing infrastructure ventures, which also folded, leaving taxpayers to cover their losses.[14]

Voters, ruined by land and infrastructure speculation, called constitutional conventions to bind corporations and corrupt state legislators. Florida's 1838–39 convention devoted a fourteen-section article to bank regulation, prohibiting election of former bank employees, limiting legislators' authority to issue debt and charter corporations, and requiring public oversight of corporations. Delegates to California's 1849 convention restricted printing currency and chartering banks, with many Western-state framers imitating these provisions. The first Midwestern constitutions, all drafted after the panic, each included at least five banking and finance regulations.[15] In total, at least nineteen constitutions regulated the printing and circulation of currency, and twelve more imposed reserve requirements on banks.[16]

Framers aggressively constrained legislators' borrowing and lending powers. Every state constitution ratified in the years after 1845 limited legislators' power to issue debt, including New York's comprehensive 1846 constitution, which tripled its predecessor in word count. With more regulations, constitutions grew longer, taking their current, wordy form. Michigan's 1835 constitution, drafted on the eve of the panic, had only one provision on corporate regulation but was replaced by an 1850 constitution that dedicated two articles and at least thirty clauses to the topic. Indianans similarly scrapped their 1816 constitution, with two sections on banking, for an 1851 document with at least thirteen sections on banks, corporations, and debt. In a few states, legislators even constrained themselves by constitutional amendment.[17] Constitutional framers also let voters constrain legislators and other officials. New York's constitution made nearly all judicial, administrative, and local offices elected and doubled the frequency of senatorial elections. As other states did the same, newly empowered voters used referenda, frequent elections, conventions, and amendments to regulate corporations, recall judges, and prohibit legislators from granting corporations special privileges, risky loans, and immunity from liability, suggesting that state-level Jacksonian democratization was in part a pragmatic response to financial crisis.[18]

State constitutional framers successfully regulated debt, banking, and incorporation. Almost all corporate regulations were drafted after 1830, cresting roughly ten years after the panic of 1837, so that nearly every constitution ratified between 1837 and 1860 constrained banks and lending.[19] In contrast, Congress, which had heard eleven national bank amendments during the first and second chartering debates of the 1790s and 1810s, considered only one proposal after Jackson's 1832 veto preempted rechartering. And with the states aggressively constraining banks after 1837, members had few reasons to constrain state lending practices, proposing only four amendments and calling two dead-end committees on the topic. Swift, competent regulation by the states let Jacksonian congressmen maintain fiscal deference to the states, obviating a federal amendment to constrain or standardize state bank policy. Martin Van Buren thus declared the national banking question dead in 1840: "in lieu of a national bank," he argued, the states had brought "the adoption of the system which is now in successful operation." Writing several decades later, the historian Herman Ames agreed: "Owing to the favor in which State banks were held, especially in the West and South, it would have been impossible to have secured an amendment, even if Congress had recommended one." In sum, Jackson's veto ended national bank amendment debates, while his surplus bill let the states fund and then strictly regulate banks, preventing a federal amendment to regulate state banking practices. This illustrates devolution and, more specifically, deference, in which state reform prevented federal reform. With this successful devolution, finance questions faded from the congressional amendment agenda until the Civil War.[20]

Federal Deference to State Slave Law

Congress also deferred slave law to the states. The 1787 Northwest Ordinance abolished territorial slavery north of the Ohio River, while the 1789 North

Carolina Cession Act forbade territorial abolition south of the Ohio River, a quasi-constitutional accord balancing free and slave seats in Congress and the Electoral College.[21] But Virginia population growth tipped seats to the South, leading Northern congressmen in the 1800s to propose nearly a dozen amendments abolishing the international slave trade and eight amendments stripping Southern states' seats representing their enslaved population. A proposed 1804 amendment to repeal the Three-Fifths Clause brought rebukes from ten state legislatures. And when Representative George Thatcher of Maine proposed abolition in the Mississippi Territory, South Carolinians Robert Goodloe Harper and John Rutledge Jr. rallied all but twelve House members against the plan, with John Nicholas declaring that it "was not for [Congress] to attempt to make a particular spot of country more happy than all the rest."[22]

Southern and moderate Northern congressmen were true to their noninterventionist rhetoric—most Jeffersonians in Congress, reading the Constitution narrowly, never conceived of slavery as within their jurisdiction—and deferred slave law to incoming territories, interfering only to keep the bisectional balance. When Indiana's territorial governor William Henry Harrison asked Congress to expressly suspend the Northwest Ordinance's abolition clause in 1802, Northern congressmen refused, and neighboring Ohio entered the Union under an antislavery constitution. Congress rejected similar proslavery 1804 and 1806 petitions undermining the bisectional accord but let new territories otherwise regulate slavery as they wished, ignoring Illinois's slave-leasing practices and Harrison's slave code in Indiana, such that, according to the historian John Craig Hammond, "the battle between slavery and freedom in Indiana shifted from Congress back to Indiana itself." Jeffersonian congressmen, wary of congressional overextension and deferential to the states' sovereign Tenth Amendment police powers, coalesced around this "nonintervention" doctrine, cemented as Northern Federalists lost seats in the 1810s and failed to abolish slavery in the new Louisiana Territory. Under nonintervention, once states ratified new constitutions, Congress relied on them to maintain the bisectional compromise, framing slavery as an issue outside of congressional authority.[23]

Presidents and Congress also pushed fugitive slave recapture onto local law enforcement. When Pennsylvania abolitionists clashed with proslavery Virginians over an escaped fugitive slave in May 1788, Pennsylvania governor Thomas Mifflin appealed to President Washington, who, on the advice of Attorney General Edmund Randolph, ignored the dispute, as would subsequent presidents. Congressmen grappled with fugitive enforcement for two years, debating one House bill and three Senate bills before settling on the 1793 Fugitive Slave Act, asking that governors accept each other's extradition requests, as required by the federal Fugitive Slave Clause. The act appeased Southerners while leaving Northern state officials and judges broad interpretive leeway. Satisfied Northern congressmen passed the act and defeated later amendments to obligate enforcement, leaving the issue to the states.[24]

State constitutional reform preserved the bisectional consensus and the Jeffersonian policy of congressional nonintervention. Eastern states maintained old laws, and so in the first two decades of the nineteenth century, all new constitutional slavery provisions were ratified by frontier states.[25] New framers in the Old Northwest maintained abolition north of the Ohio River. Swept into the territorial legislature with Jefferson's 1800 election, Democratic-Republicans dominated Ohio's 1802 convention, holding majorities on all eight committees and adopting the Northwest Ordinance's abolition clause into the state constitution, which Indiana framers then borrowed fourteen years later. Likewise, Illinois framers in 1818 almost exactly copied Ohio's abolition clause, to the satisfaction of Northern congressmen. The three states also borrowed the Ordinance's injunction to return fugitive slaves, preempting interstate disputes over runaways from neighboring Kentucky and Virginia.[26]

New Southern states kept the national balance by locally entrenching slavery. Proslavery framers voted down abolition proposals by seven ministers in Kentucky's 1792 convention, Tennessee's 1796 convention imitated Congress's 1790 Southwest Ordinance in affirming slavery, and Louisiana's territorial legislature forbade manumission and compensated emancipation. Mississippians soon drafted their own constitution, borrowing heavily from Kentucky and Tennessee, limiting compensated emancipation. With state framers peacefully accepting and elaborating Congress's Northwest and Southwest Ordinances, slavery was, as Hammond writes, "by default, a local question. Consequently, slavery entered local politics in western states and territories far more frequently and intensely than it did national politics prior to 1819."[27]

Slavery debates reentered Congress in 1818 as white settlers passed the Ohio River's free-slave dividing line, petitioning for statehood in the unregulated Missouri Territory—an area Congress had failed to address through the original Northwest and Southwest Ordinances.[28] New York's James Tallmadge Jr. proposed emancipation in Missouri; John W. Taylor, also of New York, called for abolition in the neighboring Arkansas Territory; and New Hampshire's Arthur Livermore proposed a similar national constitutional amendment. Northerners abandoned party bonds and the old bisectional compromise, voting nine to one for Tallmadge's plan, with Southerners uniformly opposed.[29]

But by December 1819, Northern congressmen tempered their ambitions, admitting Alabama under a proslavery constitution. Further compromise came by admitting proslavery Missouri alongside a free Maine and otherwise abolishing slavery north of the 36° 30′ parallel while preserving it below. Southern congressmen approved the plan, expecting that increased Southern migration would inflate their House delegation, which Northerners hoped to check with the Senate. Enforcement returned to the states. With states beginning to successfully address the issue, Jeffersonian congressmen resumed the language of nonintervention. In January 1820, Congressman John W. Taylor, now more circumspect, proposed that the Constitution's silence left slave law to the states: "The right by which this property is held is not derived from the Federal Constitution; we have neither inclination nor power to interfere with the laws of existing States in this particular."[30]

As expected, south of the Ohio and the 36° 30′ parallel, every new state constitutionally recognized slavery, while Northern ones constitutionally abolished slavery; and to the far west, only Texas constitutionally protected slavery. This let Congress pair new slave and free states, balancing Congress and the Electoral College.[31] Between 1836 and 1856, each party thus nominated a president from one section and a vice president from the other, with presidents like Jackson consequently impounding interstate abolitionist mail and congressmen uniting to gag national antislavery petitions, keeping abolition out of Congress.

Slave law remained a local constitutional issue. Save for three unsuccessful abolition amendments proposed by John Quincy Adams in 1839, Jacksonian congressmen entirely avoided proposing amendments on slavery. Senator Samuel Prentiss of Vermont captured the consensus in Congress: "I look upon slavery in the States only as the constitution of the United States looks upon it—as a state institution, existing under state laws, and subject only to state authority." And so the state constitutions, with their lower bars to amendment, entrenched the Missouri Compromise. The antebellum era's most important, stabilizing constitutional rule—bisectionalism—was constitutionalized entirely at the state level. Reading bisectionalism solely through Congress's 1787, 1820, and 1850 compromises is therefore misguided. Similarly, it would be misguided to claim that Jeffersonian congressmen felt they had no authority over slave law—they proposed over a dozen amendments on the topic—but, generally, they did not invoke this power, not only because of their restrained, strict constructionist tendencies but also because the states made such an amendment unnecessary and such noninterventionist rhetoric plausible. This nationally contentious issue, clearly within Congress's jurisdiction, was left to the states, yielding only state constitutional reform, a case of devolution broadly and deference specifically.[32]

Federal Deference to State Election Law, State Preclusion of Federal Suffrage Reform

Then there was suffrage and election law. Suffrage exclusion proved contentious. With increasing immigration and industrialization, workingmen and farmers across the country began rallying and petitioning their state legislatures to repeal long-standing property and taxpaying qualifications on the vote. Jeffersonian congressmen avoided the issue by narrowly interpreting their Elections Clause power over state suffrage law, keeping suffrage disputes local. Madison best captured the sentiment, explaining, "One uniform rule would probably have been as dissatisfactory to some of the States as it would have been difficult to the [Philadelphia] convention," with the issue best "fixed by the State Constitutions." Presidents Adams, Jefferson, and Madison accordingly only attempted suffrage reform as delegates to their home states' constitutional conventions.[33]

Election law also spurred controversy. The Elections Clause let states devise systems for selecting delegates to the Electoral College and House of Representatives. Methods for House election were diverse and sometimes dysfunctional, with some states electing members by district, some by general ticket, and in one case by two-stage election. Even strict Jeffersonians, normally wary of intervention in state politics, felt the Elections Clause empowered Congress to impose a consistent system across the states. Similarly, states imposed differing schemes to pick presidential electors by district vote, by general ticket, or by legislature, yielding occasional deadlocks in which states failed to pick electors. Between 1792 and 1849, members of Congress attempted to intervene, offering thirty-seven amendments for direct election of the president and another fifty-four amendments for the selection of electors by district, four of which passed the Senate. This was perhaps the most divisive constitutional issue of the Jeffersonian era, and like others, it was a concurrent constitutional power, inviting state intervention.[34]

Suffrage disputes, though contentious, stayed local. All thirteen original states had passed taxpaying and property requirements, disenfranchising women, Blacks, Native Americans, and white male tenant farmers and urban workers. But with the rise of urban manufacturing, workingmen, shopkeepers, and immigrants rallied for labor and suffrage reform in Baltimore, Richmond, and Milwaukee. Small farmers mobilized against their disenfranchisement and in the Hudson Valley formed roving militias, threatening to burn towns and estates and skirmishing with sheriffs and the state militia.[35]

Prudently restrained, Jeffersonian congressmen avoided these state franchise disputes, instead invoking their Territories Clause powers to reject territorial property and taxpaying suffrage restrictions. Voters in the Old Northwest Territories then elected populist tradesmen and village lawyers to their first constitutional conventions, who in turn proposed that independent employment—not property wealth—allowed independent voting. Hoping to attract new immigrants and boost tax revenues and the chances for statehood, these frontier framers competed for the broadest franchise. Indiana's 1816 framers enfranchised white males twenty-one or older after a year of state residence, and three years later, Alabama's first framers lowered the residence requirement to three months. Kentucky and Tennessee were similarly lax. Five of the next eight states admitted to the Union after Tennessee enfranchised almost all white males, with Illinois's 1847 framers expressly seeking a broad franchise to attract disempowered immigrants.[36]

In older, Eastern states, Democrats and Whigs followed suit, racing to repeal property restrictions and expand the electorate and their vote share. Congressional deference to the states coincided with a Jeffersonian sweep of nearly all state legislatures after 1800. By the 1810s, remaining Federalist strongholds like Connecticut flipped, with Jeffersonians expanding the franchise across the states in the 1810s and 1820s, proposing dozens of state constitutions and amendments.[37] Martin Van Buren, a tavern keeper's son and delegate to New York's 1821 convention, hoped to empower "mechanics, professional men, and small landholders, . . . the bone, pith, and muscle of the population of the State," by defeating a proposed freehold qualification of $250. His gamble worked. The freehold qualification failed, and along the restive Hudson Valley, Van Buren found a mass political base, nearly unseating the patrician governor DeWitt

Clinton in 1820 and winning election to the U.S. Senate the following year. A cowed Clinton quickly capitulated and amended the state constitution to remove tax and service requirements.[38] Other Eastern states did the same, and so while the number of states nearly tripled from thirteen to thirty-one between 1790 and 1855, by 1855, only three states maintained property qualifications. Similarly, legislators and framers scrapped restrictions on alien and municipal election suffrage and officeholding, expanded judicial elections and popular referenda, and reapportioned legislative districts to equitably represent these new voters. State framers entrenched these reforms in their constitutions to prevent legislative rollback. Jonas Platt reminded the New York convention that "The qualifications of voters should be fixed with precision by the constitution, and that nothing should be left to the legislature. That department of the government was fluctuating, and liable to high party excitement." Between 1790 and 1855, every state at some point constitutionally precluded, abolished, or reduced property qualifications, and all but five constitutionally did so for tax-paying requirements.[39]

Suffrage expansion and accompanying establishment of winner-take-all legislative districts created mass parties that then muscled out marginal, radical, and class-based third parties. New York Whigs, for example, absorbed the local Workingmen's Party, co-opting and moderating the party's labor rhetoric and tempering voters' radicalism and organizing. And in asserting that only wage labor allowed the material independence needed to vote, state framers firmly constrained voting to working free white men, durably foreclosing future expansion to other groups.[40]

Rhode Island showed the danger of withholding the vote from mobilized white Jacksonian men. Seth Luther, a carpenter by trade, organized Providence's disenfranchised immigrant textile workers into the Rhode Island Suffrage Association, petitioning the legislature to reapportion seats toward Providence and repeal a restrictive 1763 franchise statute. But legislators rebuffed franchise expansion in 1811 and rejected five attempts to substantially revise the state's constitution, pushing voters in 1840 to install a new cohort of Whig legislators, who then called a sixth constitutional convention in February 1841.[41] Reluctant to let the elite-led legislature modify the constitution, Luther's Suffrage Association joined the ousted Democrats in drafting an extralegal, competing constitution with universal white male suffrage, electing an equitably apportioned legislature, and picking a new governor, Thomas Dorr. Claiming that no "exigency [could] arise which the unaided power of the State could not meet," President John Tyler refused to intervene, as later did Taney's Supreme Court, deeming this a political question best left to the state. In early May 1842, Dorr mustered several thousand militiamen and laborers and marched on Providence, where he and his populist legislature were inaugurated. At dawn on May 18, Dorr rallied four hundred supporters to storm the arsenal at Providence, training their cannons on loyalist militiamen. But the cannons failed to fire, Dorr fled, and the separatist legislature dissolved. The following year, a new convention extended the vote to all males who paid a token tax, restoring peace to Rhode Island. As Keyssar concludes, there is "little reason to think that other industrializing states would have avoided similar conflict and tumult . . . had they delayed franchise reform another generation or more."[42] By expanding the white male vote, most states avoided this tumult, keeping the franchise, and to some extent, the underlying labor and class question, out of Congress and the Supreme Court.[43]

Peaceful state constitutional suffrage expansion obviated national agitation and reform. With state legislators uniformly enfranchising white workingmen, no congressional party especially benefited by enfranchising these workingmen by amendment or by invoking the Elections Clause, no congressmen proposed national suffrage amendments, and Jeffersonian nonintervention remained a viable rhetorical approach in Congress and the federal courts. Put differently, peaceful state suffrage regulation facilitated Jeffersonian nonintervention, shaping how judges and congressmen understood their own powers. This is a case of obviation, and specifically preclusion, in which state constitutional reform prevented a nationally salient issue from reaching Congress and the federal courts. This was not for lack of power—Congress could have tried using Article V to overturn state franchise law through a single federal amendment, as it later would through the Fifteenth, Nineteenth, Twenty-Fourth, and Twenty-Sixth Amendments. But in this era, state constitutional reform obviated such an amendment, preventing congressional debate on this nationally salient topic. Studying only the congressional record would therefore miss this nationally contentious and potentially destabilizing constitutional issue, misunderstanding national politics.[44]

Congress could not, however, dodge petitions to reform congressional and presidential elections. Election-reform amendments swamped Congress. With states electing U.S. House members by district, general ticket, and two-stage election, congressmen sought standardization, proposing amendments for election by district, three of which passed the Senate before failing in the House. None cleared Article V; by the time congressional Whigs settled for a statute for single-member districts in 1842, all but six of the twenty-six states had already adopted single-member districts. The issue then disappeared from the amendment agenda. As Herman Ames concludes, "The desire for local representation gradually led to the general adoption by the States of the district system of electing their Congressmen, and caused the introduction of amendments on this question to cease." State regulation made a federal amendment unnecessary.[45]

Presidential elections proved more controversial. In 1816, Democratic-Republican congressional leaders preempted an interparty nomination fight by tapping Secretary of State James Monroe for the presidency. Nominating the secretary of state was customary, but Monroe's selection by congressional caucus alienated populist members of Congress like Martin Van Buren, who offered a constitutional amendment to diffuse influence by selecting presidential electors by geographic district. Between 1816 and 1823, members proposed thirty-three presidential-selection amendments, mainly for selection of electors by district, three of which cleared the Senate, with one narrowly failing in the House. Eventual ratification of an amendment seemed likely.

In 1824, a minority of Democratic-Republican congressmen defected to nominate Treasury Secretary William Crawford, who split the Electoral College vote with Andrew Jackson, Secretary of State John Quincy Adams, and House Speaker Henry Clay. This sent the matter to the House, where Clay oversaw balloting to select Adams. Adams then nominated Clay as secretary of state and heir apparent to the presidency. Backlash was swift. In the four years following Adams's election, congressmen proposed thirty-five constitutional amendments reforming presidential election, including twenty for popular election, as well as amendments standardizing the selection of electors by general ticket, by districts, or by legislature; preventing officeholding by electors; abolishing the Electoral College; and preventing the election from devolving on the House, including a direct-election amendment that Jackson proposed to remove "impediments ... to the free operation of the public will."[46]

The issue quickly overwhelmed Congress, leading Maine's Ebenezer Herrick to propose limiting members to submit amendments decennially. Between 1824 and Jackson's election in 1828, Congress heard sixty-four amendment proposals, thirty-seven of which concerned executive selection. While none of these congressional proposals cleared Article V's supermajority threshold, the states statutorily experimented with presidential selection. Most states selected presidential electors by legislature, by district, or by general ticket, often flipping their method when new parties took power. Massachusetts alone switched its practice for selecting electors after every election from 1796 to 1820. But partisan deadlock occasionally kept states from picking presidential electors at all, forcing legislators to seek a consistent practice. In 1789, Pennsylvania became the first state to unite electors on the same general ticket, maximizing the state's influence in the Electoral College. Following the 1824 election, New York, the most populous state, followed, so that by 1828, three of the five most populous states had adopted the general ticket, increasing their proportional influence and forcing small states to scramble to imitate. New Jersey, Massachusetts, and North Carolina, having unsuccessfully petitioned Congress for a federal district selection amendment, instead adopted state-level general ticket measures. By 1828, eighteen states adopted the system, and by 1832, twenty-two of the twenty-four states used a general ticket selected by popular vote. These statutory general ticket measures, interlocking with state constitutional expansion of the franchise, alleviated congressional fear of an undemocratic presidential election. Congressmen proposed fewer amendments on the topic—only sixteen of the total sixty-five between 1832 and 1836—and the issue died the following decade. As Ames notes, thanks to state reform, "after 1832, the method of choosing electors had become nearly uniform throughout the country without the resort to an amendment to the Constitution." This exemplifies deference, with members of Congress leaving a national issue to state reform, discouraging national constitutional change.[47]

Devolution broadly, and deference specifically, described most conflict decentralization through the antebellum era, as Congress debated electoral, banking, and slavery amendments but, through Jeffersonian self-restraint, Jacksonian localism, and occasional prudence, left the difficult work to the states. The Marshall and Taney Courts also strategically shifted finance matters to the states, preventing direct confrontation with congressional Jacksonians. Antebellum state framers then tackled these issues by comprehensively regulating banking, slavery, and elections and suffrage, primarily or exclusively through constitutional reform. In response, states introduced general ticket popular selection of presidential electors and single-member House districts, appeasing reform-minded congressmen and binding members to their district, encouraging particularistic policy making. States repealed constitutional property and taxpaying qualifications, precluding congressional debate on this nationally salient issue and obviating national change. States constitutionally chartered banks and infrastructure corporations and, after 1837, constrained legislators, bankers, and corporations with elections and new finance regulations, yielding a stable locally run banking system that satisfied members of Congress. And states maintained the bisectional accord through constitutional revision, abolishing slavery in Ohio, Indiana, and Illinois and allowing it in Kentucky, Tennessee, Louisiana, and Mississippi. Through the Missouri Compromise, they extended the dividing line between free and slave states across the Mississippi in cooperation with the executive and Congress, which almost entirely avoided proposing federal constitutional reform on the issue. These three issues, the main topics of proposed amendment in the 1790s and 1800s, faded from the national amendment and court agenda by the 1840s. Through deference, national actors let the antebellum states resolve national issues, preventing national constitutional reform and guiding national political development.

4
State Reconstruction, 1850–1877

*When we have given the negro the ballot in his right hand,
the land under his feet, and a state constitution above him,
that guarantees his citizenship.*
—Wendell Phillips, National Anti-Slavery Standard,
1865

THE CIVIL WAR DESTABILIZED NATIONAL constitutionalism. An unexpected Northern population boom swung House and Electoral College control to free states by 1850, prompting Chief Justice Roger B. Taney to open Western territories to slavery in *Dred Scott*. Incensed at Taney's decision, Northerners elected Abraham Lincoln to the White House on a territorial abolition platform, abandoning the old bisectional slavery compromise. Southerners rebelled, spurring congressmen to propose hundreds of amendments, first for reconciliation, then for Reconstruction. In total, Congress attempted 834 amendments between the 1850 and 1877 Compromises, more than in all prior years combined. The Thirteenth (1865), Fourteenth (1868), and Fifteenth (1870) Amendments, ratified during Reconstruction, reversed *Dred Scott,* fundamentally revising the federal Constitution in favor of freedom and civic equality.[1]

The Civil War also unsettled the state constitutions. With Southern secession and Reconstruction, the states called ninety-nine revision assemblies, empowered ninety-one to draft new constitutions, ratifying fifty-one constitutions between 1850 and 1877, and passed dozens of amendments and clauses extending unprecedented civil, voting, labor, and education rights.[2] Why, then, did *both* the federal and state constitutions change significantly during and after the Civil War?

Article V partly explains the timing of federal amendments. With Whigs and Democrats splitting Congress through the 1850s, passage remained unlikely, and members proposed only twenty-four amendments. But Union victory and early Reconstruction in 1864 granted Republicans bicameral congressional supermajorities and control of twenty of the twenty-five Union state legislatures, enough to pass and ratify amendments. Under Lincoln's capable leadership, Unionist congressmen proposed hundreds of amendments and eventually ratified the pivotal three. Yet partisan realignment and Article V requirements cannot fully explain the slew of attempted federal amendments—in the secession winter of 1860–61, desperate congressional Democrats and Republicans, far short of Article V requirements, nevertheless proposed over two hundred longshot reconciliation amendments.[3] The state constitutions' comparatively low barriers to amendment and replacement also invited reform, but these barriers were consistently low through the era and so cannot alone explain why Southern secession and constitutional reform waited until the 1860s.[4]

Judicial and public reinterpretation also destabilized American constitutionalism. In *Prigg v. Pennsylvania* (1842) and *Dred Scott* (1857), the Supreme Court stripped free states' power to liberate fugitive slaves, sparking Northern nullification efforts and leading the abolitionist William Lloyd Garrison to publicly condemn the Constitution as a "covenant with death and an agreement with hell." As Northern citizens pondered secession and Southerners executed it, the Constitution lost much of the public veneration that had preserved it against amendment and fundamental reinterpretation. These explanations of constitutional change, focusing on Article V, congressional party realignment, executive leadership, divisive judicial reinterpretation, and waning public veneration, each capture something essential about Civil War constitutional development. Yet, as this chapter shows, even together, these solely national accounts are incomplete.[5]

National and state constitutionalism were inextricably tied through conflict decentralization during the Civil War. State constitutional reform first destabilized and then stabilized national constitutionalism. Specifically, Congress used the 1850 Compromise and 1854 Kansas-Nebraska Act to push slave law on Western territories, expecting Westerners to adopt proslavery state constitutions and rebalance the House and Electoral College. Westerners instead constitutionally abolished slavery, while Northerners defied *Dred Scott* by statutorily and constitutionally protecting fugitive slaves, pushing Southerners, a national minority, to ratify secessionist state constitutions. Deference to the states on slavery, a venting mechanism that yielded stability in 1787 and 1820, now backfired as the states diverged. But with Union victory, Republican state constitutional framers restored stability. In 1864, Lincoln and Congress called Southern Unionist state constitutional conventions to abolish slavery, grant Blacks citizenship and equal protection of the laws, disenfranchise ex-Confederates, and recognize the national government's sovereignty. Congress then carefully imitated these state constitutional provisions, passing three matching amendments, rather than a host of new amendments or a new constitution. The Reconstruction state constitutions expounded, enforced, and buttressed the brief, untested national Reconstruction Amendments. While conventional narratives focus on bold, unilateral action by Lincoln and the Reconstruction Congress, explaining Reconstruction through federal dictation to the states, these stories miss how Lincoln and Congress relied on the state constitutional reform to jointly resolve the era's central constitutional questions and preserve the Union. That is, Lincoln and Congress not only dictated state constitutional policy but also passed federal amendments that imitated and interlocked with prior state constitutional reform. Mixing dictation of state policy and convergence around prior state policy, Lincoln and Congress framed the federal amendments to dovetail with state amendments. This stabilized and supported the new national constitutional order. In this sense, Civil War constitutional development responded not only to Article V constraints, congressional party shifts, executive leadership, and court and public reinterpretation but also to state constitutional reform, which exacerbated the slavery crisis in the 1850s only to ease Reconstruction in the 1860s and 1870s.[6]

Between 1850 and 1877, Congress heard hundreds of federal amendment proposals. The most common amendment issues, in roughly descending order, were slavery, state powers and elections, executive and congressional powers, and suffrage and civil rights issues. All concerned concurrent powers, and all engaged the federal courts. This chapter therefore focuses on slavery, civil rights and equal protection, and voting rights. Two hundred amendments addressed slavery, including proposals concerning compensated and uncompensated emancipation, fugitive slaves, territorial slavery, the slave trade, and slavery in the District of Columbia. Postwar proposals restructured both the federal and state governments, addressing congressional selection and apportionment, executive powers, payment of rebel debt, and expanding Black suffrage, civil rights, and citizenship while restricting these for ex-Confederates. The three ratified Reconstruction Amendments also concerned concurrent powers and complemented similar state reforms, introducing cooperative federal and state constitutional revision to resolve national disputes. Table 4 displays the twenty-five most common topics among amendments proposed between 1850 and 1877.[7]

The chapter recounts Civil War and Reconstruction–era conflict decentralization in four chronological steps. It first describes how Congress and the federal courts used devolution, and specifically deference, to push territorial slavery, fugitive slave, and Black citizenship questions on the states, which entrenched conflicting constitutional orders, exacerbating controversy. Second, the chapter shows how the 1850 Compromise, continuing this pattern of deference, yielded divergent state slave law and finally war. The chapter then describes Confederate state constitutionalism and early attempts at presidential Reconstruction through dictation. The last section shows that Congress required the Southern states to draft Reconstruction constitutions, leading states to converge on abolition and civil and voting rights protections, aiding and guiding the later ratification of matching federal amendments. These state clauses established immediate uncompensated emancipation, equal protection, and universal male enfranchisement, often prior to and in more detail than did the federal Reconstruction Amendments. With lawmaking authority shifting from the states back to the president and Congress, patterns of constitutional reform thus shifted from deference to dictation to convergence.

From Federal Deference to State Divergence on Slavery

Territorial slavery presented the first controversy. Congress statutorily balanced free and slave states in 1787 and again in 1820, satisfying Northerners and Southerners alike. This bargain so effectively quieted the issue that even the radical William Lloyd Garrison grudgingly admitted to "recognize the compact" in 1833, declaring that the slavery question was "not a constitutional controversy, but one affecting conscience." But in 1849, antislavery delegates to California's constitutional convention refused to split the state into a free northern and proslavery southern half, potentially increasing the Senate's free-state majority to six seats, threatening the bisectional balance. The following year, the vast New Mexico territory also proposed an antislavery state constitution,

Table 4. Proposed Federal Amendments by Topic, 1850–1877

Topic	Years topic most often proposed (descending frequency)	Total	Concurrent power
Article I			
Congress	1861, 1860, 1869, 1866, 1872	78	Yes
House of Representatives	1866, 1867, 1865, 1869, 1864	66	Yes
Senate	1874, 1873, 1876, 1867, 1877	32	Yes
Article II			
Executive	1869, 1877, 1876, 1873, 1868	93	Yes
Presidency	1872, 1864, 1868, 1876, 1877	27	Yes
Article III			
Federal courts	1867, 1868, 1872, 1869, 1864	23	No
Article V			
Amendment process: general issues	1861, 1869, 1860, 1864, 1866	40	Yes
Amendment by convention	1861, 1869, 1860, 1864, 1868	28	Yes
Federal officeholding			
Term length and limits	1868, 1876, 1867, 1875, 1873	60	Yes
Elections			
Election: general issues	1869, 1877, 1876, 1872, 1873	109	Yes
Election by popular vote	1873, 1876, 1877, 1868, 1869	57	Yes
Taxes and finance			
Taxes: general issues	1866, 1865, 1864, 1876, 1877	29	Yes
National debt	1866, 1867, 1865, 1873, 1869	27	No
Rights and citizenship			
Suffrage	1869, 1866, 1868, 1867, 1861	92	Yes
Rights: general issues	1866, 1869, 1864, 1861, 1860	72	Yes
Race distinctions under law	1861, 1864, 1869, 1860, 1866	33	Yes
Slavery			
Slavery: general issues	1861, 1860, 1864, 1866, 1863	200	Yes
Territories and DC	1861, 1860, 1864, 1873, 1876	49	No
Fugitive slaves	1861, 1860, 1864, 1866, 1865	44	Yes
Compensated emancipation	1866, 1861, 1864, 1867, 1869	28	Yes
Civil War			
Ex-Confederate claims and debt	1866, 1867, 1865, 1873, 1876	33	No
Ex-Confederate rights	1866, 1869, 1867, 1872, 1864	27	Yes
Other			
State powers	1861, 1864, 1860, 1869, 1867	129	Yes
Territorial regulations	1861, 1860, 1864, 1871, 1866	72	No
Legislative apportionment: general issues	1866, 1865, 1867, 1864, 1868	48	Yes

cordoning slavery to the Southeastern states. Compounding the issue, poorer Southerners, unable to compete with the rising slave aristocracy, moved north, joining immigrants from abroad and inflating the population of the Old Northwest. By 1850, free states held 147 of the 237 House seats and 169 of the 290 Electoral College votes, enough to unilaterally select the president and thus add federal judges. Many of these new Northern congressmen were Free Soilers who sought abolition in the territories and District of Columbia and a prohibition on interstate slave transportation. Pennsylvania's David Wilmot, for example, rallied the House to interpret the Territories Clause to ban slavery in all territories seized during the Mexican-American War, though his measure failed against Southern Senate opposition.[8]

Southern radicals threatened secession. Calhoun offered Senate resolutions requiring that territories allow slavery, but these too failed against free-state majorities in both houses, which he claimed left the South "without any adequate means of protecting itself against its encroachment and oppression." Stoking secessionist rumors, the Mississippi legislature called an emergency Southern convention in Nashville in that same year, and other state legislators soon impounded, censored, and burned abolitionist literature. Meanwhile, Northern legislatures, courts, and governors passed incendiary personal liberty laws expressly nullifying the 1850 Fugitive Slave Act and blocking the recapture of runaway slaves.[9]

Panicky congressmen shoved the slavery question back on the states and territories, as they had in 1787 and 1820, hoping to again silence national debate. In 1848, Lewis Cass suggested that the Territories Clause let Congress regulate public territorial lands but not territorial slavery, leaving the latter to territorial legislators and constitutional convention delegates. Cass's Democratic platform promised Northerners territorial abolition and Southerners territorial slavery, and so even after Cass lost the 1848 presidential election, the platform claimed bisectional support, now under Democrat Stephen A. Douglas. Douglas, with the aid of Whig Daniel Webster, engineered the 1850 Compromise admitting California as a free state and letting New Mexico and Utah constitutional conventions regulate slavery as they wished.[10]

Northerners and Southerners saw divergent territorial outcomes in this "popular sovereignty" plan. Proslavery congressmen, particularly in the Deep South, trusted that the Southwest would adopt plantation and mining slavery and would elect proslavery congressmen. North Carolina representative Thomas Lanier

Clingman, recalling newspaper articles and conversations with Westerners, expected that the Colorado River would "produce sugar, cotton, rice, and tropical fruits &c." In describing California, he added, "Gold mines are known to exist there.... Wherever gold mines exist, especially surface, alluvial, or deposit mines, slave labor can be employed to greatest advantage." Northerners and some abolitionists backed popular sovereignty, predicting plantation slavery would not flourish in the dry Southwest. The Democrat John McClernand of Illinois supported the Compromise, claiming, "God and nature have traced an immutable material law in the lofty mountains and arid deserts of that Territory, forever prohibiting African slavery within its limits.... Slavery does not, nor can it, as I think, exist in Utah or New Mexico." Moreover, antislavery congressmen trusted that Southwesterners would maintain Mexican laws abolishing local slavery.[11] Douglas's plan thus passed the House and Senate with bi-sectional support partly because it did not require antislavery or proslavery congressmen to abandon their position and compromise.[12]

This devolution temporarily quieted the territorial slavery question. As Representative Boyd of Kentucky argued, deference was the plan's strength: "I am earnestly and in good faith seeking to test the sense of the House upon the doctrine of non-intervention.... I am for the Union. I am for the Constitution as it is—I want no amendment to it." Boyd got his wish. As in 1787 and 1820, the 1850 Compromise was entrenched in the state constitutions but not in the federal one. This satisfied members of Congress, who proposed only twenty-four federal constitutional amendments over the next decade, only two of which would have directly regulated territorial slavery. State constitutional revision kept slavery off Congress's constitutional agenda in the 1850s.[13] But since both Northerners and Southerners held irreconcilable expectations about territorial slavery, the state constitutions were now locked in an unstable bargain, unlike those of 1787 and 1820. Devolution of the territorial slavery question, and in this case, devolution through deference, therefore backfired. Rather than joining Congress in resolving the issue, the states merely delayed interregional confrontation. Deference lit a slow fuse on the slavery question.[14]

Fugitive slave law also split Congress and the state legislatures. The Constitution's Fugitive Slave Clause held that runaways were enslaved under their home state's laws, but the clause, and the 1793 Fugitive Slave Act, failed to charge federal or state officials with recapture and return. Northern congressmen blocked enforcement bills in 1801 and 1817, and free-state governors, legislators, and judges often ignored the clause and the act. Northern state constitutional framers instead passed abolition clauses through the early antebellum years, letting state judges emancipate runaways and state legislators pass personal liberty laws punishing slave catchers who seized free Blacks. It seemed Northerners had nullified federal fugitive slave law. Ralph Waldo Emerson triumphantly declared, "Slavery in Virginia or Carolina was like Slavery in Africa or the Feejees, for me. There was an old fugitive law, but it had become, or was fast becoming, a dead letter, and, by the genius and laws of Massachusetts, inoperative."[15]

Conversely, Southern legislators harshly limited Black people's mobility. Following Denmark Vesey's attempted 1822 slave revolt, South Carolina detained free Black sailors on shore leave from Northern ships. North Carolina, Georgia, Florida, Alabama, Louisiana, and Texas followed suit, sometimes violating the federal Privileges and Immunities right of free Black people to enjoy the same rights they held in their home states. Soon thereafter, Massachusetts's *Commonwealth v. Aves* decision freed Southern slaves entering the state with their legal owner. Between the 1836 *Aves* ruling and 1860, courts in every state considered the *Aves* precedent, and all but five Northern states accepted it.[16]

The Supreme Court similarly let the states regulate the interstate movement of free and enslaved Blacks. In *Groves v. Slaughter* (1841), Justices Smith Thompson, John McClean, and Roger B. Taney each limited the Court's jurisdiction over the interstate movement of slaves, expressly leaving the issue to state legislatures and constitutional conventions.[17] In *Prigg v. Pennsylvania* (1842), Justice Joseph Story struck down the slave catcher Edward Prigg's conviction under Pennsylvania's 1826 personal liberty law, ruling that the states could not impede enforcement of the 1793 Fugitive Slave Act, which was the duty of the federal government. Despite being an important doctrinal victory for advocates of slavery and broad national powers, in the absence of federal enforcement, this left implementing fugitive law to the states. Further, Story ruled that free-state citizens and officials could not be compelled to recapture slaves, positing that the Fugitive Slave Clause "does not point out any state functionaries, or any state action, to carry its provisions into effect. The States cannot, therefore, be compelled to enforce them, and it might well be deemed an unconstitutional exercise of the power of interpretation to insist that the States are bound to provide means to carry into effect the duties of the National Government, nowhere delegated or entrusted to them by the Constitution." The antislavery John McClean also granted each "state a power to guard and protect its own jurisdiction and the peace of its citizens," precluding recapture of fugitives. Even the proslavery, occasionally nationalist Taney concurred that returning fugitives was an Article IV power reserved to the states. In deferring implementation to the states, opposed justices avoided the difficult issue of expounding federal enforcement.[18]

With Northern states ignoring and even voiding the Fugitive Slave Clause, Southern congressmen united to pass the 1850 Fugitive Slave Act over piecemeal Northern resistance, forcing federal and state officials and citizens to return runaways. Congress then laid the issue to rest. Between 1850 and 1859, Congress proposed only one federal amendment touching on slave mobility, recognizing a right to property in slaves. The question remained whether Northern officials and citizens would capitulate to the act and appease Southerners.[19]

Tangentially related, though less contentious to Congress and the federal courts, was the question of Black citizenship. Abolitionists justified Black equality by citing the Bible, per Garrison; the Declaration of Independence, per Douglass; and centuries of uncompensated Black labor, per Martin Delany. But at Harvard University, where the Black Delany was denied entrance, Louis Agassiz's embryology studies claimed that Blacks' and Native Americans' fetal development halted too early to allow the mental capacity for citizenship. Samuel George Morton and Josiah C. Nott of the University of Pennsylvania tried to confirm this claim by studying racial differences in cranial volumes, pleasing racist abolitionists and Southern reactionaries alike and affirming state-level prohibitions on Blacks' citizenship, suffrage, and education rights nationwide. States did, however, differ on Black citizenship, inviting federal litigants to challenge these conflicting provisions under the Privileges and Immunities Clause. But the Supreme Court closed this door with *Strader v. Graham* (1851). Justice Taney asserted that on granting statehood, Congress relinquished authority to regulate slavery within a state, leaving the state courts and legislatures to regulate Blacks' freedom and citizenship rights, in lieu of the federal courts.[20] This deference quieted national debate by forcing regulation on the states.

By the 1850s, congressional and federal court deference on territorial slavery, fugitive slaves, and Black citizenship yielded incompatible proslavery and antislavery state constitutional orders. Devolution had worked in 1787 and 1820, when interstate conflicts were fewer, but now deference let the states entrench diverging state constitutional regimes, which they jealously protected from federal interference. This solidified an increasingly untenable bargain that national institutions could not arbitrate.[21]

State Divergence and the Coming War

The 1850 Compromise admitted California as a free state and allowed the legislatures and constitutional conventions of New Mexico and Utah to regulate slavery as they wished. Contrary to Southerners' expectations, agrarian plantation slavery never succeeded in these vast, dry Southwestern territories. Utah's 1849 and 1856 constitutions and New Mexico's 1848 and 1849 constitutions failed to protect slavery, and the Senate pointedly ignored New Mexico's proslavery 1850 constitution. The Supreme Court also refused to invoke its power to overrule either territory's constitution, and so by 1860, Utah and New Mexico held twenty-nine and zero slaves, respectively. This further unbalanced the House and Electoral College.[22]

California followed the same path. In 1849, mining advocates swept the state's first convention and banned slavery, which they feared would undersell wage-labor mining and allow racial intermixing. Morton McCarver, Oliver M. Wozencraft, and James McHall Jones, all born or adopted Kentuckians, proposed outlawing the immigration of free and enslaved Blacks, hoping to make California a white republic, but the convention dropped the clause, worrying that egalitarian congressmen would block California's admission to the Union. Delegates were painfully aware of the convention's national importance. Jacob Snyder, for example, asked delegates to "prevent all discussion in Congress in regard to [California's] admission into the Union" by framing a centrist, moderate constitution to "settle many important questions relative to the interests and wants of the people of this country." When the convention's Committee on Boundaries proposed enlarging California's borders to incorporate modern Nevada and thus to exclude slavery from much of the West, Winfield S. Sherwood predicted that these expansive borders would resolve the national slavery controversy. He explained, "If the Union is to be cut asunder by this one question, we shall regret it for years, that having it in our power, with no cost to ourselves, we did not settle it forever. It is this that governs my vote, and not any desire that I have to embrace that territory within our limits as a State. I want to see [the slavery debate] forever kept out of the halls of Congress." The Virginian Charles T. Botts, better attuned to the Southern mind, warned Sherwood that expansive free-state borders would provoke opposition from "the extreme faction of the South, headed by Mr. Calhoun," and from "the wise and moderate men of the North" who feared provoking Southern firebrands. Like Sherwood, Botts hoped to frame a state constitution to resolve national tensions. The convention settled on less expansive borders, and on September 9, 1850, Congress brought a free California into the Union under Douglas's Compromise. Oregon's first constitution, framed in 1857, imitated California's free-soil laws. The Compromise's deference to local custom had yielded an anti-Black, antislavery West.[23]

To Southerners' surprise, antislavery settlers quickly settled the Great Plains. Iowans placed the Northwest Ordinance's abolition clause in their 1846 and 1857 constitutions, Wisconsin's 1848 framers banned slavery and enfranchised Blacks, and Illinois's 1848 convention legally extinguished slavery, as did one in Michigan two years later and another in Indiana the year after that. Northern constitutions were now uniformly antislavery.[24]

Southern congressmen sought new, Western states, proposing the Kansas-Nebraska Act. The act, promoted by Douglas and the Missouri senator David Atchison, repealed the Missouri Compromise's prohibition on slavery above the 36° 30' parallel, leaving regulation to territorial voters, legislators, and framers. Atchison hoped this would draw new settlers from the slaveholding counties of western Missouri into eastern Kansas, while Congress's Northern Democrats expected Kansas to be climatically inhospitable to slavery. Once again, free- and slave-state congressmen saw different outcomes for devolution.

Kansans, charged with resolving this national question, failed. The politics were dirty, then violent. On election day, Atchison led his constituents across the Mississippi to install a proslavery territorial legislature. Excluded abolitionist Kansans formed a shadow government under the antislavery Topeka Constitution of 1855 but were attacked by proslavery forces in the town of Lawrence. John Brown answered by executing local slaveholders. The controversy reached the U.S. Senate when the South Carolinian Preston Brooks caned Charles Sumner of Massachusetts for a lurid speech implicating Atchison and Brooks's cousin in the crisis. The Northern-leaning House in turn accepted the antislavery Topeka Constitution, but Southern senators blocked the measure. Heartened by this, Kansas's proslavery legislature and voters proposed the proslavery 1857 Lecompton Constitution but were rejected by Congress's remaining Northern Democrats. Quarantining the free-soil issue in Kansas had not cured the controversy but rather incubated it and then spread it back to Congress.[25]

Devolution again backfired, morphing into divergence and sparking electoral and congressional realignment. While only two slave states petitioned the House Committee on the Territories to block the Kansas-Nebraska Act, citizens in all but three of the free states petitioned against the act. When the act passed with Northern Democratic support, incensed Northern voters ousted 70 percent of their Democratic congressmen in 1854, decimating the party's Northern wing. Northern Whig voters, inspired by *Uncle Tom's Cabin* and frustrated with the Kansas-Nebraska Act and the recent trial of the runaway Anthony Burns under the 1850 Fugitive Slave Act, abandoned their party's Southern wing, joining Free Soilers and rebranding themselves as Republicans. Controlling both the House and Senate after 1854, these free-state congressmen had little reason to risk further Northern voter backlash, and in 1856, they abandoned bisectional tradition and nominated the free-state antislavery candidates John C. Fremont of California and William Dayton of New Jersey. Oregon and Minnesota soon entered the Union under antislavery constitutions, with no new slave states added in the 1850s. Federal land claims now reached the Pacific, keeping proslavery settlers from retaking Congress or the Electoral College. Divergence on territorial slave regulation had elevated slavery controversies to Congress, realigning and polarizing the national parties. Republicans were now largely antislavery Northerners and Democrats largely proslavery Southerners, deadlocked and unable to pass another compromise bill.[26]

Deepening the divergence, Northern officials freed fugitive slaves. Some legislators reinterpreted *Prigg* to authorize their personal liberty statutes. Ohio congressman Joshua Giddings's 1842 *Pacificus* essays declared that *Prigg* did not infringe on the "constitutional rights of the free States"; Pennsylvania and New York judges read *Prigg* to emancipate visiting slaves; and New York governor William Seward, defending his state's liberty law, held that *Prigg* did not bind "state legislatures, directs no action by them, nor designates any possible occasion for their action."[27]

Northern framers also passed new abolition clauses, and legislators and judges reinterpreted state constitutional liberty and habeas corpus provisions to authorize antikidnapping statutes. Rhode Island contested *Prigg* by constitutionally forbidding slavery in 1842 and prohibiting slaveholders' travel with slaves; Connecticut, by abolishing slavery and the slave trade; Massachusetts, with a new personal liberty law; and Vermont, by imprisoning state officials who detained fugitives, consistent with the state constitution's abolition clause. Within weeks of the 1850 Fugitive Slave Act's passage, Vermont legislators granted fugitives habeas appeal rights, sent nullification resolutions to Congress and every governor, and passed additional personal liberty laws, defying President Millard Fillmore's threat of military intervention. As Northerners pivoted to overt nullification, Frederick Douglass soon declared, "The only way to make the Fugitive Slave Law a dead letter is to make half a dozen or more dead kidnappers." Between 1846 and 1851, framers in Illinois, Indiana, Iowa, Michigan, and Wisconsin passed, renewed, or strengthened constitutional abolition clauses. Massachusetts called for new liberty laws. Illinois's supreme court in 1852 ruled disputed fugitives to be presumed free, and Connecticut in 1855 passed a liberty law and in 1857 freed visiting slaves. That same year, legislators in the New Hampshire and Maine legislatures freed visiting slaves and in Michigan and Ohio adopted personal liberty laws, with Ohio's supreme court citing *Somerset* to free visiting slaves.[28] Finally, in *In re Booth and Rycraft,* Wisconsin judge Abram Smith repeatedly cited Jefferson's compact theory to nullify the 1850 Fugitive Slave Act. Since the state's constitution guaranteed Wisconsinites' liberty and habeas rights, Smith freed Sherman Booth and John Rycraft, who had been imprisoned under the 1850 act for aiding a fugitive. While judges led in some states and legislators in others, both groups protected fugitive slaves by reinterpreting and broadening Northern constitutions' habeas and liberty protections.[29]

Backlash was widespread. Southern courts, joined by Justice Taney, rejected *Somerset* and its Northern antislavery progeny, which the Georgia senator Robert Toombs called a scheme "to exterminate slavery by abrogating by State laws that portion of the Constitution which provides for the return of fugitive slaves." James Buchanan, a moderate "doughface" Northerner, sought to reverse the divergence, appealing to the Northern "state legislatures [to] repeal their unconstitutional and obnoxious enactments. Unless this shall be done without unnecessary delay, it is impossible for any human power to save the Union." Even the Unionist presidential candidates Abraham Lincoln and John Bell in 1860 pushed for repeal of the liberty laws, but with little success, as Northern Republican governors held the line.[30]

Northern and Southern states agreed on one thing: constraining Black citizenship. Worried that free Blacks might foment slave revolt, Southern states limited free Blacks' movement and assembly rights, assuming all Black people to be slaves unless proven otherwise. Free-soil Oregon also restricted Black immigration and movement in 1843 and 1845, as did Illinois in 1848 and Indiana in 1851, with Congress affirming these laws.[31] Southern states largely ignored state constitutional promises requiring they fund public education and nearly entirely outlawed the instruction of slaves. Northern states too forced Black residents into segregated, underfunded charity schools and largely excluded free Black people from voting and officeholding.[32] In *Crandall v. Connecticut* (1834), Connecticut formalized Black residents' partial citizenship status by rejecting their federal Privileges and Immunities rights and consequent ability to appeal to federal courts, with Pennsylvania, Kentucky, and Mississippi, among other states, adopting elements of the decision. Further, federal attorneys general had rejected Black Americans' right to federal appeal since 1821, with General Hugh Legare in 1843 deeming them mere "denizens." This, with the *Strader* decision, kept citizenship a state issue, constraining the scope of national debate.[33]

National debate therefore focused on fugitive and territorial slavery. In May 1856, Democratic Party leaders prompted Buchanan to reverse the federal policy of deference. Buchanan floated a plan for federal dictation, asking the Supreme Court to standardize the application of popular sovereignty in the territories. In the *Dred Scott* decision, Chief Justice Taney attempted to dictate territorial slave and citizenship law, asserting that no free or enslaved Black person held federal citizenship.[34] This affirmed the states' long-standing *Crandall* precedent against citizenship appeals to the federal courts, keeping the citizenship issue local. Having denied Scott's right to federal citizenship and appeal, Taney could have dismissed the case, but he instead added that the Territories Clause extended congressional authority only to territory under federal jurisdiction at the 1787 ratification of the Constitution, invalidating the later Compromises of 1820 and 1850, opening all Western territories to slavery.[35] Further still, he declared that congressional abolition would violate slaveholders' Fifth Amendment property rights to own and perhaps travel with slaves.[36]

The attempt at dictation resolved little. Northern officials worried that Taney's Fifth Amendment claims might void their liberty laws or even allow slaveholding within their borders. New Hampshire responded by freeing visiting slaves, Maine by granting fugitives a defense attorney, and New York by invoking nullification powers. Moderate Republicans rejected Taney's ruling on the territories, suggesting that since the Court had no jurisdiction over Dred Scott's case, the decision was nonbinding *obiter dictum.* Similarly, Wisconsinites ignored Taney's *Ableman v. Booth* decision to reimprison the abolitionist Sherman Booth, instead electing Booth's attorney to the state supreme court. Few of these Northern states granted Black residents full citizenship, suggesting that their objection was not over Taney's repeal of Black citizenship but rather over his reversal of Northern state statutes.[37]

In November 1860, Republicans captured 31 of 50 Senate seats and 108 of 183 House seats, bringing the antislavery congressional majority that Southerners had long feared. With Democrats divided between candidates, Lincoln took the White House with only 40 percent of the popular vote, drawing on antislavery voters and Northerners exasperated with the Buchanan administration's corruption and mismanagement in the face of an economic panic. Lincoln's platform promised to end divergence on territorial slavery for federal dictation of abolition in the territories. Proslavery Southerners saw they had little chance of regaining the Congress or presidency. They seceded and readied for war.

The Civil War and Presidential Reconstruction by Dictation

Congress scrambled to appease the South. Following Lincoln's election in November 1860, President Buchanan attempted to overturn Northern liberty laws and expand territorial slavery by convention or amendment. But the divided Congress rejected these plans and 72 similar federal amendment proposals, triple the number posed in the previous decade. In 1861, Congress saw another 167 amendments fail against Article V.[38]

On December 20, South Carolina seceded, joined in winter by the other six Deep South states and in spring by the six border states. By summer 1861, all had ratified the Confederate constitution and withdrawn from the federal Congress, expanding Congress's Northern majority. Burdened with the war and unwilling to reconcile with rebels, Congress heard only nine proposed constitutional amendments between 1862 and 1863. Federal troops now shouldered the Union's fate.[39]

Across the Southern states, delegates convened to ratify the proposed Confederate constitution and to raise funds, troops, and supplies. Most ratified new state constitutions within a year, maintaining slavery and disenfranchisement of women and people of color and adding additional provisions restricting immigration of free and enslaved Blacks. With the Confederate constitution's blessing, framers constitutionally declared their states sovereign bodies with attendant explicit rights to nullification, interposition, and secession.[40]

The documents were short-lived. Northern armies bore south along the Mississippi and through Virginia, toppling Confederate governments and letting Lincoln begin state constitutional Reconstruction and abolition. With Congress hamstrung, Lincoln seized power to dictate state Reconstruction. Even as his powers grew, Lincoln made "no claim of a right by Federal authority to interfere with slavery within State limits," particularly in the crucial, proslavery border states. The states would implement abolition themselves. After West Virginia entered the Union in 1863 under a free constitution, Lincoln proposed his "ten percent plan," readmitting any Confederate state that drafted an antislavery constitution backed by 10 percent of the state's 1860 voting population. Consequent state constitutional conventions sketched the initial contours of Reconstruction. Under Lincoln's plan, working-class Louisiana convention delegates reapportioned power away from planter parishes and to the new capital of New Orleans, gave public workers a nine-hour day and a minimum wage, funded public schools via a progressive tax, and, in another blow to the planter aristocracy, abolished slavery without compensation. Within a day of assembling, a committee of thirteen Arkansans passed a new constitution abolishing slavery without compensation and protecting Black residents' property rights, while across the Mississippi, Tennesseans proposed amendments for abolition and legislative disenfranchisement of ex-Confederates.[41]

Congress also tested Reconstruction, and dictation, by requiring state constitutional reform on the Confederacy's periphery. Congress conditioned West Virginia's admission to the Union on drafting a constitution with uncompensated emancipation, and the following year, Congress used Nevada's admission as a proving ground for Southern Reconstruction. Prodded by Union occupation, in 1864, Marylanders representing western farm counties drafted a constitution reapportioning power away from eastern slaveholders, emancipating slaves, forgiving debt, funding public schools, and enfranchising Union soldiers. In late 1864, Union troops advancing across Georgia and Virginia dismantled the remaining Confederate state governments.[42]

Congressional Reconstruction through Dictation and Convergence

As United States armies liberated Atlanta and Richmond, the Confederacy collapsed. Reunification returned power—and constitutional disputes—from the

Southern states to Washington, with Lincoln and Congress proposing separate plans to impose abolition on unwilling state governments. And while four million enslaved Black people earned freedom, many were forbidden from voting, officeholding, serving on juries, and having economic and social rights under the first Reconstruction state constitutions, curtailing Republicans' Southern electoral base. Congressional Republicans therefore debated forcing state conventions to forbid ex-Confederate voting and officeholding and even proposed dissolving ex-Confederate states into new congressionally administered territories.[43]

With ex-Confederates excluded from Congress, Northern congressmen proposed federal amendments to emancipate slaves, reapportion Congress, dispose of rebel debt, and expand Blacks' civil and voting rights while contracting ex-Confederates' rights. Congress, which had proposed only twenty-four amendments in the decade before the war, now proposed 415 amendments between 1864 and 1869, with seven proposals passing at least one house, including the three revolutionary Reconstruction Amendments. Many proposals imitated and complemented state constitutional provisions, which also eased the three Reconstruction Amendments' ratification.[44]

Emancipation came first. The House heard a pair of abolition amendments in December 1863, and weeks later, Senator Charles Sumner of Massachusetts proposed an amendment stating, "All persons are equal before the law, so that no person can hold another a slave," granting Congress necessary and proper enforcement powers. The Judiciary Committee redacted Sumner's equality provision, and on April 5, Senators Garrett Davis and Lazarus Powell of Kentucky instead proposed forbidding uncompensated emancipation and Black citizenship and officeholding. Three days later, Delaware's Willard Saulsbury presented a similar, twenty-section proposal for abolition with congressional compensation. The Senate settled for a two-sentence Thirteenth Amendment for uncompensated emancipation, attaching a congressional enforcement clause that sank the proposal in the House. By April 1864, Congress had not answered whether abolition entailed compensation, congressional enforcement, or Black citizenship and equality.[45]

Congress instead passed the Wade-Davis Bill to call Unionist state constitutional conventions. While Lincoln pocket-vetoed the bill, fearing his ten-percent-plan governments would not meet its strict criteria, by spring of 1864, Congress had opted to recognize and readmit Southern states. This subjected the proposed Thirteenth Amendment to ratification by Southern legislatures, underscoring the need to force allied state conventions.[46] Members also saw that protecting Black citizenship, education, economic, marriage, and especially franchise rights required that Southern state conventions invoke their traditional police and suffrage powers.[47] Lincoln's Reconstruction conventions offered a model. Representative Fernando Beaman deemed the Unionist Louisiana government "a beacon-light by which we may be led out of the labyrinth in which we have been groping." Two days after Appomattox, Chief Justice Salmon P. Chase asked Lincoln to readmit "state governments under constitutions securing suffrage to all citizens": "Louisiana impresses me strongly with the belief that this extension will be of the greatest benefit to the whole population. The same can be secured in Arkansas by an amendment of the State constitution, or what would be better, I think, by a new convention. . . . To all the other States the general principle may be easily applied."[48]

Cued by Lincoln and Congress, Southern convention delegates promptly abolished slavery without compensation. Constitutions in Arkansas, Louisiana, Maryland, and Virginia emancipated slaves in 1864, as did those in Alabama, Florida, Georgia, Mississippi, Missouri, and South Carolina in 1865. These abolition clauses ignored or forbade compensation. Louisiana's convention, for example, voted seventy-two to thirteen against compensation to planters, the cost of which one delegate, Alphonse Cazabat, warned would impoverish the "humble and honest farmer, the poor mechanic, the hard-working classes" and "ruin forever the people and the State," adding that "faithful, loyal citizens are almost all opposed to compensation." As Paul Herron notes, delegates strategically opposed compensation to preempt congressional intervention and protection of Black civil and voting rights. Only Georgia allowed, but did not require, compensation for emancipation, while also granting freed Blacks special protection by law.[49]

Republicans reintroduced the Thirteenth Amendment in the House in January 1865. State abolition clauses now harmonized with congressional enforcement, appeasing moderate Democrats. As the Pennsylvania Democrat Alexander Coffroth put it, "In June last my objection to this amendment was that it was taking away the property of people of the States that remained true to the Union. . . . Since that time Missouri and Maryland have abolished slavery by their own action, and the Governor of Kentucky in his message recommends to the Legislature of that State gradual emancipation. The same objection which was then urged against this amendment cannot now be urged." The New York

Democrat Anson Herrick echoed, "At the last session of Congress I voted against this resolution.... The people by a large majority ... fully indorsed the policy of the Administration on the slavery issue, and I am now disposed to bow in submission to that popular decree." Democratic support, including from Coffroth and Herrick, cleared the amendment by a narrow four votes. Alongside Republicans' logrolling and 1864 electoral gains, state abolition clauses eased the amendment's House passage, removing abolition from Congress's amendment agenda.[50]

The second, higher numerical hurdle and thus the real impediment to passage was ratification by three-fourths of the states. Near-universal uncompensated state emancipation secured ratification. Seventeen states ratified in the first month alone. Long-standing New England abolition provisions "kept the amendment from emerging there as a controversial issue," securing immediate ratification in the region, according to historian Michael Vorenberg.[51] Louisiana, Tennessee, Arkansas, Missouri, Maryland, Virginia, and Nevada, having recently constitutionally abolished slavery, easily or unanimously ratified the amendment within weeks, while Deep South framers postponed ratification votes until their states formed permanent legislatures in late 1865. After ratification, the amendment's congressional enforcement section lay dormant, largely obviated by state abolition clauses.[52] Note also that while framing the Thirteenth Amendment, the Senate added a rider allowing slavery or involuntary servitude as punishment for crime.[53] Subsequently, every Southern state passed harmonizing clauses, later read to allow private leasing of convict labor, with the unanticipated and likely unintended consequence of retrenching forced agricultural labor in the South.[54]

Lincoln's assassination in April 1865 elevated Andrew Johnson to the presidency. A Tennessee Democrat, former slaveholder, and states'-rights strict constructionist, Johnson allowed ex-Confederates holding less than $20,000 in taxable property to vote and frame new state constitutions in Mississippi, Alabama, Florida, Georgia, and the Carolinas in the summer of 1865. These states repealed legislative malapportionment and property qualifications on officeholding but still limited Black voting and citizenship and, in autumn, elected ex-Confederates to Congress and the state legislatures. Mississippi and South Carolina soon forced free Blacks into contracted plantation labor under punishment of jailing or fine, with other Southern states doing the same through facially race-neutral laws.[55]

Incensed congressional Republicans again decisively curbed the states, refusing to seat these Southern representatives and proposing the 1866 Civil Rights Act, granting Black Americans citizenship and the right to litigate and negotiate labor contracts. Congressional Democrats protested that *Dred Scott* preempted Congress from recognizing Black citizenship, and Johnson vetoed the act and an appropriations bill for the Freedmen's Bureau. Republicans overrode the veto but increasingly recognized that dictating another round of state constitutional reform could further expand Black citizenship and suffrage while skirting Johnson's veto. Even the ultranationalist senator Lyman Trumbull admitted the "right to vote and hold office in the States depends upon the legislation of the various States." In June 1866, Congress's Republican-led Joint Committee on Reconstruction therefore called for new Southern-state constitutional conventions to protect Black rights. An outmaneuvered Johnson praised the plan for promising eventual congressional representation to reconstructed states, with Republicans content to delay Southern representation in the meantime. Properly understood, Congress was not deferring to state conventions but rather dictating the agenda for state constitutional reconstruction in order to circumvent Johnson.[56]

The Joint Committee on Reconstruction also proposed the Fourteenth Amendment. Committee chair Thaddeus Stevens revived House amendment proposals to repudiate Confederate war debt and strip congressional representation from states violating Black rights, bundling these with provisions promising birthright federal and state citizenship and forbidding compensated emancipation, officeholding by ex-Confederates, and state infringement of federal due process, equal protection, and privileges and immunities rights. Congressmen had proposed dozens of amendments on each of these issues, which Stevens united into a single omnibus proposal carrying nearly the whole Republican constitutional agenda.[57]

Stevens's amendment harmonized with and, in some senses, imitated prior Southern-state constitutional regulation. Southern-state framers, facing lower bars to revision, had already forbade compensated emancipation, Confederate war debt repayment, and officeholding by ex-Confederates. Doubting that "the States would consent to surrender a [franchise] power they had always exercised, and to which they were attached," the committee assured that the amendment's congressional reapportionment clause "would be gentle and persuasive" on the states, hesitant that "Congress had power, even under the amended Constitution, to prescribe the qualifications of voters in a State, or could act directly on the subject."[58] The language masked radical Republicans' interventionist intentions but satisfied moderates, who quickly pushed the amendment through the House and Senate in May 1866.[59]

An unsold Johnson replied that Congress, in excluding Southerners, had failed the quorum needed to pass the amendment. At Johnson's behest, Delaware, Maryland, Kentucky, and all eleven ex-Confederate states, save Tennessee, rejected the amendment. Republicans were exasperated. Charles Sumner proposed coercing the states into ratification under the Thirteenth Amendment's second section and the Guarantee Clause. When critics replied that this might require enfranchising women and children across the Union, moderate Republicans balked. Republicans instead passed the Reconstruction Acts of 1867, enfranchising Southern Black men, disenfranchising ex-Confederates, and imposing army administration of Southern voter registration, elections, and state constitutional conventions until the amendment's ratification.[60]

Over ex-Confederates' boycotts, Unionist white Southerners joined Northern and Black delegates at the new state constitutional conventions, drafting rights protections that exceeded the stalled Fourteenth Amendment's minimum. In total, Black delegates made up about a third of convention attendees—of the forty-six delegates to Florida's 1868 convention, eighteen were Black and forty-three were Republicans, who together designed a new government that quickly ratified the Fourteenth Amendment. Arkansas's 1868 convention of seventy-five delegates included sixty Republicans, of whom eight were Black, and established universal male suffrage, free and unsegregated public schools, and equal protection for all races. Louisiana's radical convention, held the same year, awarded state citizenship by birthright and naturalization regardless of race or previous servitude, required officeholders to affirm racial equality by public oath, and forbade racial discrimination in state, parish, or municipally licensed public places, including schools, Louisiana's 1879 convention funded a university in New Orleans for Black students. And under army supervision, Georgians in 1867 incorporated parts of the proposed Fourteenth Amendment into their state bill of rights, enfranchised Blacks, and funded free public schools. Conventions in Mississippi, Alabama, North Carolina, and Virginia ratified similarly egalitarian state constitutions.[61]

These state clauses buttressed and elaborated the proposed federal one. The omnibus Fourteenth Amendment bundled Congress's many aims but still could not match the length and comprehensiveness of Reconstruction state constitutions. Detailed new state clauses, like those in Alabama and Georgia, mandated that birthright citizenship and equal protection be backed by legislation. Moreover, state framers invoked broad police powers to constitutionally secure fair working hours and wages, achieving labor protections that congressional Republicans could not, and allowed Blacks free integrated schooling, interracial marriage, voting, officeholding, and militia service. These constitutions also forbade ex-Confederates from voting, holding office, and framing state constitutions and subjected them to loyalty oaths, affirming the Fourteenth Amendment's section 3. These clauses, dovetailing with the federal amendment, helped Congress expound the Fourteenth Amendment and build a Black, free-labor, Republican Southern electoral coalition.[62] Imitating congressional Republicans, state framers rejected compact theory and recognized federal supremacy, snuffing out old national nullification and secession debates.[63] The state constitutional conventions, prompting the election of new Republican state legislators, eased the Fourteenth Amendment's passage in 1868. By 1868, ten Southern states had already ratified similar state constitutional equal protection clauses, assuaging fears that Congress would invoke the federal clause against the states and stripping grounds to protest the pending federal Equal Protection Clause.[64]

Finally, there was the franchise question. Abolition voided the Three-Fifths Clause, increasing Southern House and Electoral College representation and Republicans' reliance on the new Southern Black vote. Between 1866 and 1869, Congress proposed seventy-nine federal franchise amendments to legitimize and entrench the Reconstruction Acts and Southern-state franchise clauses, with most viable proposals coming after and affirming state clauses. In 1868, Republicans renewed their congressional majority, offering more suffrage amendment proposals, one of which passed the House. The Senate proposed an alternate provision, spurring a protracted reconciliation battle, ending with a barebones emergency compromise in the Fortieth Congress's last days. The brief proposal protected only American citizens' right to vote regardless of race or previous enslavement—unlike other proposals, it did not prohibit voting or officeholding restrictions based on property, origin, intelligence or literacy, or gender. Instead, the state constitutions entrenched Republicans' Black electoral base while disenfranchising ex-Confederates.[65]

State constitutional franchise reform preempted controversies over the Fifteenth Amendment. By ratification, every Southern state had reformed its franchise laws under congressional oversight, with most constitutionally enfranchising Black men. Some Northern states repealed racial franchise restrictions just before the amendment's passage, while others did so via ratification. A dozen states across the North and Deep South approved the amendment within a month, with another five following that spring, quarantining legal controversies to the border states like West Virginia, which had avoided constitutional reconstruction. Delegates to Tennessee's 1870 convention, many of them ex-Confederates, opposed the Fifteenth Amendment and Black suffrage but capitulated to Congress's proposal, as the state had already enfranchised Blacks and as other states moved the amendment to ratification. As delegate Henry R. Gibson put it, "universal suffrage will be the *supreme law* of the land, whether Tennessee *participates* in such ratification or not."[66] In sum, congressional dictation yielded state convergence, guiding and easing the drafting and ratification of the Reconstruction Amendments. This feedback between state and federal framing directed federal constitutional development, even when the power of the states reached its nadir.

Congress then quit constitutional Reconstruction, proposing only six amendments in 1870, with the yearly number of amendment proposals never exceeding a few dozen until the Great Depression. Federal troops largely withdrew from the South in 1877, depriving Congress of a means of direct enforcement against intransigent Southerners, closing this chapter of Reconstruction. The state governments entrenched Reconstruction, guiding the arc of national politics. The gains, however, were short-lived. Ex-Confederates, excluded under Reconstruction state constitutions, brooded, waiting for the end of military Reconstruction and congressional oversight, hoping to reclaim power through new, white-supremacist state constitutions.

Attending to state constitutionalism helps us better understand the Civil War and Reconstruction. The long-standing policy of deference on territorial slavery and fugitive slave law failed as Southwestern territories rejected slavery and Northerners refused to return runaway slaves, frustrating Southerners, whose control of Congress slipped away. Further attempts at deference under the 1850 Compromise and 1854 Kansas-Nebraska Act exacerbated state divergence. The long-standing antebellum practice of devolution ended as Buchanan requested that the Supreme Court dictate state law through *Dred Scott*. This worsened the conflict. Lincoln succeeded in dictation, forcing Southern-state constitutional reform, and following his assassination, Congress mixed a platform of dictation and convergence.

This lets us rethink Reconstruction. Some scholars assert that Reconstruction was a wholly national exercise, solely a matter of dictation, with Lincoln and bullish Republican supermajorities in the Thirty-Eighth and Thirty-Ninth Congresses passing the Reconstruction Acts and Amendments to strong-arm intransigent ex-Confederate states.[67] One scholar, for example, describes the Equal Protection Clause as "a child of post–Civil War mistrust of state autonomy. State constitutions were deliberately bypassed as the primary level of civil rights protection."[68] This story is somewhat misguided—the states anticipated, clarified, and supported national constitutional reform. By 1868, almost every Southern constitution included clauses for uncompensated emancipation, equal protection, and universal male suffrage. These interlocking provisions legitimized the later passage and ratification of the Reconstruction Acts and Amendments. Other state clauses elaborated the education and labor rights that Congress, hamstrung by Article V, could not. The Union-imposed state governments helped form and stabilize the new postwar constitutional order, closing the first era of American constitutional development.

5

Progressive Experimentation, 1878–1931

State constitutions furnish invaluable materials for history. Their interest is all the greater because the succession of constitutions and amendments to constitutions from 1776 till today enables the annals of legislation and political sentiment to be read in these documents more easily and succinctly than in any similar series of laws in any other country. They are a mine of instruction for the natural history of democratic communities.
—Lord Bryce, The American Commonwealth, *1888*

THE LONG PROGRESSIVE ERA BEGAN with compromise. In 1876, Democratic congressmen granted the disputed presidential election to the Republican candidate, Rutherford Hayes. Hayes then withdrew federal troops from the South, leaving the region to Democratic control. Republicans, stronger in the West and Northeast, steered Congress, the White House, and the federal judiciary, blocking national amendments and preserving old constitutional readings. Yet as the twentieth century began, reformers started experimenting with state and national constitutional amendment. Four of the 1,812 proposed federal amendments passed—the Sixteenth through Nineteenth—in a burst between 1913 and 1920. The Eighteenth Amendment's ratification in December 1919 opened a deluge of repeal proposals, culminating in 1933 with the Twenty-First Amendment. All five amendments reshaped national politics. Congress and the developing federal bureaucracy enlarged their authority by regulating prohibition and income tax collection. Parties expanded the ballot and their base, first in senatorial elections and then to women, enlarging the American polity. The Supreme Court contested these expansions with rulings on tax, corporate, labor, and marriage law. Wholesale state constitutional replacement waned as Southern Democrats entrenched stable Jim Crow constitutions and as the final Western states entered the Union, yielding sixty-one state revision assemblies, fifty-four of them authorized to draft new constitutions, and twenty-four constitutions ratified between 1878 and 1931. Implementing new referenda and initiatives, the states proposed and ratified thousands of amendments.[1]

But more important than the number of national amendments or Supreme Court decisions is the path each national reform took. Progressive academics, lawmakers, civil servants, and organizers, blocked by a conservative Supreme Court and a Senate hostile to federal amendment, intentionally took the path of least resistance, instead reforming state constitutions. They strategically targeted the states' initiative and referendum processes and reformist third parties and smaller legislatures and conventions, particularly in the West, Midwest, and South. These reformers used state constitutional revision drives to test and strengthen their federal amendment campaigns, eventually uniting electoral and congressional majorities around Article V amendments, a process of deference and then convergence.

Explaining Progressive-era constitutional development through conflict decentralization and state constitutional reform is perhaps unorthodox. Other accounts may be more familiar. Progressive reformers and modern scholars alike suggest that Article V initially thwarted national reform.[2] With Southern Democrats periodically taking the House and conservative Republicans entrenched in the Senate, neither party mustered the required two-thirds bicameral supermajority for an Article V amendment, frustrating progressive lawyers, legislators, and academics. Some historians have therefore traced the post-1913 burst of amendments to Republicans' 1912 split and Democrats' sweeping House victories in 1910 and 1912, easing Article V amendment. Others cite Theodore Roosevelt and William Howard Taft's support for the Sixteenth Amendment in 1913 or Taft's for the Seventeenth that same year or Wilson's for the Nineteenth shortly thereafter. But these stories are incomplete. They cannot, for example, explain why the conservative Senate passed reformist amendments. Other scholars read the era's constitutional development through the Court's free-market *Lochner* and *E. C. Knight* decisions.[3] Yet others have noted how progressive academics warmed to constitutional amendment and even wholesale replacement, with a supermajority of states petitioning Congress for a second convention in 1912 and with congressmen proposing loosening Article V constraints, signaling a decrease in constitutional veneration.[4]

None of these stories, emphasizing national Article V constraints, national party dynamics, national executive leadership, judicial review, and declining constitutional veneration, are wrong. But each misses how prior state-level organizing and reform bridged partisan and regional divides, nudged congressmen and the public to support amendment, and helped resolve national debates around the era's major issues. Ignoring this state constitutionalism risks misunderstanding national political development in the Progressive era.

This chapter tells a story of conflict decentralization, showing how progressive reformers, rebuffed by Congress and the Supreme Court, intentionally devolved controversy to the state legislatures and conventions, which converged on similar constitutional reform. Reformers then elevated their issue to Congress for harmonizing amendment. This pattern of deference and then convergence defined the income tax, senatorial election, and female suffrage amendments. Specifically, after the Senate blocked federal income tax amendments in the 1890s, academics, civil servants, and state legislators drafted alternative state constitutional income tax amendments. In the 1910s, these same state-level actors revived and finally passed a federal amendment, hoping for federal enforcement against state income tax evasion. As the federal tax system developed in the 1920s, more states passed income tax amendments, creating a stable, interlocking enforcement regime by the 1930s. Similarly, advocates of popular senatorial election, stymied in the 1890s by the conservative Senate, looked to the states to set the time, place, and manner for electing senators. This occurred occasionally through state constitutional reform, though more often by invoking state constitutions' initiative clauses to force state legislators to statutorily implement direct election. By the 1910s, this method elected most U.S. senators, yielding the Seventeenth Amendment in 1913, formalizing and standardizing the process established at the state level. Similarly, in these years, the suffragette Carrie Chapman Catt entrenched the female vote through state constitutional and statutory reform, tactically building a nationwide electoral base to oust congressional opponents and elect allied members of Congress, who then ratified the Nineteenth Amendment.

There were exceptions to this pattern of deference and convergence. Prohibitionists deliberately attempted this tactic of deference and convergence but failed. Blocked in Congress, reformers revived prohibition by state statute and constitutional amendment, campaigning state by state to build the supermajority for a national amendment and override remaining antiprohibition "wet" states. But state-by-state regulation merely concentrated the liquor market in wet states, spurring interstate bootlegging. Prohibitionists rushed their campaign and never achieved full convergence among the states, and so when they won a federal amendment, the amendment required federal dictation against unwilling states. This pleased old, hardline drys but was an overbearing and unstable outcome that led states to instead converge on repeal. Congress capitulated to this convergence through the Twenty-First Amendment. This restored the stable patchwork of state and local law that remains today. Prohibitionists' strategy was thus hamstrung between the nuanced Progressive-era tactic of gradual convergence and their Reconstruction-era leader Neal Dow's dream of swift, blunt, and aggressive federal dictation of state law—a movement caught between two eras and failing in both.

Finally, on matters of parochial schooling, polygamy, and child labor, reformers ended their campaigns with state reform, a case of deference without convergence. Opponents of child labor, stymied nationally by the Supreme Court, unable to push a court-curbing amendment past Article V, instead reformed some state constitutions. Similarly, reformers who failed to win federal amendments forbidding polygamy and state funding for parochial schools instead won piecemeal state constitutional reform. But generally, the era emphasized convergence and collaborative federal and state reform, with state policy and franchise experimentation narrowing, guiding, and testing options for federal reform. Progressive-era states served as constitutional laboratories to stabilize federal reform. Largely absent was divergence and stable dictation, the pattern of the previous Reconstruction years. Dictation largely became unnecessary in the progressive era as the states successfully resolved issues through deference and convergence.

The era was not without controversy. Old disputes over elections, economics, and morality regulation resurfaced during the Progressive era. The most common topics for federal amendments proposed from 1878 to 1931 were, in roughly descending order, elections, including direct election of presidents and national senators; federal terms and tenure; female suffrage and legal rights; income taxes; child labor; prohibition establishment and amendment repeal; and marriage law. These issues, all subject to concurrent regulation, also became the main concerns before the Supreme Court. Other issues faded from the national scene. Black civil rights and citizenship, the most common amendment topic in the Reconstruction Congress, disappeared from the congressional agenda after Southern Democrats swept Congress in 1892 and entrenched power under Jim Crow state constitutions. The Court refused to intervene in state reform, keeping Jim Crow law local, a case of circumvention. This chapter therefore offers case studies on four issues: income tax reform, the direct election of senators, the female franchise, and prohibition, with a concluding digression on education, marriage, Jim Crow, and child labor. Table 5 displays the twenty-five most common topics among amendments proposed between 1878 and 1931.[5]

This chapter discusses conflict decentralization in five roughly chronological steps. The first and second sections introduce the pattern of deference and convergence that defined income tax and Senate election reform, recounting how most states, in the initial absence of federal action, implemented the income tax and direct election of senators between the 1890s and 1910s, aiding the later passage of the federal Sixteenth and Seventeenth Amendments in 1913. The third section describes the long fight for female suffrage through deference and then convergence for amendment in the 1910s. The fourth concerns prohibition, a messy case of deference to the states, failed dictation of national prohibition, and convergence of states around repeal between the 1910s and 1930s. The chapter concludes with a discussion of deference without convergence, addressing parochial schooling, polygamy, and child labor and noting state circumvention of federal policy through Jim Crow.

Federal Deference, State Convergence, and the Income Tax

Proposed income taxes split Congress by party and region. Lincoln funded the Union war effort through an 1862 income tax, which stood until 1871, when heavily taxed Northeastern states blocked renewal. This quieted the issue temporarily. But in June 1892, a *New-York Tribune* article listed America's millionaires, with most living in Northeastern states. Similar muckraking newspaper articles, novels, and social science studies followed, many of the latter drafted by the reform-minded economists Richard T. Ely and Edwin R. A. Seligman. A month after the *Tribune* piece, the Midwestern, agrarian-leaning Populist Party rallied in Omaha, calling for renewing the national income tax. As Populist

Table 5. Proposed Federal Amendments by Topic, 1878–1931

Topic	Years topic most often proposed (descending frequency)	Total	Concurrent power
Article I			
Congress	1923, 1922, 1924, 1921, 1931	427	Yes
Senate	1892, 1911, 1923, 1899, 1893	289	Yes
House of Representatives	1923, 1921, 1913, 1924, 1918	202	Yes
Article II			
Presidency	1913, 1892, 1923, 1916, 1912	302	Yes
Vice presidency	1913, 1923, 1892, 1916, 1931	179	Yes
Executive	1888, 1886, 1881, 1882, 1880	60	Yes
Article III			
Federal courts	1912, 1907, 1914, 1913, 1917	93	No
Article V			
Amendment process: general issues	1919, 1921, 1913, 1923, 1931	89	Yes
Amendment: repeal proposals	1931, 1907, 1927, 1909, 1911	58	Yes
Federal officeholding			
Term length and limits	1913, 1912, 1923, 1927, 1910	284	Yes
Elections			
Election: general issues	1892, 1913, 1911, 1923, 1907	497	Yes
Election by popular vote	1892, 1913, 1911, 1923, 1907	292	Yes
Taxes and finance			
Taxes: general issues	1897, 1924, 1899, 1907, 1901	120	Yes
Taxes: income and direct	1897, 1924, 1899, 1907, 1901	93	Yes
National debt	1883, 1882, 1879, 1917, 1886	74	No
Federal appropriations	1883, 1882, 1879, 1917, 1919	76	No
Rights and citizenship			
Suffrage	1917, 1919, 1915, 1913, 1918	166	Yes
Gender distinctions under law	1919, 1917, 1915, 1923, 1913	121	Yes
Rights: general issues	1918, 1888, 1926, 1919, 1923	56	Yes
Labor			
Labor: general issues	1923, 1922, 1924, 1918, 1886	91	Yes
Labor: child labor	1923, 1922, 1924, 1918, 1921	59	Yes
Other			
State powers	1921, 1923, 1919, 1924, 1931	176	Yes
Prohibition	1917, 1913, 1931, 1927, 1916	86	Yes
Marriage and divorce	1923, 1916, 1899, 1917, 1919	70	Yes
War and emergency powers	1931, 1929, 1924, 1923, 1927	59	No

candidates sapped the Democrats' vote share and as the Panic of 1893 drained federal gold reserves, the Nebraskan William Jennings Bryan proposed a modest graduated income tax, earning Democratic president Grover Cleveland's endorsement. Weeks later, Bryan and Tennessee's Benton McMillin, serving on the House Ways and Means Committee, revised a pending tariff bill to tax 2 percent of all individual and corporate incomes over $4,000. The measure, McMillin promised, would alleviate the "antipathies that exist between the classes . . . which finds expression in violence and threatens the very foundations on which our whole institutions rest." Southern and Western Democrats on the committee backed the bill over unanimous Republican and Northeastern Democratic opposition. The bill then passed Congress along the same sectional lines. Midwestern and Western Democrats hoped the new 1894 Revenue Act would ease agrarian and populist unrest, while Southerners preferred the tax over a tariff that might hurt southern imports, leaving New York's Senator William Allen to decry the law as "unjust and sectional . . . because the people of a certain section of this country have the greatest number of incomes which are taxable."[6]

The Democrats' victory was short-lived. Two weeks after the Revenue Act's passage, the pro-business New York attorneys Joseph H. Choate and William D. Guthrie convinced the Supreme Court to overrule the act for violating the Article I requirement that direct taxes be equitably apportioned by state population. The burden, the Court agreed in *Pollock v. Farmer's Loan and Trust,* sat too heavy on Northeastern taxpayers. The five-to-four decision voided a century of Court deference on congressional direct taxes, contravened Attorney General Richard Olney's pro-tax arguments, and riled Congress and the popular press, threatening, in Justice Henry Billings Brown's dissenting words, "a sordid despotism of wealth." The Court's accompanying *E. C. Knight* ruling further exacerbated interbranch tensions by forbidding Congress from regulating monopolies over manufacturing and intrastate commerce.[7]

With the statute voided, congressional Democrats pivoted to override the Court by amendment. Justice John Marshall Harlan had called for such an amendment in his *Pollock* dissent, as did the Democrats' 1896 platform, and so between 1895, when the Court announced *Pollock,* and 1913, when the Sixteenth Amendment passed, congressmen proposed sixty income tax amendments. These amendments were proposed by Southerners and, in a few cases, Midwesterners, with only two proposed by Northeasterners. Similarly, between the 1895 *E. C. Knight* decision and 1931, members of Congress proposed thirty-six amendments to assume power to regulate trusts and corporations, twenty-nine to term limit judges, twelve to curtail judicial jurisdiction, and seven to tax inheritances. But Southern and Midwestern Democrats could not overcome the Northeastern and Republican majorities that stalled amendments well short of Article V supermajorities. The amendments were an empty gesture. With Congress divided and the Court hostile to the tax, meaningful income tax reform would not begin at the national level.[8]

This began a pattern of devolution—specifically of deference—in which thwarted national reformers took their concerns to the states. After the Court overturned the 1894 Revenue Act, national reformers and academics looked to the smaller, more populist state legislatures and constitutional conventions. Here they allied with agrarian and labor coalitions, hoping together to institute income taxes to address local wealth inequalities and revenue needs. Some states had taxed income as early as the Panic of 1837 and, in the South, during the Civil War and Reconstruction. But most states lacked the administrative capacity to reliably assess intangible property or income. Income taxes established in Alabama and Virginia in 1843, North Carolina in 1849, and Louisiana in 1865 went mostly uncollected, because, as an Alabama auditor explained, a well-off taxpayer with an "income of thousands annually, avoids a tax upon it by simply saying he has none and because of a lack of persistence on the part of the assessor." Massachusetts later taxed annual incomes over $2,000, but as a state tax collector complained, "the machinery of the Massachusetts tax laws is not adapted to the enforcement of an income tax." Most significantly, as an anticorruption measure, many antebellum states constitutionally forbade nonuniform taxes and taxes on nonproperty wealth, preventing legislators from statutorily instituting special exemptions, and as a consequence, graduated income taxes. Income tax advocates needed state constitutional amendments to repeal these uniformity clauses, and so income tax reform concerned state constitutions specifically, rather than federalism broadly.[9]

These uniformity provisions, coupled with tax evasion and revenue shortfalls, sparked local populist frustration. With few means to alleviate wealth inequality or to punish underreporting by taxpayers or assessors, most states instead taxed tangible property, especially real estate and farmland. As Lord Bryce explained in 1888, this exacerbated the "bitterness of feeling among American farmers as well as the masses against capitalists, much of whose accumulated wealth escapes taxation, while the farmer who owns his land, as well as the working man who puts his savings into the house he lives in, is assessed and taxed upon his visible property." By the 1870s, workers and small farmers sought to pass off this burden by taxing the growing incomes of corporations, banks, railroads, and industrialists. Resentment too drove the farmers, who rented expensive railroad silos and relied on steep bank loans to finance equipment. At the behest of the feminist Carrie Chapman Catt, suffragettes also backed the income tax as a substitute for tariffs on home goods. Prohibitionists joined them, hoping an income tax might also lessen states' reliance on liquor taxes and the liquor industry. And reformist economists and social scientists, their ambitions for a national tax dashed by *Pollock,* opportunistically turned their energies on friendlier state legislatures and conventions. The *Pollock* decision encouraged as much, plainly declaring, "the states have power to lay income taxes." Richard T. Ely and Delos Oscar Kinsman of the University of Wisconsin refocused their work on their own state's pioneering income tax, as did the University of California's Carl C. Plehn on his state's tax. As the legal historian Ajay Mehrotra concludes, "*Pollock* channeled reform efforts toward improving state and local fiscal regimes. By foreclosing, at least for the time being, the possibility of a national income tax, the U.S. Supreme Court indirectly pushed fiscal reformers to concentrate their efforts at the subnational level." By the turn of the century, this network of national reformers and local populists together pushed for new state income taxes.[10]

These coalitions backed reformist legislators and framers, who passed stringent income tax provisions to boost flagging state revenue after the Panic of 1893. Addressing corporate and personal income evasion required new, centralized state commissions and offices that could fine or override lax local assessors and collectors. Indiana's Tax Commission led centralization efforts in the early 1890s. North Carolina's legislature was similarly aggressive, reinstituting the income tax in 1893, doubling the tax in 1895, and in 1901 placing a 10 percent tax on annual incomes over $1,000. These North Carolina laws voided local taxes and created a central State Tax Commission to supervise and fine local assessors five dollars for every blank line on their reports. Between 1895 and 1907, the number of North Carolina counties reporting the tax jumped from thirty-nine to eighty-one of ninety-seven total, with income tax revenue increasing tenfold. The state's auditor dubbed it "the best law . . . we can have in the state and keep within bounds of the constitutional limitations."[11]

Rigorous income tax implementation required state constitutional reform. Some Western and Midwestern framers scrapped uniformity clauses, constitutionally allowing graduated income taxes and new central tax offices. In 1864, the Nevada delegate Albert Hawley proposed taxing mining corporations' "princely fortunes" to relieve the small farmer from taxation on "the few acres of sterile land from which he ekes out his scanty existence."[12] Hawley's proposal failed, and Colorado's 1876 framers also disappointed local agrarians by capping taxes at a fraction of a cent on the dollar, making a graduated tax unconstitutional according to the state supreme court and "crude and ineffective" per a Colorado Revenue Commission report.[13] Mirroring the congressional response to *Pollock,* state legislators and framers increasingly proposed amendments overriding these state court decisions and the uniformity clauses on which they rested. The University of California economist Carl C. Plehn later agreed that his state's farmers "as a class are now bearing far more than their share of public burdens," while the wealthy underreported their income assets, making the property tax "highly conducive to political immorality and [a] veritable school for perjury." For progressives like Plehn, income tax enforcement doubled as an anticorruption and civil service reform measure. Workingmen's Party and Granger delegates to California's 1878 convention constitutionally empowered the state legislature to tax corporate and joint-stock income, shifted taxes on land mortgages from small farmers to banks, and regulated railroad rates. Utah's 1896 framers also expressly allowed a graduated income tax. And in 1907, Oklahoma's populist convention specifically enabled the legislature to pass a graduated income tax, which, instituted the following year, held that individuals or assessors who underreported income could be charged with perjury and empowered a state auditor to oversee local assessors. Revenue from the tax nevertheless remained low. Constitutional amendment initiatives in South Dakota and Minnesota similarly sought to let the legislature institute a graduated income tax but met with failure.[14]

Southern states also constitutionalized the income tax. In 1845, Texas and Louisiana passed the first constitutional income tax clauses, later adding new provisions to fund Reconstruction, as did North Carolina, Virginia, and Tennessee. The Panic of 1893 pushed states to raise revenue by centralizing income, inheritance, corporate, and property tax assessment and collection. South Carolina, for example, had long neglected its tax until the state's 1895 convention specifically authorized the legislature to raise revenue though a centralized graduated income tax. The legislature then held county collectors and auditors responsible for enforcement, tripling the total state tax yield within a decade. Virginia's 1902 convention approved taxing income from rent, wages, interest, and profits, which increased under the guidance of a state tax commission, though this tax remained marginal to the state's total tax revenue. The following year, Kentucky too added an income tax by amendment. But without rigorous enforcement, states still struggled to collect these taxes.[15]

Wisconsin's income tax fared best. In 1898, state tax commissioner Nils P. Haugen proposed taxing corporate and personal income, noting that there was "no class of people who feel the direct burden of [property] taxation more keenly than the farmers." Two years later, these farmers elected the tax reformer Robert La Follette as governor, with Haugen as his deputy on the commission. The legislature amended the state constitution's uniformity clause and passed a graduated personal and corporate income tax statute, with the approval of state courts. The commission, which helped draft the law in collaboration with Delos Oscar Kinsman at the University of Wisconsin, then appointed civil servants for three-year terms to assess and collect the tax. As a safeguard, employers reported workers' incomes directly to the commission, with false income reports triggering fines of up to $500 and a year in prison.

The centralization scheme worked. Underreporting plummeted. By one lawyer's estimate, less than 5 percent of reports misrepresented income, yielding $3.5 million in tax revenue in the first year, roughly a hundred times that of North Carolina's locally assessed tax, quintupling by 1920. Because the tax was graduated, less than 0.5 percent of the tax came from the predominantly rural districts inhabited by small farmers, while Milwaukee, home to the state's wealthy industrialists, brokers, and manufacturers, shouldered 40 percent of the tax.

In response, the Wisconsin Manufacturers Association urged local industries to reincorporate and operate in neighboring Illinois to dodge the tax. Edwin R. A. Seligman, the era's foremost tax scholar, lauded the law's "revolution in administrative methods" but concluded that if "there is any lesson to be drawn from the short experience of Wisconsin with the income tax it is, that while much can be accomplished by improved and centralized administrative methods, some form of federal regulation is necessary." State Tax Commissioner Thomas Lyons also called for congressional intervention, asking, "If Wisconsin cannot tax income derived from this source no other state can do so, and the result is a legal no-man's-land where vast and prosperous organizations may operate.... Why should not Congress, which has supreme control of the subject, authorize the several states to tax either property or income from interstate commerce?" To Lyons's point, without concurrent federal taxation and enforcement, interstate capital flight would keep state income tax revenue marginal. State tax officials could only benefit from a companion federal income tax. The Wisconsin Supreme Court dryly added that "income taxation is no new and untried experiment.... It has been used at various times by nearly or quite twenty of our own states, and is now in use in several of them ... and is now in successful operation in practically all of the great nations of the civilized world, except the United States."[16]

These state officials joined national lawmakers and academics in advocating federal tax reform. The constituency for the national amendment grew, incorporating states that hoped to institute their own income tax. In 1907, New York's Special Tax Commission urged a federal amendment as a prelude to state reform, explaining that a federal tax would keep individuals from shifting their income receipts to banks in tax-free states. The commission concluded that "interstate comity can probably be forced on the American commonwealths only from above.... For New York State to act independently in this matter would be ... highly inexpedient." Since locally administered state income taxes were unevenly enforced and took only pennies on the dollar of income, many contributed only a small percentage of a state's tax revenue. Colorado's Revenue Commission thus warned of underreporting by local assessors and instead called for a new, more lucrative federal income tax administered by impartial federal agents. Some states implemented the tax, while others abstained, but increasingly, states harmonized in support of a federal income tax.[17]

Progressive social scientists also felt that state tax reform validated a federal amendment. Some held that this piecemeal state experimentation, success, and frequent failure might guide better national law. Ever skeptical, Richard T. Ely held that the income tax "never worked very well in any one of our commonwealths, and it appears with us to be better adapted for national purposes." Ely's student Delos Oscar Kinsman was more sanguine. Reflecting on the states' response to the 1895 *Pollock* decision, Kinsman declared, "What political laboratories our forty-six states are! How many a costly venture could be avoided if the experiments tried and the results obtained in each were studied by all! ... The keen interest in the [income tax] during recent years is evidenced by the fact that since 1895 sixteen states and three territories have paid attention to the tax either by constitutional amendment, legislative enactment, or in commission reports.... Indeed, [state] legislatures have already done something, tax commissions more, but constitutional changes most, to prepare the way for a sane and scientific law." Mabel Newcomer, another young progressive and a student of Edwin R. A. Seligman, agreed that the "increase in state tax commissions and commissioners, and the widening powers of state boards," spurred a broader, "growing and widely commended tendency in the United States to centralize administration in financial matters." Joined by state legislators, tax commissioners, civil servants, and journalists, these scholars formed the National Conference on State and Local Taxation and the National Tax Association to regularly convene and petition for both state constitutional reform and a federal amendment.[18]

The states meanwhile began reshaping broader tax law. Bowing to populists, state legislators taxed corporations, particularly in the West, and overrode uniformity clauses and related court decisions, implementing inheritance taxes in six states by 1890. By 1913, the number of inheritance tax states jumped to thirty-five. With the rise of the inheritance tax, the old general property tax proportionally declined in twenty-nine states in the decade before the Sixteenth Amendment's passage. As the historian Robert Stanley notes, by 1913, only six states could effectively collect the income tax, contributing a fraction of a percent of total state revenue. Because states collected only marginal income taxes, they had little reason to worry that a federal tax would cut into this meager revenue; rather, with concurrent federal enforcement, state income tax receipts could only increase. State officials trusted that a federal tax would support, rather than compete with, a state tax. Per Stanley, low state income tax revenue made state officials all the "more receptive to federal overtures in the comparatively empty arena of income taxation."[19]

This convergence in state support for the income tax elevated the issue to Congress. Congress and the White House warmed to an income tax amendment. Republicans initially opposed the income tax, with Theodore Roosevelt in 1906 instructing congressional Republicans to accept *Pollock* and William Howard Taft favoring a statutory inheritance tax. But as the Panic of 1907 increased federal deficits, Roosevelt reversed position, Democrats readopted the amendment plank, and Taft followed, hoping to siphon pro-tax Democratic votes to his presidential campaign. In spring of 1909, Senator Nelson Aldrich, Republican of Rhode Island, drafted a revenue-raising tariff bill, to which the progressive congressmen Joseph Bailey and Albert Cummins appended a steeply graduated income tax. On June 16, 1909, President Taft reminded Congress that they were still bound by *Pollock* and that this income tax rider required an accompanying constitutional amendment to override the decision. Aldrich, a plutocrat and veteran Senate tactician, switched the Bailey-Cummins tax with a meager 2 percent excise tax on corporate incomes, which later dropped to 1 percent. On June 28, Nebraska's Norris Brown then proposed the necessary constitutional amendment in the Senate Finance Committee. Chairing the committee, Aldrich rushed the amendment to a floor vote on July 5, with the amendment passing seventy-seven to zero, essentially as proposed. Aldrich admitted that he intended the amendment as a ruse, using the amendment and accompanying "corporation tax as a mere means to defeat the income tax," trusting that the Northeastern and Republican state legislatures would kill the amendment. The House debated the measure for only four hours, offering no major revisions. There was little disagreement over the proposal, as conservative Republicans backed the accompanying token corporate income tax and progressive Republicans and Democrats supported the longshot amendment—though as the progressive Robert La Follette admitted, "the success of any given amendment is very improbable." The amendment passed the House 314 to 14, with 55 abstentions, and went to the states for approval in July 1909.[20]

Ratification initially seemed unlikely. Under Aldrich's direction, Rhode Island rejected the amendment in early 1910. So too did New York after Governor Charles Evans Hughes warned that the measure would allow federal taxation of state and municipal bond income, decreasing the value and demand for state bonds and leaving the "borrowing capacity of the State and of its governmental agencies at the mercy of the federal taxing power." Such an amendment, cutting into state income, would be "an impairment of the essential rights of the State." But few state lawmakers bought the claim, especially after Democrats, retaining their pro-tax plank, took seven legislatures in November 1910, flipping holdouts New York and Connecticut. Then in 1912, Roosevelt and Taft split the Republican vote, leaving Democrats the White House, both houses of Congress, and three more state legislatures, building the interstate coalition needed for ratification. To Aldrich's chagrin, the Sixteenth Amendment was ratified in 1913. As many scholars note, Democrats' sudden legislative gains in 1910 and 1912 helped secure ratification, making approval, in Sheldon Pollack's words, "a foregone conclusion."[21]

But prior state reform also aided ratification. Decades before the Democrats' 1910 and 1912 state legislative sweeps, economists joined state judges, lawmakers, and civil servants in calling for a federal amendment to buttress the states' constitutional tax clauses and enforcement efforts. Robert Stanley traces this shift to the 1890s, noting that since "at least 1890 the climate within the state legislatures toward progressive taxation had grown increasingly favorable." Legislators in these income tax states led the charge in ratification. Alabama, Kentucky, South Carolina, Oklahoma, and Texas, all income tax states, quickly ratified in 1909, joined by Georgia, Mississippi, Maryland, and Illinois. Addressing the Senate Judiciary Committee the following year, Norris Brown promised, "the proposed amendment will not authorize any additional burden on the several States in the exercise of their sovereign rights" to issue tax-exempt bonds, reiterating that "the tax would not impair the credit of the states." Thus, Brown explained, "Governor Hughes stands alone in his fight against the amendment." Affirming Brown's claim, twenty states ratified in 1911, fifteen of them west of the Mississippi. Southern state legislators revived class-redistribution arguments from their own states' tax debates, paired with the specter of an alternative, costly tariff on Southern raw goods. In these Western and Southern states, the long-standing agrarians' and workingmen's factions that first organized for state tax reform also pushed the amendment to ratification.[22]

Pre-amendment state reforms, piecemeal and experimental, did not single-handedly resolve the national income tax question. Post-amendment state constitutional reforms, widespread and stable, harmonized with the new federal tax, firmly establishing a nationwide income tax regime. As expected, federal enforcement aided state enforcement, encouraging state reform. Specifically, Congress gave state officials federal records on taxpayers' names, addresses, and tax returns in 1926, intangible property income records in 1932, and all income records in 1934. State commissioners and assessors and the federal Bureau of Internal Revenue jointly pursued state income tax evasion, particularly across states, such that by 1939, all but four income tax states requested federal tax return records. Automatic distribution of federal records from Washington, DC, to local district offices aided the process.[23]

With the evasion problem addressed, state income tax laws quickly proliferated. Backed by state judges, state legislators circumvented uniformity clauses, passing income taxes, mainly by statute, in at least twelve states between 1912 and 1923.[24] In other states, framers used constitutional amendments to override uniformity clauses and stalwart judges, passing constitutional reforms in Arizona and Ohio in 1912, Massachusetts in 1916, South Dakota in 1918, Nebraska in 1920, and Louisiana in 1921.[25] Interstate imitation was common, as Massachusetts and New York borrowed elements of the Wisconsin model, and South Carolina and Georgia state courts upheld schemes to peg state income tax to federal rates. Later state framers, hoping to slow state revenue loss during the Great Depression, constitutionally authorized income taxes in Utah in 1930, Kansas in 1931, West Virginia and Kansas in 1932, Alabama in 1933, Montana in 1934, and Colorado in 1936. Additional Depression-era income taxes came, primarily by statute, in Arkansas, California, Georgia, and Oregon in 1929; Idaho, Utah, and Vermont in 1931; Minnesota, Montana, and New Mexico in 1933; Iowa in 1934; Rhode Island in 1935; Kentucky in 1936; and Maryland in 1937. By 1937, at least thirty-three of forty-eight states had established individual or corporate income taxes, with income taxes contributing a tenth of total state tax revenue.[26]

In sum, tax reformers took the path of least resistance, one of deference and then convergence, moving from Congress and the Supreme Court to the state legislatures and courts and then back to Congress for the Sixteenth Amendment. Specifically, with congressional statutes blocked by *Pollock* and with federal amendment proposals failing, national reformers, particularly progressive academics, joined local prohibitionists, suffragettes, and agrarian and workers' parties in petitioning friendlier state legislatures, conventions, and tax commissions in the 1890s. Piecemeal state-level successes reiterated the need for a national amendment. As Mehrotra puts it, "Although the development of an effective state-level income tax may have precluded other, more radical fiscal changes, the early success of the tax reform movement emboldened other activists and politicians at the state and national level to pursue a similar set of fundamental reforms." State tax commissioners' appeals revived the national amendment in 1909, and with Aldrich's miscalculation, the proposed amendment went to the states for ratification. As Steven Weisman notes, this then let the states resolve the issue: "For many years, the country had been debating whether the income tax and the inheritance tax would destroy society, incite a class war, or lead to the confiscation of the wealth of the few by the many.... The states were resolving the issue by enacting taxes, preparing a climate that would permit ratification of a constitutional amendment." The state legislatures and conventions then affirmed the new, somewhat accidental Sixteenth Amendment by passing their own, complementary laws, such that by 1937, a supermajority of states had passed reforms dovetailing with federal tax law. Opponents' repeal amendments failed, signaling the stability of this cooperative income tax regime. The resolution of the income tax question occurred through interdependent national and state constitutional reform, as a case of convergence. Put differently, one cannot fully understand the development and expansion of congressional taxation powers without studying the state constitutions.[27]

Federal Deference, State Convergence, and Direct Senatorial Election

Progressives also called for direct election of U.S. senators. While congressmen had proposed seven direct-election amendments in the antebellum years and, with President Andrew Johnson's endorsement, another sixteen between 1868 and 1877, a sustained national reform movement began only in the 1880s, as party bosses used closed meetings to arrange nominations, hiding "the real fight in the caucus behind the scenes," per the progressive professor George H. Haynes. The caucus, Haynes explained, "meets behind closed doors; its proceedings are not a matter of record," nominating state legislators who, conferring with local bosses and industrialists, then picked loyal plutocrats for the Senate. The *Saturday Review* reported that through bribes "senatorships are directly bought ... [or] are indirectly bought by contributions to party funds," so that "localism has been gaining ground, and Senators are heard to speak of themselves as ambassadors from their several States." Local partisan splits often derailed the selection process, deadlocking legislatures forty-six times between 1891 and 1905. Bribes sometimes broke ties, spurring ten Senate investigations and a few resignations. In the 1890s, another nine split state legislatures failed to fill Senate vacancies. In total, between 1893 and 1907, the U.S. Senate was fully seated only for the 1903–5 session. Senator Elihu Root of New York thus proposed lowering the selection bar from majority to a mere plurality, but U.S. senators, loyal to their state's sitting majority party, refused, compounding the problem. Deadlock seemed unavoidable. As Haynes concluded, "there is never a long contest over a senatorial election which does not do serious harm to the interests of the Commonwealth."[28]

Congress and the White House struggled to resolve the issue. Presidents James Garfield and Grover Cleveland deferred to state machines, as did President William McKinley, himself selected by the national Republican boss Mark Hanna. As press coverage stirred public indignation, the Populist Party adopted a direct-election plank in 1892, and the Democratic Party did the same in 1900. The House proved friendliest to reform. Beginning in 1881, House Democrats and some Western Republicans nationalized the issue, proposing direct-election amendments over Northeastern and Republican resistance, with amendments passing in 1893, 1894, 1898, 1900, and 1902. The 1900 amendment, for example, passed the House 242 to 15 but, like the other amendments, never received a Senate vote, dying in the Committee on Privileges and Elections. House members proposed dozens of additional amendments, but the Senate remained unmoved, closing the congressional reform path. The federal courts, unable to significantly restructure the Senate, were no more helpful. While controversy had gone national, reform had not. Reform would not come through the Supreme Court, Congress, or White House.[29]

The road to the Seventeenth Amendment, like the road to the Sixteenth, wound from Congress to the state legislatures and back, another case of deference yielding convergence. With five direct-election amendments dying in the Senate, prominent progressive political scientists like Woodrow Wilson, Charles Edward Merriam, and George H. Haynes proposed that the states unilaterally set the time, place, and manner of senatorial elections. State legislators also sought to reform Senate selection. Between 1891 and 1905, forty-six senatorial selection votes deadlocked, on average for thirty-eight days, nearly the length of a normal legislative session. Whole sessions derailed. For example, in 1897, a faction of Oregon legislators blocked quorum for an entire session to prevent a Senate vote, while four other deadlocked states had to call special sessions, and six left their Senate seat vacant, with Delaware forgoing any Senate representation in 1901. As anticorruption measures weakened state party bosses, state legislators urged broader reforms. For example, Washington State legislators, hoping to prevent another "tedious repetition of ballots," resolved in 1903 to cast only two ballots and then return to "matters and things of vital interest to the people."[30]

Fearing legislative corruption, reformers proposed selection by popular vote. Haynes held that legislative selection brought gridlock to "the whole range of state and local politics" and underrepresentation and "misrepresentation in the Senate" and so required that "elections be placed directly in the hands of the people." Populist and agrarian parties soon proposed a popular vote amendment to the Constitution, with five state Democratic parties and two Republican parties following by 1892. Reformist third parties joined the cause, and by 1913, 220 different state party platforms had called for direct election. State legislators swung into action. In the 1890s, twenty-seven states across the country sent Congress forty-five petitions asking for an amendment. Amendments that passed the House in 1893 and 1894 failed decisively in the Senate. Chastened, state legislators submitted only one petition in 1898.[31]

Stymied by the Senate, state legislators unilaterally reformed Senate elections. Allowing the popular vote in primaries was a first step. Between 1901 and 1907, most Southern legislatures statutorily allowed or mandated that the Democratic Party hold popular primary elections, which effectively picked state officers, including U.S. senators. Wisconsin, Minnesota, Michigan, Indiana, Illinois, and Massachusetts also considered or instituted direct primaries for senators, though legislators in these states could still ignore the results and make their own selection. Some Western and Great Plains states thus went further, allowing a popular vote in the general election. Nebraska voters appended to their 1875 constitution a provision letting the legislature call nonbinding popular elections for senators, though counties rarely placed Senate candidates on the ballot, leaving turnout low and legislators free to ignore the results. Similarly, in 1899, Nevada legislators required that ballots include Senate candidates but still did not bind themselves to follow the popular vote. State legislators, constrained only by statute, often ignored primary rules and outcomes.[32]

Oregon voters solved this issue through state constitutional initiatives. In 1901, Oregon legislators, recalling their deadlocked sessions of 1895 and 1897, resolved to follow their state's popular vote. Governor Theodore Geer reminded legislators to obey the "general demand from the people and press of the state," especially since "this first attempt at the popular vote for United States senators is watched with much interest . . . in other States." But the experiment failed, as legislators ignored Geer and slipped their statutory bond to the state's popular vote, picking an alternate candidate after a five-week deadlock. Frustrated voters in 1904 thus invoked the state constitution to pass an initiative requiring that legislators publicly pledge to accept the next popular vote and circulated an accompanying petition promising to oust legislators who reneged. The legislators, mainly Republicans, could not statutorily block this constitutionally implemented initiative, and so in the following election, they folded and picked the popularly selected candidate—a Democrat—after only twenty minutes of balloting. Oregon voters had succeeded in using their state constitution to constrain legislators and implement popular senatorial elections.[33]

Eleven states imitated Oregon. Nebraska adopted Oregon's public oath verbatim, additionally marking on the ballot which state legislative candidates had not signed the oath, while North Dakota bumped these candidates from the ballot entirely. South Carolina imposed a similar oath, and the Colorado legislature promised to expel members who voted against the popularly elected candidate. Woodrow Wilson, who had once thought reform impossible without federal amendment, as New Jersey governor now came "to believe in the popular election of Senators and the primary devices by which the thing is virtually brought about without a Constitutional amendment": "What I said in my [gubernatorial] Inaugural address about the Oregon system was simply that I commended it most warmly to the studious attention of our own legislature."[34] Between the optional party primary, the mandatory party primary, and the Oregon system, by 1913, thirty states had implemented direct senatorial elections, as a Senate report observed.[35]

State legislatures used several tactics to nudge the Senate toward amendment. First, between 1901 and 1905, nineteen state legislatures sent thirty-two petitions calling for an Article V constitutional convention. Pennsylvania's legislature organized an interstate committee of correspondence to coordinate appeals, pushing the number of petitions to twenty-seven in 1910, then to thirty-one by 1912, just short of the thirty-two-state threshold needed to trigger the convention and override the Senate. The usually circumspect Professor Haynes declared, "we are on the eve of seeing the final step taken in the proposing of the long-desired amendment." In calling a convention, the state legislatures also threatened broader national reform. Senator Weldon Heyburn warned that a radical runaway convention would challenge Jim Crow and reopen the "bitterness of the race question." Worrying that "enough States will act to take it out of our hands," Senator Fred DuBois urged his colleagues to instead preempt a convention by agreeing to "debate this question" of amendment. Amendment, once radical, became the conservative, stabilizing option to recognize the status quo established by the states.[36] Further, as petitions mounted in the late 1900s, additional states implemented direct-election laws, which reformist senators periodically presented to their chamber. Praising the accumulation of these democratic laws and petitions, in 1910, Senator Robert Owen of Oklahoma told the chamber that now "37 States . . . have expressed themselves (in one form or

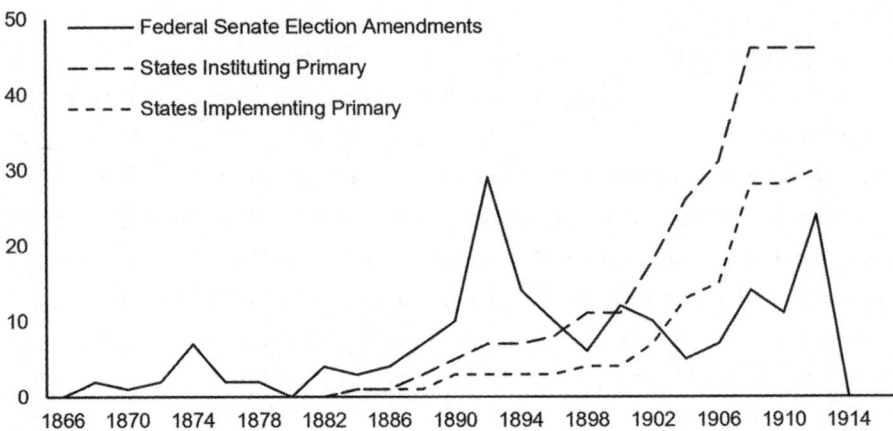

Fig. 6. State and federal measures for U.S. Senate elections, 1866–1914. State data from Schiller and Stewart, *Electing the Senate*, 112–13. The y-axis indicates proposed federal senatorial direct election amendments and states allowing senatorial primaries.

another) favorably to the election of Senators by direct vote." Joined by Oregon's Johnathan Bourne, Owen effusively praised Oregon and other states for instituting direct election and warned that continued obstruction by Northeastern Senate Republicans, including the obstinate Nelson Aldrich, would not deter the states from a unilateral convention or further state-level reform. Moreover, this state-level reform convinced senators that there was indeed a national constituency backing the impending convention. Finally, with the proliferation of these laws, the proportion of senators selected by direct election increased, from a fifth in 1905 to four-fifths in 1909 (figure 6). These factors probably inclined the Senate to support an amendment.[37]

Proposed amendments gained traction. On February 24, 1911, George Sutherland derailed a promising amendment by appending a clause letting Congress intervene in state elections, including in the South, threatening Jim Crow. Conferring with Maryland's Isidore Rayner, Judiciary Committee chairman William Borah recognized that the next amendment would have to cut such language to win required Southern votes. Michigan's William Smith agreed: "It would have been better to have confined the resolution to the direct election of Senators without complicating the question, . . . mindful of the fact that this joint resolution must receive the sanction of two-thirds of the States. . . . We can not afford to involve this question with sectional or race problems." A short amendment, deferential to existing state electoral practice, would satisfy populists, Southerners, and the conservatives who sought to preempt a convention. The House passed such an amendment on April 13, and Borah sponsored a matching amendment, to which Republican Joseph Bristow attached a weak federal regulation rider, which cleared the Senate by a single vote. After sixteen weeks of foot-dragging, House Democrats in the conference committee accepted the Bristow rider as sufficiently innocuous and passed the measure. The states, having vociferously backed an amendment for nearly a decade, ratified the amendment decisively, completing the process on April 8, 1913.[38]

Scholars have suggested that rising populism and frustration with legislative deadlocks and corruption pushed U.S. senators to pass the amendment. This is not wholly wrong, for reformist senators did indeed mention these issues through the 1890s and 1900s.[39] But mounting state constitutional and statutory reform also inclined the Senate to amendment. This, combined with state-level reform, averted an open-ended, potentially destabilizing national convention. As the historian C. H. Hoebke explains, "the direct primary had done its work before the convention became necessary." Twenty-nine states had instituted the direct senatorial primary, most of them tightening the rein on legislative discretion with enactments similar to those of the "Oregon system." Finally, it is worth noting that states stripped legislative discretion both constitutionally and statutorily. Prior to the Seventeenth Amendment, several states entrenched direct senatorial election in their constitutions. Most of the thirty states to secure direct election did so statutorily. A third of these statutory states also constitutionally allowed the citizen initiative. In these ten states, voters could invoke the constitution to constrain or punish state legislators who bucked their statutory obligation to the popular vote, as Oregon voters decisively demonstrated. Put differently, the threat—though not always the use—of the state constitutional initiative was essential to enforcing these direct-election laws. Between these ten states and those that constitutionalized direct election, senatorial elections in nearly half the popular election states relied directly or indirectly on state constitutional reform. The claim here is not that state constitutional and statutory reform unilaterally resolved the senatorial election question but rather that one cannot fully understand the Seventeenth Amendment's passage without attending to these democratic state constitutional reforms. As with the Sixteenth Amendment, resolution of the selection question and the passage of the Seventeenth Amendment was a collaborative, joint effort by national and state legislators, academics, and voters, with reformers opportunistically shifting venues to resolve this national conflict, a pattern of deference and then convergence.[40]

Federal Deference, State Convergence, and Female Suffrage

Suffragettes also followed a path from deference to convergence and victory. The road was long. Delegates to the 1848 Seneca Falls convention demanded the vote, attempting scattered state and local reform until early 1866, when Elizabeth Cady Stanton and Susan B. Anthony petitioned Congress to enfranchise women alongside Black men. Senator Charles Sumner and Representative James Brooks presented the petition, with Brooks proposing to modify the draft Fourteenth Amendment to decrease congressional representation for any state disenfranchising persons by race or sex. The revision, though simple, voided longstanding state constitutional disenfranchisement practices, doubling the electorate and letting women claim other, broader legal and social rights, expanding the American polity.[41]

Congress was unsold. The old abolitionist Wendell Phillips, once a firebrand, now a gradualist, suggested that the pending amendment forbid only racial disenfranchisement: "[The] amendment to the Constitution . . . shall read thus—'No state shall ever make any distinctions in civil privileges among those born on her soil, of parents permanently resident there, on account of race, color, or descent.' I hope in time to be as bold as [John] Stuart Mill and add the last clause 'sex'! But this hour belongs to the negro." Congress agreed, limiting the Fourteenth Amendment's prohibition on disenfranchisement expressly and solely to males. As the Pennsylvania Republican John Broomall explained, it was "time this Government should recognize the rights of the Black man, and should arm him with the ballot" to counterbalance disloyal ex-Confederates, with "women and children . . . mediately represented" through their husbands and fathers. Broomall admitted that this phrasing failed the Guarantee Clause's promise of republican state government and "would meet the requirements of the [clause] much better if the right of suffrage were extended to all adults without regard to sex," but such an expansion required that more women "demand the right of suffrage for themselves." Thus, in the spring of 1866, Congress reserved the Fourteenth Amendment's second section to Black men. Months later, Stanton and Anthony joined the veteran suffragists and abolitionists Lucretia Mott, Frederick Douglass, Henry Blackwell, and Lucy Stone to form the American Equal Rights Association, campaigning for state constitutional and statutory enfranchisement in Maine, Massachusetts, New York, New Jersey, Ohio, and Kansas. But state legislators were no more sympathetic, and further, in Kansas, Stanton and Anthony funded stump speeches by the racist huckster George Francis Train, excluding Blackwell and Stone and alienating Douglass. The Kansas campaign ended with neither women nor Black residents earning the vote.[42]

The movement further frayed in debating the proposed Fifteenth Amendment. In 1869, Congressmen James Brooks, Samuel Pomeroy, and George Julian each separately proposed that the pending amendment forbid states from both racial and gender disenfranchisement. But as Representative William Robinson objected, these proposals trampled the franchise authority of the "sovereign and coequal States," and so Congress instead copied existing Reconstruction franchise clauses. The clauses, drafted by the 1867–68 Reconstruction constitutional conventions, forbade only racial disenfranchisement, ignoring sex. The consequent Fifteenth Amendment made no mention of sex, prohibiting only racial disenfranchisement. Stanton and Anthony attacked the amendment and so earned Douglass's condemnation at the 1869 American Equal Rights Association convention.

The association dissolved in acrimony, and the female suffrage moment split, with reformers seeking both national and state constitutional revision. Two organizations emerged. Stanton and Anthony's National Woman Suffrage Association (NWSA) advocated an additional national amendment. Stanton wanted the female vote "incorporated in the Federal Constitution, there to remain forever. To leave this question to the States and partial acts of Congress, is to defer indefinitely its settlement, for what is done by this Congress may be repealed by the next; and politics in the several States differ so widely, that no harmonious action on any question can ever be procured." Stanton and Anthony sought dictation. But congressional Republicans, satisfied that the Southern Black male vote would maintain their power, rejected the few female franchise amendments offered in the late 1860s and early 1870s. Lucy Stone and her husband, Henry Blackwell, organized the competing American Woman Suffrage Association (AWSA) in November 1869 to enfranchise women through congressional action in the territories and District of Columbia and through state constitutional and statutory reform. They sought deference. State reform promised to assuage not only states'-rights congressmen like William Robinson but also

Southern conservatives. Blackwell penned a letter to Southern legislators, proposing a Faustian bargain whereby the enfranchisement of "4,000,000 of Southern white women will counterbalance your 4,000,000 of negro and women, and thus the political supremacy of your white race will remain unchanged." He and Stone hoped Southern state enfranchisement of white women would build the interstate coalition needed to ratify an eventual national amendment. The Supreme Court's 1875 *Minor v. Happersett* ruling affirmed both national and state amendment approaches, holding that "the Constitution of the United States does not confer the right of suffrage upon any one" through citizenship, including women, but rather forbade the states only from racial disenfranchisement. Otherwise, "each State determined for itself who should have [the] power" to vote.[43]

Having "puttered with State rights for thirty years without a foothold anywhere," Susan B. Anthony, alongside Elizabeth Cady Stanton and other NWSA members, kept petitioning and testifying before the House and Senate Select Committees on Woman Suffrage. Speaking before the Senate committee in 1884, Anthony admitted that prior state-level referenda had failed against the uneducated "vast masses of the people [and] the laboring classes," asking instead that "intelligent and liberty-loving" congressmen and state legislators back a federal amendment. She promised that the female vote would then split equally and impartially between parties: "Some of us like one party and one candidate and some another. Therefore we cannot promise you that women will vote as a unit when they are enfranchised. Suppose the Democrats shall put a woman-suffrage plank in their platform in their Presidential convention, and nominate an open and avowed friend of woman suffrage to stand upon that platform; we cannot pledge you that all the women of this Nation will work for the success of that party." The Senate committee, convinced, reported in 1886 that the few but "unqualified success[es]" in some local elections, territorial enfranchisement, and "petitions . . . from all parts of the country" validated a national amendment, which the pro-temperance Senator Henry W. Blair of New Hampshire proposed the following year. But Senator George Vest of Missouri derided the suffrage experiments of the "sparsely-settled Territories of the West," asking, "Where are their large cities?" Adding that women were "essentially emotional" and so "not adapted to the political work of this world," Vest especially warned against giving the "negro women of the South the right of suffrage, utterly unprepared as they are for it." Fearing federal dictation of state policy, Southern senators rallied to block the amendment, thirty-four to sixteen, with twenty-six absent. The *Chicago Daily Tribune* concluded that a female suffrage amendment required additional support: "There are twelve million female adults in the United States and 700,000 in Illinois. How many of them have petitioned for, lobbied for, or expressed a desired to have a female suffrage amendment submitted to the people of the United States, or have indicated the slightest wish for the possession of the franchise? Not one in a hundred.... Changing the Constitution in so vital a respect before a single State has even seriously thought of adopting female suffrage looks a little premature." Aside from a favorable committee report in 1893, Congress ignored subsequent amendment petitions, and the NWSA dissolved in 1890. The organization's twenty-one-year tenure saw seventeen amendments before Congress, with half sponsored by the same three sympathetic Northeastern congressmen. Suffragettes needed a broader coalition to satisfy Article V requirements.[44]

Lucy Stone and Henry Blackwell's American Woman Suffrage Association meanwhile sought state-level enfranchisement. Results were mixed. In the winter of 1869–70, Utah's and Wyoming's small territorial legislatures let women vote, and through the 1870s and 1880s, fourteen states, mainly but not solely in the West, enfranchised women on matters related to schooling. Local lawmakers similarly allowed voting in tax, municipal, and liquor board elections, affirming traditional ideas of women's domestic authority. Fights for the full franchise came in Michigan in 1874, Colorado in 1877, Nebraska in 1882, Oregon in 1884, Rhode Island in 1887, Washington in 1889, and South Dakota in 1890. While all faltered against local opposition, the campaigns forced the issue into state constitutional conventions. Pro-suffrage convention delegates' arguments varied. Framers in Illinois in 1868, Texas in 1875, and California in 1878 debated the female franchise, some proposing that it would counterbalance the votes of immigrants, the poor, and people of color. Conversely, Governor James Harvey of Kansas objected to these "social or ethnological distinctions," proposing that a "true republic" forbade a "favored class of 'white male citizens.'" As a congressman in 1866, John Broomall had unsuccessfully argued that the Guarantee Clause required that the states enfranchise women, and now as a delegate to Pennsylvania's 1872 constitutional convention, he instead sought state reform, citing the female franchise "experiment that has succeeded so well in Wyoming." State and territorial reform had convinced him that "this thing is coming. It is only a question of time." Others adopted the Wyoming argument, but with suffrage still local and limited, female turnout stayed low, bolstering opponents' claims that women did not want the vote. Henry Blackwell's speech on the Wyoming experiment failed to convince delegates at North Dakota's 1889 convention, leading delegate J. W. Scott to declare that the suffrage "question is not one that has been sufficiently thought of by the public, or demanded sufficiently by the public for us to take this step at this time. There has been no serious discussion of the question—it has only been agitated by a few." The full franchise required further organizing.[45]

United by frustration, in 1890, the NWSA and AWSA merged into the National American Woman's Suffrage Association (NAWSA). Alice Stone Blackwell, the daughter of Lucy Stone and Henry Blackwell, led the union, proposing that women enfranchised at the state level could then force their congressmen to back a national amendment. They thus reconceived the AWSA's state-level enfranchisement strategy as a means to the NWSA's federal amendment. The NAWSA began building a local base. At the 1893 NAWSA convention, Alice Blackwell suggested rotating subsequent conventions throughout the states. This frustrated Anthony. "Our younger women," Anthony declared, "naturally can not appreciate the vast amount of work done here in Washington by the National Association." But Ohio delegate Claudia Quigley Murphy replied, "It seems better to sow the seed of suffrage throughout the country by means of our national conventions. . . . We have found the average legislator to be but a reflex of the sentiments of his constituents. If we wish representation at Washington, . . . let us get down to the people and sow the seed among them." The measure passed, and the NAWSA began state campaigns. Even Anthony eventually accepted the tactic, admitting, "I don't know the exact number of States we shall have to have, but I do know that there will come a day when that number will automatically and resistlessly act on the Congress of the United States to compel the submission of a federal suffrage amendment."[46]

The NAWSA initially struggled at the state level. While women won the vote in Colorado in 1893 and in Idaho and Utah in 1896, Kansas women capitulated to local Republican opposition in 1894, Massachusetts women organized against a franchise referendum in 1895, and California women lost the vote in 1896 thanks to counterorganizing by the liquor lobby, which resisted enfranchising prohibitionist women. No further state-level franchise expansions occurred until 1910. In total, between 1870 and 1910, 480 campaigns across thirty-three states yielded seventeen amendment referenda, mainly in the West. These succeeded only in Colorado and Idaho. Even with forty-seven more campaigns petitioning state constitutional conventions, in these years, only six states constitutionally recognized school election franchise and two granted tax or bond election franchise. Statutory reforms were more common, occurring in sixteen and four states for each type of election, respectively.[47]

Suffragettes, still undeterred, added states. When the NAWSA requested that Theodore Roosevelt support suffrage in his 1908 State of the Union Address, Roosevelt famously replied, "Go, get another state." President Taft, addressing the NAWSA 1910 convention, echoed skeptical state legislators and framers, holding that "woman suffrage has not been a failure, . . . but it has been tested only in those States where population is sparse and where the problem of entrusting such power to women in the concentrated population of large cities is not presented." Missouri's George Vest had used almost this exact language to block a Senate vote a quarter century earlier. Alice Blackwell therefore concluded that Taft "was not a strong suffragist and might not even be wholly with us," reaffirming the need for Eastern and Southern states.[48]

The message was clear. Following Roosevelt's and Taft's injunctions, reformers canvassed by car in Washington State in 1910 and California in 1911, allied with local labor organizations, and won the vote. Oregon, Arizona, and Kansas referendum victories followed the next year, though fraud and the liquor lobby defeated ballot measures in Michigan, Ohio, and Wisconsin. With the suffragettes' referendum bid blocked by the Illinois governor, they pushed the Illinois legislature to grant the presidential vote, increasing suffrage states to seventy-three electoral votes, over a tenth of the Electoral College. The state-by-state strategy got another boost in 1914 when the Supreme Court refused to overturn the Illinois law, consistent with its policy in *Minor* of deferring the female franchise question to the states. White-collar Southern "New Women" had organized NAWSA affiliates in every Southern state by 1913 but were ignored by Democratic state legislators, secure in their seats and loathe to risk enfranchising Black women. A federal suffrage amendment and the prospect of attendant congressional intervention seemed even less palatable to Southern elites.[49]

Buoyed by these victories, the NAWSA returned to Washington, DC. Alice Paul, a newly recruited graduate student trained by militant British suffragettes, reassembled the NAWSA's dormant Congressional Committee in 1912 and rallied a five-thousand-person march along Pennsylvania Avenue on the eve of the

1913 inauguration. NAWSA state affiliates lofted placards bearing their state's name, displaying the organization's nationwide reach to the noncommittal President Woodrow Wilson. Lucy Burns, another veteran of the British movement, joined Paul to form the Congressional Union as an autonomous affiliate of the NAWSA Congressional Committee, submitting national amendments and promising to organize female voters against opposed congressional incumbents. Western Democrats brought amendments to vote in 1913 and 1914, the first since Senator Blair's 1887 proposal. The NAWSA joined the amendment campaign. NAWSA president Carrie Chapman Catt, frustrated to see state referenda defeated by the most "ignorant, most narrow-minded, most un-American" voters, floated a test amendment before the "higher court of the Congress." Senator John Shafroth of Colorado and Representative A. Mitchell Palmer of Pennsylvania sponsored a proposal to require each state to call a suffrage referendum on the petition of 8 percent of the state electorate. This aimed to further lower the bar for state-level referenda and appease states'-rights and Southern opponents of the female franchise, but the proposal failed against uniform Southern resistance, 174 to 204 in the House and 35 to 34 in the Senate, short of Article V's two-thirds threshold. Still, the Shafroth-Palmer amendment was the first since 1878 to earn a congressional vote, reenergizing the national amendment campaign. Between the NAWSA's 1890 founding and 1916, Congress heard forty-nine amendment proposals, all but seven of which came from Great Plains or Western congressmen, with most proposed after 1910.[50]

The movement sought still more states. Seeing that the "amendment will pass when there are enough Suffrage states," NAWSA Congressional Committee chair Ruth McCormick advocated a forty-eight-state campaign and presented a four-hundred-thousand-signature petition to Congress. The failure of five Western referenda in 1914 and four Northeastern ones the following year did not slow organizing. Eastern defeats were narrow, marked by corruption and saloon-lobby counterorganizing that only stiffened suffragettes' resolve to return the question to the ballot. Two nights after their New York loss, activists raised over $115,000 for the next campaign. The Women's Trade Union League recruited more working women and men to the suffrage cause, nudging the American Federation of Labor to endorse enfranchisement in 1915.[51]

By 1916, the NAWSA and Congressional Union had enfranchised enough women to threaten congressional and presidential incumbents. The NAWSA marched outside the 1916 Republican Convention, and the Congressional Union regrouped in Chicago as the National Woman's Party (NWP) to secure, in the words of party leader Maud Younger, the "defeat of Mr. Wilson and the national Democratic ticket in the twelve equal suffrage states": "One thing we have to teach Mr. Wilson and his party—and all on-looking parties—that the group that opposes national suffrage will lose women's support in twelve great commonwealths controlling nearly a hundred electoral votes; too large a fraction to risk." These states, representing only a fifth of the Electoral College, were concentrated in the West, which Wilson won handily. While both parties adopted a state-level enfranchisement plank in 1916, the full federal amendment required an interregional coalition.[52]

Catt therefore developed a "Winning Plan" to add suffrage states and force amendment. This was a blueprint for convergence. On reassuming the NAWSA presidency in 1915, Catt abandoned the old Shafroth-Palmer amendment for the original Anthony amendment forbidding state-based disenfranchisement. Marshaling the NAWSA's state-level heads in a "crowded, stuffy" meeting at the 1916 NAWSA convention in Atlantic City, Catt sketched on a wall map her strategy to pass the new amendment—the NAWSA would mobilize for the full franchise in Southern and Eastern states and replicate "the Illinois law [for presidential franchise] in a number of other states," paired with party primaries or other limited votes in hostile states. Catt planned to then assemble "thirty-six, and [then], forty-eight divisions [to] move on Congress with precision," adopting the Congressional Union's militancy but adding strategic patience, building nationwide, interregional consensus before appealing to Congress. As Catt recounted in her notes, "When thirty-six state associations, or preferably more, enter into a solemn compact to get the Amendment submitted by Congress and ratified by their legislatures; when they live up to their compact by running a red-hot, never ceasing campaign in their own states designed to create sentiment behind the political leaders of these states and to aim both these forces at the men in Congress as well as the legislatures, we *can* get the Amendment through." Catt saw that Congress would not accept a national amendment until the constitutional question had been resolved by the state legislatures and constitutional conventions. And so suffragettes again answered Roosevelt's challenge to "Go, get another state."[53]

Suffragettes made three advances between the 1916 and 1920 elections. First, states extended the federal franchise. In the late 1910s, political machines in Boston, Philadelphia, Pittsburgh, Cleveland, and Chicago followed their working-class voters in backing suffrage—in New York City, the Democratic machine's conversion pushed a state referendum to victory in 1917. Further, women's wartime labor and the NAWSA's campaigning and civic volunteering led state legislators to propose over a hundred bills for full franchise and to grant the presidential vote in fourteen states between 1917 and 1919, with all but five of these presidential states in the South, Old Northwest, or Northeast. Three other states added the full franchise, including the federal vote, in these years, giving the resulting twenty-nine federal election suffrage states 339 of 531 Electoral College votes in 1919, spread evenly across the country, save for the Deep South. Second, following this Electoral College realignment and growing publicity around NWP White House pickets and Paul's hunger strikes, Wilson in 1917 pushed the House to reestablish a suffrage committee. Third, while the proportion of suffrage states had hovered just short of three-fifths since 1898, thanks to this recent state-level surge, in 1918 the proportion passed three-fourths, enough to ratify an amendment.[54] By 1919, forty states had enfranchised women in some capacity at some point. The same nationwide base could also oust resistant congressional incumbents. The NAWSA, meeting in Washington, DC, in December 1917, therefore instructed the recently reconvened Sixty-Fifth Congress "to submit the Federal Amendment before the next congressional election" or face "a compact of State associations willing and ready to conduct such campaigns" to "effect change in both Houses of Congress sufficient to insure [the amendment's] passage." Members of Congress proposed thirty-six federal amendments between 1917 and 1919—nearly as many as in the previous two decades combined—with all but six sponsored by Great Plains or Western members of Congress representing the NAWSA's core base (figure 7).[55]

State-level franchise expansion pushed the president and Congress toward amendment. A 1917 House Judiciary Committee minority report suggested that a federal amendment would complement but not override state law, leaving Southern states "to impose restrictions on the elective franchise . . . [and] strengthen Anglo-Saxon supremacy." Southerners, still wary of federal intervention, rejected a January 10, 1918, House proposal, which nonetheless passed with support from Western and new federal suffrage states. In an unprecedented step, Wilson then spoke before the Senate on September 30, urging passage of the amendment as a "vitally necessary war measure." But the following day, four Northeastern senators defected and allied with the Southern bloc to defeat the proposal by two votes. The NAWSA ousted two of these Northeastern sen-

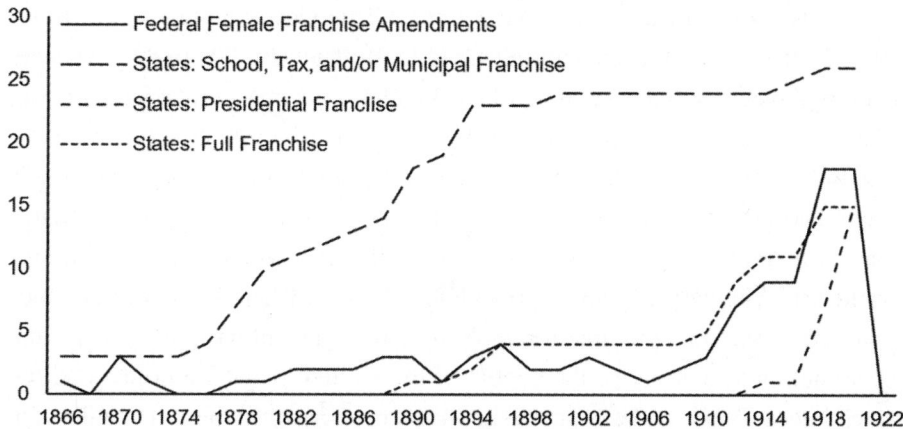

Fig. 7. State and federal female suffrage regulation, 1866–1922. State data from Keyssar, *Right to Vote*, 365–68. The y-axis indicates proposed federal female franchise amendments and states allowing the female franchise.

ators, John Weeks of Massachusetts and Willard Saulsbury of Delaware, in November 1918. Further, with the Eighteenth Amendment's ratification in January 1919, the antisuffrage saloon lobby folded, helping the NAWSA add six presidential suffrage states, including Maine, whose Senator Frederick Hale flipped to support the amendment. Another Senate vote failed on February 10, 1919, but with the seating of the new Sixty-Sixth Senate in March, the NAWSA estimated that it now had the votes. The House considered another proposal on May 21, with Edward Little of Kansas advocating an amendment by citing "the Western States": "where we have had woman suffrage in one form or another for years." Texas's Rufus Hardy warned of federal encroachment "first as to race and now as to sex qualification. Next, perhaps it will be taken over as to educational or property qualifications." But rebuking Hardy, fellow Texan Thomas Blanton adopted the language of convergence, answering that the amendment "does not infringe on the rights of the sovereign States," as the issue had been settled by "the majority in the interest of the whole people" in favor of enfranchisement. California's John Raker gave the numbers: "There are 15 States which have full woman suffrage. There are 29 states where women can vote for President. These 29 States control 306 electoral votes." Adolphus Nelson of Wisconsin also saw the new electoral reality in which the "28 States in which women now have presidential suffrage now control about 55 percent of the Electoral College, over one-half of the Senate, 45 percent of the House, and 55 percent of the votes in the party conventions." This electoral shift was demonstrated concretely when the House passed the amendment 304 to 89. The same pattern played out in the Senate on June 3 and 4. Alabama's Oscar Underwood, Idaho's William Borah, and New York's James Wadsworth, now the minority, also railed against the amendment on states'-rights grounds, with Connecticut's Frank Brandegee condemning the amendment as "an outrage upon the States that do not want it. It does not make any difference whether 45 or 47 States wanted it." Convergence again prevailed. Democrat Charles Thomas of Colorado answered that "the time for applying that argument has gone, for ... the overwhelming majority of the people of the United States are in favor of the amendment. There can be no more significant evidence than the fact that the vote about to be taken will be confined to no particular section of the country." Even Mississippi's John Sharp Williams admitted that the amendment would not override his state constitution's poll tax clause, which "may be made to apply to the Negro women" under *Williams v. Mississippi*. As a final ploy, Underwood tried derailing the amendment by proposing ratification by state conventions, rather than by legislatures, where the NAWSA was stronger, but his measure failed. The amendment passed, with forty-one of the fifty-six supporting senators representing states that had already established suffrage.[56]

Prior state-level reform eased ratification. Even during the congressional endgame, Catt kept NAWSA state affiliates operating in anticipation of the ratification campaign. Accordingly, NAWSA affiliates and allies quickly pushed ratification through special legislative sessions in the newer suffrage states. In older Western suffrage states, where state-level organizations had atrophied, ratification followed slowly and haphazardly, punctuated by near defeats. Texas, Arkansas, and Tennessee, which had recently extended presidential suffrage, joined Kentucky and West Virginia to ratify the proposal over Deep South opposition.[57]

Scholars have attributed the Nineteenth Amendment's passage to women's wartime labor and volunteering, to strategic alliances between national suffrage and labor organizations, to Wilson's sudden intervention, and to the defeat of the liquor lobby with the Eighteenth Amendment. These stories are not wholly wrong. But, focusing on national phenomena, they miss how state-level NAWSA campaigns and enfranchisement convinced congressmen that women could and did vote competently and that these state laws could exclude Black women to maintain Jim Crow. Catt later mused that the states so decisively settled the national issue that they nearly obviated a federal amendment entirely. As Catt explained, with a few more state-level reforms in the 1870s, "State amendments . . . [for] woman suffrage would have swept from West to East long before corporate interests had gained sway over party councils. The East and South would have yielded then to the momentum of the triumphant movement, as they did forty years later, and there would probably have been no need for a federal woman suffrage amendment." So universal was state suffrage reform that the movement nearly yielded deference without subsequent convergence for federal amendment. But suffragettes wanted the amendment. In practice, the states moved more slowly, and the path was not one of deference alone but rather deference and then convergence. Through this reform, the states addressed the suffrage question in a way that complemented the Nineteenth Amendment and stabilized national constitutionalism.[58]

Federal Deference and Dictation on Prohibition, State Convergence on Repeal

Like suffragettes, prohibitionists failed in their initial amendment campaign. Liquor law began locally. Responding to scattered group organizing and dry, anti-liquor pressures, towns and counties tailored liquor laws to their needs, banning or taxing liquor sales and saloon licenses, with Indiana first formalizing the deferential "local option" approach in 1832 and Georgia passing a similar law the following year. In the 1850s, suffragettes, nativists, and Protestant traditionalists sought to eliminate statewide liquor access in order to force sobriety on resistant cities and itinerant alcoholics, workers, and immigrants. The temperance crusader Neal Dow led Maine to ban liquor statewide in 1851, with ten other "dry" New England and upper Midwest states and two territories following by 1855. But public frustration and liquor-industry lobbying pushed state judges and legislators to dilute these statutes, which were further undermined as the post–Civil War boom in railroads let "wet"-state distillers ship liquor into dry ones.[59]

As increased interstate shipping undermined dry-state enforcement, reformers sought congressional dictation of a uniform national prohibition law. Dow became the chief advocate of federal dictation of state liquor law. He rallied absolutists to the Prohibition Party in 1869, aiming to break dry voters from the moderate national parties, win congressional seats, and eliminate wet jurisdictions. Middle-class Midwestern women formed the Woman's Christian Temperance Union (WCTU) in 1874, protesting and occupying neighborhood saloons and, in lieu of voting, lobbying and petitioning legislators. Both organizations, led by old abolitionists, consciously imitated the early Republicans' partisan wedge tactics, mass moral appeals, and platform of federal dictation of state policy, by 1890 building a national audience of one hundred thousand readers between the WCTU's *Union Signal* and the Prohibition Party's *Voice* and *Lever*. They wanted a national amendment. Ada Bittenbender, the chief—and sometimes sole—staffer of the WCTU Office of National Legislation, explained that with increasing interstate rail shipment, the "quasi-prohibitory legislation of individual States is expected to accomplish that which is impossible." Facing conflicting state laws and failing dry-state enforcement, she deemed the movement's aim to be "a national one. The traffic is carried on everywhere. No place and no person of this great nation is free from its polluting influence. How to end its pernicious existence is peculiarly a national question—more of a national question than was slavery." Her goal was thus to "introduce into the National Constitution provisions of the same general character as those which now confer power in Congress to establish uniform laws respecting bankruptcies, slavery, involuntary servitude, and the like"—federal dictation of state policy. But prohibition amendments garnered little support in Congress. The Prohibition Party and WCTU rejected the two morally compromised major parties and represented only six dry states in 1890—Kansas and the Dakotas joined holdouts Maine, New Hampshire, and Vermont—and so won only fringe votes in presidential or congressional elections. Congressmen ignored prohibition as a constitutional concern, considering only eighteen amendments between 1876 and 1907, thirteen of which came from Kansas's Preston Plumb and New Hampshire's Henry W. Blair.[60]

The Supreme Court seemed friendlier to state-level prohibition. In 1887, the Court upheld the Kansas Constitution's ban on intrastate liquor manufacture and sale, emboldening WCTU legislative director J. Ellen Foster to propose that the Supreme Court also affirm state-level bans on interstate sale. The Court did the opposite. In *Bowman v. Chicago & Northwestern Railway* and *Leisy v. Hardin,* the Court blocked states from banning interstate rail shipment and from seizing alcohol kept in the original shipping package, which remained under Congress's interstate commerce jurisdiction. In *Leisy,* the Court did, however, leave a door open for drys, holding that Congress could "remove the restriction upon the state in dealing with imported articles of trade within its limits" and thus allow state bans on out-of-state liquor imports. Given "the late decision of the Supreme Court," the WCTU's 1888 convention resolved that "suppression of the liquor traffic must come through National Legislation" to authorize state bans. The WCTU Office of National Legislation joined WCTU local chapters and the Prohibition Party in petitioning Congress for a statute authorizing state-level bans on interstate shipping, pushing the United States' Brewers Association to counterlobby Congress in 1890.[61]

Congress bent to WCTU pressure and allowed state bans on interstate liquor imports. The stalwart dry senator Henry Blair, his prohibition amendments having failed, backed a national statute affirming state import bans, a compromise crafted at the behest of the moderate drys William Frye, Alfred Colquitt, John H. Reagan, and Isaac S. Struble. According to the wet Missouri Democrat George Vest, moderate Republican backers intended the bill to silence the divisive national prohibition question—a growing wet Democratic cause—by reframing regulation as a duller "question as to the power of Congress of the United States and as to what are the reserved powers of the States." This deference to state regulation helped preserve Republican control of Congress and won over even Mississippi Democrat James George, who loathed expanding federal power, especially when the same Congress considered monitoring Southern elections under the 1890 Lodge Federal Elections Bill. Like a few Senate Democrats, George defended the pending temperance bill as a matter of states' rights, explaining that "Congress may create the [regulatory] power and donate it to the states" and thus affirm the states' "necessary and essential police powers." As the historian Richard F. Hamm confirms, members like George interpreted *Leisy* to push regulation on the states and so "remove prohibition, always a troublesome political issue, from the Senate debates." The resulting 1890 Wilson Act, introduced by James Falconer Wilson in a swift and overt response to *Leisy,* authorized state-level importation bans, subjecting alcohol shipments to state regulation upon arrival. In Wilson's words, the act aimed to let the states adopt the "local option, [and] to allow them to do as they please in regard to the liquor question." The Court affirmed the act the following year, and so, with federal amendment unlikely and the state-level path reopened and encouraged by Congress and then the Court in 1891, prohibitionists founded the Anti-Saloon League in 1893 to revive the original state-by-state strategy. The constitutional issue quieted at the national level. Save for four more amendments, prohibition would not reappear on the congressional amendment agenda until 1913.[62]

Prohibitionists looked to reform state constitutions. Reformers worked haltingly, failing, reevaluating, and forming new groups and plans. WCTU Washington staffer Ada Bittenbender returned to Nebraska to run for state judicial office, and Legislative Superintendent J. Ellen Foster instructed local chapters to join Prohibition Party candidates in sponsoring statewide prohibition amendments, sixteen of which cleared at least one state legislative chamber between 1880 and 1883. But wet-county voters and legislators blocked nearly all amendments, with scattered local option clauses passing in convention. Capitalizing on this, brewers formed the National Protective Association to buy newspaper articles, speeches, and occasional legislators, and voters across twelve states rejected prohibition measures between 1887 and 1890, approving temperance only in the sparsely settled Dakotas. Prohibition Party membership dwindled after a failed 1892 merger with the Populist Party, sending supporters to the new Anti-Saloon League, which Foster joined as a trustee.[63]

Rejecting the Prohibition Party's immediate ban strategy, the Anti-Saloon League instead worked gradually and locally. The league began by organizing members through church congregations, opportunistically promising these voters to supportive Democratic and Republican candidates, and sponsoring local option bills to capture populous counties. State legislators passed these local option bills to punt prohibition debate to the counties, which often allowed personal liquor possession while closing saloons. Saloon closures deprived pro-liquor activists of meeting places, weakening local wet opposition. Local bans followed. In the West, growing agrarian counties overrode older, wet mining counties to pass local option bills. In the South, where the league chapters were poorest and weakest, middle-class churchgoing whites pushed the local option to force sobriety on Black and white workers and farmers, so that by 1907, 825 of the 994 ex-Confederate counties were dry. And nationwide, brewers, distillers, and saloons backed local option and licensing bills to shutter competitors in neighboring counties and preempt tougher reform. A 1910 Anti-Saloon League newspaper described the organization's strategy as "the line of least resistance. It began in the rural communities, its first conquests being against the crossroads bar rooms. . . . The next object of attack was the village saloon. . . . From the villages and townships, the scene of battle very naturally shifted to the counties, ... one thousand seven hundred and twenty-nine [of which] have outlawed the liquor traffic, leaving only one thousand one hundred and fifty-six in which saloons are permitted.... The outposts have largely been taken; the enemy has been constantly on the retreat, until the real strength of the liquor army is entrenched in comparatively few cities." The prohibitionist academic Norman E. Richardson noted that to conquer these cities, "the next step in the rural States was naturally for State-wide prohibition."[64]

The breakthrough to statewide reform came between 1907 and 1909. Legislators in Tennessee, Georgia, Mississippi, and North Carolina affirmed the local dry consensus with statewide bans, as did Oklahoma's first state constitutional framers. Like many Southern states, Georgia first went dry by local option, implemented in 125 of 137 counties by 1907, excluding only Atlanta and a few other cities. Dozens of dry-county state legislators, satisfied with this status quo, opposed statewide ban and faced little pressure from the WCTU or Anti-Saloon League, their state chapters nearly disbanded by 1905–6. The precipitating factor seems to have been the 1906 Atlanta race riot, which sensationalistic local papers used to stoke white fears of Black drunkenness and violence. Thereafter, Atlanta closed Black saloons and segregated and regulated the rest, encouraging the WCTU and the Anti-Saloon League to seize on racial anxieties in lobbying the legislature and winning statewide reform. Elsewhere, early state bans mirrored existing local law, limiting saloons, breweries, distillers, and liquor licenses while allowing personal possession. Oklahoma and Maine, for example, constitutionally exempted medicinal liquor, leaving Maine sheriffs to ignore other, unauthorized possession.[65]

These statewide bans gave prohibitionists an imperfect and brief victory. Brewers soon formed the Personal Liberty League to counterorganize locally, and as wet urban and immigrant populations grew, voters rejected eight prohibition measures between 1909 and 1913. In Ohio, voters amended their constitution in 1912 to allow licensing. Further, in *Rhodes v. Iowa,* the Supreme Court held that the Wilson Act, letting states ban out-of-state alcohol imports on arrival, only applied *after* receipt by the consignee, impeding dry-state enforcement. Thanks to this limitation and to wet-state brewing and distilling, by 1911, twenty million gallons of liquor flowed annually into nine dry states, mainly in the South. The Anti-Saloon League's 1911 convention declared that under "the Rhodes case, the Federal Government now protects a system which goes far to nullify State prohibitory laws, by which, in response to circular appeals, sent to citizens in 'dry' territory by manufacturers and wholesalers in other States, an extensive interstate traffic in liquors is carried on." The convention proposed that Congress statutorily subject interstate liquor shipments to state regulation, protecting dry laws, which wets then claimed overextended congressional Commerce Clause powers.[66]

Anti-Saloon League strategy evolved in 1913. Ernest Cherrington, the league's national legislative strategist, proposed flipping additional states, counties, and congressmen to then win a national amendment. An amendment promised to resolve the Commerce Clause question and dry out remaining, uncooperative Northeastern states. National Superintendent Purley Baker helped draft a new organization constitution in 1913 centralizing policy planning, dues collection, chapter budgeting, selection and compensation of state superintendents, and distribution of league print material, including national maps targeting remaining dry counties and states. The strategy of planned state convergence for federal amendment mirrored that of the suffragettes—perhaps not coincidentally given the movements' overlap. For example, an Anti-Saloon League "anti-liquor warfare" circular mapped the counties won in Arkansas, Delaware, South Carolina, and Florida, predicting that increasingly dry states would domino, tipping Florida: "With prohibition in every state across [Florida's] northern border . . . it is altogether likely that the people will take the suggestion seriously and vote accordingly in the election next November, which is to decide whether prohibition shall go into the constitution of the State of Florida." A 1914 flyer, mapping the nation's dry counties and states in white, reminded members of the league's true aim, to "make the map all white by constitutional amendment—thirty-six states can do it."[67]

Congress aided Cherrington's convergence strategy. With increased Anti-Saloon League pressure, the addition of five dry states, and House reapportionment toward dry rural districts in 1910, Congress passed the 1913 Webb-Kenyon Act, forbidding railroads from purchasing, selling, or importing alcohol into "bone dry" jurisdictions that forbade possession. William Kenyon sponsored the act not to expand congressional power or dictate state policy but rather to defer to state dry laws, assuring that "each State should be free to determine its own policy in regards to the liquor traffic." This reversed *Rhodes*, strengthening enforcement in dry jurisdictions and stemming interstate rail transportation of liquor, albeit without stoppering wet-state brewing and distilling. Imitating Alice Paul's recent suffrage parade, on December 10, 1913, the WCTU and Anti-Saloon League led a three-thousand-person march on the Capitol, presenting an ambitious amendment prohibiting liquor manufacture, sale, and transportation nationwide, which Representative Richmond Hobson and Senator Morris Sheppard proposed the following year. Representative Martin Morrison offered an alternative, weaker amendment constitutionalizing the Webb-Kenyon Act by prohibiting interstate liquor traffic. But Representative Edwin Webb, cosponsor of the act, dismissed Morrison's watered-down proposal as redundant given that the Court had already affirmed the Webb-Kenyon Act's constitutionality. With Anti-Saloon League support, the stronger Hobson-Sheppard amendment cleared the House by simple majority in 1914. The amendment push had begun. Congress, which had heard only twenty-one prohibition amendments prior to 1913, received another thirty-eight between 1913 and 1917, roughly half narrowly tailored like the Morrison amendment to outlaw only interstate traffic and half following the expansive Sheppard-Hobson amendment in prohibiting all sale, manufacture, and transportation.[68]

The Anti-Saloon League captured additional states. With Purley Baker's blessing, Ernest Cherrington developed the league's *New Plan of Campaign,* raising $5 million through newspaper subscriptions, which funded additional advertisements, trade newspapers, and pamphlets in twenty languages, a bid to win urban immigrants and workers. In 1914, league presses printed ten tons of material daily. Income tax reform further decreased the states' dependence on the liquor tax and interstate trade, already declining with the Webb-Kenyon Act, leading state legislators to call new prohibition referenda. Between 1914 and 1917, prohibitionists added eighteen states, eleven by popular vote and nine by constitutional revision, almost exclusively in the South, Great Plains, and West. Arizona, Colorado, Oregon, Virginia, and Washington led the charge in 1914, going dry by initiative, with only California and Ohio opposed. These statewide bans closed more breweries, shifting growing beer demand to St. Louis and Milwaukee companies, which backed additional bans, hoping to corner the wet-state market through interstate rail shipment. Popular initiatives passed again in Colorado, Oregon, and Washington in 1916 and in Alaska, Arkansas, Idaho, Michigan, Montana, Nebraska, and South Dakota, while Missouri and Vermont joined California in voting against prohibition. By the end of 1917, prohibitionists held a slim, twenty-seven-state national majority, reflecting moderate, if growing, public support for prohibition—between 1914 and 1919, 2,347,000 people voted for prohibition in state referenda. Though this was a narrow national majority, with the passage of the Sixteenth and Seventeenth Amendments and the introduction of the female suffrage amendment, Anti-Saloon League legislative strategist Wayne Wheeler felt the time had come for the prohibition amendment. Purley Baker called again for an amendment, recommending a twenty-year campaign for gradual, decisive convergence. Richmond Hobson, joining the league after losing reelection to Congress, backed Ernest Cherrington in accelerating the campaign in March 1917, hoping to pass the measure the following year, before 1920 congressional reapportionment added more urban, wet seats. Looming reapportionment pushed Cherrington to accelerate the campaign, perhaps to Baker's dismay. Baker warned that in this "next and final step," the league should "go just as far and just as fast as public sentiment would justify."[69]

Congress seemed receptive, especially as Anti-Saloon League grassroots organizing turned additional seats dry. After the Court upheld the Webb-Kenyon Act, Congress prohibited mailing liquor ads to dry jurisdictions. Congress's Lever Act also let the president divert grain from liquor production to war needs. Wartime nationalization of railways and mines, bans on sale to servicemen, and anti-German sentiment hobbled brewers, many of them German, and aided prohibitionists, who added seven dry states by 1919, including the holdout Ohio, which had rejected four prior temperance measures. In total, between 1907 and 1919, sixteen state amendments bumped the national count to twenty constitutional provisions across thirty-four prohibition states. State constitutional reform had created a narrow dry national consensus and a sense, if illusory, of broader convergence for federal amendment.[70]

Congress renewed amendment debate in 1917. Senator Morris Sheppard reintroduced the Anti-Saloon League's amendment prohibiting alcohol sale, manufacturing, and transportation, pitching the measure as an affirmation of prior state reform. He noted, "Prohibition by State or local option now prevails in an area equal to two-thirds of the United States, and that area contains more than half of the American people. Millions of American people have petitioned Congress to submit an amendment." The amendment's second section, he added, allowed "joint national and State action against the liquor traffic," preserving state sovereignty. Edwin Webb, sponsor of the Webb-Kenyon Act, agreed that this let the states "enforce the constitutional amendment in their own way": "My understanding of section 2 of the amendment is that it makes both the state and the federal government sovereign in enforcement of the prohibition law."

Judiciary Committee Chair Andrew Volstead affirmed that "the states have courts and police forces equipped to do that work" and that the federal amendment should not be interpreted as "annulling state laws on the same subject." Even Idaho's William Borah, a states'-rights voice on the committee, backed "national prohibition through constitutional amendment—not for the purpose of destroying local self-government but really in aid of it. There was no other way by which a State could be dry," especially given neighboring wet states. On December 18, 1917, the proposal cleared both houses with bipartisan support, and dry states pushed the amendment to ratification within weeks of their assembly in early 1919.[71] Similarly, after Congress's Volstead Act provided for federal enforcement, dry states quickly passed harmonizing enforcement statutes. Even wet-state legislators, concentrated in New England, ratified the amendment, accepted federal enforcement under the Volstead Act, and passed eleven concurrent state enforcement acts by 1923.[72]

The difficulty was that under Cherrington's plan, the Anti-Saloon League went a little further and faster than public sentiment would justify. The national dry consensus existed more in law than in practice. Cherrington rushed the convergence strategy, passing a federal amendment before winning sufficient, durable state and public support. Instead of convergence around federal amendment, Cherrington won federal dictation by amendment against a sizable wet constituency—the platform that Neal Dow had proposed at the height of federal power during Reconstruction. With the Anti-Saloon League uncommitted to either party, many state legislators were uncommitted to the league, merely passing local option bills to punt regulation to counties and cities. This local option, coupled with the *Rhodes* decision and hodgepodge state laws, resulted in uneven enforcement, concentrating liquor consumption and sale. Virginia, for example, added sixteen dry counties between 1908 and 1914, funneling liquor traffic into remaining wet jurisdictions, which licensed over three hundred new liquor vendors in these years. Some statewide bans had prohibited sale, manufacturing, and saloon licensing but allowed consumption and possession. Oregon's constitution, for example, forbade sale and manufacturing while allowing possession, prompting distributers to deliver monthly bulk shipments to Portland for subsequent distribution. As the local option and statewide bans proliferated through the 1910s, wet jurisdictions doubled down, and national beer consumption increased. Similarly, the Volstead Act interpreted the amendment to forbid manufacture, sale, and transportation of liquor over 0.5 percent alcohol by volume but exempted liquor consumption and the possession of sacramental wine and home-brewed hard cider. While the states had gone dry, prompting the federal amendment, they did so in a way that allowed and sometimes concentrated consumption of liquor and beer, creating staunchly wet legislative districts and constituencies, often in cities. Dictation under the Eighteenth Amendment faltered.[73]

A few wet-state governors and legislators weakened state enforcement statutes. Initially, resistance came from Northeastern states with big, wet cities. Organized in 1918, the Association Against the Prohibition Amendment (AAPA) asserted that overlapping state and federal enforcement acts subjected violators to double jeopardy and unreasonable search and seizure, concerns that nudged Governors Al Smith of New York and Edward Edwards and George Silzer of New Jersey to suggest softening state enforcement in the early 1920s. Maryland outright refused to pass an enforcement act, while Californians and Nevadans moved to repeal their acts, the latter claiming that federal agents should enforce the Volstead Act on the state's federal lands. Georgia, Massachusetts, and Pennsylvania lawmakers also proposed nonenforcement.[74]

Congress, however, remained unmoved. During the 1924 presidential and congressional campaign, neither major party addressed the enforcement question, while the November election added dry members to Congress. Against an uninterested Congress, the AAPA unsuccessfully pitched bills restricting double jeopardy and exempting beer and wine from enforcement. Save for a rogue Michigan proposal, between 1919 and 1926, repeal amendments came only from members representing the handful of states contesting enforcement, namely, Massachusetts, Connecticut, New York, New Jersey, and Maryland. The AAPA's base was too narrow, urban, and Northeastern to sway Congress, which, at the Anti-Saloon League's request, skipped 1920 reapportionment toward urban districts.[75]

Just as the Anti-Saloon League flipped states and then Congress, so too would the AAPA. Wisconsin AAPA leader Henry Curran observed, "Prohibition was won state by state," as would be repeal. While most governors and state legislators refused to undermine the Volstead Act by overtly refusing enforcement, urban voters and legislators proved more sympathetic. Pro-brewery Milwaukee legislators sponsored a nonbinding ballot measure asking Congress to modify Volstead, as did Republican New York legislators, hoping to vent wet voters' frustrations. In California, Montana, Colorado, and Illinois, the AAPA circumvented dry legislators by calling nonbinding citizen initiatives against state enforcement statutes and constitutional clauses and, in Nevada and Missouri, against the Volstead Act and Eighteenth Amendment. The tactic worked, as referenda carried in five states by 1926, winning decisive supermajorities in Illinois, Wisconsin, New York, and Nevada. Wet legislators in Maryland and Massachusetts lost narrow votes to call referenda the following year, and in 1928, Massachusetts wets won their advisory referendum. North Dakota, an early dry state, narrowly voted to retain its prohibition laws. Following a second wet referendum in 1929, the Wisconsin legislature repealed state enforcement laws. Repeal planks were passed by both parties in Connecticut, Illinois, New Jersey, New York, Rhode Island, Washington, and Wisconsin and by Democrats in Delaware, Maryland, Massachusetts, New Hampshire, North Dakota, Vermont, and Pennsylvania.[76]

Wets renewed calls for federal reform. The Women's Organization for National Prohibition Reform argued that the Eighteenth Amendment encouraged bootlegging, lawlessness, and disregard for the national Constitution, with the AAPA blaming the amendment for the "distortion of our Federal Constitution by compelling it to carry the burden of a task which is an affair for the police power of each of our forty-eight separate and sovereign states." Conversely, repeal and proper constitutional deference to the states would strengthen the federal Constitution. Congressional amendment sponsorship widened between 1924 and 1930, as members from Illinois, Massachusetts, New York, and Wisconsin, each of which had recently passed anti-prohibition referenda, joined those from Michigan, Mississippi, and Pennsylvania and from the old wet bastions of Maryland, Missouri, and New Jersey to propose twenty-six amendments for repeal of national prohibition. New York's wet governor Al Smith then secured the 1928 Democratic presidential nomination, appointing national party chair John Raskob to stack Democratic leadership with wet loyalists, leading the Anti-Saloon League to back the staunchly dry Republican Herbert Hoover. The league began fracturing over declining revenue and leadership conflicts between Cherrington and Wheeler.[77]

The AAPA kept adding states. The Anti-Saloon League's dream of a dry-state supermajority never fully materialized, yielding federal dictation of prohibition against unwilling states. This unpopular platform encouraged convergence for a federal repeal amendment. Henry Curran, now AAPA president, declared in January 1931 that twelve wet states, nineteen senators, and 113 representatives supported a repeal amendment, with a dozen to follow by 1933. "As to the probability of the people of thirty-six States voting for repeal," he predicted that "twenty-four States would do so within the shortest time possible after the submission of the question by Congress, and that twelve more States would do so within a further period of two years." In 1931, the AAPA lost state repeal campaigns but gained new members and state legislators, boosted by the growth of the nation's urban, wet population and the formation of the allied Women's Organization for National Prohibition Reform. After the 1931 Wickersham Report detailed the difficulty of enforcement against bootlegging and speakeasies—illustrating the divergent status quo—wets co-opted drys' anticorruption arguments, turning them against the Eighteenth Amendment. Republicans answered with an amendment letting states regulate alcohol, subject to federal oversight. In a move to undercut wet rival Al Smith, at the 1932 Democratic convention, Franklin Delano Roosevelt endorsed repeal of the Eighteenth Amendment, winning the nomination and emboldening wet-state legislators. The same year, New Jersey, Louisiana, Arizona, California, Colorado, Michigan, Oregon, and Washington repealed enforcement by referendum, and Rhode Island did so by statute. These nine repeal measures boosted the national count to fifteen states by 1932—shy of a national majority but enough to imperil the Eighteenth Amendment's enforcement.[78]

New urban and Democratic members tilted the Seventy-Second Congress toward repeal. Congress's 1930 reapportionment, long overdue after skipping the 1920 reapportionment, shifted seats to cities. This added four wet senators and thirty wet representatives in 1931, many of whom urged reopening urban breweries and distilleries to employ their constituents during the Great Depression. Then, in November 1932, wets won eleven referenda, and Democrats, running a repeal platform, added ninety-six representatives and twelve senators. Representative Leonidas Dyer declared that voters had picked Democrats to "hasten the repeal of the eighteenth amendment." His colleague John Nelson, an unconvinced Maine dry, answered that the "recent election was an economic revolution, a demand on the part of the people, not for rum, but for better economic and social conditions. That demand has not yet been met, nor will this [repeal] resolution meet it." Members like Nelson might dismiss Democrats' gains, but they could not ignore the emerging state-level wet consensus. Representative Clarence McLeod gave "proof of the deep root of this sentiment against prohibition" by noting that "seventeen States have either repealed or never had State prohibition laws; twenty-six that have retained their State laws to date are refusing to spend a cent for enforcement, while the five remaining States are making but a negligible effort to assist Federal enforcement officers." Members began to reframe the Eighteenth Amendment, not as a case of gentle convergence around state policy but rather as a case of overzealous, untenable federal dictation against opposed states. Frederick Britten noted that "the sentiment of Ohio, New Jersey, and Pennsylvania is opposed to national prohibition. If they are added to the nine States which have repudiated national prohibition, as heretofore shown, we find that the group represents a population of 52,281,311, or 42.74 per cent of our country's total." Further, "although not a single State platform contained a repeal plank in 1928, there was a call for repeal in 21 different State platforms in 1930." Progressive academics also attacked the amendment for quashing local, democratic policy experimentation, forcing, in Michael Musmanno's words, the same law on "each State, city, town, and home and demand[ing] certain conduct there." Members representing the fifteen states repealing enforcement pushed the Seventy-Second Congress to amendment, accounting for most of the proposals, with John Blaine's broad repeal amendment clearing the Senate on February 16, 1933, and the House four days later. With many rural-state legislators still loyal to the Anti-Saloon League, the AAPA convinced the Senate Judiciary Committee to let voters elect ratification convention delegates. Under the guidance of the AAPA and the Voluntary Committee of Lawyers, legislators in all but five states called ratification conventions, most within sixteen weeks of congressional passage. Seventy-three percent of voters electing delegates favored repeal, sweeping the Twenty-First Amendment to ratification by wide margins in hasty, perfunctory conventions. The amendment's second section, prohibiting alcohol importation in violation of a state's laws, reaffirmed the states' authority to regulate liquor, keeping the issue local. State-level reform had helped Congress to restore the stable pre-prohibition consensus (figure 8). Convergence had finally come.[79]

The difference between prohibition and female suffrage campaigns can help us better understand Progressive-era American political development. Both the prohibition campaign, under Neal Dow, and the suffrage campaign, under Stanton and Anthony, rooted in Reconstruction-era reform politics, sought federal dictation against noncompliant states. Both movements initially lacked widespread electoral support and, rebuffed by Congress and the Supreme Court, abandoned dictation for deference, building support among the states. The NAWSA

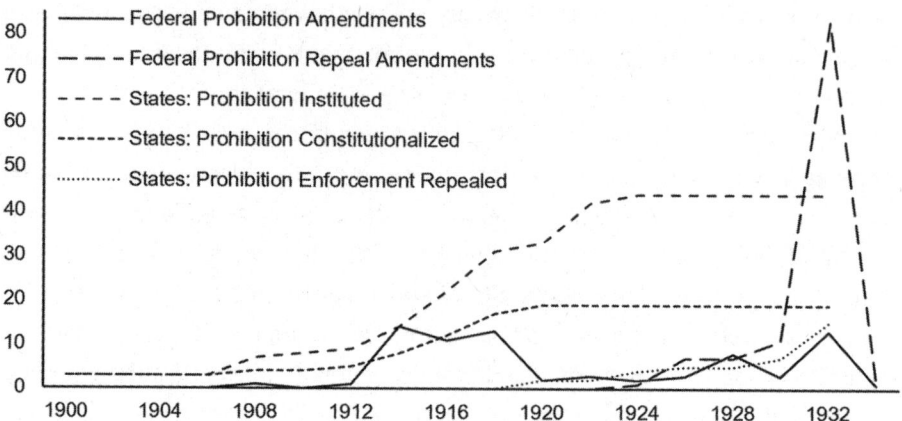

Fig. 8. State and federal prohibition regulation, 1900–1934. State data from Beienburg, *Prohibition, the Constitution, and States' Rights,* appendix. The y-axis indicates proposed federal prohibition amendments and states regulating prohibition.

did so gradually under Catt, drawing a national voting base that converged on federal amendment. Under Cherrington, the Anti-Saloon League attempted a nearly identical convergence plan, accelerated to pass an amendment before congressional reapportionment in 1920. This acceleration won an amendment without nationwide state-level support, yielding dictation, Dow's original aim, which forced federal agents to struggle to stopper the interstate flow of liquor, a problem unique to the prohibition cause. Unpopular federal dictation of prohibition brought convergence for repeal. Cherrington's mistake was to attempt in half a decade what the NAWSA did in three decades.

Federal Deference on Polygamy, Schooling, and Child Labor; State Circumvention on Jim Crow

While income tax, Senate election, female suffrage, and prohibition reform occurred through joint federal and state constitutional revision, constitutional regulation of parochial schools, polygamy, Jim Crow, and child labor occurred exclusively at the state level, reducing pressure for, and preventing, federal amendment—cases of deference or circumvention without convergence. This section offers short digressions on these four examples.

Morality legislation, dormant in Congress during the Civil War and Reconstruction, returned to the fore with debates over parochial school funding. In

Ulysses Grant's December 1875 presidential message to Congress, he requested an amendment forbidding state legislators, including the growing cohort of German and Irish Catholic Democrats, from granting religious organizations and schools funding or tax exemptions. Days after Grant's call to preserve "the education of the masses" against "the demagogue and [the] priestcraft," Maine Republican James G. Blaine proposed the amendment in the House Judiciary Committee. House Democrats passed the measure 180 to 7, sending the bill to the Senate. New York's Catholic Democratic senator Francis Kernan rejected the proposal, declaring that "the perpetuity and strength of the Federal Government" required that Congress defer this police power to the states. He felt it best if "the people of each State managed these local affairs for themselves. It makes the Federal Government strong to leave local affairs to the people of the State, because the people of different States then do not come in conflict in the Halls of Congress as to local government and policy." Republican William Edmunds also trusted that citizens "will, as they have done in State constitutions and otherwise, defend this fundamental ground-work of the Republic" and maintain separation between church and state. Urban and Southern Democrats, eager to keep Congress out of their schools, helped defeat the proposal by two votes. On losing the 1876 Republican nomination, Blaine abandoned the measure. Article V supermajority requirements had blocked the Blaine amendment in Congress.[80]

Parochial schooling remained contentious through the late nineteenth century. Irish and German Catholic immigration triggered widespread nativist mobbing and backlash, with framers in seventeen states constitutionally blocking parochial institution funding and tax exemptions, often using secularist, school neutrality claims. Grant's 1875 State of the Union Address and Representative Blaine's accompanying, failed federal amendment fueled this ongoing state-level movement, pushing Colorado, New Hampshire, Nevada, and Minnesota to pass analogous constitutional provisions in 1876 and 1877. Congress's 1889 enabling act conditioned statehood in the Dakotas, Montana, and Washington on such constitutional clauses, bumping the national total to twenty-nine clauses. Additional Western states, admitted under the same congressional requirement, slowly inflated the national count to thirty-eight. Congress had abandoned the amendment route in favor of enabling acts, using the state constitutions to vent national pressure on the issue. Save for three lonely proposals, Blaine amendments disappeared from the congressional agenda after 1889. Surveying the situation in 1897, Herman Ames concluded that the "state constitutions are in almost all instances adequate on this subject, and no amendment is likely to be secured." More recently, David E. Kyvig found the same: "Congressional committees generally ignored [the Blaine amendment] but on one occasion recommended against its passage. They regarded state constitutions as adequate in this era." State constitutional reform made a federal amendment unnecessary.[81]

Utah's statehood petitions incited a related polygamy scare. Grant's 1875 address also warned that Utahan polygamy threatened "free, enlightened, and Christian" American customs, asking for a congressional statute criminalizing the practice. While the Supreme Court's 1879 *Reynolds* decision upheld the 1862 Morrill Anti-Bigamy Act and Utah's 1896 constitution outlawed polygamy, in 1898 Utahans elected the polygamist Brigham H. Roberts to Congress. Congressmen refused to seat Roberts and proposed dozens of amendments regulating marriage, polygamy, and divorce, noting that mere statutes had not compelled Utahans' compliance. One such amendment empowered the Supreme Court to regulate marriage in all of the states, prompting Representative Dorsey Shackleford of Missouri to object, "States are undoubtedly better able to deal with this matter than we can possibly hope to do through a constitutional amendment." The amendment movement soon fractured, in Representative George Ray's words, between "three or four different committees," with each "reporting upon the same subject without any uniformity of action," stalling the amendments without addressing the polygamy question.[82]

Western-state constitutional reform also deterred a federal antipolygamy amendment. With the proposed congressional amendment split between four committees, Congress instead prohibited polygamy by conditioning Western statehood on antibigamy clauses. Between 1889 and 1912, at least six states, all Western, constitutionally limited or banned polygamy, including the holdout Utah.[83] Southerners, wary of federal interference with their antimiscegenation laws, also wanted the "states to take upon themselves the power, as they now have, of caring for their own internal affairs," per Representative John Maddox of Georgia. Tennessee Democrat Nicholas Cox agreed: "There is not a State in the Union that has not a statute against bigamy, and men are punished continuously for it. . . . I am against the whole [amendment]. I do not think it amounts to anything." Antipolygamy amendments faded from Congress's amendment agenda after the 1920s. In David Kyvig's words, congressional "representatives overwhelmingly believed authority over marriage should remain with states, [and] that existing law could be used to deal with the specific problem of polygamy."⁸⁴

Jim Crow also expanded in these years, as Congress, the Court, and Southern state framers together rolled back Southern Blacks' rights. Ex-Confederates, expressly excluded under Reconstruction suffrage, officeholding, and loyalty clauses, rallied as the Ku Klux Klan, waiting to return to electoral politics. Allied "Redeemer" Democrats in Tennessee's 1870 convention and Arkansas's 1874 convention, capitalizing on weak federal oversight and splits among state Republicans, moved to reenfranchise ex-Confederates. Alabaman and North Carolinian Democrats ousted their Republican governors and state legislators and called conventions in 1875. Interlocking federal and state voting and equal protection clauses, no longer buttressed by military occupation and congressional oversight, buckled across the South. Federal troops' withdrawal from the old Confederacy in 1877 and the Supreme Court's deferential 1883 *Civil Rights Cases* helped constitutional convention delegates erode Reconstruction in Georgia in 1877, Louisiana in 1879, and Florida in 1885–86.

Congress considered but ultimately avoided intervention. Henry Cabot Lodge proposed a Federal Elections Bill to let voters petition a federal judge to supervise Southern registrars, but in July 1890, Democrats stalled the bill. Meeting weeks later, emboldened Mississippi convention delegates renewed Jim Crow disenfranchisement with vigor, devising facially race-neutral state poll tax, residency, literacy, and understanding requirement clauses to circumvent the Fourteenth and Fifteenth Amendments, confident that Congress would not intervene. Sweeping the House in November 1892, Democrats killed Lodge's "Force Bill." Alongside the Supreme Court's affirmation of state segregation law in *Plessy* in 1896, convention delegates framed Jim Crow constitutions in Kentucky in 1891, South Carolina in 1895, Louisiana in 1898, Alabama in 1901, and Virginia in 1902, all mirroring the Mississippi model. The Fifteenth Amendment, worded not to guarantee the Black vote but rather to forbid the states from explicit racial disenfranchisement, enabled inexplicit disenfranchisement. The Alabama convention Suffrage Committee chair Thomas Coleman thus claimed that the amendment "in no way interferes with the sovereign power of a State to fix a standard of fitness, applicable to all alike," though the committee minority report recognized that this "confers the right of suffrage on members of the white race" alone, inviting "an attack on [the] suffrage plan through the courts."⁸⁵

The federal courts did not oblige. While Senator James Vardaman of Mississippi bragged, "In Mississippi we have in our constitution legislated against the racial peculiarities of the Negro and in that way we have practically eliminated them from politics," the Supreme Court in 1898 refused to overturn the Mississippi Constitution's facially race-neutral poll tax clause. With the 1903 *Giles v. Harris* decision, the Court added a wrinkle, speculating that the Alabama Constitution's character test clause "would exclude, perhaps, a large part of the black race," inviting congressional intervention under the Fourteenth and Fifteenth Amendments. Hoping to silence the issue, Vardaman asked Congress for outright "repeal of the fifteenth, [and] the modification of the fourteenth amendment, . . . making this Government a government for white men, of white men, for all men, which will be but the realization of the dream of the founders of the Republic." Between 1900 and 1920, congressmen proposed twenty-two amendments to repeal the Fifteenth Amendment and twelve to repeal the Fourteenth Amendment's second section, concentrated around the Seventeenth Amendment debates of 1909–13. But the issue remained marginal in Congress—Southern framers' race-neutral language effectively preempted judicial intervention per *Williams,* and only vitriolic white supremacists like Vardaman campaigned for further action by Congress. The defeat of a congressional enforcement rider to the Seventeenth Amendment appeased most congressmen, quieting the repeal question. Racial disenfranchisement and discrimination began as a state concern, gained little attention in Congress or the Supreme Court, and continued unabated at the state level, a case of state circumvention of federal policy making. Civil and voting rights had "belong[ed] to the negro" in Reconstruction, per Wendell Phillips, but no longer. Joint federal and state constitutional reform advanced Reconstruction and then, in the 1890s, repealed Reconstruction.[86]

Finally, with Eastern industrialization and Western expansion, miners, smelters, railroad workers, and factory laborers, some mere children, worked long, hazard-filled days at low wages. The Progressive-era Congress statutorily protected laborers in dangerous interstate industries like railroad work but rejected dozens of amendments proposing broader, cross-industry reforms. Labor organizers instead revised state constitutions to protect wages, hours, and labor conditions for workers in hazardous industries. The U.S. Supreme Court repeatedly supported this extension of state police powers, affirming an 1891 Kansas law guaranteeing state employees an eight-hour workday, an 1896 Utah law promising smelters and miners an eight-hour workday, a 1903 Illinois law prohibiting child labor in hazardous occupations, a 1903 Oregon law promising female factory and laundry workers a ten-hour workday, and a 1913 law, also from Oregon, guaranteeing male and female factory workers a ten-hour workday with overtime pay. Empowered by the Supreme Court, between the 1870s and 1920s, legislators and convention delegates constitutionally protected laborers' injury compensation rights in fifteen states, working hours in twelve, safety in eleven, and wages in four. These Court decisions and constitutional clauses undergirded further statutory reform—in the eight years after the Court upheld Oregon's first law, nineteen states adopted new laws supporting female workers, and twenty strengthened existing laws.[87]

But as states considered extending protections to workers in nonhazardous occupations, the Supreme Court intervened, rejecting New York's ten-hour workday for bakers in *Lochner v. New York* (1905). *Lochner* allowed states to protect only those laborers working in hazardous industries. Some states, like Ohio, nevertheless allowed a broad minimum wage, while Oregon and Mississippi limited working hours across industries. But most states, like California and Nebraska, extended constitutional working hours, wage, and working-condition protections only to state employees or those laborers they deemed vulnerable, namely, women and children, and men in hazardous trades. Forty-one states secured maximum hours for women, mainly between 1909 and 1917, and fifteen promised women a minimum wage. The American Federation of Labor (AFL) supported these narrowly tailored bills, worried that tightfisted employers would interpret a general, cross-industry minimum wage as the maximum wage. Women's clubs and church organizations also pushed for state-level child-labor regulations on humanitarian grounds through the 1910s.

After the Supreme Court struck down a women's minimum wage law, reformers increasingly focused on child labor. In most Western states, convention delegates limited working age and hours in mines, workshops, factories, or other hazardous places. Often accompanying pension and poor-relief clauses, these provisions suggested that Western framers felt some moral responsibility for the young and vulnerable. Oklahoma's clause, for example, forbade work that was physically demanding or "injurious to health or morals." This wording influenced Arizona's 1912 framers, including Patrick Connelly, who explained, "I have known girls under 15 years of age working in 'hash houses,' working 14 hours a day. These are the kids we want to take care of. . . . And I have seen young girls working in the smelter. We want to take care of these children whether in a factory, mine or anywhere." Sometimes this required passing additional constitutional amendments to expressly override free-market judges. As Joseph Walker told Massachusetts's constitutional convention of 1917–18, "Suppose we want to limit the hours of labor for men. Undoubtedly the courts would declare that unconstitutional.... Workingmen's compensation laws, laws affecting the hours of labor, laws protecting the health, laws to prevent industries being carried on in tenement-houses,—it is that kind of legislation that we wish and it is that kind of legislation that is frequently declared unconstitutional." In California, Louisiana, Ohio, Nebraska, New York, and Utah, reformers passed child-labor clauses to empower legislators and override opposed judges and, in other states, to recall these judges. Yet other states, like Wyoming, merely grandfathered child workers under existing safety, maximum working hours, and minimum wage protections. By 1909, forty-two states imposed constitutional or statutory limits on child factory labor. Hostile judges, constrained and cowed, joined progressive judges to uphold state labor protections, in nine states broadly affirming child-labor protections. State courts similarly affirmed protections for women and for men working in hazardous or state-run industries. The trend was not universal—Southern states, stubbornly reliant on child textile mill workers, refused to forbid child labor.[88]

Hoping to discourage child labor nationwide, the National Child Labor Committee (NCLC) also backed Congress's 1916 Keating-Owen Act. The act capped working hours for children between fourteen and sixteen and forbade companies from interstate sale of goods produced by children under fourteen. In *Hammer v. Dagenhart* (1918), the Court voided the act for overextending Congress's commerce authority. Congress failed to override *Hammer* by amendment, prompting a grander plan by Senator Robert La Follette. Addressing the 1921 AFL convention, La Follette declared that he would not settle for an "amendment which will merely meet the objection to the Child Labor Law raised by a majority of the Supreme Court," instead proposing that a two-thirds congressional supermajority be able to veto the Court. The NCLC, meanwhile, resumed the statutory reform effort with a congressional tax on goods produced by child workers. After the Court rejected the new tax in 1922, Congress over the next decade proposed several amendments constraining the Court via term limits, elections, and congressional veto and fifty amendments regulating child labor.

Congress debated the Child Labor Amendment through the 1920s. Representative Finis Garrett of Tennessee, for example, attacked the Child Labor Amendment, which he felt "could be better wrought out through the sovereign States under the powers they now possess." Anticipating this objection, the NCLC drafted an amendment leaving the "power of the several States unimpaired" when consistent with federal law. This convinced all but the most stalwart states'-rights members. The measure, sponsored by Pennsylvania Republican George Pepper and Montana Democrat Thomas Walsh, cleared the House on April 26, 1924, and the Senate a week later, sending the issue to the states.[89]

The states refused ratification. The NCLC, confident that its proposal would follow the previous four amendments to swift approval, waited until late summer 1924 to plan a ratification campaign. Meanwhile, the Sentinels of the Republic, a newly formed alliance of legal conservatives, plutocrats, and defeated antisuffrage advocates, cast the amendment as a socialist plot to restructure the family. The Georgia Senate took little convincing, warning of a scheme to "destroy parental authority and responsibility throughout America, . . . destroy local self-government," and establish "a system of slavery, with public ownership substituted for private ownership." The amendment died in February 1925 after a thirteenth state refused ratification. Reformers settled for piecemeal state constitutional clauses protecting women, children, and men in hazardous occupations. In this sense, state framers achieved what their federal counterparts could not, venting locally the national pressure to protect young and vulnerable workers.[90]

Through the Progressive era, reformers, thwarted by Article V and a conservative Senate and Supreme Court, instead intentionally targeted state legislatures, constitutional conventions, and initiatives and referenda. State constitutional reform campaigns united national voting and congressional majorities around direct election of senators, the female franchise, and prohibition. State reform also proved untested measures, like the income tax, before a skeptical Congress. In this sense, state constitutionalism quieted and guided national debates around the progressive amendments, stabilizing national constitutionalism. In other cases, like regulation of polygamy, parochial schools, Jim Crow, and child labor, state constitutional change skirted national amendment entirely.

The failure of the child-labor and prohibition amendments in the 1930s upended progressives' faith in the Article V process. The Eighteenth Amendment, the culmination of a half century of dry social engineering and experimentation, seemed initially to be a sound, tested measure, a case of deference and convergence like the Sixteenth, Seventeenth, and Nineteenth Amendments. Regarding prohibition, Senator Thomas Walsh declared in 1926 that "there was not the faintest ground for hope that any material alteration would be made in the law, or that the idea of repealing the amendment would be entertained at all." Morris Sheppard similarly boasted in September 1930 that "there is as much chance of repealing the Eighteenth Amendment as there is for a hummingbird to fly to Mars with the Washington Monument tied to its tail!" Two years later, in the last hours of the Seventy-Second Congress, Sheppard quietly voted to repeal his old amendment.

A new, graver crisis had emerged. The economy, once so robust that the Yale economist Irving Fisher declared, "Stock prices have reached what looks like a permanently high plateau," collapsed in late October 1929. Fisher, like many Americans, lost his shirt. Congress pivoted from social reform by amendment to economic reform by statute. On repealing the Eighteenth Amendment, New York's Fiorello La Guardia told the House, "Twelve years' experimenting has demonstrated the impossibility of enforcement and the widespread use of liquor.... We are now too weary and too law-abiding to celebrate our victory. Congress will now be able to give its undivided attention to economic matters, less controversial but far more important."[91]

6

Welfare States, 1932–1979

> *It is one of the happy incidents of the federal system that a single courageous state may, if its citizens choose, serve as a laboratory; and try novel social and economic experiments without risk to the rest of the country.*
> —Justice Louis Brandeis, New State Ice Co. v. Liebmann, *1932*

CHASTENED BY THE FAILED PROHIBITION and child-labor amendments, New Dealers and Great Society reformers circumvented Article V. Between 1932 and 1979, Congress proposed 6,329 amendments but ratified only seven, three narrowly regulating voting and four clarifying presidential selection and succession. Congress instead used the 1935 Social Security Act, 1964 Civil Rights Act, and 1965 Voting Rights Act, affirmed by landmark Supreme Court decisions, to statutorily enlarge labor, welfare, voting, and civil rights. Scholars therefore describe the era as one of transformative federal judicial and statutory reform, rather than one of significant constitutional amendment.[1]

State constitutionalism complicates this story. In these years, the states called 145 constitutional revision bodies, empowering sixty-six to draft new constitutions, ratifying sixteen new documents; proposed and passed thousands of amendments; and reworked and expanded their judicial commitments to welfare, civil, and voting rights programs. These state constitutional provisions entrenched labor, welfare, voting, and civil rights, often supporting and sometimes exceeding federal statutory minimums.[2] The United States' constitutional welfare clauses therefore exist *only* in the state constitutions, not in the federal

Constitution. But perhaps more important than the content of these positive rights is the neglected fact that these state-level positive rights reforms guided national constitutional development. The New Deal's and Great Society's pioneering federal statutory and judicial reforms are best understood through complementary, interlocking state constitutional provisions. Since many scholars have ignored these state reforms, they give an incomplete story of national political development during the New Deal and Great Society.

Canonical accounts explain that high Article V requirements blocked some proposed federal amendments in the New Deal and Great Society years. After the Child Labor Amendment failed Article V ratification, Franklin Delano Roosevelt warned against future amendments, explaining, "It would take months or years to get substantial agreement upon the type and language of the amendment. It would take months and years thereafter to get a two-thirds majority in favor of that amendment in both Houses of the Congress. Then would come the long course of ratification by three-fourths of all the States. No amendment which any powerful economic interests or the leaders of any powerful political party have had reason to oppose has ever been ratified within anything like a reasonable time." Gender-equality reformers learned this firsthand as their Equal Rights Amendment languished before Congress and then before opposed state legislatures in the 1960s, 1970s, and 1980s.[3]

High Article V barriers cannot, however, fully explain midcentury constitutional development. New Deal Democrats swept Congress, holding two-thirds supermajorities in one or both chambers between 1932 and 1942 and claiming thirty state senates and thirty-four state lower houses in 1932, nearing Article V ratification thresholds. Yet they implemented federal New Deal laws statutorily, rather than by amendment. Similarly, Great Society Democrats held Senate supermajorities for 1958–60 and 1962–66 and in 1964 claimed a House supermajority, thirty-four state senates, and thirty-nine state lower houses, clearing Article V. But these Democrats too relied on federal statutes and judicial rulings.

Reformers had several reasons to avoid Article V amendment. Even with necessary congressional supermajorities, New Deal and Great Society Democrats could not push Article V civil rights amendments past their powerful Southern bloc. Roosevelt instead passed detailed statutory reforms, some with elaborate carve-outs for Southerners, that used taxation, with the prospect of eventual benefits payback, to earn durable public support, forgoing amendment to build atop "the Constitution 'a system of living law.'" President Johnson too passed "super-statutes"—the Civil and Voting Rights Acts—while the National Association for the Advancement of Colored People (NAACP), rebuffed by the state and federal legislatures, litigated before the Supreme Court and entrenched rights judicially. Conservative legal groups like the Sentinels of the Republic also discouraged Article V tinkering and encouraged veneration, as did the Constitution's 1937 sesquicentennial commission and 1952 interment in the grand National Archives. Commentaries on the era thus emphasize debate, innovation, and expansion of power by the White House, Congress, the Supreme Court, and national parties and lobbies. This, some argue, sidelined the states as constitutional actors. Per Bruce Ackerman, "The New Deal revolution, then, broke with Article Five. . . . It substituted a model of Presidential leadership of national institutions for a model of assembly leadership based on dialogue between the nation and the states." William Eskridge and John Ferejohn also emphasize national statutory reform, rather than state reform or amendment. William Leuchtenburg, Barry Cushman, and Robert McCloskey also largely understate the role of states, focusing on the federal courts.[4]

But the states proposed dozens of constitutions and ratified thousands of amendments, guiding and stabilizing national constitutional politics. New Dealers used state constitutional conventions and amendments to protect workers' wages, hours, labor conditions, and unemployment, disability, and old-age benefits in the 1930s. Ackerman's and Eskridge and Ferejohn's attempts to contort federal New Deal and Great Society statutes into quasi-amendments would perhaps be unnecessary if they looked to the state constitutions, which expressly entrenched and authorized New Deal and Great Society projects. Further, in the 1930s, 1940s, and 1950s, state constitutional framers repealed poll taxes and legislative malapportionment, in nearly all cases repealing poll taxes before and without federal oversight, guiding later congressional debates over the 1964 Twenty-Fourth Amendment and 1965 Voting Rights Act. And state constitutional gender-equality debates filtered into Congress, discouraging ratification of the Equal Rights Amendment in the 1970s. State constitutional reform thus channeled national constitutional debates through the New Deal and Great Society years.

The most common topics among federal amendments proposed from 1932 to 1979 concerned, in roughly descending order, equal gender rights; executive, congressional, and judicial powers and selection; elections and suffrage, including the youth vote; public prayer, public school regulation; state powers; federal budgeting and taxes; and legislative apportionment. This chapter therefore offers case studies on gender, voting, and welfare and labor rights. Table 6 displays the twenty-five most common topics among amendments proposed between 1932 and 1979.

This chapter recounts conflict decentralization during the New Deal and Great Society years in three chronological steps. The first section outlines the labor and pension debates that gripped Congress and the Court through the 1930s and 1940s, noting how New Dealers built federal labor and welfare protections atop existing state constitutional wage, hours, and pension protections, appeasing the Supreme Court—a case of convergence. The second section recounts a similar pattern of convergence as the NAACP, AFL, CIO, and other groups worked to amend state constitutions to repeal poll taxes and legislative malapportionment, affirming and elaborating federal Voting Rights Act (VRA) and Court protections, which also incorporated elements of dictation. Dictation was clearer in the case of the youth vote, as Congress lowered the national voting age to eighteen in the face of state inaction. Finally, as the 1973 Equal Rights Amendment failed, reformers entrenched gender equality through state constitutional reform, stifling further attempts at federal reform, a case of deference.

State Convergence on Labor and Welfare Protection

The Great Depression brought systemic crisis. As businesses collapsed, unemployment climbed and wages fell, and consumers struggled to afford basic goods. Lagging food sales created agricultural surpluses, deflating crop prices and bankrupting dustbowl farmers. Across industries, Americans worked longer hours under worse conditions to make ends meet. Few could turn to welfare. Some state constitutions offered pensions for single mothers, the elderly, and the disabled and guaranteed fair wages, hours, and working conditions for women, children, and men in hazardous jobs. Implemented in some states but not others and protecting only the most vulnerable, these clauses could not address nationwide, cross-industry labor and welfare crises.

The Seventy-Third Congress, the first of the New Deal, quickly assumed new, broad commerce and tax powers to repair the economy and support the needy. In 1933, Congress passed the National Industrial Recovery Act to create boards setting industrywide prices, wages and hours, and labor conditions; the Agricultural Adjustment Act to tax and curb crop overproduction; the Tennessee Valley Authority to run hydroelectric plants; and the Securities Act to check

Table 6. Proposed Federal Amendments by Topic, 1932–1979

Topic	Years topic most often proposed (descending frequency)	Total	Concurrent power
Article I			
Congress	1937, 1973, 1967, 1965, 1975	675	Yes
House of Representatives	1969, 1979, 1971, 1937, 1973	333	Yes
Senate	1979, 1971, 1973, 1945, 1977	192	Yes
Article II			
Presidency	1969, 1961, 1973, 1977, 1965	1094	Yes
Vice presidency	1969, 1965, 1977, 1973, 1961	844	Yes
Article III			
Federal courts	1969, 1971, 1968, 1973, 1937	427	No
Supreme Court	1968, 1969, 1962, 1971, 1937	298	No
Federal officeholding			
Term length and limits	1977, 1979, 1965, 1973, 1947	458	Yes
Nomination	1979, 1969, 1973, 1971, 1972	181	Yes
Elections			
Election: general issues	1969, 1961, 1977, 1973, 1971	885	Yes
Election by popular vote	1969, 1977, 1973, 1979, 1975	199	Yes
Electoral College	1955, 1953, 1961, 1949, 1957	174	Yes
Taxes and finance			
Federal budgets and deficits	1979, 1977, 1978, 1975, 1973	302	No
Taxes: general issues	1937, 1939, 1959, 1933, 1935	299	Yes
Rights and citizenship			
Rights: general issues	1969, 1961, 1977, 1973, 1971	1708	Yes
Gender distinctions under law	1969, 1961, 1967, 1963, 1971	1097	Yes
Suffrage	1969, 1967, 1971, 1970, 1961	406	Yes
Apportionment			
Legislative apportionment: states	1965, 1964, 1967, 1977, 1975	271	Yes
Legislative apportionment: general issues	1965, 1964, 1967, 1963, 1969	248	Yes
Other			
Public prayer	1963, 1971, 1969, 1973, 1967	702	Yes
School regulation: general issues	1963, 1973, 1971, 1967, 1962	682	Yes
State powers	1965, 1964, 1937, 1959, 1977	535	Yes
Abortion: general issues	1975, 1977, 1973, 1979, 1976	223	Yes
Regulation of DC	1967, 1975, 1969, 1971, 1970	169	No
Treaties	1953, 1969, 1955, 1945, 1952	177	No

investment fraud. Congress claimed that these acts rested on existing commerce and tax powers, requiring no new amendments, save for twenty-five proposals affirming the National Industrial Recovery Act's taxes on government securities income, exempted by the Sixteenth Amendment's framers, which the wealthy had long used as a tax-exempt investment loophole.

But the Supreme Court's unanimous *Schechter* ruling of May 27, 1935, overturned Congress's National Industrial Recovery Act. Justice Louis Brandeis worried that the act overextended commerce powers and delegated legislative power to central regulatory boards, allowing industry capture. He instead urged regulatory decentralization: "We must come back to the little unit," he wrote in early 1935. Minutes after the Court announced the *Schechter* decision, Brandeis summoned Roosevelt lawyer Thomas Corcoran to his chambers with a message: "Tell the President that we're not going to let this government centralize everything. It's come to an end. As for your young men, you call them together and tell them to get out of Washington—tell them to go home, back to the states. That is where they must do their work." In a press conference four days later, Roosevelt condemned the Court's "horse-and-buggy definition of interstate commerce," which gave the states "practically all control over economic conditions." He sought further centralization, by congressional amendment if needed. Having campaigned for the Sixteenth, Seventeenth, and Child Labor Amendments, Roosevelt kept a progressive's faith in deliberate Article V reform. The American Federation of Labor, the National Consumers League, and the Democratic National Committee also urged overriding the Court by amendment. The New Deal Congresses of 1933–41 proposed eighty-three amendments taxing wealthy investors' securities income; forty on labor, including wage, age, and hour limits; thirty-one on business and commerce, including thirteen on authorizing agricultural regulation; twelve on old-age pensions; and a few letting Congress regulate banking, prices, transportation, insurance, and manufacturing. Between the Court's contentious 1935 decisions and 1939, Congress offered forty-six amendments on court powers, including twenty limiting jurisdiction, twelve imposing term limits, and seven for removal of justices. The November 1936 elections granted Democrats congressional and state legislative supermajorities, enough to pass and ratify amendments fundamentally restructuring the Court and the national balance of powers.[5]

As Congress struggled to overcome the Court, the states constitutionalized labor and pension protections. Labor and pension regulation had long been state prerogatives, letting state lawmakers swiftly confront the Depression by granting many adults the work and welfare protections once reserved to women, children, and civil servants. Between 1929 and 1933, seven states secured a minimum wage, and seventeen expanded old-age pensions. Wisconsin's 1931 unemployment compensation plan required companies to support fired workers, while Ohio's 1932 plan pooled workers' and employers' contributions into a single unemployment fund, earning endorsements from Roosevelt and the 1932 Democratic Convention. These tax-funded, constitutionally entrenched state unemployment and pension programs informed the drafters of the 1935 Social Security Act, which funded additional state programs, encouraging further state constitutional welfare expansion. The resulting cooperative "second" New Deal, interlocking state and federal reform, appeased skeptics on the Court, easing tensions with Congress and Roosevelt.

Labor reform came first. States ratified workers' compensation clauses through the Progressive era—after New York judges voided a state workers' compensation statute for using public money to reimburse private workers, voters reversed the court by amendment in 1913. Noting the New York example, legislators constitutionally protected workers' right to hold their employer liable for injury in fifteen states and to injury compensation in eleven states, passing compensation statutes in forty-three states.[6] A few state constitutions and courts affirmed tax-funded pensions for firefighters, police officers, and civil servants. Progressives in twelve states constitutionally capped working hours, binding hostile judges, while AFL chapters overrode judges with eight-hour workday amendments in Montana in 1936 and in New York in 1938.[7]

New Deal state legislators further expanded workers' protections to incorporate a minimum wage. With the federal Child Labor Amendment stalled against Article V, the National Consumers League focused on comprehensive state-level wage reform, drafting a model state minimum wage bill. In a sudden boon to the league, Democrats flipped twelve state legislatures between 1931 and 1932, including one or both chambers in Connecticut, Illinois, New Jersey, New York, Ohio, and Utah, and gained seats in New Hampshire. In 1933, these seven states passed new minimum wage laws based on the model bill. The Supreme Court upheld these laws in *Parrish,* and months later, New York guaranteed competitive wages for public workers. By 1938, twenty-three states regulated wages across industries, genders, and age groups, sixteen statutorily, two constitutionally, and five both statutorily and constitutionally. New York also constitutionally guaranteed workers' bargaining rights in 1938, as soon did Florida, Missouri, New Jersey, and Hawaii.[8] These New Deal protections layered atop prior Progressive-era ones, with judges affirming protections both new and old. As Keith Whittington concludes, "Judicial review in the state courts and the elaboration of state-level constitutional law are characterized by continuity rather than transformation during this period."[9]

Beyond protecting workers, New Deal lawmakers expanded state pensions. At least twenty-two state constitutions allow poor relief, but with varied commitment. Most state constitutions' charity clauses, plenary and vague, left legislators and counties to devise and implement statutory poor-relief programs, often through pensions. A few clauses charged specific actors with enforcement— Montana's 1889 constitution, for example, required that counties support the elderly, infirm, and misfortunate. Empowered by these clauses, New Deal state lawmakers enlarged and transformed pensions from special labor protections for public servants to societal, tax-funded protections encompassing single mothers, the elderly, and the blind.[10]

States passed pensions for the indigent through the late Progressive and early New Deal years. With widows and single mothers often working overtime and with poor children abandoned to overcrowded orphanages, progressive moralists, women's clubs, and trade unions pushed states to cap women's and children's working hours and grant cash payments to female-headed families. Spurred by the 1909 White House Conference on the Care of Dependent Children, in 1911, Illinois passed the first mothers' pension law. By 1913, the National Congress of Mothers and the Federations of Women's Clubs spread these laws to eighteen states, mainly in the West and Midwest; by 1919, to thirty-nine states; and by 1934, to all states but two. Pensions for the elderly and blind came next. Corporate and state pensions covered few retirees, leading Pennsylvania, Montana, and Nevada to pass the first old-age pension laws in 1923, as did eight more states by 1928. California first mandated statewide funding and implementation for pensions in 1929, and by 1933, another sixteen states followed. The blind also claimed state vocation, medical, and pension assistance, first in Ohio in 1904, and by 1931 won pensions in twenty-four states.

Some states amended their constitutions to authorize these pensions. As pension programs proliferated, taxpayers sued, citing Gilded Age state constitutional clauses that forbade funneling public tax funds into private or charity programs. Some state judges and pension commissioners rejected these arguments, reinterpreting state charity clauses to authorize tax-funded pensions. The Ohio Supreme Court, for example, used a state constitutional provision authorizing homes for the blind to uphold the state's statutory pension for the blind. But not all judges were convinced. Some voided tax-funded pensions for lack of clear constitutional authorization or by citing clauses forbidding public funding for private aims. In response, state legislators amended their constitutions to specifically authorize tax-funded pensions. Legislators and voters constitutionally authorized tax-funded pensions for mothers in California in 1920 and Louisiana in 1921, for the elderly in Missouri in 1932, and for the blind and disabled in Missouri in 1916, California in 1928, and Pennsylvania in 1933. Through the 1920s, Congress proposed few statutes and no amendments addressing pensions, showing little interest in the area. As Mark H. Leff concludes, before the Depression, the "belief that public aid and other social services were a local responsibility rendered them a dead issue on the national level." This let the states experiment, devising novel constitutional amendments and judicial doctrine to divert public tax funds to private citizens' pensions—mechanisms that would later serve as models for convergent statutory federal pensions.[11]

But spotty state pensions could not address systemic Depression-era poverty. Many charity clauses left pension implementation to counties. In forty states, county children's boards and juvenile courts paid mothers' pensions, often unevenly and with strict behavioral stipulations, leaving meager benefits for rural, Southern, and Black women. Only 6 percent of female-headed families nationwide claimed coverage in 1931. States relaxed eligibility during the Depression, but laxer standards, growing agency costs, and declining tax revenue strained state program funding.[12] Old-age pensions, subject to special judicial scrutiny, fared little better. By the depth of the Depression in 1932, no Kentucky counties implemented their optional pension, while only one West Virginia county did so. Nationally, only 40 percent of pension-state counties actually paid benefits, covering 102,500 participants at a total cost of $22 million. California's, Massachusetts's, and New York's mandatory laws accounted for nearly all national pension spending in 1932, while new mandatory laws in Arizona, Indiana, Maine, Michigan, and North Dakota thinned state resources across a growing poor population, decreasing the average monthly payout in all but one of the seventeen old-age pension states. Similarly, only eleven of the twenty-four states with pensions for the blind spent state funds, while the other thirteen offered negligible county benefits. Expanded pensions strained municipal governments—in eighty-one cities, combined public relief grew from $42 million in 1929 to $170 million in 1931.[13]

Beyond passing pensions for the indigent unemployed, states supported the able under unemployment insurance. Following Massachusetts's experimental 1916 unemployment insurance bill, the University of Wisconsin economist John R. Commons and his students Edwin E. Witte, Arthur J. Altmeyer, Elizabeth Brandeis, and Paul Raushenbush together designed the pioneering 1932 Wisconsin law requiring individual employers to reserve funds compensating fired employees. The Ohio Commission on Unemployment instead proposed a pooled state fund so workers would not rely on employers. Aided by the American Association for Labor Legislation, legislators introduced twenty-three unemployment bills across sixteen states in 1931 and another sixty-eight bills across twenty-five states by the 1933 session but passed only five before 1935, rejecting the rest for fear of hobbling their employers against competitors in neighboring, regulation-free states. Congress intervened, passing two emergency measures, the 1933 Wagner-Peyser Act, making grants-in-aid to new state unemployment offices, and the 1934 Federal Emergency Relief Act, funding state programs meeting administrative minimums.[14]

Justice Louis Brandeis sought a permanent, state-run solution. In fall 1933, he introduced his daughter, Elizabeth Brandeis, and her husband, Paul Raushenbush, authors of Wisconsin's unemployment plan, to the Labor Department lawyer Thomas H. Eliot and to Thomas Corcoran, Roosevelt's legislative strategist and go-to Washington operator. Working from Brandeis's Washington apartment, they combined the Wisconsin and Ohio schemes into a plan funding state unemployment programs through pooled federal payroll taxes. The tax was Justice Brandeis's idea, built on the 1926 Federal Estate Tax Act, upheld in *Florida v. Mellon*. Brandeis, Raushenbush, and Eliot then wrote the tax into the Wagner-Lewis Social Security bill in February 1934. With the Seventy-Third Congress concluding, in May 1934, Roosevelt's cabinet agreed to push the bill to the next session.

The following month, Roosevelt named Frances Perkins to lead the new Committee on Economic Security and elaborate the planned system. The University of Wisconsin brain trust ran the committee, with Witte serving as executive director, Altmeyer as technical committee head, and Alvin H. Hansen, another Commons student, leading the Subcommittee on Unemployment Insurance. Witte and Altmeyer expected judicial objections to any sweeping, nationalized labor or pension reform, the latter writing his 1932 doctoral dissertation on the topic. After internal debates, the subcommittee endorsed Brandeis's plan granting "wide latitude to the States," hoping for a Court decision reaffirming *Florida v. Mellon*. Witte and Altmeyer then pitched the plan to Roosevelt and Labor Secretary Frances Perkins in late August 1934. Roosevelt and Perkins, having endorsed the Wisconsin plan for New York in 1931, backed the scheme. According to Perkins, the bill allowed "different problems to be solved by the different States according to their own particular genius and to be administered locally by these States in the best interest of all people." Roosevelt, having read the progressive scholar James Bryce's *American Commonwealth,* similarly trusted state innovation. Altmeyer recalled an early meeting with Roosevelt in the summer of 1934: "The President's desire to rely on the states as much as possible was based upon his lifelong belief in our federal form. . . . He was particularly interested in Bryce's thesis that a major advantage of our federal system was the opportunity it afforded for the individual states to serve as laboratories." Altmeyer added, "Roosevelt has often been charged with having had a desire to build up the central government at the expense of the state governments. . . . I am certain this allegation was not true of his ideas concerning his social security program." Roosevelt informed Congress of his administration's national pension plan on January 17, 1935.[15]

The Committee on Economic Security deferred pension regulation to the states. A January 1935 committee report rejected a blanket national mothers' pension, instead offering the Aid to Dependent Children (ADC) program, making grants-in-aid to state programs for direct cash payments to single mothers. As the committee put it, these "recommendations regarding security for children do not set up any new or untried methods of procedure, but build upon experience that has been well established in this country." Addressing Congress, Roosevelt repeated that the plan was "not an untried experiment. Lessons of experience are available from States," and he promised "a maximum of cooperation between States and the Federal Government." Surveying the framing of the Social Security Act (SSA), Nancy Cauthen and Edwin Amenta agree: "Proposals for ADC were constructed with the best state mothers' pension programs in mind. Similarly, about one-half the states had means-tested old age pension laws and programs by the end of 1934, and Old Age Assistance (OAA) was constructed to reinforce the best of these." The 1935 Social Security Act, exemplifying the cooperative federalism of the second New Deal, provided federal funds to subsidize state programs. Title III mandated that the Treasury Department fund qualified state unemployment programs. In late 1935, remaining states passed unemployment compensation laws in special session. By mid-1939, all states enforced these laws, and by 1945, seventeen states provided supplementary funding, all states increased payable benefits, and nearly all cut waiting periods to three weeks or less. Title IV and Title V allowed quarterly federal grants to fund qualified state widows' and mothers' pension program expenses, conditioned on expanded eligibility and statewide implementation via a single state agency. By 1950, nationwide coverage expanded to a quarter of female-headed families, many of them headed by Black women, particularly in postwar Northeastern cities. But Southern members of Congress curtailed federal oversight for state OAA and ADC programs, so that some states, particularly those in the South and with decentralized, optional pension administration, barely cleared federal ADC minimums, forbidding or reducing pensions for unmarried, separated, divorced, or Black mothers. In 1940, the Roosevelt administration's National Resources Planning Board proposed eliminating cooperative ADC administration, and Senator Robert Wagner of New York sponsored a supporting bill; but the measure failed, maintaining joint implementation.[16]

SSA subsidized other state pensions. Title I, the Old Age Assistance program, mandated quarterly Treasury Department grants covering half of expenses for qualified state old-age assistance programs. Between 1932 and 1937, eleven states constitutionally affirmed new pension programs, with Nevada repealing county pensions, Colorado overriding opposed state judges, and New York promising broad welfare rights. By 1936, Witte triumphantly declared, "Old age assistance is no longer debatable. Thirty-nine states and the District of Columbia now have old age assistance laws. American public opinion revolts against forcing old people who are dependent upon the public for support to go into poor-houses or to subsist on uncertain and degrading outdoor poor-relief." By July 1939, expenditures and receipts for old-age assistance increased tenfold from their February 1936 baseline, covering eight times as many beneficiaries. Expenditures and receipts for the blind quadrupled, thanks to Title X, the Aid to the Blind program, which authorized federal grants to cover half of state expenses for pensions for the blind. New York's 1938 constitutional convention expressly let legislators fund programs for the blind, disabled, and sick, and California boosted state benefits to the blind in 1948. While there were elements of federal dictation—the federal SSA set uniform standards for state pension eligibility and implementation—consequent grants incentivized, rather than forced, state compliance.[17]

The SSA's cooperative federalism appeased Justice Brandeis. The justice, who on May 27, 1935, had told Roosevelt lawyer Tommy Corcoran to send New Deal administrators "back to the states" and "back to the little unit," by August 2, days before the act's passage, admitted that Roosevelt's plan addressed his centralization concerns in *Schechter:* "F.D. is making a gallant fight and seems to appreciate fully the evils of bigness." In early 1936, Brandeis supported New Deal programs, voting to uphold the 1933 Agricultural Adjustment Act and a New York State minimum wage law. Yet Brandeis voted in dissent, as the Court rejected both laws.[18]

A frustrated Roosevelt considered packing the Court. Congress debated court-constraining amendments through mid-1936, but as a revived Child Labor Amendment sputtered against opposed states, Roosevelt soured to the Article V amendment process. On Felix Frankfurter's advice, he instead pitched a court-packing statute to Congress's newly elected Democratic supermajority on February 5, 1937. Roosevelt told Congress that the bill would obviate a difficult, radical amendment, preventing "fundamental changes in the powers of the courts or the constitution of our Government—changes which involve consequences so far-reaching as to cause uncertainty as to the wisdom of such course." In the winter of 1936–37, the Court affirmed New Deal wage and pension regulations. Democrats' 1936 electoral gains and court-packing amendments may have swayed the Court. Days after the Associated Press leaked Roosevelt's court-packing bill, Justice Owen Roberts voted in conference to uphold a Washington State minimum wage law that was nearly identical to the New York law he had overturned months earlier.[19] The Court then invoked state pension doctrine to affirm the SSA. In the May 24, 1937, *Carmichael* decision, Justice Harlan Stone upheld Alabama's pension program for serving "the public purposes of [the] state, for which it may raise funds by taxation, [and] embrace expenditures for its general welfare." The Court next adopted this state-level "public purpose" doctrine to uphold SSA taxes in *Helvering v. Davis* and *Steward Machine Co. v. Davis,* issued alongside *Carmichael.* In *Steward,* Justice Benjamin Cardozo surveyed state tax law, holding that Congress, like the state legislatures, could issue a tax to fund SSA pensions. As he explained, "The statute books of the states are strewn with illustrations of taxes laid on occupations pursued of common right. We find no basis for a holding that the power in that regard which belongs by accepted practice to the legislatures of the states, has been denied by the Constitution to the Congress of the nation." Cardozo also commended Wisconsin's pioneering pension plan and praised the SSA for enabling states to implement their own pension programs without fear of capital flight. He noted that before the SSA, many states proposed pension programs but "held back through alarm lest, in laying such a toll upon their industries, they would place themselves in a position of economic disadvantage as compared with neighbors or competitors." After the SSA, in "1936, twenty-eight other states fell in line, and eight more [followed in 1937]," demonstrating in the states a "sympathetic interest" in the cooperative federalism of the SSA. Similarly in *Helvering,* Cardozo noted that the SSA helped the states overcome the disincentive to act first on old-age pensions. These decisions and the retirement and replacement of the hardline conservative Justice Willis Van Devanter swayed at least forty-five senators to kill the president's court-packing bill. Roosevelt's other three consistent opponents, Justices Pierce Butler, James McReynolds, and George Sutherland, soon retired, shifting the Court left. The Court's 1938 *Carolene Products* ruling reaffirmed the states' economic regulatory powers; *Helvering v. Gerhardt* allowed taxing state employees' incomes and, by extension, state bonds; *U.S. v. Darby* upheld the 1938 Fair Labor Standards Act's prohibition on child labor; and *Wickard v. Filburn* gave Congress sweeping commerce powers. This quieted Congress's amendment campaign. After *Helvering v. Gerhardt,* Congress proposed only fourteen more bond tax amendments and, after the 1941 *Darby* decision, only one Child Labor Amendment, down from eleven over the previous five years. In affirming the cooperative second New Deal, the Court deterred court-constraining amendments and statutes, preserving judicial independence and the rough balance of powers.[20]

In sum, state constitutional pension experimentation informed, guided, and interlocked with New Deal statutory framing and litigation, a case of convergence. At Justice Brandeis's behest, Perkins, Witte, and Altmeyer imitated the Wisconsin and Ohio plans, pooling SSA taxes for dispersal to states, which soon constitutionally authorized new pensions for the unemployed, disabled, elderly, and single mothers. State judges, using state constitutions' charity clauses, affirmed the legitimate "public purpose" of these means-tested, tax-funded pension clauses and statutes. This public purpose doctrine anticipated and shaped Harlan Stone's and Benjamin Cardozo's arguments in *Carmichael, Steward,* and

Helvering v. Davis. Susan Sterett explains this influence in greater detail, noting that "state supreme courts approved these [pension] programs before the United States Supreme Court did: as legislation proliferated, state courts acceded to the position that what constituted public purpose was a matter for the legislature to determine, not the courts." Sterett thus concludes that "state constitutional governance of pensions is significant in its own right, but it also had implications for interpreting the national Constitution. Once Roosevelt signed the Social Security Act in 1935, and corporate lawyers challenged the programs toward which employers were required to pay taxes—unemployment insurance and old age social security—it was state constitutional debates concerning public payments that provided the groundwork for explaining why the programs were indeed constitutional." Melvin Urofsky reaches a similar conclusion on state doctrine.[21] While state pension clauses presented little controversy in federal courts, they did invite challenge in state courts, which state judges affirmed under the public purpose doctrine. The Supreme Court applied this doctrine to approve analogous SSA taxes, deescalating confrontation with the New Dealers in Congress. Put differently, in 1935 and 1936, federal lawmakers and judges compromised and defused conflict by together drawing on state constitutional pension clauses and doctrine.

The textbook story of the SSA, focusing on the national branches, is a bit different. This story, told by Ackerman, McCloskey, and Leuchtenburg, emphasizes the Court's novel arguments and Roosevelt's and Congress's transformative, bullish national statutory reforms. Ackerman, for example, argues that New Dealers eschewed constitutional amendment for revolutionary, quasi-constitutional federal "super-statutes" like the SSA that endured through intergenerational public support. This story is not wrong but, rather, is incomplete.[22] A complete story notes that alongside these federal super-statutes, New Deal state legislators, overriding and preempting judges, passed dozens of amendments durably—and constitutionally—entrenching fair working conditions and pensions. These state clauses and programs guided the Committee on Economic Security to compromise with the Court, which then echoed state pension doctrine in *Carmichael, Steward,* and *Helvering v. Davis,* appeasing the White House. Finally, some scholars emphasize variation in state welfare protections, noting that some states, particularly those without mandatory pension clauses, particularly in the South, narrowed benefits, particularly for Black women. Suzanne Mettler convincingly demonstrates this, concluding that the "lesson of the early development of ADC at the state level is that rights are never really rights when they are determined through the system of American federalism." But national protections too were weak, as Congress's Southern reactionaries modified the SSA to deny benefits to Black Americans. And Mettler's "never" is too strong a word. The United States' constitutional welfare rights, binding or nonbinding, exist only in the state constitutions, not in the federal Constitution or through Supreme Court doctrine. State constitutional labor and pension provisions preceded, supported, and sometimes exceeded federal statutory minimums.[23]

State Convergence and Federal Dictation on Voting Rights

Congress also considered repealing civil and voting rights restrictions. Between 1870 and 1921, twenty-five states enacted poll taxes, twelve constitutionally, six statutorily, and seven through both methods. Legislators also used literacy and residency requirements to disenfranchise Northeastern immigrants and Southern Blacks. All eleven old Confederacy states constitutionalized residency requirements and the poll tax, six letting unpaid taxes accumulate, while seven states constitutionalized literacy tests, dropping Black turnout to single digits by 1912. And after 1929, rural legislators nationwide disempowered urban voters by refusing to reapportion new seats to growing cities.

Widespread poll taxes drew special ire. Repeatedly and decisively rebuffed by the Supreme Court, which held that poll taxes did not violate the Equal Protection Clause, the NAACP pivoted to legislative action in 1941, founding the National Committee to Abolish the Poll Tax. The committee, backed by the AFL and the Congress of Industrial Organizations (CIO), found a hesitant ally in Franklin Roosevelt, who attacked the tax in 1938, hoping to reenfranchise poor Southerners and oust their reactionary congressmen. Progress was halting. Working with the committee, New Dealers in Congress introduced bans annually, one of which passed the House 254 to 84 in October 1942, only to fail against the Southern filibuster, as did four others by 1949. Congress passed a limited bill exempting Black servicemen from the tax, albeit with a rider letting the states pass enabling legislation. Since Article I, Section 2, let the states administer elections, in 1944, Roosevelt and the Republican Party endorsed an Article V amendment to expressly disallow poll taxes. Republicans regained Congress in 1949, pitching a poll tax statute, and Southern Democrats answered with an Article V amendment, trusting states to refuse ratification or, in event of passage, to deploy literacy tests. In total, between the honest and bad-faith proposals, Congress heard thirty-one amendments addressing poll tax and property requirements and seven on literacy qualifications from 1941 to 1962.[24]

State legislative reapportionment also riled Congress. As reformers attacked state poll tax, literacy, and residency requirements, white, rural, conservative state legislators increasingly relied on malapportionment to disempower Black, urban, and liberal voters. Sweeping 1962 and 1964 Supreme Court decisions invalidated this malapportionment, spurring congressional conservatives to propose hundreds of amendments restoring state malapportionment. By 1967, legislators in thirty-two states submitted federal convention petitions, two short of the Article V requirement needed to call a convention to completely rewrite the Constitution.[25]

Midcentury reformers largely circumvented Article V. Between 1953 and 1979, Congress proposed 5,294 amendments—nearly half of those proposed in U.S. history—but ratified only four. Three narrowly tailored amendments enlarged the vote: the Twenty-Third (1961), Twenty-Fourth (1964), and Twenty-Sixth (1971) enfranchised, respectively, District of Columbia residents in presidential elections, citizens paying poll taxes, and those eighteen or older. The Twenty-Fifth Amendment (1967) codified the long-standing order of presidential succession.

Given the amendments' constrained scope, scholars including Bruce Ackerman, David Kyvig, Gerald Rosenberg, and Richard Valelly have instead credited reform to Democrats' coordinated, sweeping doctrinal and statutory reform efforts. Congressional Democrats, holding a bicameral supermajority in one or both chambers through the 1960s, transformed American constitutionalism statutorily, insuring the poor and elderly by amending the SSA in 1966, desegregating schools and public places through the 1964 Civil Rights Act and 1965 Elementary and Secondary Education Act, and combating racial disenfranchisement through the 1965 Voting Rights Act. Franklin Roosevelt's long tenure stacked the Supreme Court with liberal allies, who upheld these laws under landmark Commerce and Equal Protection Clause cases, obviating court-constraining amendments. Ackerman thus concludes, "it is these statutes, not formal amendments, that provided the primary vehicle for the legal expression of popular sovereignty in the twentieth century."[26]

But Americans did pass transformative civil rights amendments. They did this at the state level, ratifying thousands of constitutional amendments in the 1960s and 1970s. State constitutional reform forbade poll taxes, legislative malapportionment, and racial and gender discrimination, sometimes before Congress or the Supreme Court intervened by amendment, statute, or judicial review.

Poll tax repeal began with the states. Buoyed by ongoing New Deal reform, Southern populists, Roosevelt Democrats, and union organizers attacked the poll tax for disenfranchising poor whites during the Depression. Reform came by piecemeal state constitutional amendment. Appalachian North Carolina voters banned poll taxes and residency requirements by amendment in 1920, defeating eastern Black-belt planter resistance. In 1934, Huey Long and the AFL forced a constitutional amendment through the Louisiana legislature, adding 110,000 white voters in primary elections by 1940. And in 1936, the New Deal Florida legislator Claude Pepper won statutory poll tax repeal as an anti-vote-buying measure and, with boosted turnout, beat his reactionary opponent, James Wilcox, in the 1938 U.S. Senate race.

State reformers earned little White House support. Roosevelt, impressed by Pepper's win, quietly backed Arkansas's abolition efforts but, when confronted by Mississippi's patrician Democratic senator Pat Harrison in October 1938, denied his earlier support for a congressional ban and in February 1939 refused to directly aid Tennessee's repeal push or other "campaigns of state issues." That same month, Roosevelt opened the Department of Justice's Civil Rights Section to explore federal judicial challenges to the tax. But the Supreme Court refused an appeal against Texas's tax in 1941, and a chastened Attorney General Francis Biddle redirected efforts against the white primary.[27]

Reformers looked to Congress. In November 1938, delegates met in Birmingham for the inaugural Southern Conference on Human Welfare (SCHW), tackling the twin evils of poverty and the poll tax, deeming the latter "the key to other problems." Earning Roosevelt's tacit support, the conference left repeal efforts to the Committee on Civil Rights, which soon was replaced by the National Committee to Abolish the Poll Tax (NCAPT). The NCAPT, headquartered in Washington, DC, with a small permanent staff, coordinated lobbying and bill drafting between the SCHW, NAACP, AFL, CIO, and allied workers' groups. NCAPT arguments strategically emphasized labor and white poverty, not Black enfranchisement, but Southern congressmen, fearing federal intervention in state elections, still killed an SCHW-sponsored repeal bill in 1939, citing successful state reform. Several other bills died against Southern filibuster, and by 1944, both Roosevelt and his opponent in that year's presidential election, Thomas Dewey, called for a federal amendment, by then a purely symbolic gesture. On assuming the presidency, Harry Truman rejected even this, declaring that repeal "was a matter for the Southern states to work out." Postwar anticommunism made the CIO cut funding to the communist-friendly NCAPT, which went bankrupt and dissolved in 1948.[28]

In contrast, state campaigns gained traction through the 1940s. As the Depression waned, poll taxes, many constitutionally fixed at a dollar or two, devalued with rising inflation, nudging lawmakers toward abolition. All Northern states banned poll taxes by 1940. The Southern Electoral Reform League, founded in 1941 with AFL and CIO funding, was steered partly by Claude Pepper toward repeating Florida's state-level success, establishing local chapters and newspapers to lobby moderate Democratic lawmakers. As the NAACP paid Black voters' devalued taxes, conservative Democrats also abandoned the tax for literacy and residency requirements and voter intimidation. Georgia's reactionary former governor Eugene Tallmadge urged repeal to enfranchise poor whites against the sitting liberal governor, Ellis Arnall. A December 1944 SCHW conference in Atlanta called for a ban, and soon Roosevelt privately telephoned Arnall, who fell in line and pushed a repeal bill through the statehouse weeks later. South Carolina state senators, conferring with their congressional delegation, passed a 1951 repeal amendment to preempt federal intervention. Tennessee's legislature statutorily abolished the tax in 1943 and, reversing state courts, did so by constitutional amendment in 1953.

A few states resisted full repeal. Alabama's NAACP, AFL, CIO, and populist governor "Big Jim" Folsom did not win an outright ban but rather made the $1.50 tax noncumulative and appointed liberal registrars. The NAACP, AFL, and CIO also attempted amendments in Virginia through the late 1940s and early 1950s. Arkansas, a diehard poll tax state, rejected a 1937 AFL-sponsored amendment but passed a 1944 amendment exempting Black servicemen, in tandem with Congress's Soldier Voting Act. Mississippi did the same two years later, though paying the conventional tax remained prohibitively difficult. By 1953, poll tax laws remained only in Alabama, Arkansas, Mississippi, Texas, and Virginia.[29]

Despite the near unanimity of state bans, Congress stalled for another decade. Senate Judiciary Committee chair James Eastland of Mississippi consistently blocked voter protections, forcing Florida's Spessard Holland to modify a congressional succession amendment to include a national poll tax ban. Appeasing Southerners, Holland invoked the language of convergence, promising that the ban would not trigger aggressive federal enforcement against Southern states, since "so many of the Southern States recently have eliminated the poll tax requirement." Senator Jacob Javits instead backed a statutory ban against the remaining "five States where it still stands," adding, "we do not need a constitutional amendment" given that the "poll tax is not necessarily a prohibitive factor in regards to voting in most other States." The amendment passed the Senate floor in 1960 but failed against anticipated Southern resistance in the House. Holland repeated the Senate maneuver in 1962, and House Judiciary Committee chair Emanuel Celler suspended the rules to sneak a matching measure to a quick vote. Like his New York colleague Javits, Celler sold the measure as innocuous, given that "45 states do not have a poll tax." Ohio's William McCulloch agreed that it was "a mild proposal, indeed, in view of the limited use of poll tax laws." The measure easily passed the Senate 294 to 86, and thirty-eight states, largely excepting the South, swiftly ratified the Twenty-Fourth Amendment by January 23, 1964. Narrow in scope, the amendment affected only federal elections and only directly in the five remaining unreformed states. Arkansas repealed the tax by state constitutional amendment, while Alabama, Mississippi, Texas, and Virginia, unrepentant, retained their taxes, promising to tax voters in state elections.[30]

In response, Congress and the Supreme Court closed this loophole. In 1965, Lyndon Johnson steered Democratic supermajorities in the Eighty-Ninth Congress to pass the Voting Rights Act, claiming broad Fourteenth and Fifteenth Amendment powers to oversee state poll taxes under Section 10(b). Sections 4(a) and 4(b) applied this power specifically to the Jim Crow South. Section 10(c) invited federal judicial affirmation, which the Court delivered in *Harper v. Virginia Board of Elections,* though the Court noted that few states still used the tax.

Scholars disagree on whether to credit poll tax repeal to the Twenty-Fourth Amendment, the VRA, or *Harper.* Roger Hartley and Richard Bernstein and Jerome Agel praise the amendment for repudiating Southern reactionaries, Bruce Ackerman shows that the VRA enlarged federal oversight, and Alexander Keyssar lauds Justice William O. Douglass's *Harper* opinion for recognizing a right to vote regardless of wealth. Each measure, applying to all of the states, prevents franchise rollback, so none of these answers are wholly wrong.

Nor are they wholly right. We should also remember the grinding struggles of local NAACP organizers, union workers, lobbyists, and New Deal state legislators, who, rebuffed by Congress, the White House, and the Court through the 1930s, 1940s, and 1950s, abolished the poll tax by state constitutional amendment, aiding congressional and Court intervention in the 1960s. In the case of poll tax repeal, myopically focusing only on national politics risks misreading the Twenty-Fourth Amendment as a case of dictation, rather than convergence, and thus misunderstanding national political development.[31]

As the poll tax folded, Southern lawmakers tried excluding Black voters through residency requirements, literacy tests, and white primaries. Texas legislators initially forbade Black residents from voting in the Democratic primary that determined general elections. When the Supreme Court overruled the Texas legislature, the state Democratic Party, a voluntary association beyond the Court's reach, then reinstituted the rule, earning the Court's approval in 1935. But new Roosevelt appointees, the NAACP, and the Department of Justice forced the Court to reverse itself in 1944, using the Fifteenth Amendment to abolish white primaries.[32]

Jim Crow lawmakers fell back on old literacy tests. Largely a relic of late nineteenth- and early twentieth-century state constitutions—Oregon passed the last test in 1924—these also faltered against rising Black and immigrant literacy. In response, registrars, particularly in rural counties, posed increasingly byzantine, racially biased literacy tests in Alabama, the Carolinas, and Virginia, an impossible "understanding" exam in Mississippi, and arbitrary additional "moral character" tests in Georgia and Louisiana. The few voters to clear these examinations faced Klan and White Citizen Council intimidation. By 1960, thirteen tests lasted outside the South, in New York disenfranchising immigrants, including many Puerto Ricans.[33]

Unlike poll tax bans, literacy test repeal was primarily a federal, not state, project, a case of federal dictation. In 1962, the Department of Justice recommended overseeing Southern registrars, and in 1965, the VRA banned literacy tests, initially in jurisdictions with turnout or registration under 50 percent and then permanently nationwide under 1970 and 1975 amendments, which the Court promptly upheld under the Fifteenth Amendment. By 1968, the test was dead, save scattered, illegal implementation in Texas and some North Carolina counties. So too went residency requirements under the 1970 amendments.[34]

The Court next targeted malapportionment. In 1929, Congress stopped requiring that states equally apportion congressional districts, letting rural state legislators gerrymander cities into multimember state legislative districts, ignore state constitutional reapportionment requirements, and refuse calls for new state constitutional conventions and apportionment schemes. Between 1930 and 1960, only four conventions ratified new state constitutions, and twelve state chambers refused redistricting outright. Dwight Eisenhower's 1955 Kestenbaum Commission asked states for modernization and "fundamental review and revision of their constitutions," a sentiment shared by the National Municipal League, the National Governors Conference, and state Leagues of Women Voters. The Court's *Baker* (1962), *Wesberry* (1964), and *Reynolds* (1964) rulings broke the logjam by allowing and then forcing state and congressional reapportionment into equal single-member districts. The decisions empowered urban, Southern, and Black voters by mandating redistricting in forty-six states by 1966.[35]

Rural state and congressional legislators faced electoral ouster. In July 1962, mere weeks after *Baker,* Southern state legislators convened in Biloxi, Mississippi, for the Southern Branch Meeting of the nonpartisan Council of State Governments, proposing an Article V convention to reverse the Court's decision. The proposal won support from conservatives at the council's National Legislative Conference in September and from thirteen state legislatures by the end of 1963. Chief Justice Earl Warren, the American Civil Liberties Union, the AFL-CIO, and the American Bar Association warned of a runaway convention through 1963, prompting ten states, six of them Southern, to petition Congress to instead submit an apportionment-specific amendment, which crept into the 1964 Republican platform. The Court's 1964 *Wesberry* and *Reynolds* reapportionment decisions riled additional congressional conservatives to action—between 1962 and 1967, members of Congress, many of them Southern, proposed 206 state apportionment amendments, mainly reversing the Court. After two amendments proposed by Republican Senate Minority Leader Everett Dirksen narrowly failed floor votes in 1965 and 1966, Dirksen helped the Council of State Governments lobby additional states for convention resolutions, admittedly a ploy to goad liberal members of Congress, scared of a runaway convention, into accepting his narrower alternative amendment. Council lobbying and backlash to *Wesberry* and *Reynolds* nevertheless jump-started the convention campaign. Following council guides, legislators in twelve states soon followed by 1965, and by March 1967, thirty-two states submitted petitions, two short of

Article V requirements to rewrite the whole Constitution. Troublingly, many state legislators cursorily supported convention petitions without debating, investigating, or sometimes even understanding the motion.[36]

Meanwhile, suburban, urban, and progressive state legislators, no longer sidelined, quickly redrafted their constitutions to entrench new, equitable districting plans. Between 1962 and 1979, states empowered thirty-nine commissions, twelve conventions, and six legislative sessions to draft or amend constitutions, ratifying nine new documents. Commissioners and convention delegates debated *Baker* and *Reynolds* in detail, passing varied reforms. Several proactive states constitutionally established bipartisan, independent, or advisory redistricting commissions to preempt backsliding, and by 1964, twenty-six states approved reapportionment plans. New conservative suburban districts appeased Republicans. In noncompliant states like Georgia, Louisiana, Mississippi, and the Carolinas, preclearance denials under the 1965 VRA effectively eliminated multimember districts, adding new majority-Black single-member districts and hundreds of Black state legislators. By 1966, forty-six legislatures were reapportioned, with thirty contemporary state constitutions clearly and thoroughly forbidding population malapportionment.[37]

With the state constitutional logjam broken, revision spread beyond reapportionment to broader rights and policy issues. Connecticut's 1965 constitutional convention, called only to redistrict seats, drafted a new constitution with a new clause guaranteeing civil and political rights regardless of race. Florida's 1968 constitution also broadly forbade any rights denial by race. And Michigan's 1961–63 constitutional convention included a new environmental rights and protection clause. Between 1962 and 1980, state legislators, convention delegates, and constitutional commissioners ratified at least seventy civil rights amendments and ninety-five elections and voting rights amendments.[38]

The Article V convention movement stalled. A March 18, 1967, *New York Times* front-page story condemned the states' haphazard petition votes, and days later, New York's Senator Javits decried the process on the Senate floor, predicting a "wide-open convention." Prominent liberal senators Robert Kennedy, William Proxmire, and Joseph Tydings also warned of a runaway convention, as did the conservative Southerners Willis Roberts and Sam Ervin. Moreover, prior apportionment by state constitutional reform made a federal amendment unnecessary. Proxmire, joined by Claiborne Pell, pointed to near-universal state reapportionment. Tydings added, "conservative suburbs have been the real gainers in the 40 States which have already reapportioned on the one-man, one-vote principle." Javits agreed: "Reapportionment is a dead horse. It is already just about an accomplished fact in every State, and it is not even a political issue. . . . [In 1966] Republicans made a net gain of 153 seats in State senates and 387 seats in State lower houses." Javits was right—by 1966, all but four states had finished reapportionment, adding conservative suburban seats, appeasing Republicans and sapping conservative congressional support for an amendment or convention. In November 1969, Wisconsin rejected a convention petition, and Illinois, Kansas, North Carolina, and Texas soon withdrew theirs. Congress heard only four apportionment amendment proposals after 1970, and the Court reaffirmed state legislators' redistricting reforms. State constitutional reform obviated a court-constraining amendment or runaway convention, preserving the interbranch balance of powers.[39] In sum, through the 1960s, the federal courts and Department of Justice pushed some civil and voting rights reforms on the states though dictation, as was the case for the repeal of literacy tests and white primaries, while in other cases, like poll tax repeal and reapportionment, widespread state constitutional reform detailed and stabilized the new electoral order—examples of convergence.

The era's final suffrage debate concerned the voting age. Reform came in fits and starts, first at the state level. Between the Second World War and the Korean War, members of Congress, led by Senator Arthur Vandenburg and Representative Jennings Randolph, proposed thirty-three amendments to enfranchise servicemen and all others eighteen or older, but with Gallup polls registering public opposition, only one amendment won a hearing. Oklahoma and South Dakota voters also rejected state constitutional amendments, though a 1945 Georgia amendment enfranchised people eighteen and older, as did constitutional reforms in Kentucky, Alaska, and Hawaii after the Korean War. By the late 1960s, teenage Vietnam draftees remained disenfranchised in all other states. The Vietnam generation, politically active, their ranks stacked with baby boomers, mobilized for reform, and by spring 1967, Gallup polling showed moderate support for enfranchising eighteen-year-olds. In 1969, members of Congress offered nineteen amendments to lower the national voting age to eighteen—the first proposals in nearly a decade. States also considered constitutional reform. In 1966, Michigan ventured a voting age reduction amendment, and by 1969, state legislators and constitutional convention delegates proposed at least twelve more measures to constitutionally lower the voting age. Wary of student radicalism and protests, voters soundly rejected all of these proposals and another eleven state amendments in 1970, while approving amendments in Alaska, Maine, Massachusetts, Minnesota, Montana, and Nebraska.

Focus shifted to Congress. Senate Judiciary Committee chair Birch Bayh, a longtime proponent of youth voting, called hearings in February 1970, offering a federal constitutional amendment to vent young protestors' frustration. Weeks later, Congress instead amended the 1965 Voting Rights Act to enfranchise all citizens eighteen or older—the measure's main opponent, House Judiciary Committee chair Emanuel Celler, allowed passage, expecting the Court to overturn the amendment. Surprising Celler, the Court narrowly upheld the amendment to the VRA, and Congress, faced with contradictory state qualifications, opted for a federal constitutional amendment to void the state laws. A defeated Celler backed Jennings Randolph's franchise amendment, which easily cleared Congress on March 23, 1971. Cued by Congress's dictation, state legislators ratified by July, with Maine, Nevada, and Oklahoma passing matching state constitutional amendments and Massachusetts, Montana, Mississippi, and Nebraska reforming their constitutions the following year. While seventeen states opted to constitutionally lower the voting age by 1974, congressional leaders including Bayh and Randolph deserve more credit for addressing this national debate. State constitutional reform, though parallel and complementary to federal reform, did not alone resolve the issue. Rather, Congress dictated a uniform policy for the states.[40]

Federal Deference on Gender Discrimination

Finally, Congress considered gender-equality measures. In 1921, the National Woman's Party (NWP) proposed a federal amendment and state bills forbidding gender discrimination under the law. NWP head Alice Paul instructed Massachusetts's chapter to exempt women's labor-protection laws, imitating Wisconsin's pioneering statute. But NWP research secretary Sue Shelton White, surveying diverse state-level gender regulations, instead drafted a model state bill without labor exemptions. The pro-business NWP Lawyer's Committee chair Gail Laughlin then sold this unexempted, broadly applicable "blanket" bill to Paul. Paul's endorsement of a blanket bill, threatening state-level women's labor protections, alienated the AFL, the Women's Trade Union League, the National Consumers League, and the League of Women Voters. League of Women Voters chair Maud Wood Park, trained in the NAWSA by the more moderate Carrie Chapman Catt, doubted Paul's uncompromising tactics, and in a December 4, 1921, meeting warned Paul that the blanket bill would "divide the women's movement."[41]

The NWP forged ahead with the blanket-bill strategy. In February 1922, the NWP's National Advisory Council endorsed a blanket federal amendment to override state laws. The following year, equal rights measures failed or were repealed in Connecticut, Illinois, Massachusetts, Michigan, New York, North Dakota, Ohio, Oklahoma, and Rhode Island, which *Equal Rights,* the NWP weekly, declared "an example of the insecurity of State Equal Rights legislation . . . and of the consequent desirability of establishing Equal Rights by the more permanent method of a national amendment." NWP research secretary Burnita Shelton Matthews added in December 1923, "Discriminations against women that are written in a state constitution can only be removed by amending the state constitution. . . . In every state, except Delaware, an amendment to the state constitution must be ratified by a vote of the people." Recalling the recent "great cost and the great labor involved in state referendums" for the female vote, Matthews noted that a single federal Equal Rights Amendment (ERA) "would render unnecessary any further Equal Rights amendments to state constitutions." The NWP abandoned state constitutional referenda campaigns for a grand July 21, 1923, Seneca Falls convention to unveil the federal ERA, which Kansas's Charles Curtis submitted before the Senate Judiciary Committee on December 10, 1923.[42]

Testimony from unions and women's groups killed the federal measure in hearings. As Melinda Scott, a United Textile Workers organizer, told the Senate Judiciary Committee, "The National Woman's Party does not know what it is to work 10 or 12 hours a day in a factory; so they do not know what it means to lose an eight-hour day or nine-hour day law. The working women do know." Adopting a League of Women Voters argument, Senator Thomas Walsh held that state constitutional experimentation with labor protections made a blanket amendment undesirable: "We have passed all manner of laws in the various states to protect women—factory laws, for instance, hours of labor, etc. I can see no sense in a constitutional amendment that will wipe these laws off the books." The white-collar NWP, based in a new Washington, DC, headquarters and bankrolled by Alva Vanderbilt, maintained the old Congressional Union strategy of threatening to rally supporters to oust opposed congressional incumbents, but with steep ten-dollar annual dues and anemic grassroots membership—a result of forgoing state campaigns—the NWP's threat rang hollow. Charles Curtis, Indiana's Louis Ludlow, Delaware's John Townsend, and a few other stalwart allies pitched twenty-seven other ERA proposals by 1943, none of which garnered broad support. The ERA, briefly contentious, fell dormant. For the time, state constitutional labor protections obviated a federal amendment.[43]

Mobilization continued for federal amendment. The ERA won endorsements from the National Federation of Business and Professional Women's Clubs in 1937, the Republican Party in 1940, and, with women facing wartime workplace discrimination, the Senate Judiciary Committee in 1942, the Democratic Party in 1944, and both the Senate and House Judiciary Committees in 1945. But during Senate hearings, Labor Department Women's Bureau director Frieda Miller praised state protective laws, highlighting New York's recently constitutionalized workers' rights, and condemned the ERA for striking "directly at the right of the states to exercise such police power." Growing opposition to a federal ERA sought to preserve old state labor protections alongside new federal ones. The following year, Eleanor Roosevelt, joined by Carrie Chapman Catt and Frances Perkins, warned Congress against an ERA that would "wipe out the legislation which has been enacted in many states for the special needs of women in industry." Emanuel Celler, the old-line pro-labor House Judiciary Committee chair, blocked ERA measures, rejecting even labor-exempted Senate bills in 1950 and 1953. To preserve state laws, labor advocates stalled the ERA in Congress—between 1945 and 1958, fifty members from nineteen states offered eighty-nine ERA proposals, often in a rough dozen to start each Congress, with none clearing the House.[44]

During the Eisenhower and Kennedy administrations, labor advocates sidelined the ERA to maintain state statutory and constitutional labor provisions. Eisenhower pushed the amendment in 1956 and 1957 speeches, appointing the sympathetic Alice K. Leopold, author of Connecticut's equality bill, as the Women's Bureau director. But John F. Kennedy replaced Leopold with the AFL-CIO lobbyist Esther Peterson, who led his Commission on the Status of Women. Rejecting a federal ERA, the commission report explained, "State legislation, applicable to both men and women, should be enacted, or strengthened and extended," including stronger wage, hours, unionization, pension, and property rights.[45]

Title VII of the 1964 Civil Rights Act invalidated these state laws. Congresswoman Martha Griffiths drafted Title VII, outlawing workplace gender discrimination, which the segregationist Virginian Howard Smith appended to the act to tank House labor support. But House liberals swallowed Title VII to advance the bill, and the Senate forwent a vote, passing the act. After the Labor Department interpreted the 1963 Equal Pay Act to invalidate state gender-specific wage laws, unions girded for a similar, if broader, interpretation of Title VII, and states quickly repealed gender-protective legislation.[46] The fight for state laws lost, labor advocates reconceived the ERA as a workplace-protection measure. The National Organization of Women (NOW), formed with labor support in 1966, endorsed the ERA in 1967, as soon did the United Auto Workers. Public support grew, and Presidents Johnson and Nixon and the Congress followed. Between 1959 and 1971, 414 members from all fifty states proposed 971 ERAs in the most intense single-issue amendment push in U.S. history.

Congressional ERA passage still took maneuvering. Circumventing Celler, Griffiths gathered 218 signatures to discharge her ERA bill for a House floor vote, which passed 352 to 15 in 1970. The ERA then got mired in Senate Judiciary Committee debates over labor, draft, and domestic-violence exemptions and chair Birch Bayh's proposed seven-year ratification deadline, never making a floor vote. But NOW lobbying won a 1969 Equal Employment Opportunity Commission (EEOC) decision dismantling remaining women's labor protections and union opposition. The following session's House Judiciary Committee passed the ERA 32 to 3, endorsing the amendment to expressly override discriminatory state education, occupation, property, and jury service laws. Bayh's Senate committee passed the ERA, rejecting Sam Ervin's bad-faith riders and implausible objection that the few surviving state gender laws obviated a federal amendment. The ERA easily cleared the House 354 to 24 on October 12, 1971, and the Senate 84 to 8 on March 22, 1972, with an attached seven-year deadline.[47]

Supporters expected quick ratification. After the EEOC ruling and a companion Ninth Circuit case invalidated remaining state protective laws, twenty-two states ratified by the end of 1972, and eight more followed by the end of 1973. Heartened by this progress, the Ratification Council, an umbrella coalition of pro-ERA groups, waited until April 1973 to appoint an Action Committee to coordinate lobbying in the remaining states. But, confident of ratification, the committee met only once before disbanding and being replaced by a similar Operation Taskforce, and many state coalitions did not form until 1974.[48]

Conservatives immediately countermobilized. In *Reed, Frontiero,* and *Boren,* the Supreme Court interpreted the Fifth and Fourteenth Amendments to require intermediate scrutiny of legal gender distinctions, a standard somewhat below the proposed ERA. These rapid-fire decisions, followed by *Roe v. Wade,* flipped conservatives against further expanding women's access to abortion, shared bathrooms, and military service, which Phyllis Schlafly's STOP ERA campaign linked to the pending amendment. STOP ERA lobbying won Republican state legislators, particularly those in safe seats, stalling ratification. Idaho's, Nebraska's, and Tennessee's legislatures attempted rescinding ratification, as did South Dakota's legislature, contingent on the ERA's expiration, and Kentucky's legislature before being vetoed by Governor Thelma Stovall. While ratifications came from Maine, Montana, and Ohio in 1974, North Dakota in 1975, and Indiana in 1977, a renewed NOW campaign in 1977 made no inroads against STOP ERA allies. Even after a 1979 congressional resolution extended the approval deadline three years, President Ronald Reagan opposed the amendment, and Congress failed to renew the deadline in 1982.[49]

Why did the ERA fail? Scholars pin the ERA's defeat on high Article V ratification requirements, contentious deadline-extension procedures, STOP ERA's proactive countermobilization and scaremongering, NOW's delayed and discordant ratification campaign, Reagan's opposition, and the Supreme Court's preemptive expansion of gender equality.[50] Each of these claims is plausible, but to the extent that they all focus mainly on national institutions, they are incomplete. State constitutional reform also complicated ERA ratification.

As the ERA stalled, states proposed constitutional gender-equality clauses. Pennsylvania, Virginia, and Illinois ratified equal rights provisions in 1971, as did another twelve states by 1976. Motivations varied. New Mexico, anticipating federal ratification, passed a 1972 ERA to void gender distinctions under state law, and Maryland and Texas jointly passed state and federal ERAs under NOW and Business and Professional Women's Clubs lobbying, Maryland after only brief debate under suspended rules. In other states, lawmakers debated and passed ERAs to guide judges. Rather than trust "court interpretation [of] whether or not women are, in fact, 'persons,' and entitled to equal protection," the Illinois constitutional convention delegate Odas Nicholson proposed an equal rights clause to make state judges switch from intermediate to strict scrutiny. Conversely, Pennsylvania's cursory and unrecorded state ERA passage, like Maryland's, left judges broad interpretive leeway, and Washington's legislature reported that its 1972 ERA would not force judges to use a particular standard.[51]

By 1976, eighteen states ratified equality clauses, which judges in eleven states interpreted to require strict scrutiny or even absolute abolition of gender distinctions. Legislators voided gender distinctions in jury service, employment, education, and criminal, probate, and marriage and family law, stripping some gender protections and stoking fears of broader judicial activism. Texas's attorney general preemptively declared that the state ERA did not let judges recognize same-sex marriage, and in debates over New York's proposed ERA, state senator Richard Schermerhorn added, "My wife is not equipped to earn her own way. . . . If the [state] ERA had passed, she could have lost my retirement benefits, my Social Security benefits, everything. These issues would be up to the courts, and I don't trust the judges. I don't want to put the lives and rights of women in the hands of some freaky judge."[52]

State equal rights amendments flagged after the mid-1970s. Attacks on the federal ERA filtered into state campaigns, forcing Florida's Ruth Gokel to promise that her state's ERA required only "state action in Florida, not federal action in Washington." But skeptical voters rejected Florida's ERA in 1978, as well as ones in Wisconsin in 1973 and New Jersey and New York in 1975. New York homemakers lobbied against their proposed ERA, perceived as a radical ploy by "an elitist minority fringe that didn't give a damn about homemakers or women at the bottom of the labor market," according to the *New York Times*. One New York woman explained her vote against the state ERA: "I didn't know what the ERA meant, but I thought it was a women's libber type thing—how they don't want men to have their own clubs, they don't want Mother's Day." Schlafly, who led New York counterlobbying, seized on mounting opposition to state ERAs. The *Schlafly Report*'s August 1979 national mailer cast state ERAs as ruses to legalize abortion, prostitution, and same-sex marriage, claiming, "The experience of the State ERAs is more than adequate to convince us that ERA is unnecessary to achieve any beneficial goal for women or society, unreasonable in its absolute refusal to recognize obvious differences between the sexes, and unwanted in its potential to upset traditional objections to homosexual marriages, massage parlors, government funded abortions, and other imaginative uses of the term 'sex.'" State-level opposition entered a new phase in the early 1980s, as Christian lobbies defeated state ERA referenda in Iowa in 1980, Maine in 1984, and in Vermont in 1986 over concerns about abortion and same-sex marriage.[53]

Surprisingly, successful state ERA campaigns set back federal ratification. State ERAs and judicial strict scrutiny exceeded federal standards, perhaps obviating a federal ERA and cornering ratification advocates into making nationally unpopular arguments for the federal amendment on solely federal grounds, including for expanded federal abortion funding and women's military service. This occurred in Illinois, where ratification advocates, mired in draft debates, never cleared the legislature's three-fifths ratification vote requirement. Schlafly also successfully reframed aggressive state ERA enforcement as an assault on traditional family values presaging a federal ERA: "The experience of the seventeen states which allegedly have State ERAs provides conclusive proof [the federal] ERA is not needed." As Mary Frances Berry explained in 1986, "Vigorous implementation of state ERAs and court decisions tending toward more equality only helped to undermine any sense of urgency and to build consensus against ratification."[54]

State ERA campaign failure also set back federal ratification. When New York's state ERA failed, Schlafly gloated that the amendment's defeat "by more than 400,000 votes in November 1975, was the start of a mighty swing against [federal] ratification." New York then proposed rescinding its federal ERA ratification, to State Senator Schermerhorn's satisfaction: "Now the state ERA was rejected in 58 out of 62 counties, and I think the senators and assemblymen finally have gotten the message. What we've got to do now is rescind the Federal ERA." A February 1983 NOW report estimated a second New York state ERA campaign at $7 million, sapping federal ERA lobbying funds. By March, NOW proponents and allies "who counseled immediate attention to state ERAs and indefinite delay at the national level had been overrun.... Were campaigns for state ERAs to fail—as they had earlier failed in New York, New Jersey, and Florida at crucial times—the national effort would be weakened if not discredited in Congress." ERA supporter Janet Boles concluded in 1978 that further state ERA campaigns, whether successful or unsuccessful, would sideline federal ratification: "If the state ERA should fail, the federal amendment would not be ratified. If the state ERA were approved, the argument would be that the federal amendment is not needed." Unlike the suffragists, neither NWP nor NOW built a strong grassroots network for state constitutional change. They quickly and decisively lost state campaigns, which opponents turned against them, hobbling their federal campaign.[55]

State ERA controversies armed ERA opponents in Congress. In 1977 and 1978 ERA extension hearings, ERA opponents cited "as a gauge of public opinion, New York, New Jersey, and Wisconsin['s] recently rejected attempts to inject an Equal Rights Amendment into their state constitutions." And cataloguing state ERAs and gender rights cases, the law professor William Stanmeyer predicted that the federal ERA would force "judicial involvement in the affairs of our daily lives unprecedented in scope," a claim that Schlafly's testimony echoed. Proponents cited narrow case law allowing extension, which carried by simple majorities in both chambers. No additional states ratified, and the Equal Rights Amendment expired on June 30, 1982.[56]

Members proposed a new federal ERA in 1983, reopening hearings. Citing litigation in Connecticut, Hawaii, Massachusetts, and Pennsylvania seeking to use state ERAs to guarantee abortion funding, witnesses warned that a federal ERA would do the same. Senator Orrin Hatch, surveying state ERAs, concluded, "There is clearly a genuine controversy here. . . . The [federal] ERA may significantly enhance abortion rights," a worry that Senator Chuck Grassley, who opposed Iowa's ERA, and James Sensenbrenner repeated in Senate and House hearings. The new amendment did not pass Congress, and after 1984, Congress heard only twenty-nine ERA proposals from five members. Protections would be piecemeal, through state ERAs and federal jurisprudence.[57]

Attending to state constitutional reform helps us understand the federal ERA's failure. Most legal scholarship on state ERAs, couched in the "new judicial federalism" of the 1970s and 1980s, catalogues which states' jurisprudence meets or exceeds federal judicial intermediate scrutiny standards, presenting state ERAs as an alternate track for antidiscrimination litigation.[58] Most histories and postmortems on the federal ERA address social movements and conservative backlash to the amendment.[59] Both approaches, though useful, are largely disconnected and miss an important causal point—we rely on federal judicial scrutiny, and lack a federal ERA, partly *because of* these state clauses. State constitutional reform campaigns complicated, and sometimes impeded, the federal ERA's ratification.

Specifically, during and after the New Deal, union lobbyists, Labor Department experts, and mainline feminists preserved state constitutional labor laws by contesting the federal ERA in House Judiciary Committee hearings. But postwar feminism, emphasizing workplace equality rather than special protections, culminated in Title VII of the 1964 Civil Rights Act, voiding these state constitutional clauses, opening a window for the federal ERA. Labor lobbyists and feminists then pushed the federal ERA through Congress as a women's labor equality measure. State ERAs sometimes impeded federal ratification—when state provisions failed, they threatened federal ratification campaigns, and when they succeeded, they seemed to obviate the federal ERA, closing the window for federal reform. State constitutional clauses, first for women's labor rights and then for gender equality, consistently complicated, and sometimes thwarted, efforts to pass a federal ERA. This is not to claim that state constitutional reform singlehandedly blocked federal ERA ratification but rather that national reformers settled for state constitutional reform, which guided and often deterred national amendment ratification, a case of devolution by deference.

This understanding helps us rethink New Deal and Great Society constitutional development. Ackerman claims that "the twentieth century was an age of political pygmies ... [with] no constitutional amendments defining the nature and limits of activist national government, none codifying the central achievements of the civil rights revolution."[60] While this is true of federal constitutionalism, it misses the thousands of state amendments, including those protecting labor, welfare, voting, and gender rights. These provisions shaped, buttressed, and often exceed federal statutory minimums and, with the failure of analogous proposed federal amendments, are the *only* American constitutional clauses expressly protecting workers', welfare, and gender rights.

State constitutionalism also helps us rethink the exercise of federal power in these years. Democratic congressional majorities waxed during the New Deal and Great Society, dictating and sometimes overturning state welfare, franchise, and segregation law, particularly in the South. But this federal dictation coincided with state constitutional convergence and federal imitation. State lawmakers authorized tax-funded pensions by constitutional amendment, binding judges to affirm these programs. State pension programs guided the framing of the SSA, which the Supreme Court upheld by citing and imitating state pension doctrine, a case of convergence. Similarly, nearly all states constitutionally or statutorily converged on poll tax repeal, which the Twenty-Fourth Amendment,

VRA, and *Harper* decision affirmed and entrenched against rollback. Finally, ERA advocates, stymied by Article V ratification barriers, settled for deference to state ERAs. In this sense, state constitutionalism helped resolve national constitutional disputes in the New Deal and Great Society eras.

7

Contemporary Constitutionalism, 1980–2020

> *State constitutions, too, are a font of individual liberties, their*
> *protections often extending beyond those required by the Supreme*
> *Court's interpretation of federal law. The legal revolution which*
> *has brought federal law to the fore must not be allowed to inhibit*
> *the independent protective force of state law—for without it,*
> *the full realization of our liberties cannot be guaranteed.*
> —Justice William Brennan, "State Constitutions and the
> Protections of Individual Rights," 1977

ALMOST ALL MODERN CONSTITUTIONAL reform occurs at the state level. Federal amendment has declined. Between 1980 and 2020, Congress proposed 2,169 Article V amendments and passed none, while the Twenty-Seventh Amendment, pending since 1789, finally cleared the states, capping congressional salaries. Relative to previous eras, federal amendment proposals were few and focused on limiting federal power. Small federal government in the Reagan years entailed deference to the states, where constitutional amendment continued unabated. Fearing runaway conventions, lawmakers called twenty-five revision bodies, twenty-one of them with limited agendas, including sixteen limited commissions, yielding only two new constitutions. Instead, between 1980 and 2018, the states proposed 4,928 amendments and ratified 3,713, many constraining legislators. State judges, emboldened by a philosophy of "new judicial federalism," reinterpreted their constitutions. Why, then, did most constitutional change occur at the state and not federal level?

Consider the familiar explanations. Republicans, empowered by suburban growth and legislative reapportionment, challenged Democrats' long-standing dominance in Congress, claiming slim majorities that left both parties far short of amendment supermajority requirements. "Article V stood as a barrier to change sought by minorities or even slight majorities of citizens or states," according to David Kyvig. Kyvig, joined by Bruce Ackerman, Darren Latham, Aziz Huq, and David Strauss, notes that in the contemporary era, members of Congress have therefore offered symbolic, unabashedly partisan amendments as reelection ploys, foreclosing serious Article V reform. As Senator Dale Bumper of Arkansas admitted, "Constitutional amendments are palpable nonsense," because they are "all crafted for political advantage." With Article V disused, the Constitution, particularly during the 1987–88 bicentennial, gained the patina of "veneration which time bestows on everything," further deterring amendment. Strauss therefore concluded in 2001 that "constitutional amendments have not been an important means of changing the constitutional order." Members of Congress, particularly Republicans, similarly shied from expansive quasi-constitutional, super-statutory reforms, and the Court, from sweeping, activist rulings. The federal Constitution ossified.[1]

The states meanwhile proposed and ratified thousands of amendments. Since 1980, judges, lawmakers, and voters in all but four states have rejected constitutional conventions, for as an Oklahoman explained, "Having a convention would be like putting a patient on an operating table and opening him up when you don't know what you are going to find or what you are going to improve."[2] Similarly, New Yorkers rejected convention calls in 1997 and 2017 in order to preserve provisions for bipartisan gerrymandering, gubernatorial term limits, and labor, pension, and environmental protections. And in Iowa in 2000 and Alaska and Missouri in 2002, voters rejected convention ballot measures for lack of interest and information. Reformers have instead pitched amendments, circumventing legislatures by initiative. In 1994, Michigan voters rejected a convention to instead consider fifty-one bundled amendments and pass seventeen, since, as a Michigander noted, "individual elements of the Constitution— even the most important ones—can be changed by elected officials and citizens without an open-ended effort at overall constitutional revision."[3] Since 1980, the states have ratified three-quarters of the four thousand amendments proposed. State judges too have joined the fray. Building on mounting skepticism of federal power, U.S. Supreme Court Justice William Brennan and Oregon

Supreme Court Justice Hans Linde pushed state judges to expand their review powers, interpreting states' civil rights and liberty protections to exceed federal minimums, inviting occasional court-constraining amendments.[4]

While Article V and congressional fractiousness and polarization have hampered federal constitutional reform, the state constitutions' laxer amendment, initiative, and referenda processes vent reform pressure. This final chapter proceeds in two steps. The first section briefly recounts how Article V and Supreme Court resistance thwarted congressional balanced-budget, tax-cap, item-veto, and term-limits amendments and statutes, forcing fiscal reformers to instead pass state amendments. These state amendments vented national pressure for fiscal reform, such that after the 1990s, Congress largely abandoned balanced-budget, tax, and item-veto amendments, a case of issue devolution. The second section concludes the book with broader lessons on American constitutional development.

Federal Deference on Fiscal Reform

Between 1980 and 2020, Congress considered amendments curtailing federal fiscal powers, including proposals for a balanced budget, a tax cap, and an item veto, and amendments limiting congressional terms, abortion access, and flag-burning rights. Most of these proposals to restrain government reversed progressive Warren and Burger Court decisions. These electioneering ploys by conservative lawmakers stood little chance of passage. But a balanced-budget amendment cleared the House in 1995, falling a vote short in the Senate, and another passed the House in 2011. Through the 1980s and 1990s, thirty-two states called for a convention for a federal balanced budget and twenty-one for an abortion ban, potentially allowing broader reform in convention. And members of Congress threatened to reverse recent Supreme Court decisions with amendment proposals outlawing flag burning and authorizing school prayer, an item veto, and a balanced budget. Table 7 displays the twenty-five most common topics among amendments proposed between 1980 and 2020.[5]

Many of these federal proposals concerned concurrent powers, inviting parallel state amendment and reform. Addressing popular frustration with rising congressional incumbency, the advocacy group U.S. Term Limits helped twenty-three states cap congressional tenure. In an instance of supersession, the Supreme Court overrode Arkansas's state constitutional limit on congressional terms but allowed limits on state legislators' tenure, which passed in twenty-one states,

Table 7. Proposed Federal Amendments by Topic, 1980–2020

Topic	Years topic most often proposed (descending frequency)	Total	Concurrent power
Article I			
Congress	2013, 1989, 2017, 1987, 2015	371	Yes
House of Representatives	1993, 1995, 1983, 1981, 1991	234	Yes
Senate	1993, 1983, 1995, 1981, 1991	187	Yes
Article II			
Presidency	1993, 1981, 1983, 1991, 1989	248	Yes
Vice presidency	1981, 1983, 1992, 1985, 1993	139	Yes
Article III			
Federal courts	1981, 1983, 1989, 1987, 1991	90	No
Article V			
Amendment repeal proposals	1983, 1997, 1981, 1995, 1991	69	Yes
Federal officeholding			
Term length and limits	1983, 1993, 1981, 1989, 1995	307	Yes
Elections			
Election: general issues	1993, 1981, 1983, 1989, 2011	261	Yes
Campaign finance	2011, 2013, 1993, 1997, 1987	102	Yes
Election by popular vote	1981, 1993, 1983, 1992, 1989	73	Yes
Taxes and finance			
Federal budgets and deficits	1981, 1985, 1989, 1991, 1995	437	No
Federal appropriations	1991, 1993, 1981, 1989, 1983	139	No
Taxes: general issues	1981, 1993, 1991, 1983, 1999	134	Yes
National debt	1981, 1983, 1982, 2013, 1993	58	No
Rights and citizenship			
Rights: general issues	1983, 1987, 1981, 1989, 2011	316	Yes
Citizenship: general issues	2005, 1995, 2003, 1997, 1993	106	Yes
Residency rights	1993, 1985, 1987, 1991, 1981	58	Yes
Abortion			
Abortion: general issues	1981, 1983, 1987, 1985, 1989	110	Yes
Abortion: state regulation	1983, 1995, 1997, 1981, 2011	70	Yes
Schools			
School regulation: general issues	1981, 1993, 1985, 1989, 1983	108	Yes
Busing and school choice	1981, 1985, 1983, 1993, 1989	88	Yes
Other			
State powers	1995, 1997, 1981, 2011, 2015	187	Yes
Item veto	1993, 1991, 1989, 1995, 1985	113	No
Flag desecration	1989, 1991, 1995, 1997, 2003	107	Yes

mainly by amendment.⁶ And while Congress tried and failed to pass dozens of amendments reversing the Court's authorization of flag burning in *Texas v. Johnson,* the states uniformly statutorily banned the practice. Other national constitutional reform issues, like marijuana control, affirmative action, same-sex marriage, and gambling, rarely or never yielded congressional amendment proposals but brought widespread state constitutional amendment, suggesting that state amendment may have helped obviate congressional action in the modern era.⁷

In the case of fiscal reform, the states passed constitutional amendments mirroring those that routinely failed in Congress against Article V requirements. This was a case of congressional deference to state constitutionalism. Through the mid-twentieth century, conservatives in Congress repeatedly tried to cap spending. While emergency Treasury bonds financed expansive Depression and wartime projects, postwar Congresses hesitated to accordingly raise taxes, leading fiscal hawks to propose ninety budget-constraint amendments between 1943 and 1973. The 1974 Budget and Impoundment Control Act further expanded Congress's budget drafting powers, leading moderates Paul Simon and Carl Curtis to back a 1975 amendment tethering congressional spending to taxes. That year, the newly founded National Taxpayers Union (NTU) and National Tax Limitation Committee (NTLC) proposed stricter tax caps, alleging that the federal government, like a family, had to balance yearly accounts. This oversimplified argument ignored the government's sovereign debt powers but mobilized disaffected white suburban voters and lawmakers already chafing at expansive federal integration and busing plans. With the Curtis amendment trapped in the Senate Judiciary Committee's Subcommittee on the Constitution, the NTU instead pushed Maryland and Mississippi to directly petition Congress for a balanced-budget convention in 1975, reaching twenty-two states by 1978 and thirty by summer 1979, nearing the thirty-four-state threshold. This was a misstep. President Jimmy Carter and even the libertarian Senator Barry Goldwater predicted a runaway convention, and Judiciary Committee chair Birch Bayh's staff noted that a dozen state petitions were incorrectly filed and thus void. The subcommittee instead recommended an amendment in December 1979.

Republican gains in 1980 boosted prospects for an amendment. NTLC chair Lewis Uhler urged President Ronald Reagan to statutorily cut taxes, which Reagan did while increasing defense spending in 1981, pushing the 1982 budget deficit over $100 billion. Reagan then decried this deficit in summer 1982, requesting a balanced-budget amendment. Members answered this budget and deficit growth with detailed, quasi-statutory amendments. Charles W. Stenholm's eight-section proposal required the president to transmit an annual budget to Congress tying expenses to revenue and capping annual debt, with specified exemptions allowed by a bicameral congressional supermajority, letting Congress also override these limits following a declaration of war or of a national security emergency, given bicameral majorities. These amendments lumbered toward passage. Replacing Democrat Bayh as Senate Judiciary Committee chair, the Republican Strom Thurmond joined Orrin Hatch in drafting an amendment, which, with NTU and NTLC endorsement, barely cleared the Senate on August 4, 1982.

But fortunes quickly reversed. Democrats added twenty-seven House seats in November 1982, and in 1984 and 1985, California, Michigan, and Montana rejected convention petitions. Article V again thwarted reform. Frustrated with hardline Republicans' simultaneous deficit spending and increasingly byzantine, detailed budget-constraint amendments, the liberal Republican Senator Charles Mathias argued that Congress should avoid amendment: "I do not think we should use the Constitution as a fig leaf to cover our embarrassment over the deficit." In 1985, Congress settled for a balanced-budget statute, the Gramm-Rudman-Hollings Act. But the Supreme Court promptly overturned the act, spurring new, albeit increasingly symbolic court-constraining budget amendments. On February 4, 1986, Reagan addressed Congress with an alternate request: "I ask you to give me what 43 Governors have: Give me a line-item veto this year. Give me the authority to veto waste." He reiterated this call in his 1987 address, and members of Congress proposed dozens of item-veto amendments, some members citing the state clauses as models, which scholars credited for constraining state budgets.[8] Between feasible and longshot proposals, from 1980 to 1994, Congress proposed 272 amendments on balancing budgets, 103 on appropriations, 82 on item vetoes, and 45 on the national debt.[9]

Stifled in Congress by Article V, fiscal reformers instead passed state constitutional amendments limiting taxes and balancing budgets. While these amendments could not balance the federal budget, reformers found the states to be a more hospitable venue. Grassroots suburban canvassing against busing and property taxes and for the Nixon and Reagan campaigns built strong Sunbelt and Southern networks for state-level fiscal-reform measures. And while some members of Congress balked at adding detailed budget amendments to the brief federal Constitution, the state constitutions, with lower bars to amendment, already included dozens of lengthy clauses checking legislative budgeting practices, many passed by nineteenth-century framers after cyclical economic crises. Indiana's budget clause, dating to 1851, and West Virginia's, from 1872, forbid legislators from assuming debt, while Ohio's 1851 clause caps debt at $750,000, and Nevada's 1864 clause tethers debt to taxes, which reformers strengthened by amendment in 1989. Nevadans were not unique—through the 1970s and 1980s, fiscal reformers, facing economic stagnation, amended their state constitutions to update old budget checks and institute new ones. Convention delegates imposed balanced-budget amendments in Illinois in 1971 and in Tennessee and Hawaii in 1978, as did voters in Maryland in 1974, North Carolina in 1977, Virginia in 1984, and Rhode Island in 1986. By 1993, thirty-five state constitutions had balanced-budget clauses, and including statutory provisions, forty-nine states now mandate balanced budgets. These detailed measures mirrored Congress's rejected amendments, requiring executives or legislators to provide or pass a budget in which annual or biennial revenue exceeds expenses or debt, unless exempted by legislative supermajority.[10]

Voters also passed tax-limitation amendments. By initiative and referendum, voters imposed absolute limits or legislative supermajority requirements on property tax increases, restricted nonproperty taxes, and capped statewide tax expenditure by population. California pioneered each approach. In 1973, Lewis Uhler, chairing then-Governor Reagan's Tax Reduction Task Force, drafted Proposition 1 to force legislators to curb state spending and rising property taxes. When the attempt failed in 1978, fiscal conservatives Howard Jarvis and Paul Gann proposed Proposition 13 to limit property taxes and Proposition 4 to tether state expenditures to population growth. Californians backing the initiatives, many of them conservative homeowners, tended to see the state's lawmaking process as unresponsive, inefficient, and wasteful, soundly rejecting the legislature's alternate, more moderate Proposition 8. The same conservative suburbanites who shifted Congress right after the 1970 reapportionment now increasingly focused on state constitutional reform.

California triggered a landslide of tax initiatives. National media coverage introduced Proposition 13 to three-quarters of Americans outside California, two-thirds of whom supported similar reforms, according to November 1978 polls. Voters used initiatives and referenda to force lawmakers to make swift change. Constitutional convention delegates in Tennessee and Hawaii, sensing the nation's anti-tax tenor, proposed referenda capping state taxes and expenses. Other states followed. In total, seventeen states attempted tax initiatives in 1978; by 1981, forty-three states stabilized or reduced taxes; and by 1984, forty-four had called fiscal referenda. Congress also took note, proposing twenty-eight amendments for national referenda between 1977 and 1983, the first such amendment proposals since the New Deal. The movement spread, with Lewis Uhler advising Michigan's 1978 initiative capping state revenue and California's 1990 term-limits initiative and with Missourians passing a similar revenue initiative in 1980. Massachusetts's Proposition 2½ of 1980 statutorily reduced the state's relatively high property taxes, and by 1985, voters approved legislative-initiated tax-reduction amendments in seven more states. Through the 1990s, the states passed another five amendments initiated by citizens and eight initiated by legislators. These measures continued the fiscal-reform efforts of the 1980s—for example, in the 1990s, Arizonans, Oklahomans, and Nevadans passed amendments requiring legislative supermajorities for tax increases. Remarkably, survey respondents in California, Massachusetts, and Michigan supported broad tax cuts while favoring program-specific spending increases. Something had to give.[11]

Voters rolled back some of these clauses. Although Colorado initially imposed relatively low state and local taxes, through the 1980s, state legislators tried and failed to further lower taxes, leading Douglass Bruce, who had observed California's Proposition 13 campaign, to propose circumventing the legislature by constitutional initiative. Paul Gann, who authored Propositions 13 and 4, also advised Colorado's amendment campaign, which culminated in 1992 when voters passed a briefly worded ballot initiative, the "Taxpayer's Bill of Rights," constitutionally forbidding legislators from increasing state revenue over that of a previous year and distributing the excess as taxpayer refunds. Rife with populist symbolism, the much longer, more complex amendment text promised to "restrain most of the growth of government," holding that "limits on district revenue, spending, and debt may be weakened only by future voter approval," while financing taxpayer suits against legislative nonenforcement. Coloradans did not expect a decrease in public services, but predictably, the amendment's procrustean budget constraints hobbled the state government, as state revenue ratcheted down year after year. By 2000, primary and secondary education funding plummeted to forty-sixth nationally, forcing voters to pass an amendment exempting K–12 education spending. A 2001 recession then forced legislators to cut $1 billion from the state's $13 billion budget, yielding deep cutbacks to higher education, infrastructure, and child health care budgets, hampering child immunization, which voters also exempted in 2005. Across the states, lawmakers exempted necessary hospital, university, public housing, and infrastructure projects from debt caps and allowed exempted entities to assume debt for nonexempt ones, leading Richard Briffault to conclude that three-quarters of state debt escaped these strict, and increasingly rhetorical, state constitutional constraints. Surveying these carve-outs and the differences between state and federal budgeting processes, a 1993 General Accounting Office report to the House Budget Committee concluded that state balanced-budget clauses were not a successful model for Congress to emulate.[12]

Congress failed to pass budget amendments in the 1990s. In November 1994, Republicans gained nine Senate seats and fifty-four House seats on a fiscal-restraint platform and in 1995 proposed twenty-nine balanced-budget amendments, one of which cleared the Republican House but failed in the Senate by a single vote. Congress attempted alternate reforms, passing a House rule requiring a three-fifths vote for tax increases and proposing ten item-veto amendments. As Reagan noted, nearly all governors had item vetoes—Progressive-era state framers and voters had checked pork-barrel legislative appropriations through the gubernatorial item veto, constitutionalized in forty-four states, and through governor-initiated budgets constitutionalized in several.[13] But none of the analogous federal amendments cleared Congress, which in January 1997 instead passed the Line Item Veto Act. The Supreme Court promptly rejected this law in 1998, holding that the item veto required an amendment, only seventeen of which have since appeared on the congressional agenda. The item veto remained a matter for the states. The Court meanwhile upheld California's anti-tax initiatives.[14]

Congressional budget, tax, and item-veto amendments and statutes failed against Article V supermajority requirements and the Supreme Court. Reformers instead harnessed popular sentiment to pass fiscal-restraint measures through states' laxer initiative and referendum processes. Applying only to state finance, these state amendments could not address federal fiscal concerns or replace federal amendment proposals, but they did vent popular disaffection, channeling discontent, and reform efforts, to the states, following a pattern of devolution through deference.

Other issues followed the same path. Flag-burning amendments, dominating Congress's constitutional agenda in the early 1990s, yielded only state statutory reform. Victims' rights amendments, granting crime victims special procedural protections, uniformly failed in Congress in the 1990s, while thirty-five states passed analogous amendments, mainly in the 1980s and 1990s. Other national reform issues like marijuana regulation, affirmative action, same-sex marriage, and gambling brought inconsistent or delayed federal intervention and widespread state constitutional amendment.[15] Contemporary constitutional amendment belongs to the states.

Conclusion

The federal framers signed the Constitution in Philadelphia on September 17, 1787. The following July 4, Philadelphians celebrated the Constitution's ratification with a mile-long "Grand Federal Procession," led by a six-horse coach ornamented by a thirteen-foot gilded copy of the Constitution held by an eagle bearing the phrase "THE PEOPLE." Boston, Baltimore, Charleston, and New York hosted similar parades. A schoolbook printed eight years later declared the Constitution "the greatest by far that any people ever had; and it can scarcely be expected that any ever should be greater." That same year—1796—the original Constitution was placed under the care of Secretary of State Thomas Jefferson and then deposited in Treasury Department storerooms. On the eve of British occupation of Washington in August 1814, three government clerks spirited the Constitution in a linen sack across the Potomac to a Virginia gristmill. It later was returned to a Treasury Department archive, then placed in the Washington Orphan Asylum, and finally in a secured State Department storage basement. After a transfer to a Library of Congress cellar in 1921 and to Fort Knox during the Second World War, the document was brought back to Washington, DC, sealed in a bulletproof case, and escorted down Pennsylvania Avenue by two tanks and a detachment of four servicemen bearing submachine guns. The Constitution was interred in the vast, dim rotunda of the National Archives Building, flanked by the Declaration of Independence and Bill of Rights, where it has since remained under armed guard in a bomb-proof vault that nightly descends into the floor.[16]

The Constitution is nearly untouchable. For nearly two and a half centuries, Americans have avoided amending or fundamentally reinterpreting the Constitution. Scholars attribute the Constitution's stability to Article V, to the rarity of national partisan and legislative realignment, to Supreme Court gradualism, and to popular veneration. These accounts focus mainly or exclusively on national political institutions, often ignoring the hundreds of state constitutions and thousands of state amendments.

This book argues that through conflict decentralization, state constitutional reform guides and stabilizes national political development. Specifically, reformers thwarted by Article V or entrenched federal judges may instead attempt state constitutional revision. Regular, ongoing state constitutional reform resolves national controversies, deterring radical federal amendment and judicial review. State constitutional instability secures federal stability.

I suggest that conflict decentralization can take several paths. Congressional party development follows punctuated equilibrium, with extended periods of party parity in Congress discouraging Article V amendment. Long stretches of congressional parity and federal court gradualism affect state constitutionalism in a few ways. Congressional or federal judicial debate, if followed by inaction, can channel reformers to the states, a case of deference, in which constitutional reform occurs only at the state level. State debate and experimentation can yield convergence, elevating a constitutional issue to the federal level, allowing federal imitation by amendment, statute, or court ruling. States may also obviate federal reform entirely, precluding federal reform debates or, if federal debate occurs, circumventing federal actors to unilaterally address national concerns. Cases of preclusion are akin to the dog that did not bark, revealing in state constitutional debates those nationally salient issues largely absent in congressional and federal judicial records and therefore often ignored. Importantly, in each of these cases—deference, convergence, preclusion, and circumvention—active state constitutionalism resolves national issues for federal actors. Not all cases follow this pattern. Deference also allows divergence, conflict, and dysfunction in state constitutionalism, requiring federal intervention. Similarly, federal debate may incite active dictation of state policy. And federal actors may frame some national constitutional issues in ways that entirely preempt state intervention. But even in these cases, state constitutional reform shapes the choices of federal actors.

Conflict decentralization follows different paths in different eras. Since the power and cohesiveness of national party coalitions vary over time, so too do patterns of conflict decentralization. National party parity and gridlock encourage federal deference to the states, state experimentation, and convergence and federal imitation of state policy, while periods of one-party dominance allow federal dictation and intervention against divergent state policy. Since these coalition conditions vary cyclically, we similarly see long periods of passive federal deference and convergence give way to moments of active federal dictation and intervention against state constitutionalism.

The book defends this claim in several parts. It first notes how Revolutionary-era state constitutional framing settled national debates over slavery, frontier regulation, and legislative sovereignty and unicameralism, quieting these issues at the federal Constitutional Convention and subsequent ratifying conventions. The book then recounts how state constitutional reform stabilized the young Constitution. The antebellum era, with a weaker federal government and an emerging party system, was one of deference to state constitutionalism. Left by Congress to their own devices, Northern state framers abolished slavery, and Southern ones protected it, maintaining a peaceful, though unjust, bisectional compromise and preventing congressional intervention or a national amendment addressing slavery. Similarly, while Jeffersonian congressmen proposed national amendments regulating elections, state framers enfranchised almost all adult white males, disenfranchising all others, and selected House members by single districts and presidential electors by popularly selected general ticket, deferring federal suffrage and electoral reform. Successful state constitutional regulation made Jeffersonian and Jacksonian deference and strict constructionism a viable ideological position. And after the states passed comprehensive constitutional provisions regulating local banks, the antebellum Congress abandoned fiscal-reform amendments.

The Civil War era saw divergence yield to dictation and convergence. Fracturing national coalitions and continued congressional deference on slavery allowed divergent, clashing state slavery law, failed federal dictation under *Dred Scot,* and the Civil War. This brought presidential Reconstruction and federal dictation of state constitutional law. Consequent Reconstruction-era state constitutional conventions resolved national debates in favor of uncompensated abolition and expanded Black citizenship and enfranchisement, helping congressmen pass the later Reconstruction Amendments and ensuring swift ratification by the states. Even during congressional Reconstruction, at the height of federal power, dictation mixed with convergence. These many, detailed state clauses dovetailed with and strengthened the brief and ambiguous federal Reconstruction Amendments, guiding national constitutional reform.

As Republican majorities waned at the nineteenth century's end, and as Reconstruction faded with them, Congress and the courts again released their grip on the states, beginning the Progressive years. The era was one of federal deference and of state constitutional experimentation, circumvention of federal lawmaking, and sometimes convergent state policy guiding the framing of national amendments. Progressive social movements intentionally took the latter path. Reformist academics, lawmakers, civil servants, and organizers, their Article V amendments blocked by a conservative Senate and their litigation campaigns thwarted by an inflexible Supreme Court, sought state constitutional reform. The states' popular referenda, initiatives, and smaller legislatures and constitutional conventions, with their radical third parties, invited change, especially in the West, Midwest, and South, where reformers tested income tax and direct-election schemes and rallied voters to female enfranchisement and prohibition proposals. This pattern of deference and then convergence allowed Congress to pass Article V amendments for the income tax, direct Senate election, female enfranchisement, and prohibition and repeal. State constitutional regulation of other issues, like polygamy, parochial school funding, Jim Crow, and child labor, largely blocked or obviated active federal constitutional reform in these areas. The era emphasized cooperative reform, with state constitutional revision often narrowing, guiding, and legitimizing options for federal amendment.

The New Deal and Great Society years, bringing commanding Democratic congressional and federal judicial majorities, let federal actors steer state constitutional reform. Recalling the failure of the prohibition and child labor amendments, New Deal and Great Society Congresses reworked the Constitution by statute rather than amendment. Alongside this federal statutory reform, the states proposed and passed dozens of constitutions and thousands of amendments, constitutionally protecting workers' wages, hours, and labor conditions and unemployment, disability, and old-age benefits, guiding the drafters of the Social Security Act. The act mixed federal dictation of state pension policy with imitation of convergent state policy. This cooperative constitutional federalism earned approval from the Supreme Court and deterred confrontational court-constraining amendments and statutes. State legislators and framers repealed poll taxes and at federal behest addressed literacy tests, legislative malapportionment, and youth disenfranchisement while selectively guaranteeing gender equality, guiding and narrowing debates over the Twenty-Fourth Amendment, and discouraging ratification of the proposed Equal Rights Amendment. Reagan, elected by conservative Southern and Sunbelt suburbanites to roll back federal authority, opened the modern era, which has largely been one of federal constitutional inaction, deference, and state constitutional experimentation by amendment.

The introduction to this book offered four lessons on American constitutional development. I revisit them here. First, national partisan and coalition realignments shape patterns in conflict decentralization. Long periods of congressional party parity and federal judicial nonintervention allow federal deference to state constitutionalism, state constitutional experimentation, and occasional state constitutional convergence. Rarer are the electoral realignments that allow one party momentary bicameral congressional supermajorities and the power to reform national constitutionalism by amendment, super-statute, or judicial review. These moments can also allow federal dictation of state policy and intervention against divergent state policy. The logic of conflict decentralization, following that of national coalition realignment, is therefore cyclical, with long stretches of federal passivity, deference, and occasional state convergence interrupted by periodic moments of active federal dictation against divergent states. But state constitutionalism, precluding or delaying nationally salient issues from reaching Congress or the federal bench, can also delay national partisan realignment. State constitutional reform and congressional party development affect each other in ways we have missed.

Second, I suggest that state constitutional reform sometimes causes national outcomes that scholars may attribute to national political actors or institutions. The example given in the introduction, elaborated in chapter 6, was poll tax repeal. Congress forbade state poll taxes under the Twenty-Fourth Amendment of 1964 and Voting Rights Act of 1965, which the Supreme Court affirmed in *Harper v. Virginia Board of Elections* in 1966. Subsequently, all states abandoned the poll tax. This poll tax abolition occurred *after* federal dictation but not *because of* federal dictation. By *Harper,* all but four states had already constitutionally or statutorily outlawed the poll tax, thanks to pressure from New Deal state lawmakers and local NAACP chapters. These reformers, rebuffed by Congress, the Department of Justice, and the Supreme Court, fought for and won state constitutional poll tax repeal with little federal help, instead organizing local, grassroots campaigns in the 1930s, 1940s, and 1950s. The Twenty-Fourth Amendment, VRA, and *Harper* are significant moral achievements, victories for suffrage expansion and hedges against state-level franchise rollback. But they are largely not responsible for initiating poll tax repeal in the United States, and to describe them as such while ignoring state constitutionalism is to misunderstand them and to overlook the work of state reformers.

Third, by comparing state and federal constitutional amendments, we can better understand the passage and ratification of federal amendments. The Twenty-Fourth Amendment, empowering Congress to forbid states from disenfranchising persons on the basis of fixed characteristics, in this case wealth and race, is textually nearly identical to the Fifteenth, Nineteenth, and Twenty-Sixth Amendments, which let Congress void state disenfranchisement on the basis of race, gender, and age. But this textual similarity masks different, somewhat opposed patterns in amendment ratification and expansion of congressional power. The ratification of the Nineteenth and Twenty-Fourth Amendments followed patterns of deference and convergence, in which Congress let states address and ultimately converge on repeal of gender and poll tax disenfranchisement, encouraging corresponding federal amendments. Conversely, the states diverged and lagged in their efforts at racial and age disenfranchisement, forcing Congress to dictate and overrule state constitutional clauses with the Fifteenth and Twenty-Sixth Amendments. Though textually similar to the Nineteenth and Twenty-Fourth Amendments, the Fifteenth and Twenty-Sixth Amendments operate differently when understood alongside comparable state clauses. Reading the federal amendments through accompanying state reform helps us better understand the evolution and meaning of the Constitution.

This book offers a final lesson, this one for political and constitutional theorists. Conflict decentralization helps overcome national constitutional dysfunction. Liberal constitutions face a dilemma. These constitutions invoke popular sovereignty but impose amendment supermajority requirements that impede democratic reform. The U.S. Constitution sets exceptionally high bars to amendment, entrusting amendment proposal and ratification not to ordinary voters but to elected legislators and convention delegates. In contrast, the state constitutions encourage democratic reform. Americans revise their state constitutions through initiatives, referenda, conventions, and commissions that set lower thresholds for reform. Conventions have ranged from summits between former presidents and federal framers to nighttime meetings of farmers and pioneers in frontier taverns. These state constitutions, unlike their federal counterpart, are democratically responsive. Through the states, Americans secure popular sovereignty.

APPENDIX A: STATE CONSTITUTIONAL REVISION ASSEMBLIES, 1776–2020

State	Duration	Procedure	Limited agenda	Popular vote	Proposal passage	Ratification outcome	Source
AK	1949	Commission: preparatory	Yes	No	No	None	G
	1955	Commission: preparatory	Yes	No	No	None	B
	1955–56	Convention	No	Yes	Yes	Constitution	G
	1979–80	Legislature	Yes	No	No	None	B
	1980–81	Legislature	Yes	No	No	None	B
	1993–95	Commission: study	No	No	No	None	B
AL	1819	Convention	No	No	Yes	Constitution	B
	1861	Convention	No	No	Yes	Constitution	O
	1865	Convention	No	No	Yes	Constitution	T
	1868	Convention	No	Yes	Yes	Constitution	O
	1875	Convention	No	Yes	Yes	Constitution	O
	1901	Convention	No	No	Yes	Constitution	O
	1969–76	Commission: study	Yes	Yes	Yes	Amendment(s)	B
	1978	Commission: study	No	No	No	None	B
	2003	Commission: study	Yes	Yes	Yes	Amendment(s)	B
	2011–13	Commission: study	Yes	Yes	Yes	Amendment(s)	B

State	Duration	Procedure	Limited agenda	Popular vote	Proposal passage	Ratification outcome	Source
AR	1836	Convention	No	No	Yes	Constitution	T
	1861	Convention	No	No	Yes	Constitution	T
	1864	Convention	No	Yes	Yes	Constitution	T
	1868	Convention	No	Yes	Yes	Constitution	T
	1874	Convention	No	Yes	Yes	Constitution	T
	1917–18	Convention	No	Yes	No	None	G
	1967–68	Commission: study	Yes	No	No	None	O
	1968–69	Commission: preparatory	Yes	No	No	None	S
	1969–70	Convention	No	Yes	No	None	G
	1974–75	Commission: study	Yes	No	No	None	O
	1978–80	Convention	No	Yes	No	None	G
	1978	Commission: preparatory	Yes	No	No	None	B
	1995	Commission: study	No	Yes	No	None	B
AZ	1860	Convention	No	No	No	None	O
	1891	Convention	No	Yes	No	None	G
	1911	Convention	No	Yes	Yes	Constitution	G
CA	1849	Convention	No	Yes	Yes	Constitution	T
	1878–79	Convention	No	Yes	Yes	Constitution	T
	1929–30	Commission: study	No	No	No	None	G
	1947–49	Legislature	No	Yes	Yes	Amendment(s)	O
	1959–61	Commission: study	Yes	Yes	Yes	Amendment(s)	O
	1959–60	Commission: study	Yes	Yes	Yes	Amendment(s)	O
	1962–74	Commission: study	No	Yes	Yes	Amendment(s)	O
	1994–97	Commission: study	Yes	No	No	None	O
CO	1859	Convention	No	Yes	No	None	G
	1859	Convention	No	Yes	Yes	None	G
	1864	Convention	No	Yes	No	None	O

State	Duration	Procedure	Limited agenda	Popular vote	Proposal passage	Ratification outcome	Source
	1865	Convention	No	Yes	Yes	None	O
	1875–76	Convention	No	Yes	Yes	Constitution	T
CT	1776	Legislature	No	No	Yes	Amendment(s)	G
	1818	Convention	No	Yes	Yes	Constitution	T
	1902	Convention	No	Yes	No	None	G
	1965	Commission: preparatory	Yes	No	No	None	S
	1965	Convention	Yes	Yes	Yes	Constitution	G
DE	1776	Convention	No	No	Yes	Constitution	T
	1792	Convention	No	No	Yes	Constitution	T
	1831	Convention	No	No	Yes	Constitution	T
	1852–53	Convention	No	Yes	No	None	G
	1896–97	Convention	No	No	Yes	Constitution	G
	1967–70	Commission: study	Yes	No	No	None	G
FL	1838–39	Convention	No	No	Yes	Constitution	T
	1861	Convention	No	No	Yes	Constitution	T
	1865	Convention	No	No	Yes	Constitution	T
	1868	Convention	No	Yes	Yes	Constitution	T
	1885–86	Convention	No	Yes	Yes	Constitution	T
	1954–55	Commission: study	Yes	No	No	None	S
	1955–57	Commission: study	No	Yes	No	None	G
	1958–59	Commission: study	Yes	No	No	None	B
	1965–68	Commission: study	Yes	Yes	Yes	Constitution	G
	1977–78	Commission: study	Yes	Yes	No	None	O
	1990	Commission: study	Yes	Yes	Yes	Amendment(s)	B
	1997–98	Commission: study	Yes	Yes	Yes	Amendment(s)	O
	2008	Commission: study	Yes	Yes	Yes	Amendment(s)	B

State	Duration	Procedure	Limited agenda	Popular vote	Proposal passage	Ratification outcome	Source
	2017–18	Commission: study	Yes	Yes	Yes	Amendment(s)	O
GA	1776–77	Convention	No	No	Yes	Constitution	T
	1788	Convention	No	No	No	None	T
	1789	Convention	No	No	No	None	T
	1789	Convention	No	No	Yes	Constitution	T
	1795	Convention	No	No	Yes	Amendment(s)	O
	1798	Convention	No	No	Yes	Constitution	G
	1833	Convention	No	Yes	No	None	O
	1839	Convention	No	Yes	No	None	O
	1861	Convention	No	Yes	Yes	Constitution	T
	1865	Convention	No	Yes	Yes	Constitution	T
	1867–68	Convention	No	Yes	Yes	Constitution	T
	1877	Convention	No	Yes	Yes	Constitution	G
	1943–45	Commission: study	No	Yes	Yes	Constitution	G
	1963–64	Commission: study	No	No	No	None	G
	1969–70	Commission: study	Yes	No	No	None	G
	1975–76	Legislature	Yes	Yes	Yes	Constitution	G
	1977–82	Commission: study	Yes	Yes	Yes	Constitution	G
HI	1950	Convention	No	Yes	Yes	Constitution	G
	1968	Convention	No	Yes	Yes	Amendment(s)	B
	1978	Convention	No	Yes	Yes	Amendment(s)	G
IA	1844	Convention	No	Yes	No	None	G
	1846	Convention	No	Yes	Yes	Constitution	G
	1857	Convention	No	Yes	Yes	Constitution	G
ID	1889	Convention	No	Yes	Yes	Constitution	G
	1965–70	Commission: study	Yes	Yes	No	None	G
IL	1818	Convention	No	No	Yes	Constitution	T
	1848	Convention	No	Yes	Yes	Constitution	T
	1862	Convention	No	Yes	No	None	G
	1869–70	Convention	No	Yes	Yes	Constitution	T
	1920–22	Convention	No	Yes	No	None	G

State	Duration	Procedure	Limited agenda	Popular vote	Proposal passage	Ratification outcome	Source
	1949–50	Commission: study	Yes	Yes	Yes	Amendment(s)	B
	1965–67	Commission: study	No	No	No	None	S
	1967–69	Commission: preparatory	Yes	No	No	None	B
	1969–70	Convention	No	Yes	Yes	Constitution	G
IN	1816	Convention	No	No	Yes	Constitution	G
	1850–51	Convention	No	Yes	Yes	Constitution	G
	1967–72	Commission: study	No	Yes	Yes	Amendment(s)	S
KS	1855	Convention	No	Yes	Yes	None	T
	1857	Convention	No	Yes	Yes	None	T
	1858	Convention	No	Yes	Yes	None	T
	1859	Convention	No	Yes	Yes	Constitution	T
	1957–61	Commission: study	No	No	No	None	B
	1961–63	Commission: study	No	Yes	Yes	Amendment(s)	G
	1968–69	Commission: study	Yes	Yes	Yes	Amendment(s)	O
KY	1792	Convention	No	No	Yes	Constitution	T
	1799	Convention	No	No	Yes	Constitution	T
	1849–50	Convention	No	Yes	Yes	Constitution	T
	1890–91	Convention	No	Yes	Yes	Constitution	G
	1953–56	Commission: study	Yes	Yes	No	None	G
	1960	Commission: study	No	Yes	No	None	G
	1964–66	Commission: study	No	Yes	No	None	G
	1978	Commission: study	Yes	No	No	None	B
	1987	Commission: study	Yes	Yes	Yes	Amendment(s)	O
LA	1812	Convention	No	No	Yes	Constitution	T
	1845	Convention	No	Yes	Yes	Constitution	T

State	Duration	Procedure	Limited agenda	Popular vote	Proposal passage	Ratification outcome	Source
	1852	Convention	No	Yes	Yes	Constitution	T
	1861	Convention	No	No	Yes	Constitution	T
	1864	Convention	No	Yes	Yes	Constitution	T
	1867–68	Convention	No	Yes	Yes	Constitution	T
	1879	Convention	No	Yes	Yes	Constitution	T
	1898	Convention	No	No	Yes	Constitution	G
	1913	Convention	No	No	Yes	Constitution	G
	1921	Convention	No	No	Yes	Constitution	G
	1970–72	Commission: study	No	Yes	Yes	Amendment(s)	B
	1973–74	Convention	Yes	Yes	Yes	Constitution	G
	1992	Convention	Yes	Yes	No	None	O
MA	1778	Convention	No	Yes	No	None	G
	1779–80	Convention	No	Yes	Yes	Constitution	G
	1820–21	Convention	No	Yes	Yes	Amendment(s)	G
	1853	Convention	No	Yes	No	None	G
	1917–19	Convention	No	Yes	Yes	Amendment(s)	G
	1917	Commission: preparatory	Yes	No	No	None	O
	1962–67	Commission: study	Yes	Yes	Yes	Amendment(s)	G
MD	1776	Convention	No	No	Yes	Constitution	T
	1850–51	Convention	No	Yes	Yes	Constitution	T
	1864	Convention	No	Yes	Yes	Constitution	T
	1867	Convention	No	Yes	Yes	Constitution	T
	1965–67	Commission: study	No	Yes	No	None	S
	1967–68	Convention	Yes	Yes	No	None	G
ME	1819	Convention	No	Yes	Yes	Constitution	T
	1875	Commission: study	Yes	Yes	Yes	Amendment(s)	G
	1948–49	Legislature	No	Yes	Yes	Amendment(s)	O
	1961–63	Commission: study	No	Yes	Yes	Amendment(s)	O
	1965	Legislature	Yes	No	No	None	G
MI	1835	Convention	No	Yes	Yes	Constitution	T
	1850	Convention	No	Yes	Yes	Constitution	G

State	Duration	Procedure	Limited agenda	Popular vote	Proposal passage	Ratification outcome	Source
	1867	Convention	No	Yes	No	None	G
	1873	Commission: study	No	Yes	No	None	G
	1907–08	Convention	No	Yes	Yes	Constitution	G
	1938	Commission: preparatory	Yes	No	No	None	G
	1941–42	Commission: study	No	Yes	No	None	G
	1960–61	Commission: study	Yes	Yes	No	None	S
	1961–63	Convention	No	Yes	Yes	Constitution	S
	1961	Commission: preparatory	Yes	No	No	None	S
	1961	Commission: study	No	Yes	No	None	S
MN	1857	Convention	No	Yes	Yes	Constitution	G
	1947–48	Commission: study	Yes	Yes	Yes	Amendment(s)	O
	1962	Commission: study	Yes	No	No	None	S
	1971–72	Commission: study	Yes	Yes	Yes	Amendment(s)	G
MO	1820	Convention	No	No	Yes	Constitution	G
	1845–46	Convention	No	Yes	No	None	T
	1861–63	Convention	No	Yes	Yes	None	T
	1865	Convention	No	Yes	Yes	Constitution	T
	1875	Convention	No	Yes	Yes	Constitution	T
	1922–23	Convention	No	Yes	Yes	Amendment(s)	O
	1943–45	Convention	No	Yes	Yes	Constitution	O
	1961–62	Commission: study	No	Yes	No	None	S
MS	1817	Convention	No	Yes	Yes	Constitution	T
	1832	Convention	No	Yes	Yes	Constitution	T
	1851	Convention	No	No	No	None	O
	1861	Convention	No	No	No	None	O
	1865	Convention	No	No	No	None	O
	1869	Convention	No	Yes	Yes	Constitution	T

State	Duration	Procedure	Limited agenda	Popular vote	Proposal passage	Ratification outcome	Source
	1890	Convention	No	No	Yes	Constitution	O
	1985–86	Commission: study	Yes	No	No	None	G
MT	1866	Convention	No	No	No	None	G
	1884	Convention	No	Yes	Yes	None	G
	1889	Convention	No	Yes	Yes	Constitution	G
	1967–68	Legislature	Yes	No	No	None	G
	1969–71	Commission: study	Yes	No	No	None	B
	1971–72	Convention	No	Yes	Yes	Constitution	G
	1971	Commission: preparatory	Yes	No	No	None	G
NC	1776	Convention	No	No	Yes	Constitution	T
	1823	Convention	Yes	No	No	None	O
	1835	Convention	No	Yes	Yes	Amendment(s)	G
	1861–62	Convention	No	No	No	None	T
	1865–66	Convention	No	Yes	No	None	T
	1868	Convention	No	Yes	Yes	Constitution	T
	1875	Convention	Yes	Yes	Yes	Amendment(s)	G
	1912–13	Commission: study	Yes	Yes	No	None	O
	1932–33	Commission: study	No	No	No	None	G
	1958–59	Commission: study	Yes	No	No	None	G
	1968–70	Commission: study	Yes	Yes	Yes	Constitution	G
ND	1889	Convention	No	Yes	Yes	Constitution	T
	1963–66	Legislature	No	Yes	No	None	B
	1971–72	Convention	No	Yes	No	None	G
	1975	Commission: study	No	No	No	None	B
	1977	Commission: study	No	No	No	None	B
NE	1864	Convention	No	No	No	None	G
	1866	Legislature	No	Yes	Yes	Constitution	T
	1871	Convention	No	Yes	No	None	G

State	Duration	Procedure	Limited agenda	Popular vote	Proposal passage	Ratification outcome	Source
	1875	Convention	No	Yes	Yes	Constitution	T
	1919–20	Convention	No	Yes	Yes	Amendment(s)	G
	1967–68	Legislature	Yes	Yes	Yes	Amendment(s)	S
	1969–70	Commission: study	Yes	Yes	Yes	Amendment(s)	G
	1995–97	Commission: study	Yes	Yes	Yes	Amendment(s)	O
NH	1776	Convention	No	No	Yes	Constitution	T
	1778–79	Convention	No	Yes	No	None	T
	1781–84	Convention	No	Yes	Yes	Constitution	T
	1791–92	Convention	No	Yes	Yes	Amendment(s)	G
	1850–51	Convention	No	Yes	Yes	Amendment(s)	G
	1876	Convention	No	Yes	Yes	Amendment(s)	G
	1889	Convention	No	Yes	Yes	Amendment(s)	G
	1902	Convention	No	Yes	Yes	Amendment(s)	G
	1912	Convention	No	Yes	Yes	Amendment(s)	G
	1918–23	Convention	No	Yes	No	None	G
	1930	Convention	No	Yes	Yes	None	G
	1938–41	Convention	No	Yes	Yes	Amendment(s)	G
	1948	Convention	No	Yes	Yes	Amendment(s)	G
	1956–59	Convention	No	Yes	Yes	Amendment(s)	G
	1963–64	Commission: study	Yes	No	No	None	S
	1964	Convention	No	Yes	Yes	Amendment(s)	G
	1971	Commission: study	Yes	No	No	None	B
	1973–74	Commission: study	No	No	No	None	B
	1974	Convention	No	Yes	Yes	Amendment(s)	G
	1983–84	Convention	Yes	Yes	Yes	Amendment(s)	G
	1984	Commission: study	No	Yes	Yes	Amendment(s)	B
NJ	1776	Convention	No	No	Yes	Constitution	G
	1844	Convention	No	Yes	Yes	Constitution	T
	1852	Commission: study	Yes	No	No	None	O

State	Duration	Procedure	Limited agenda	Popular vote	Proposal passage	Ratification outcome	Source
	1854	Commission: study	Yes	No	No	None	O
	1873	Commission: study	No	Yes	Yes	Amendment(s)	O
	1881–82	Commission: study	No	No	No	None	O
	1894	Commission: study	Yes	No	No	None	O
	1905	Commission: study	Yes	Yes	No	None	O
	1941–42	Commission: study	No	No	No	None	O
	1943–44	Commission: study	No	Yes	No	None	O
	1947	Convention	Yes	Yes	Yes	Constitution	O
	1966	Convention	Yes	Yes	Yes	Amendment(s)	O
NM	1848	Convention	No	No	No	None	O
	1849	Convention	No	No	No	None	O
	1850	Convention	No	Yes	Yes	None	G
	1872	Convention	No	Yes	No	None	G
	1889–90	Convention	No	Yes	No	None	G
	1907	Convention	No	No	No	None	O
	1910–11	Convention	No	Yes	Yes	Constitution	G
	1963–66	Commission: study	No	Yes	Yes	Amendment(s)	G
	1969	Convention	No	Yes	No	None	G
	1993–95	Commission: study	No	Yes	Yes	Amendment(s)	B
NV	1859	Convention	No	No	No	None	G
	1863	Convention	No	Yes	No	None	G
	1864	Convention	No	Yes	Yes	Constitution	G
NY	1776–77	Convention	No	No	Yes	Constitution	T
	1801	Convention	Yes	No	Yes	Amendment(s)	G
	1821	Convention	No	Yes	Yes	Constitution	G
	1846	Convention	No	Yes	Yes	Constitution	T
	1867–68	Convention	No	Yes	Yes	Amendment(s)	G

State	Duration	Procedure	Limited agenda	Popular vote	Proposal passage	Ratification outcome	Source
	1872	Commission: study	No	Yes	Yes	Amendment(s)	O
	1875	Commission: study	Yes	No	No	None	O
	1890–91	Commission: study	Yes	No	No	None	O
	1894	Convention	No	Yes	Yes	Constitution	T
	1915	Convention	No	Yes	Yes	Amendment(s)	G
	1921	Commission: study	No	Yes	Yes	Amendment(s)	G
	1936	Commission: preparatory	Yes	No	No	None	O
	1938	Convention	No	Yes	Yes	Amendment(s)	G
	1956–58	Commission: study	No	Yes	No	None	O
	1958	Commission: study	Yes	Yes	Yes	Amendment(s)	G
	1959–61	Commission: study	No	Yes	Yes	Amendment(s)	G
	1965–67	Commission: preparatory	Yes	No	No	None	S
	1967	Convention	No	Yes	No	None	S
	1993–95	Commission: preparatory	Yes	No	No	None	O
	1997–98	Commission: study	No	Yes	Yes	Amendment(s)	B
OH	1802	Convention	No	No	Yes	Constitution	T
	1850–51	Convention	No	Yes	Yes	Constitution	G
	1873–74	Convention	No	Yes	No	None	G
	1912	Convention	No	Yes	Yes	Amendment(s)	G
	1969–77	Commission: study	Yes	Yes	Yes	Amendment(s)	G
	2011–17	Commission: study	Yes	Yes	Yes	Amendment(s)	B
OK	1906–07	Convention	No	Yes	Yes	Constitution	G
	1947–48	Commission: study	No	Yes	No	None	O

State	Duration	Procedure	Limited agenda	Popular vote	Proposal passage	Ratification outcome	Source
	1968	Commission: study	Yes	No	No	None	O
	1969	Commission: study	Yes	Yes	No	None	O
	1988–89	Commission: study	Yes	Yes	Yes	Amendment(s)	O
OR	1857	Convention	No	Yes	Yes	Constitution	T
	1953–54	Commission: preparatory	Yes	No	No	None	S
	1961–63	Commission: study	No	No	No	None	O
	1969–70	Legislature	Yes	Yes	No	None	O
PA	1776	Convention	No	No	Yes	Constitution	T
	1789–90	Convention	No	No	Yes	Constitution	T
	1837–38	Convention	No	Yes	Yes	Constitution	T
	1872–73	Convention	No	Yes	Yes	Constitution	T
	1918–20	Commission: study	No	Yes	No	None	O
	1935	Commission: study	No	Yes	No	None	O
	1957–59	Commission: study	Yes	Yes	No	None	S
	1963–64	Commission: study	No	Yes	Yes	Amendment(s)	O
	1967–68	Commission: preparatory	Yes	No	No	None	S
	1967–68	Convention	No	Yes	Yes	Constitution	G
RI	1776	Legislature	No	No	Yes	Amendment(s)	T
	1824	Convention	No	Yes	No	None	G
	1834	Convention	No	No	No	None	G
	1841	Convention	No	Yes	Yes	None	G
	1841	Convention	No	Yes	No	None	G
	1842	Convention	No	Yes	Yes	Constitution	G
	1882	Legislature	No	No	No	None	G
	1896–99	Commission: study	Yes	Yes	No	None	G

State	Duration	Procedure	Limited agenda	Popular vote	Proposal passage	Ratification outcome	Source
	1912–15	Commission: study	No	No	No	None	G
	1944	Convention	Yes	Yes	Yes	Amendment(s)	G
	1951	Convention	Yes	Yes	Yes	Amendment(s)	G
	1955	Convention	Yes	Yes	Yes	Amendment(s)	G
	1958	Convention	Yes	Yes	Yes	Amendment(s)	G
	1962	Commission: study	No	Yes	No	None	G
	1964–69	Convention	No	Yes	No	None	G
	1973	Convention	Yes	Yes	Yes	Amendment(s)	G
	1982–83	Commission: preparatory	Yes	No	No	None	B
	1986	Convention	Yes	Yes	Yes	Constitution	G
	2004	Commission: study	Yes	Yes	No	None	O
SC	1776	Legislature	No	No	Yes	Constitution	T
	1778	Legislature	No	No	Yes	Constitution	T
	1790	Convention	No	No	Yes	Constitution	T
	1861	Convention	No	No	Yes	Constitution	T
	1865	Convention	No	No	Yes	Constitution	T
	1868	Convention	No	Yes	Yes	Constitution	T
	1895	Convention	No	No	Yes	Constitution	G
	1948–51	Commission: study	No	No	No	None	S
	1966–69	Commission: study	No	Yes	Yes	Amendment(s)	B
SD	1883	Convention	No	Yes	Yes	None	G
	1885	Convention	No	Yes	Yes	None	G
	1889	Convention	No	Yes	Yes	Constitution	T
	1969–76	Commission: study	Yes	Yes	Yes	Amendment(s)	B
	2004–07	Commission: study	Yes	Yes	Yes	Amendment(s)	B
TN	1796	Convention	No	No	Yes	Constitution	T
	1834–35	Convention	No	Yes	Yes	Constitution	T
	1870	Convention	No	Yes	Yes	Constitution	G

State	Duration	Procedure	Limited agenda	Popular vote	Proposal passage	Ratification outcome	Source
	1945–46	Commission: study	No	No	No	None	B
	1953	Convention	Yes	Yes	Yes	Amendment(s)	G
	1959	Convention	Yes	Yes	Yes	Amendment(s)	G
	1965	Convention	Yes	Yes	Yes	Amendment(s)	G
	1971	Convention	Yes	Yes	Yes	Amendment(s)	G
	1977	Convention	Yes	Yes	Yes	Amendment(s)	G
TX	1845	Convention	No	Yes	Yes	Constitution	T
	1861	Convention	No	Yes	Yes	Constitution	T
	1866	Convention	No	Yes	Yes	Constitution	T
	1869	Convention	No	Yes	Yes	Constitution	T
	1874	Legislature	No	No	No	None	O
	1876	Convention	No	Yes	Yes	Constitution	T
	1957–59	Commission: study	No	No	No	None	B
	1967–68	Commission: study	No	Yes	Yes	Amendment(s)	G
	1973–74	Commission: study	Yes	No	No	None	B
	1974	Convention	Yes	Yes	No	None	G
UT	1849	Convention	No	No	No	None	O
	1856	Convention	No	No	No	None	O
	1862	Convention	No	No	No	None	O
	1872	Convention	No	Yes	Yes	None	O
	1882	Convention	No	Yes	Yes	None	O
	1887	Convention	No	No	No	None	O
	1895	Convention	No	Yes	Yes	Constitution	G
	1969–2011	Commission: study	Yes	Yes	Yes	Amendment(s)	B
VA	1776	Convention	No	No	Yes	Constitution	T
	1829–30	Convention	No	Yes	Yes	Constitution	T
	1850–51	Convention	No	Yes	Yes	Constitution	T
	1861	Convention	No	No	No	None	T
	1864	Convention	No	Yes	Yes	None	G
	1869	Convention	No	Yes	Yes	Constitution	G
	1901–02	Convention	No	No	Yes	Constitution	O

State	Duration	Procedure	Limited agenda	Popular vote	Proposal passage	Ratification outcome	Source
	1927–28	Commission: study	Yes	Yes	Yes	Amendment(s)	G
	1945	Convention	Yes	No	Yes	Amendment(s)	G
	1956	Convention	Yes	No	Yes	Amendment(s)	G
	1970–71	Commission: study	Yes	Yes	Yes	Constitution	G
VT	1777	Convention	No	No	Yes	Constitution	T
	1786	Convention	No	No	Yes	Constitution	T
	1793	Convention	No	No	Yes	Constitution	G
	1814	Convention	Yes	No	No	None	G
	1822	Convention	Yes	No	No	None	G
	1828	Convention	Yes	No	Yes	Amendment(s)	G
	1836	Convention	Yes	No	No	None	G
	1843	Convention	Yes	No	No	None	G
	1850	Convention	Yes	No	Yes	Amendment(s)	G
	1857	Convention	Yes	No	No	None	G
	1870	Convention	Yes	No	Yes	Amendment(s)	G
	1910–13	Commission: study	No	Yes	Yes	Amendment(s)	O
	1949–50	Commission: study	Yes	No	No	None	S
	1959–60	Commission: study	Yes	Yes	Yes	Amendment(s)	S
	1968–71	Commission: study	Yes	Yes	No	None	B
WA	1878	Convention	No	Yes	Yes	None	O
	1889	Convention	No	Yes	Yes	Constitution	T
	1933–34	Commission: study	No	No	No	None	S
	1965–66	Commission: study	No	No	No	None	B
	1968–69	Commission: study	No	No	No	None	B
	1975–76	Commission: study	No	Yes	No	None	B
WI	1846	Convention	No	Yes	No	None	G
	1847–48	Convention	No	Yes	Yes	Constitution	G

State	Duration	Procedure	Limited agenda	Popular vote	Proposal passage	Ratification outcome	Source
	1960	Commission: study	No	No	No	None	S
	1964–65	Commission: study	Yes	Yes	Yes	Amendment(s)	B
WV	1861–63	Convention	No	Yes	Yes	Constitution	T
	1861	Convention	No	No	No	None	G
	1861	Convention	No	No	No	None	G
	1872	Convention	No	Yes	Yes	Constitution	G
	1929	Commission: study	No	Yes	Yes	Amendment(s)	G
	1957–61	Commission: study	No	Yes	Yes	Amendment(s)	B
	1963	Commission: study	No	Yes	Yes	Amendment(s)	B
WY	1889	Convention	No	Yes	Yes	Constitution	T

Note: "Popular vote" indicates whether the proposal was subject to a popular ratification vote.

Sources: B: Council of State Governments, *Book of the States* (1942–2019); G: Greenwood/Oxford Commentaries on the State Constitutions of the United States; O: other; S: Sturm, *Methods of State Constitutional Reform* (1954); *Thirty Years of State Constitution-Making* (1970); T: Thorpe, *Federal and State Constitutions* (1909).

APPENDIX B: STATE CONSTITUTIONS AND THE DECLARATION OF INDEPENDENCE, JANUARY–JULY 1776

Provisions	NH	NJ	SC	VA	US 1	US 2
Preamble						
Appeal to natural rights, law, and equality	X		X		X	X
Appeal to life, liberty, happiness, and/or property	X		X		X	X
Appeal to government by consent	X	X			X	X
Right to alter and abolish government		X			X	X
Right to institute new government	X	X			X	X
Abolition of government after long train of abuses		X		X	X	X
Grievances against the Crown and/or Parliament						
Refusing assent to laws				X	X	X
Suspending gubernatorial powers	X		X	X	X	X
Refusing legislative representation				X	X	X
Calling colonial legislatures at inconvenient times and places						X
Suspending colonial legislatures	X		X	X	X	X
Refusing elections, leaving colonies vulnerable				X	X	X
Refusing colonies' authority over naturalization and land				X	X	X
Refusing colonies' laws establishing courts					X	X
Controlling judges' salaries and tenure, suspending courts	X		X		X	X

Provisions	NH	NJ	SC	VA	US 1	US 2
Establishing new offices					X	X
Establishing armies without colonial legislative consent	X		X	X	X	X
Rendering military power superior to civil power	X		X	X	X	X
Subjecting colonists to Parliamentary jurisdiction				X	X	X
Quartering troops				X	X	X
Protecting troops and officers from colonial trial					X	X
Suspending colonial trade with foreign nations or each other	X		X	X	X	X
Imposing taxes without consent			X	X	X	X
Suspending jury trial			X	X	X	X
Requiring trial in Britain for colonists			X	X	X	X
Passing the Quebec Act of 1774			X			X
Suspending or altering colonial charters			X			X
Letting governors assume colonial legislatures' powers				X	X	X
Suspending government by declaring war against colonists		X			X	X
Making war against colonists' seas, coasts, and towns	X		X	X	X	X
Hiring foreign mercenaries				X	X	X
Imprisoning or impressing colonists into military service			X		X	X
Inciting domestic insurrection and Indian revolt			X	X	X	X
Inciting domestic insurrection by promising reward			X	X	X	
Prohibiting abolition of slavery and encouraging slave revolt			X	X	X	
Conclusion						
Petitions to the Crown unanswered			X	X	X	X
Petitions to the British people unanswered					X	X
Necessity of rebellion			X		X	X
Colonies declared independent					X	X
Renunciation of ties to the British		X		X	X	X
Appeal to reconciliation with Britain	X	X	X	X		

Note: US 1 indicates Jefferson's "original rough draught" Declaration, and US 2, the final Declaration.

APPENDIX C: STATE CONSTITUTIONAL SLAVERY AND RECONSTRUCTION CLAUSES, 1776–1877

	Antebellum: 1776–1861						Civil War–Reconstruction: 1862–1877			
	Slavery abolished	Slave trade abolished or regulated	Black or slave immigration regulated	No uncompensated abolition	Humane treatment of slaves required	Slave jury and due process rights	Slave taxation and representation	Slavery abolished	No compensated abolition	Universal adult male vote	Equal rights or protection under law
AL 1819		Art. VI S.§1	Art. VI S.§1	Art. VI S.§1	Art. VI S.§3	Art. VI S.§2					
AL 1861			Art. VI S.§3	Art. VI S.§1	Art. VI S.§§2, 5	Art. VI S.§4					
AL 1865								Art. I §34*			
AL 1867								Art. I §35*		Art. I §35	Art. I. §2
AL 1875								Art. I §33*		Art. I §36	Art. I. §2
AR 1836		Art. IV §25	Art. IV §23	Art. VII, S.§1	Art. IV §25	Art. IV §25				Art. I §§34, 38	
AR 1864								Art. V §1*			
AR 1868								Art. V. §37*	Art. V §38	Art. I §19	Art. I §3
AR 1874								Art. II §27*		Art. III §2	Art. II §3
CA 1849	Art. I §18*										
CO 1876								Art. II §26*		Art. II §5	
DE 1776		Art. XXVI									

FL 1839			Art. XVI §3				Art. IX §1		
FL 1861				Art. XVI §1		Art. IV §27			
FL 1865				Art. XV §1					
FL 1868								Art. XVI §1* Art. I §19*	Art. XV §1	Art. XVI §1 Art. XVII §28
GA 1798			Art. IV §11						
GA 1861			Art. II §7	Art. IV §11			Art. IX §1		
GA 1865				Art. II §7			Art. IV §22, Art. IX §1	Art. I §20*	Art. II §2
GA 1868					Art. IV §12	Art. II §7	Art. IX §1	Art. I §4	Art. II §1
GA 1877			Art. II §7				Art. I §7 (1843)	Art. I §1*	
IA 1846	Art. I §23*								
IA 1857	Art. I §23*								Art. II §1 (1868)
IL 1818	Art. VI §1*								
IL 1848	Art. XIII §16*	Art. XIV							
IL 1870										Art. VII §7
IN 1816	Art. VIII §1*								
IN 1851	Art. I §37*	Art. XIII §1								Art. I §2

	Antebellum: 1776–1861							Civil War-Reconstruction: 1862–1877			
	Slavery abolished	Slave trade abolished or regulated	Black or slave immigration regulated	No uncompensated abolition	Humane treatment of slaves required	Slave jury and due process rights	Slave taxation and representation	Slavery abolished	No compensated abolition	Universal adult male vote	Equal rights or protection under law
KS 1859	Bill of Rights §6*										
KY 1792		Art. IX §1	Art. IX §1	Art. IX §1	Art. IX §1						
KY 1799		Art. VII §1	Art. VII §1	Art. VII §1	Art. VII §1	Art. VII §2					
KY 1850		Art. X §1	Art. X §1	Art. X §1, Art. XIII §3	Art. X §1	Art. X §§2–3					
LA 1864								Title I Art. 1–2*			
LA 1868								Title I Art. 3*	Title VI Art. 129	Title VI Art. 98	Title I Art. 2, 13
MD 1776				§26 (1837)							
MD 1851				Art. III §43							
MD 1864								Dec. of Rights Art. 24*	Art. III §36		

State & Year									
MD 1867						Art. III §37			Dec. of Rights Art. 24*
MI 1835	Art. XI*								
MI 1850	Art. XVIII §11*								
MN 1857	Art. I §2*								
MS 1817		Art. VI S. §1	Art. VI S.§1	Art. VI S.§1	Art. V §7, Art. VI S.§2				
MS 1832		Art. VII S.§2	Art. VII S.§1	Art. VII S.§1	Art. VII S.§3	Art. VII (1865)*			
MS 1869						Art. I §19*			
MO 1820		Art. III §26	Art. III §26	Art. III §26	Art. III §26	Art. III §26 (1863)*			
MO 1865						Art. I §2*			
MO 1875						Art. II §31*	Art. IV §29		
NE 1867						Art. I §2*			
NE 1875						Art. I §2*		Art. VIII §2	Art. VII §1
NV 1864						Art. I §17*			Art. II §1 (1877)
NC 1776							Art. IV §3 (1835, 1861)		
NC 1868						Art. I §33*			Art. I §6

Art. II §1 (1870)

	Antebellum: 1776–1861							Civil War–Reconstruction: 1862–1877			
	Slavery abolished	Slave trade abolished or regulated	Black or slave immigration regulated	No uncompensated abolition	Humane treatment of slaves required	Slave jury and due process rights	Slave taxation and representation	Slavery abolished	No compensated abolition	Universal adult male vote	Equal rights or protection under law
NC 1876								Art. I §33*			
OH 1802	Art. VIII §2*										
OH 1851	Art. I §6*										
OR 1857	Art. I §35*										
SC 1865								Art. IX §11*			
SC 1868								Art. I §2*	Art. IV §34	Art. I §34	Art. I §39
TN 1796							Art. I §26				
TN 1835				Art. II §31			Art. II §28	Art. I §1 (1866)*	Art. I §1 (1866)*		
TN 1870								Art. I §33*		Art. I §5	

	1	2	3	4	5	6	7	8	9	10	11
TX 1845	Art. VIII §1										
TX 1861	Art. VIII §1	Art. VII §3									
TX 1866	Art. VIII §1	Art. VII §§1–2		Art. VIII §1*					Art. I §16	Art. I §16	Art. I §2, VIII §1
TX 1869				Art. I §22*							Art. I §§2, 21
TX 1876										Art. VI §1	
RI 1843	Art. I §4										
VA 1851	Art. IV §§19–20		Art. IV §21								
VA 1870					Art. IV §§22–23, 36	Art. I §19*		Art. III §1			Art. I §20
VT 1777	Ch.1 §1										
VT 1786	Ch.1 §1										
VT 1793	Ch.1 §1										
WI 1848	Art. I §2										
WV 1863	Art. VI §7						Art. VI §7				
Total	19	14	14	20	13	11	8	7	33	22	13

Note: * indicates slavery or involuntary servitude allowed as punishment for crime; amendments indicated by year in parentheses.

NOTES

Chapter 1. Rethinking American Constitutional Development

1. As the world's shortest and oldest codified constitution, the two-century-old federal Constitution is too extreme an outlier to represent other national constitutions, which on average last nineteen years. While the current fifty American state constitutions, averaging a 121-year lifespan, better resemble many national constitutions, this book does not speculate on constitutions or constitutionalism outside the United States. Versteeg and Zackin, "Constitutions Unentrenched"; Elkins, Ginsburg, and Melton, *Endurance of National Constitutions,* 129.
2. Constitutional reform or amendment is desirable because it is a powerful political tool. More durable and legitimate than a statute, an amendment can invalidate past constitutional provisions and statutes, can guide and constrain existing and future institutional actors, and can empower and create future voting and political constituencies.
3. The federal Constitution enumerates national powers, denying some, but not all, to the states. The remaining national powers not denied to the states are shared concurrent powers. In 1787, the federal framers, divided over the balance of national and state powers, largely avoided defining these concurrent powers. Philadelphia convention delegates rejected James Madison's proposal for a congressional veto on state legislation and instead passed the brief Supremacy Clause instructing federal judges to uphold federal law over conflicting state law but never defined what sort of conflict might trigger the clause, leaving the issue to debate. The clause itself may apply to federal or state judges, each of which may be biased, preventing impartial arbitration. See U.S. Constitution, Article VI, Clause 2, and Tenth Amendment.
4. See U.S. Constitution, Article I, Section 8, Clauses 3, 7, 11, Article II, Section 2, Clause 2, Article IV, Section 2, Clause 2; and *Gibbons v. Ogden,* 22 U.S. 1 (1824). Note also dormant Commerce Clause doctrine.
5. See U.S. Constitution, Article I, Section 4, Clause 1, Article IV, Section 1, Section 2, Clause 1, Section 3, Clauses 1 and 2, Section 4, Clause 1; *Luther v. Borden,* 48 U.S. 1 (1849).

6. Agency in American constitutional change thus lies with both elites and reformers—reformers provide the driving force for revision, while national elites often steer this away from national politics and toward the states.
7. Schattschneider, *Semi-Sovereign People;* Whittington, *Political Foundations of Judicial Supremacy,* 109.
8. See *Prigg v. Pennsylvania,* 41 U.S. 539 (1842); *Dred Scott v. Sandford,* 60 U.S. 393 (1857); *New State Ice Co. v. Liebmann,* 285 U.S. 262; U.S. Constitution, Thirteenth Amendment. Madison offered a similar logic in *Federalist* 10. Hamilton, Madison, and Jay, *Federalist,* 40–46.
9. Tarr, *Understanding State Constitutions,* 99–135; Dinan, *American State Constitutional Tradition,* 3; Fritz, *American Sovereigns;* Zackin, *Looking for Rights in All the Wrong Places,* 1–35, 52–61, 64.
10. In most state legislatures, amendments must pass a two-thirds supermajority, but twenty-one states require only a simple legislative majority to approve a legislative amendment, though eleven of these require approval over two sessions. Initiatives are available in eighteen states. In Massachusetts, a proposed initiative must receive a number of signatures over twenty-five thousand and equal to or greater than 3 percent of the total votes cast in the preceding gubernatorial election, the lowest bar in any state. See Massachusetts Constitution of 1780, Article XLVIII. New Hampshire requires a two-thirds majority of voters for approval; Florida, a three-fifths majority; and Colorado, a 55 percent majority. Illinois has a provision for majority voting in election or three-fifths voting on amendment, while Delaware does not require voter approval at all. There have been 11,635 amendments proposed to the fifty standing state constitutions, 7,695 of which have been ratified as of 2017. Data on state revision procedure and amendment rates from May, "Constitutional Amendment and Revision Revisited," 155–62; Dinan, *State Constitutional Politics;* Council of State Governments, *Book of the States.* See also Dixon and Holden, "Constitutional Amendment Rules."
11. Proposal for a convention takes a simple majority in fifteen states and a two-thirds majority in others. Approval is by simple majority in all states. In all but three states, voters ratify the resulting document by only a simple majority. In total, the states have called 290 assemblies to draft new constitutions, yielding 144 ratified documents. See also May, "Constitutional Amendment and Revision Revisited," 155–64; Lutz, "Toward a Theory of Constitutional Amendment"; Besso, "Constitutional Amendment Procedures," 71–75.
12. Berkowitz and Clay put the average state constitution at 28,000 words, though flexible state constitutions tend to be longer and more specific. Alabama's constitution, with a lax amendment procedure often invoked to address local governance, is 388,882 words long, fifty-one times longer than the 7,591-word federal document. Sturm, "Development of American State Constitutions"; Elazar, "From the Editor of Publius"; Lutz, "Purposes of American State Constitutions"; Lutz, "Toward a Theory of Constitutional Amendment," 357–59; May, "Constitutional Amendment and Revision Revisited," 164–70; Fritz, "Alternative Visions of American Constitutionalism," 35–36; Berkowitz and Clay, "American Civil Law Origins," 69; Zackin, *Looking for Rights in All the Wrong Places,* 22–27.
13. State judges are constrained by familiar appointment and enforcement issues, by juris-

diction-limiting state constitutional amendments, by the length and specificity of state constitutions, and by federal statutes and court rulings. See Graber, "Nonmajoritarian Difficulty," 40, 56–59; Dinan, "Court-Constraining Amendments"; Marshfield, "Amendment Creep."

14. Only 52 percent of respondents to a 1991 survey knew that the states have constitutions, 37 percent were unsure, and 11 percent believed the states did not have constitutions. Respondents to a 2014 survey, when informed they had a state constitution, approved of it, but this approval reflected respondents' pride in their state more than their political knowledge and had little association with the constitution's content. Louisiana, with a French civil law tradition, has had eleven lengthy documents, enough for a Louisiana historian to quip that "constitutional revision in Louisiana, whether in convention or by amendment, has been sufficiently continuous to justify including it with Mardi Gras, football, and corruption as one of the premier components of state culture." Tarr, *Understanding State Constitutions*, 2n4; Cayton, "Why Are Some Institutions Replaced While Others Persist?," 3–4, 19n3; Stephanopoulos and Versteeg, "Contours of Constitutional Approval," 26–29, 36–39, 66–67; Brown and Pope, "Measuring and Manipulating Constitutional Evaluations." For the quote on Louisiana, see Carleton, "Elitism Sustained." For more on path dependence, see Pierson, *Politics in Time*, 10.

15. Key, "Theory of Critical Elections"; Key, *American State Politics;* Key, *Southern Politics in State and Nation*.

16. Sundquist, *Dynamics of the Party System;* Carmines and Stimson, *Issue Evolution;* Skowronek, *Politics Presidents Make*.

17. Key, Mayhew, and Carmines and Stimson show that partisan and ideological realignment is often gradual. If parties faithfully and constantly follow demographic changes, this would probably be the case. However, if self-interested political parties resist these demographic changes, through civic or franchise exclusion, they exacerbate the pressure that can cause sudden critical realignments. And even if this incremental model described all partisan realignment, it would not describe the development of the Constitution, which is designed through Article V to resist minor, incremental change. Key, "Secular Realignment and the Party System"; Carmines and Stimson, *Issue Evolution;* Mayhew, *Electoral Realignments*, 15–20.

18. See *Breedlove v. Suttles*, 302 U.S. 277 (1937); *Harper v. Virginia Board of Elections*, 383 U.S. 663, 666 n.4 (1966). For more on Harper, see Bernstein and Agel, *Amending America*, 136–38; Keyssar, *Right to Vote*, 218–21; Ackerman, *We the People*, vol. 3, 84–88; Hartley, *Failed Attempts to Amend the Constitution*, 81–82.

19. Dahl, "Decision-Making in a Democracy"; Graber, "Nonmajoritarian Difficulty"; Tushnet, *Taking the Constitution Away from the Courts;* Kramer, *People Themselves;* Perry, *Deciding to Decide*.

20. Justices Oliver Wendell Holmes, William Rehnquist, and Sandra Day O'Connor devolved controversies to the states on democratic grounds, a practice that Roger B. Taney enshrined in the political question doctrine in *Luther v. Borden* (1849). Note also that Supreme Court justices often defer to state amicus briefs. See Lindquist and Corley, "National Policy Preferences." Chief Justice John Marshall deferred to the states on tactical, pragmatic grounds—an arch-Federalist, he stripped states' economic regulatory

power in *Fletcher v. Peck* (1810), *McCulloch v. Maryland* (1819), and *Gibbons v. Ogden* (1824), until the 1828 election of the states'-rights Democrats and Andrew Jackson forced Marshall to defer to states' commerce regulations in *Willson v. Black-Bird Creek Marsh Co.* (1829) and *Barron v. Baltimore* (1833).
21. For example, in *Taylor v. United States*, 495 U.S. 598 (1990), the Court interpreted the term "burglary" according to "the generic sense in which the term is now used in the criminal codes of most States," using the same standard for interpreting theft in *Gonzales v. Duenas-Alvare*, 549 U.S. 183 (2007), and again in *Esquivel-Quintana v. Sessions*, 581 U.S. __ (2017), where the Court deferred to a standard adopted by thirty-one states. For discussions of how the Court used this reasoning to preempt congressional court-constraining amendments, see the banking and Social Security Act cases in chapters 3 and 6.
22. See, for example, Sundquist, *Dynamics of the Party System;* Skowronek, *Politics Presidents Make;* Kramer, *People Themselves;* Whittington, *Political Foundations of Judicial Supremacy;* Milkis and Tichenor, *Rivalry and Reform.*
23. Chapters 4 and 6 expound this reading of the Fifteenth and Twenty-Fourth Amendments and the conventional readings of these amendments.
24. *Dillon v. Gloss*, 256 U.S. 368, 376 (1921); *Coleman v. Miller*, 307 U.S. 433 (1939).
25. Burgess's contemporary Herman Ames agreed that Article V raises "insurmountable constitutional obstacles" before necessary constitutional reforms, concluding that the "majorities required are too large." John R. Vile summarizes the progressives' special dislike for the Article V process. See Bryce, *American Commonwealth*, 360; Ames, *Proposed Amendments*, 301–4; Burgess, *Political Science and Comparative Constitutional Law;* Vile, *Encyclopedia of Constitutional Amendments.*
26. Musmanno, *Proposed Amendments;* Orfield, *Amending of the Federal Constitution;* Leedham, *Our Changing Constitution;* Vose, *Constitutional Change;* Grimes, *Democracy and the Amendments to the Constitution*, 1978; Kammen, *Machine That Would Go of Itself;* Ackerman, *We the People*, vol. 1; Lynch, "Other Amendments," 309; Dahl, *How Democratic Is the American Constitution?*, 144–45; Kramer, *People Themselves*, 251; Levinson, *Our Undemocratic Constitution*, 159–66. For a review of these and other scholarly works on Article V, see Kyvig, *Explicit and Authentic Acts*, ix–xviii; Guerra, *Perfecting the Constitution.*
27. For example, Democratic-Republicans held sufficient congressional supermajorities between 1802 and 1824, and Democrats did between 1934 and 1938, with according power in the states, but only one amendment passed in these years.
28. Elkins, Ginsburg, and Melton, *Endurance of National Constitutions*, 81–83, 99–101, 140–41, 163. The American political scientist George H. Haynes observed roughly the same in 1912: "No written law, however great authority it may claim, can long withstand the determined will of the people. . . . The more rigid the Constitution, so much the more inevitable and the more radical becomes this subversive interpretation." Haynes, *Election of Senators*, 130–31.
29. Key, "Theory of Critical Elections"; Key, "Secular Realignment and the Party System"; Burnham, *Critical Elections;* Sundquist, *Dynamics of the Party System;* Ackerman, "Storrs

Lectures"; Skowronek, *Politics Presidents Make;* Kramer, *People Themselves;* Milkis and Tichenor, *Rivalry and Reform.*
30. For a summary of these arguments, see Elkins, Ginsburg, and Melton, *Endurance of National Constitutions,* 84–88, 107–9.
31. Dahl, "Decision-Making in a Democracy"; Graber, "Nonmajoritarian Difficulty," 41; Whittington, *Political Foundations of Judicial Supremacy;* G. Rosenberg, *Hollow Hope;* Hirschl, "Juristocracy," 6; Hirschl, *Towards Juristocracy.*
32. For Kramer, popular constitutionalism has a conservative tradition: "Details, applications, even institutions might change, but the fundamental law itself remained constant and retained its essential substance." Kramer, *People Themselves,* 14–15.
33. As Dahl concludes, because many Americans "regard the Constitution as a sacred document," amendments "have very little chance of coming about in the indefinite future." With difficult and infrequent amendment, as Levinson notes, "citizens are encouraged to believe that change is almost never desirable, let alone necessary." Kammen, *Machine That Would Go of Itself,* 38; Levinson, "Pledging Faith in the Civil Religion"; Dahl, *How Democratic Is the American Constitution?,* 154–55; Levinson, *Our Undemocratic Constitution,* 165.
34. Madison predicted that Article V would allow revision only on "certain great and extraordinary occasions ... [for] frequent appeals would in great measure deprive the government of that veneration which time bestows on everything, and without which perhaps the wisest and freest governments would not possess the requisite stability." Hamilton, Madison, and Jay, *Federalist,* 245–46, 309.
35. Elkins, Ginsburg, and Melton, *Endurance of National Constitutions,* 141–42.
36. A few have noted that in divided societies federal systems allow for power sharing and constitutional longevity. See De Figueiredo and Weingast, "Self-Enforcing Federalism"; Elkins, Ginsburg, and Melton, *Endurance of National Constitutions,* 168. Conversely, others have argued that American federalism breeds interstate controversy and division. See Kettl, *Divided States of America.* I argue that it is not so much federalism broadly as subnational *constitutions* specifically that stabilize American constitutionalism.
37. For this progressive history, see Lutz, "Purposes of American State Constitutions," 27–31. For exemplary Progressive-era accounts of the state constitutions, see Jameson, *Treatise on Constitutional Conventions;* Bryce, *American Commonwealth,* 427–62; Thorpe, "Recent Constitution-Making in the United States"; Dodd, "Judicial Control over the Amendment of State Constitutions"; Dealey, *Growth of American State Constitutions.*
38. For a description of this problem, see Margolick, "State Judges Are Shaping Law"; Lutz, "Purposes of American State Constitutions," 27–31; Friedman, "State Constitutions in Historical Perspective," 33–35; Tarr, *Understanding State Constitutions,* 1–5; Dinan, *American State Constitutional Tradition,* 1–6; Williams, *Law of American State Constitutions,* 1–11; Onuf, "State Politics and Republican Virtue," 388–90; Levinson, *Framed,* 1–32; Zackin, *Looking for Rights in All the Wrong Places,* 1–36; Herron, *Framing the Solid South,* 17–18.
39. Kaye, "State Courts at the Dawn of a New Century," 3; Bannon and Robbins, "Nation's Top State Courts."

40. For example, on Revolutionary-era state constitutionalism, see Wood, *Creation of the American Republic;* Wood, *Radicalism of the American Revolution;* Lutz, *Popular Consent and Popular Control;* Kruman, *Between Authority and Liberty;* W. Adams, *First American Constitutions.*
41. On culture, and particularly the South, see Elazar, *American Federalism;* Elazar, "Principles and Traditions Underlying State Constitutions"; Fehrenbacher, *Constitutions and Constitutionalism;* Hall and Ely, *Uncertain Tradition.*
42. On state constitutions and republicanism, for example, see Wood, *Creation of the American Republic;* Wood, *Radicalism of the American Revolution;* Scalia, *America's Jeffersonian Experiment;* Henretta, "Rise of 'Democratic-Republicanism'"; Onuf, "State Politics and Republican Virtue."
43. For a legal perspective on positive rights, and state constitutional rights generally, see, for example, Hershkoff and Loffredo, "State Courts and Constitutional Socio-economic Rights"; Hershkoff, "Positive Rights and the Evolution of State Constitutions"; Sutton, *51 Imperfect Solutions.*
44. For "a very preliminary" and "purely anecdotal" study of state constitutional duration, see Friedman, "Endurance of State Constitutions." For a broader but still brief account, see Cayton, "Why Are Some Institutions Replaced While Others Persist?"
45. Dinan, *American State Constitutional Tradition;* Dinan, *State Constitutional Politics.*
46. Novkov, "Bringing the States Back In"; Zackin, *Looking for Rights in All the Wrong Places;* Stohler, "Slavery and Just Compensation"; Beienburg, "Neither Nullification nor Nationalism"; Beienburg, *Prohibition, the Constitution, and States' Rights.*
47. Bridges, "Managing the Periphery in the Gilded Age"; Bridges, *Democratic Beginnings;* Herron, *Framing the Solid South.*
48. Sturm, "Development of American State Constitutions"; Friedman, "State Constitutions in Historical Perspective"; Tarr, *Understanding State Constitutions;* Dinan, *American State Constitutional Tradition;* Hall, "Mostly Anchor and Little Sail."
49. Lutz, "Purposes of American State Constitutions"; Lutz, "United States Constitution as an Incomplete Text"; Hall, "Mostly Anchor and Little Sail"; Marshfield, "Models of Substantial Constitutionalism"; Tarr, "Explaining Sub-national Constitutional Space"; Burgess and Tarr, "Introduction."
50. Reform is necessary but not sufficient for instability. Frequent reform or amendment alone may not signal instability—the nature of reform also matters.
51. Note that the national Constitution does not specify a process for wholesale replacement, which has never been attempted. Kammen, *Machine That Would Go of Itself,* 11; Strauss, "Irrelevance of Constitutional Amendments"; Latham, "Historical Amendability of the American Constitution," 157, 201; Huq, "Function of Article V," 1169; Vile, *Encyclopedia of Constitutional Amendments;* Hartley, *Failed Attempts to Amend the Constitution.*
52. To code amendments by topic, I identify all terms that occur at least five times in amendment descriptions for each year for 1788 to 2020. I exclude common policy-irrelevant terms, mainly prepositions and conjunctions like "of" and "and" and prefatory language like "proposing" or "resolution," yielding remaining policy-relevant terms. I combine similar policy-relevant terms like "congress" and "congressional" into shared topic variables and use conditional text string matching to identify amendments containing these

terms and to match the amendments to these topic variables. I then check each variable for false-positive matches by sampling 5 percent of variable matches for errors, updating coding rules as needed to eliminate these errors, and check for false negatives by randomly selecting ten variables and sampling 1 percent of nonmatches. As an additional check, I identify all policy-relevant terms that occur at least fifty times for 1788 to 2014, deriving similar results. I also check this against John R. Vile's subjective summary of common amendment topics by year. Vile, *Encyclopedia of Constitutional Amendments*, 547–64.

53. As the English jurist Matthew Hale argued, the flood of minor amendments to the English Constitution reaffirmed the Constitution's fundamental principles. In the American context, a few individual amendments, like the Thirteenth, have rebuilt the nation, while many other proposed amendments and some peripheral ratified amendments, like the Twentieth Amendment setting the date for Inauguration Day, do not significantly affect core American commitments. William S. Livingston rightly observes that a simple count of proposed amendments "is of little significance. Many of the proposals were identical, or at least were concerned with the same questions; many were trivial; many were ridiculous; and many were unnecessary. But the most significant explanation of the large number of proposals is the unlimited right of American Congressmen to introduce as many resolutions as they like," mainly engaging in position-taking to satisfy constituents, so that many proposals "command no public support whatsoever." Hale, *History of the Common Law of England*, 84; Livingston, *Federalism and Constitutional Change*, 200–201. For more on this, see Roznai, *Unconstitutional Constitutional Amendments;* Albert, *Constitutional Amendments*.

54. A constitution's identity exists through its central normative commitments. An amendment violating these core normative commitments fundamentally reforms and destabilizes the constitution. Kramer, *People Themselves,* 9–18; Jacobsohn, "Constitutional Identity"; Jacobsohn, *Constitutional Identity;* Jacobsohn, "Rights and American Constitutional Identity."

55. Commitments blend across clauses. As Justice Oliver Wendell Holmes Jr. stated, "Great ordinances of the Constitution do not establish and divide fields of Black and white. Even the more specific of them are found to terminate in a penumbra shading gradually from one extreme to the other." *Springer v. Government of the Philippine Islands,* 277 U.S. 189, 276 (1928).

56. State constitutions have been proposed by convention, commission, and legislative committee. For data on conventions from 1776 to 1909, I rely on Thorpe's compendium of state constitutions (1909); from 1938 to 1968, on Sturm (1954, 1970); from 1776 to 2006, on Dinan (2006); and from 1942 to 2018, on the Council of State Governments' *Book of the States*. For data on commissions from 1776 to 1968, I rely on Sturm (1954, 1970); and from 1965 to 2010, on Kogan (2010). To check and expand this data and add missing observations, I hand code every reference to a state constitutional commission from 1943 to 2018 in *The Book of the States*. Sturm and Kogan derive data from *The Book of the States* reports, to which Dinan is a contributor, such that data is comparable across these different sources. For legislative proposals, I use Sturm (1954, 1970), Connor and Hammond (2008), and *The Book of the States*. See Thorpe, *Federal and State*

Constitutions; Sturm, *Methods of State Constitutional Reform;* Sturm, *Thirty Years of State Constitution-Making;* Dinan, *American State Constitutional Tradition;* Connor and Hammond, *Constitutionalism of American States;* Kogan, "Irony of Comprehensive State Constitutional Reform."

57. I code only assemblies under U.S. jurisdiction, excluding state constitutional assemblies outside U.S. territorial jurisdiction, like the preannexation 1836 Convention of the Republic of Texas. I also exclude assemblies to draft territorial organic laws and overseas territorial and District of Columbia constitutions. I define a proposal for a new state constitution as the assembly of a state constitutional revision body with the authority to draft a new state constitution. This does not require that the body complete the drafting process. This rule excludes unofficial citizen groups' proposals, limited conventions, commissions, and legislative committees authorized exclusively to amend but not draft a constitution, and preparatory commissions used to aid conventions. My list of ratified constitutions matches that of other scholars; see Sturm, "Development of American State Constitutions," 57; Dinan, *State Constitutional Politics*, 23.

58. I use *The Book of the States* to derive state-level counts of proposed and ratified amendments for all states biennially for 1942–2001 and annually for 2002–2019. I also extract amendments from the texts of state constitutions available through the NBER–University of Maryland State Constitutions Project, which covers forty-one states for 1776–2000, checking these counts against a sample of a third of states in Thorpe's compendium, covering 1776–1906. State-level biennial counts from *The Book of the States* and the NBER-Maryland data differ, sometimes significantly, but are more closely associated in the aggregate, so I use the *Book of the States* data in the aggregate and sparingly. Thorpe, *Federal and State Constitutions;* Council of State Governments, *Book of the States,* 100; Wallis, "NBER–Maryland State Constitutions Project."

59. States relied on wholesale replacement by constitutional convention until switching to expert commissions in the Progressive era and in the years after court-mandated redistricting under *Baker v. Carr,* 369 U.S. 186 (1962). These commissions often proposed piecemeal amendments, which, abetted by initiatives and referenda and a wariness of runaway conventions, have largely displaced wholesale replacement by convention. For scholarly work on the decline in conventions, see Benjamin and Gais, "Constitutional Conventionphobia"; Dinan, "Political Dynamics"; Kogan, "Irony of Comprehensive State Constitutional Reform"; Levinson and Blake, "When Americans Think about Constitutional Reform"; Williams, "Evolving State Constitutional Processes"; Williams, "Are State Constitutional Conventions Things of the Past?" There is some disagreement on the number of conventions: Dinan counts 236; Hall, 239; and I find 255, due to slightly broader coding conditions that include prestatehood conventions. See Hall, "Mostly Anchor and Little Sail," 394; Dinan, *State Constitutional Politics,* 295n124.

60. In 1780, Massachusetts's framers forbade legislators from making laws that were "repugnant or contrary to this constitution," suggesting that some core provisions of the constitution ought to be impervious to legislative amendment. See the Massachusetts Constitution of 1780, Frame of Government, Chapter I, Section I, Article IV. For a similar provision, see the New Hampshire Constitution of 1784, Form of Government, Section 2. And the New Jersey Supreme Court declared, "Not all constitutional provisions are of

equal majesty.... The task of interpreting most if not all of [the New Jersey Constitution's] 'great ordinances' is an evolving and on-going process." See *Vreeland v. Byrne*, 72 N.J. 292, 370 A.2d 825 (1977); Williams, *New Jersey State Constitution*, 42. See also *Corum v. University of N.C.*, 413 S.E.2d 276, 289 (N.C. 1992); *Raven v. Deukmejian*, 801 P. 2d 1077, 1085 (Cal. 1990). However, in *Omaha National Bank v. Spire*, 223 Neb. 209, 389 N.W. 2d 269 (1986), the Nebraska Supreme Court implied that the Nebraska Constitution had no core provisions. See also Pope, "Approach to State Constitutional Interpretation"; Schapiro, "Identity and Interpretation in State Constitutional Law."

61. Between 1781 and 1894, over seventy compilations of state constitutions were printed. Dinan, "Court-Constraining Amendments," 14–16; Tarr, *Understanding State Constitutions*, 98–99.
62. Consistently selecting the three or four most common congressional amendment topics prevents cherry-picking topics. As subsequent chapters show, these amendment topics tend to reflect the main issues for federal judicial review in each era, suggesting that the amendment list is an accurate representation of national constitutional disputes.
63. I rely on *Book of the States* amendment data for 1960–2018. Data I extracted from the NBER–University of Maryland State Constitutions Project also show that biennial counts of ratified state amendments are closely associated with proposed federal amendments for 1776–2000. I use the Pearson correlation coefficient here. A higher absolute value suggests a stronger association on a 1 to –1 scale; a positive value suggests that when one variable increases, the other increases; and a negative value suggests that when one variable increases, the other decreases. This measure suggests that it is highly unlikely that there is no association between aggregate federal and state constitutional reform.
64. Equally important is the number of proposals weighted by the number of existing states. For example, between 1787 and 1791, the fourteen states proposed six constitutions, while between 1912 and 1916, also a five-year span, the United States saw also six proposals, but these were diluted across forty-eight states. This pattern of periodic peaks holds, even when weighted by the increasing number of states over the course of American history, suggesting that national expansion does not drive this pattern in state constitutional revision. The pattern also remains the same when splitting the total number of state constitutional proposals into ratified and unratified proposals. Federal and state data also diverge periodically. This occurred in the 1890s, when Congress incorporated many Western states with new constitutions but proposed relatively few federal amendments, and during the Great Depression and after the civil rights movement, the two nadirs of wholesale state constitutional replacement.
65. W. Wilson, *Constitutional Government in the United States*, 173.

Chapter 2. First Conventions, 1760–1791

1. Between 1776 and 1780, every state save Connecticut and Rhode Island called a convention in what Gordon Wood calls "the most creative and significant period of constitutionalism in modern Western history." Wood, "Foreword," 911.
2. "Provincial Conference," 41; Braxton, "Address to the Convention," 670.
3. Farrand, *Records*, 2:278.

4. At the federal convention, James Wilson reminded the drafters that Americans were "the first instance of a people assembled to weigh deliberately and calmly, and to decide leisurely and peaceably, upon the form of government by which they will bind themselves and their posterity." J. Wilson, *Substance of a Speech*, 5.
5. Pennsylvania's 1681 charter granted William Penn and his heirs "full and absolute power, licence and authorities" over the colony's land, "to time hereafter forever." Maryland's 1632 charter, the 1669 Fundamental Constitutions of Carolina, and Georgia's 1732 charter similarly empowered a few families, even after the gradual repeal of charters in the eighteenth century. The Carolina charter of 1669, for example, rejected "numerous democracy," authorizing later disenfranchisement. Keyssar, *Right to Vote*, 5–6; Burke, "Speech on Conciliation with America," 186.
6. Virginia formally established Black chattel slavery in 1661, and Maryland in 1662. After 1682, Virginia's House of Burgesses initially classed Native Americans not as indentured servants but as slaves, akin to Blacks. But with Native Americans' escapes from plantations and costly wars with the Tuscarora and Yamasee tribes between 1715 and 1718, white Carolinians shifted primarily to purchasing Blacks, and other colonies followed suit. New York passed the 1702 Act for Regulating Slaves, and Pennsylvania's 1726 Act for Better Regulating Negroes in the Province was similarly harsh to free Blacks. Countryman, *American Revolution*, 34–37, 51; R. Smith, *Civic Ideals*, 59–67, 521n53; Nash, *Unknown American Revolution*, 32–33; Ablavsky, "Making Indians 'White,'" 1466–71; Gillman and Graber, *Complete American Constitutionalism*, 409–26.
7. *Somerset* held that slavery might be allowed under flawed colonial laws but not under the higher natural law. Where positive slave law was unclear or contradictory, Mansfield ruled that slaves could not be removed from Great Britain without the liberty of habeas corpus review. British precedent since *Smith v. Brown and Cooper* (1702) allowed colonial slavery, and each of the American colonies clearly and consistently legalized slavery, preventing Mansfield from abolishing or modifying colonial slave laws. See *Somerset v. Stewart*, 98 ER 499 (1772); *Smith v. Brown and Cooper*, 90 Eng. Rep. 1172 (1702); Wiecek, "Somerset," 114–15; Wood, *Radicalism of the American Revolution*, 51; Oldfield, *Popular Politics and British Anti-Slavery*, 5–7; Nash, *Unknown American Revolution*, 21–23, 39–43, 62–65, 157–66; Gillman and Graber, *Complete American Constitutionalism*, 406–9.
8. For example, the Livingstons, Van Renssalaers, and Beekmans controlled tenant estates of hundreds of thousands of acres in New York, while over 70 percent of New Jersey legislators were related to previous legislators in the late colonial era. And in the city of Philadelphia in 1775, only a tenth of male taxpayers could raise the fifty pounds required to vote, locking the city under elite control. Wood, *Radicalism of the American Revolution*, 42–49; R. Smith, *Civic Ideals*, 67–69.
9. The 1701 charter specified that Pennsylvania's three easternmost counties elect four legislators each but did not explain how to apportion representation to new counties. With reapportionment, peripheral Berks, Northampton, and Cumberland Counties received a total of five seats, but easterners refused to incorporate additional growing western counties; and so in total, the three eastern counties kept a legislative majority of twenty-six to ten. These eastern Quaker legislators, insulated from and morally opposed to war with

western Native Americans, refused western petitions to fund militias and forts. A tavern keeper named John Hambright led three hundred to seven hundred German frontiersmen to march on Philadelphia in 1755, extracting funding for western troops, but in 1763 the governor dismissed a reapportionment petition made by a similar mob, who dubbed themselves the "Paxton Boys." While the Assembly in 1771 and 1772 relaxed western taxes, funded canals and turnpikes to the region, and added five western seats to the legislature, it required these representatives to reside in their district, keeping them from serving in distant Philadelphia. Selsam, *Pennsylvania Constitution of 1776*, 4–8, 18–42; Thayer, *Pennsylvania Politics and the Growth of Democracy*, 127–39; Hutson, *Pennsylvania Politics*, 24–28, 96–98, 103–5; Branning, *Pennsylvania Constitutional Development*, 9–16.

10. The 1696 and 1701 charters limited the vote to any Protestant male over twenty-one with two years residency and fifty acres of land or fifty pounds of property. McKinley, *Suffrage Franchise*, 284–92; Selsam, *Pennsylvania Constitution of 1776*, 8–9, 33; Thayer, *Pennsylvania Politics and the Growth of Democracy*, 3–6; Countryman, *American Revolution*, 117; Wood, *Radicalism of the American Revolution*, 119–20, 129, 184.

11. Two years later, in 1765, William Prendergast led New York tenant farmers' to successfully revolt against a reduction in their land leasing rights. McKinley, *Suffrage Franchise*, 284–92; Bailyn, *Ideological Origins of the American Revolution*, 118; R. Smith, *Civic Ideals*, 57, 61; Nash, *Unknown American Revolution*, 2–8, 72–87.

12. Bailyn, *Ideological Origins of the American Revolution*, 99–104; Countryman, *American Revolution*, 10–11.

13. A few years later, Dickinson wrote that without American delegates, the Commons could not represent the American people's taxation powers. Dulany, "Considerations on the Propriety of Imposing Taxes"; Dickinson, "Letters from a Farmer in Pennsylvania"; Jensen, "Introduction," xl–xli, xxix–xxxii; Bailyn, *Ideological Origins of the American Revolution*, 99–104; Countryman, *American Revolution*, 10–11, 41–52, 63–69; R. Smith, *Civic Ideals*, 70–86; Greene, *Constitutional Origins of the American Revolution*, 67–88.

14. James II dissolved New England's colonial charters to create the Dominion of New England under Governor Edmund Andros in 1686, and perhaps more offensive to Massachusetts Puritans, on May 1, 1687, Andros's government planted a maypole in Charlestown, inciting the townspeople to dance. Enraged Bostonians seized a royal heavy frigate, then Andros's officials, and then Andros himself; Connecticut colonists challenged their charter's revocation, and New Yorkers dispossessed officeholders and the wealthy and overthrew Andros's deputy, Francis Nicholson. William and Mary capitulated with the restoration of the charters. Haffenden, "Crown and the Colonial Charters," 456–59; Sosin, *English America and the Revolution of Sixteen Eighty-Eight*, 76–80, 153–56.

15. Under the era's Lockean contractarianism, individuals could only hold overawing, executive power when they combined their private powers as a group, which they could then leave at will, so long as they did not violate the group's rules. For colonists, a plural, shifting, popular executive was a part of contractarian theory and custom.

16. The Virginia planter Landon Carter claimed that self-government was "an Englishman's inherent Birthright," while New Hampshire's John Sullivan wrote that Massachusetts's written charter was "only a confirmation of those Liberties which the God of nature had

given" and Richard Bland argued that subjects "have a natural Right to quit the Society of which they are Members, and to retire into another country. . . . If they unite, and by common Consent take Possession of a new Country, and form themselves into a political Society, they become a sovereign State." Bland, "Inquiry into the Rights of the British Colonies," 112, 116; Bailyn, *Ideological Origins of the American Revolution*, 118–19; Maier, "Popular Uprisings and Civil Authority," 428–48; Countryman, *American Revolution*, 52–56; R. Smith, *Civic Ideals*, 72–86; York, "First Continental Congress," 366; McConville, *King's Three Faces*, 29–39; Greene, *Constitutional Origins of the American Revolution*, 82–90.

17. Recalling Otis's fiery speech, Samuel Adams held that "the child independence was there born." See *Paxton's Case*, Quincy's Mass. Rep. 51 (1761), *Entick v. Carrington*, EWHC KB J98 (1765); J. Adams, "Letter to William Tudor, March 29, 1817," 248; Lovejoy, "Rights Imply Equality," 478–82; Bailyn, *Ideological Origins of the American Revolution*, 74–75, 105–9; Maier, "Popular Uprisings and Civil Authority," 429–32; Countryman, *American Revolution*, 43, 59; Kramer, *People Themselves*, 35–39; Nash, *Unknown American Revolution*, 21–23; Greene, *Constitutional Origins of the American Revolution*, 140–41; Gillman and Graber, *Complete American Constitutionalism*, 485–92.

18. In Virginia, sitting justices advised the governor's nominations, keeping the courts a closed cabal. See the Massachusetts Bill of Rights, Article XIV; Massachusetts Constitution of 1780, Ch. III; Wiecek, "Somerset," 113; Jordan, "Enslavement of Negroes in America," 258–68; Countryman, *American Revolution*, 32; Nicholls, "Squint of Freedom," 48; Nash, *Unknown American Revolution*, 79–82; Ablavsky, "Making Indians 'White,'" 1458, 1476–78.

19. New Hampshire's emergency congress met for barely two weeks, concluding on January 5, 1776, then appointed itself the state legislature and continued to modify the constitution using statutes. South Carolina's provincial assembly, operating without a governor and facing domestic insurrection, passed a constitution on March 26, 1776, and another on March 19, 1778. The beleaguered Virginia Provincial Convention passed a state constitution as if it were ordinary legislation on June 29, 1776, as did New Jersey's congress three days later. Save for South Carolina's, each meeting lasted less than eight weeks, and none of the conventions submitted their work for popular review. W. Ford, *Journals of the Continental Congress*, 2:79; Nevins, *American States*, 75–95, 108–16, 125–27; Wood, *Creation of the American Republic*, 130–32, 306–10; Countryman, *American Revolution*, 113–21; Greene, *Negotiated Authorities*, 27–28; Maier, *American Scripture*, 8–14; Kruman, *Between Authority and Liberty*, 16–20; W. Adams, *First American Constitutions*, 26–27, 54–57, 68–72; Nash, *Unknown American Revolution*, 159–60, 178–82, 194–99.

20. Working in a subcommittee of the First Continental Congress, John Adams quietly drafted his Declaration and Resolves, declaring, "the power of making laws for ordering or regulating the internal polity of these Colonies, is, within the limits of each Colony, respectively and exclusively vested in the Provincial Legislature of each colony." The final draft passing on October 14, 1774, redacted Adams's insurrectionary language. John Adams's second cousin and fellow Bay Stater Samuel Adams agreed that Congress saw Massachusetts as too "intemperate and rash." Congress also rejected John Rutledge's

separation declaration on May 16, passing instead on July 6 a "Declaration on Taking Up Arms" that Dickinson had softened from the insurrectionary original draft, and defeated at least three more proclamations against Great Britain that summer, each shying from independence. J. Adams, "Letter to Joseph Palmer, September 26, 1774," 154–55; J. Adams, "Letter to Timothy Pickering, August 6, 1822," 535–42; Jefferson, "Notes of Proceedings in the Continental Congress," 309; W. Ford, *Journals of the Continental Congress*, 1:63–74; Maier, *American Scripture*, 6–25; W. Adams, *First American Constitutions*, 51, 57.

21. Adams confided to his journal that the delegates to Congress "knew not to what Plunder or Massacres or Cruelties [Bostonians] might be exposed." He decided that Congress ought to resolve the crisis by recommending "to the People of all the States to institute Governments for themselves, . . . then to inform Great Britain [colonists] were willing to enter into Negotiations with them for the redress of all Grievances, and a restoration of Harmony between the two Countries." J. Adams, "Diary," 406–7; J. Adams, "Letter to John Taylor, April 9, 1814," 94–96.

22. Confiding to fellow congressman Patrick Henry, Adams wrote, "It has ever appeared to me, that the natural Course and order of Things, was this—for every Colony to institute a Government—for all the Colonies to confederate, and define the Limits of the Continental Constitution—then to declare the Colonies a sovereign State, or a Number of confederated Sovereign States—and last of all to form Treaties with foreign Powers. But I fear We cannot proceed systematically, and that We Shall be obliged to declare ourselves independant [sic] States before We confederate, and indeed before all the Colonies have established their Governments." J. Adams, "Letter to Patrick Henry, June 3, 1776," 386–87; J. Adams, "Letter to John Taylor, April 9, 1814," 95; J. Adams, "Autobiography," 3:44–46; W. Ford, *Journals of the Continental Congress*, 4:199–201, 342, 357–58; Nevins, *American States*, 125–26; Wood, *Creation of the American Republic*, 131–32; Kruman, *Between Authority and Liberty*, 20; Maier, *American Scripture*, 37–38; W. Adams, *First American Constitutions*, 58–59.

23. For nearly another century, proponents of states' rights pointed to Adams's sweeping delegation of power. Maier, *American Scripture*, 94; W. Adams, *First American Constitutions*, 47.

24. Past Anglo-Americans understood their constitution as an informal accretion of royal and Parliamentary practices, laws, and charters. These four new constitutions were explicit pacts, with terms for amendment and dissolution. Greene, *Negotiated Authorities*, 27–28.

25. Dickinson, Wilson, and other middle-colony delegates attacked the measure as imprudent, and so Lee's measure was postponed until the delegates of New York, New Jersey, Pennsylvania, Delaware, and Maryland were willing to vote for independence. Jefferson, "Notes of Proceedings in the Continental Congress," 309–15.

26. Jefferson wrote, "The fact is, that the [Virginia Constitution's] preamble was prior in composition to the Declaration; and both having the same object, of justifying our separation from Great Britain, *they used necessarily the same materials, and hence their similitude.*" Jefferson, "Letter to Augustus B. Woodward, April 3, 1825," 407–8. Pauline Maier argues that the preamble to the Virginia Constitution of 1776 in turn came from the

English Declaration of Rights. Maier, *American Scripture*, 126. For an extended discussion of Jefferson's drafting of the Declaration of Independence, see Maier, 97–153.

27. While serving in Congress in Philadelphia, Jefferson drafted a constitution for Virginia, which he then sent to Edmund Pendleton, president of Virginia's constitutional convention. On June 29, the convention ratified a constitution including much of Jefferson's preamble, cataloguing grievances against George III. While the Virginians were deliberating, Jefferson incorporated these grievances, largely unmodified, into his draft of the Declaration. Excluded from the Declaration's final draft was Jefferson's original abolition provision and the claim that George III had abdicated power "By answering [the colonists'] repeated petitions for redress with a repetition of injuries: And finally, by abandoning the helm of government and declaring [the colonists] out of his allegiance and protection." Language from the Virginia bill's first and third sections reappeared in the opening of the Declaration, as did other sections. Boyd, "Editorial Note: The Declaration of Independence," 413–17; Boyd, "Editorial Note: The Virginia Constitution," 229–39.

28. Since May 1775, Adams had advised Joseph Warren, the president of Massachusetts's Provincial Convention, on a Massachusetts constitution, George Wythe, Richard Henry Lee, and Patrick Henry on drafting the Virginia Constitution, and Jonathan Dickinson Sergeant on the New Jersey Constitution. Adams also recorded in his diary independence resolutions from New Hampshire, South Carolina, and Maryland made in these months. Adams, "Autobiography," 3:18–21, 53–55; Adams, "Letter to John Taylor, April 9, 1814," 94–96; Nevins, *American States*, 122–25; Gutzman, *Virginia's American Revolution*, 24–27; Unger, *Lion of Liberty*, 113–16.

29. Jefferson later recalled the tenor of the Committee of Five and of the era: "All American whigs thought alike on these subjects. . . . This was the object of the Declaration of Independence. . . . Neither aiming at originality of principle or sentiment, nor yet copied from any particular and previous writing, it was intended to be an expression of the American mind, and to give to that expression the proper tone and spirit called for by the occasion. All its authority rests then on the harmonizing sentiments of the day, whether expressed in conversation, in letters, printed essays, or in the elementary books of public right, as Aristotle, Cicero, Locke, Sidney, &c." Jefferson, "Letter to Henry Lee, May 8, 1825," 408.

30. New Hampshire's conciliatory 1776 convention delegates listed only a dozen grievances, objecting mainly to the seizure of property and impediment to trade under the Navigation Acts and to George III's suspension of the colony's governor, legislature, and courts, asking for a restoration of English rights and peace with Britain. New Jersey's convention also listed few grounds for independence and, like New Hampshire's, closed by appealing to conciliation. South Carolina's 1776 constitution systemically catalogued many grievances against George III with the same vitriol as the Declaration. Both Virginia's and South Carolina's constitutions anticipated the Declaration's complaint that George III instigated revolt among "the merciless Indian savages." For a systematic comparison of the first state constitutions to drafts of the Declaration, see appendix B.

31. These state declarations drew on Congress's Declaration. New York copied the congressional Declaration verbatim. The following states listed grounds for independence and

dissolution of government in their constitutions: Pennsylvania (1776), Maryland (1776), North Carolina (1776), Georgia (1777), New York (1777), Vermont (1777), and Massachusetts (1780). For a discussion of the state and local declarations, see Maier, *American Scripture*, 47–96.

32. The clause added that the royal slave trade violated the "most sacred Rights of Life and Liberty in the Persons of a distant People who never offended him." For the full clause, see Jefferson, "Fragment of the Composition Draft," 420n10.

33. Jefferson, "Notes of Proceedings in the Continental Congress," 314–15; Becker, *Declaration of Independence*, 171–72; Maier, *American Scripture*, 146–47.

34. For example, Gary Nash calls it "the most important deletion made to Jefferson's draft." For similar accounts, see Boyd, "Editorial Note: The Virginia Constitution," 414; Rogin, "Two Declarations of American Independence," 14–15; Fehrenbacher, *Slaveholding Republic*, 17; Nash, *Unknown American Revolution*, 208–9; Beaumont, *Civic Constitution*, 61; Kettl, *Divided States of America*, 9.

35. Jefferson's provision, as passed in the Virginia Constitution of 1776, provided this reason that George III had lost authority over the colony: "By prompting our negroes to rise in arms against us, those very negroes whom, by an inhuman use of his negative, he hath refused us permission to exclude by law." Jefferson originally drafted this complaint in his *Summary View of the Rights of British America*. See Maier, *American Scripture*, 112–13.

36. Many of the sponsors of colonial Virginia's nonimportation bill were themselves wealthy slaveholders who stood to benefit from such a law and were upset when the law was vetoed by the loyalist Governor Dunmore. One such slaveholder, George Mason, blamed the governor's veto, which he felt, in combination with his incitement to slave revolt, "proved dangerous" to Virginia slaveholders. John Adams speculated that the Georgia and South Carolina delegates were not opposed to Jefferson's nonimportation argument— they may even have supported it—but rather rejected his lofty antislavery "tone and flights of oratory." Later, in the federal convention, Charles Cotesworth Pinckney was more direct in describing the Virginian justification for nonimportation: "Virginia she will gain by stopping the importations. Her slaves will rise in value, & she has more than she wants." J. Adams, "Letter to Timothy Pickering, August 6, 1822," 514; Farrand, *Records*, 2:370–71; Maier, *American Scripture*, 122, 265n33.

37. The historian Robert McColley writes, "By removing foreign competition, Virginia could hope to maintain attractive prices for slaves, and could also expect enough of them to be carried out of the state to maintain a safe proportion between the races of the Old Dominion. . . . The laws against slave importation were by no means intended to attack, or even criticize, the holding of slaves itself." McColley, *Slavery and Jeffersonian Virginia*, 164–67; Nicholls, "Squint of Freedom," 51, 54–55; Wax, "Negro Import Duties."

38. See Article 26 of the Delaware Constitution. Note that Pennsylvania also considered such an act in 1778, before passing one in 1785, but faced less pressure from slave revolts than did Southern colonies.

39. It is not clear whether Jefferson intended to protect states' rights to regulate slavery. In his 1775 "Address to the Inhabitants of Great Britain," his "Declaration of Causes and Necessity of Taking Up Arms," and his *Summary View*, Jefferson condemned injuries to

free Blacks and slaves under royal government. The extent to which Jefferson genuinely sympathized with African Americans, whom he considered physiologically inferior to whites, is suspect. Jefferson, "Composition Draft," 419n1.

40. Rhode Island and Connecticut kept their colonial charters and did not call conventions. In Pennsylvania, Delaware, and Virginia, the state constitutional conventions doubled as temporary legislatures. New Hampshire, Georgia, New York, and Vermont called special legislative sessions to draft new constitutions.

41. Conference delegates took popular authority so seriously that they redrafted their original notes, capitalizing every mention of "the People." Convention delegates later held that "the people have a right, by *common* consent" to change government and that "the *community* hath an indubitable, unalienable and indefeasible right to reform, alter, or abolish government" (emphasis added). As Gordon Wood concludes, it was in Pennsylvania "where the distinction between constitutional and legislative law was most sharply appreciated." The dialogue and quotes appeared in the May 16, 1776, edition of the *Pennsylvania Evening Post* and the May 22 *Pennsylvania Journal*. See "The Alarm; or, an Address to the People of Pennsylvania on the Late Resolve of Congress" and "Pennsylvania Provincial Conference of Committees Minutes," (#Am.289), Historical Society of Pennsylvania, Philadelphia; Pennsylvania Constitution of 1776, Preamble and Article V; "Provincial Conference," 38; Nevins, *American States,* 107, 129; Wood, *Creation of the American Republic,* 308, 332–40; Williams, "State Constitutions of the Founding Decade," 552; Kruman, *Between Authority and Liberty,* 25; W. Adams, *First American Constitutions,* 61; Carter, "Religion and State Constitution Making," 133; "*Boston Gazette,* 19 November*,*" 274.

42. After the Pennsylvania Council reauthorized the Constitution in 1783, legislators rallied for abolition of the Council and Constitution, arguing that ongoing legislative amendment would more closely track the shifting popular will. In 1790, Pennsylvania's anti-Constitutionalists scored a convention that revised amendment procedures. Demophilus quoted in Selsam, *Pennsylvania Constitution of 1776,* 435. See the Virginia Constitution of 1776, Bill of Rights, Section 15; Shaeffer, "Public Consideration of the 1776 Pennsylvania Constitution," 416, 432; Kruman, *Between Authority and Liberty,* 24–26, 57–59; Maier, *American Scripture,* 66; W. Adams, *First American Constitutions,* 74–77, 267–69; Paine, *Rights of Man,* 297.

43. New York, New Jersey, Virginia, North Carolina, and South Carolina refused to specify the legal process for constitutional amendment, and Delaware and New Jersey prohibited the legislature from amending provisions on rights and on legislative powers, perhaps reflecting a growing fear of majoritarian tyranny. Maryland allowed the legislature to amend the state's 1776 constitution only if the amendment represented a united popular will, indicated by a two-thirds majority in both houses over two years. But note that Nevins, against Wood, Kruman, and Adams, argues the conventions frequently engaged in legislation. Further, of the twenty-eight conventions between 1776 and 1799, only half a dozen assemblies, held in Massachusetts, New Hampshire, and Georgia, submitted their work for a vote of public approval. See the Maryland Constitution of 1776, Article LIX; Nevins, *American States,* 127–37; Wood, *Creation of the American Republic,* 328–33; Vile, *Constitutional Amending Process,* 25; Kruman, *Between Authority and Liberty,*

20–24, 28–33, 53–57; W. Adams, *First American Constitutions*, 64–66, 72–85, 134–42; Dinan, *State Constitutional Politics*.

44. Massachusetts's 1780 constitution called for a referendum in 1795, while New Hampshire's 1784 constitution required one every seven years. See Massachusetts Constitution of 1780, Frame of Government, Chapter I, Section I, Article IV, and Chapter VI, Article X; New Hampshire Constitution of 1784, Form of Government, Section 2; Nevins, *American States*, 175–81; Wood, *Creation of the American Republic*, 339–43; Kruman, *Between Authority and Liberty*, 30–33; W. Adams, *First American Constitutions*, 83–90.

45. With fifty-seven Philadelphia delegates and fifty from the outlying counties, the Provincial Convention rolls roughly reflected the colony's population distribution. By my count from the original Provincial Conference minutes, westerners constituted exactly half of the 108 delegates to the conference, mainly men of humble background, nearly all captains, majors, or colonels in the Continental army, joined by a few country lawyers and several scholars, including Benjamin Franklin and Benjamin Rush. At the constitutional convention, western delegates outnumbered those from the city of Philadelphia and the three eastern counties thirty-two to sixteen, and many of the Philadelphia delegates were themselves radicals. Theodore Thayer writes, "When one considers the composition of the Constitutional Convention, it becomes apparent that almost any procedure adopted in choosing a drafting committee would have given it a radical majority. . . . The opposition could do little more than register its protest." This radical majority rejected Whig bicameralism and suffrage qualifications for an older, simpler unicameral Saxon model espoused in two pamphlets printed in Philadelphia in 1776: Paine's *Common Sense* and the anonymous *Genuine Principles of the Ancient Saxon, or English Constitution*. Selsam, *Pennsylvania Constitution of 1776*, 71, 118; Thayer, *Pennsylvania Politics and the Growth of Democracy*, 184, 191; Wood, *Creation of the American Republic*, 226–32; Branning, *Pennsylvania Constitutional Development*, 9–16; Nash, *Unknown American Revolution*, 273–74.

46. The popular, or radical, party was led by wealthy Presbyterian Philadelphia radicals, including George Bryan, James Cameron, James Cannon, and Franklin, the convention's president. Despite their wealth, as Thayer puts it, their minds were unfettered by "traditional concepts concerning the proper form of civil government," including mixed government. Instead they had a "tendency to approve the democratic aspirations of the common man." Consequently, they allied with the west's "motley throng of backwoods farmers and country politicians" and a handful of populist German delegates from the middle counties. A few wayward Philadelphia Quakers like Timothy Matlack joined the radicals. Most conservative leaders like George Ross, George Clymer, and James Smith came from wealthy Philadelphia families. A Quaker leader in the Assembly, Ross was presiding officer in the convention. Clymer admired Montesquieu's separation of powers and the moderate Whig theory of mixed government. And per Thayer, Smith "feared an unrestrained democracy. . . . The end product of [the convention], he concluded, was forcing upon Pennsylvania a thoroughgoing democratic 'Agrarian constitution.'" P. Ford, "Adoption of the Pennsylvania Constitution of 1776," 432–34; Thayer, *Pennsylvania Politics and the Growth of Democracy*, 182–90.

47. Ben Franklin, George Bryan, and James Cameron proposed the unicameral legislature as

the Constitution's centerpiece and the locus of institutional power in the state. See the Pennsylvania Constitution of 1776, Sections 1, 8, 10, 13–15, 22, and 47.

48. The Pennsylvania Constitution established a university; subsidized public schools in each county; exempted debtors from prison on attempting repayment; guaranteed debtors reasonable bail; provided lands, commons, and game for public hunting; and let foreigners own property, assume the rights of a freeman after a year, and vote after two years. See Pennsylvania Constitution of 1776, Sections 5, 17, 20, 26, 28–29, and 43; Selsam, *Pennsylvania Constitution of 1776,* 192, 202–4; Thayer, *Pennsylvania Politics and the Growth of Democracy,* 192–96; Bailyn, *Ideological Origins of the American Revolution,* 72–79; Nash, *Unknown American Revolution,* 268–77.

49. After public review, delegates dropped an original provision granting "the rights of an elector on taking an oath or affirmation of fidelity to the Common-Wealth, if required." This excluded Quakers. As noted, framers kept a similar oath requirement for legislators. For the redacted proposal, see "The proposed plan or frame of government for the commonwealth or state of Pennsylvania: printed for consideration," Rare Book and Manuscript Library—Rare Book Collection, Van Pelt Library, University of Pennsylvania, Philadelphia.

50. Evidently this was the first use of the phrase "constituent power." The idea gained traction in France, where on the eve of their revolution, the Girondist leader Jacques Pierre Brissot circulated a French printing of the Pennsylvania Constitution with accompanying essays, which was later translated into Italian. The constitution was also reprinted in Germany. J. Adams, "Autobiography," 508; Young, "To the Inhabitants of Vermont," 76; Selsam and Rayback, "French Comment on the Pennsylvania Constitution of 1776," 311–25; Williams, "State Constitutions of the Founding Decade," 563; W. Adams, *First American Constitutions,* 63.

51. See Vermont Constitution of 1777, Declaration of Rights, Article I, and Frame of Government, Section II, XIII–IV, XVI–XIX; Georgia Constitution of 1777, Article II; Maryland Constitution of 1776, Articles I–II; Wood, *Creation of the American Republic,* 148n40, 150, 226n41; W. Adams, *First American Constitutions,* 73, 78–80; Nash, *Unknown American Revolution,* 280–84.

52. Adams pushed his May 10 and 15 resolutions through a subcommittee, rather than the Committee of the Whole, worrying that the latter might recommend unicameral governments for the states. J. Adams, "Autobiography," 506–7; W. Adams, *First American Constitutions,* 54.

53. Note that Adams's *Thoughts,* following Parliament's familiar "established modes," placed the state executive within the legislature and equivocated on the extent of veto power, perhaps in response to Massachusetts's authoritarian royal governor Thomas Gage. But considering the Virginian case specifically, he instructed Richard Henry Lee to separate powers more carefully: "It is by ballancing each of these Powers against the other two, that the Effort in humane Nature towards Tyranny, can alone be checked and restrained and any degree of Freedom preserved in the Constitution." Lee spread the letter and with his colleague George Wythe printed and disseminated Adams's final draft of *Thoughts.* Adams sent *Thoughts* to his Virginian confidant Patrick Henry, who reprinted it in Williamsburg's *Virginia Gazette* on May 10 for other members of the state constitutional

convention. Even more conservative than Adams, Braxton drafted for his fellow convention delegates a pamphlet warning against "a reckless spirit of innovation" by "advocates of popular governments" and the consequent "tumult and riot incident to simple democracy." Braxton's proposal limited lower-house elections to every third year, granted life tenure in the upper house, and urged delegates to retain their English laws and customs, including a strong executive and upper house. The pamphlet derided Adams's *Thoughts* as too trusting of democracy and public virtue. In a June 3 letter to Patrick Henry, Adams scoffed that Braxton's "little pamphlet . . . will make no fortune in the world. It is too absurd to be considered twice." Richard Henry Lee offered his own "Government Scheme" in the *Gazette,* reiterating Adams's plan and calling for an upper house and a supreme court to check the people's house. While serving in Congress, Jefferson also developed a tripartite plan of government, which he sent the Virginia convention. J. Adams, "Letter to Richard Henry Lee, November 15, 1775"; Braxton, "Address to the Convention of the Colony," 670–72; J. Adams, "Thoughts on Government," 195; J. Adams, "Letter to Patrick Henry, June 3, 1776," 387; Nevins, *American States,* 122–25, 131–46, 208, 579; Williams, "State Constitutions of the Founding Decade," 544; W. Adams, *First American Constitutions,* 118–22; Gutzman, *Virginia's American Revolution,* 24–27; Unger, *Lion of Liberty,* 113–16.

54. To Jefferson's frustration, large western counties had only two legislative seats, the same as their smaller eastern counterparts. Note also that the legislature was the state's dominant branch, electing delegates to the Continental Congress, state judges, the secretary of state, and the attorney general. See Virginia Constitution of 1776, Section 6, Bill of Rights, Section 3; Nevins, *American States,* 146–48; Wood, *Creation of the American Republic,* 156; Williams, "State Constitutions of the Founding Decade," 569–74; Kruman, *Between Authority and Liberty,* 41, 91, 117–21, 141–44; W. Adams, *First American Constitutions,* 204–5, 234–40, 265–66.

55. Adams so thoroughly promoted his treatise across the states that the historian Gordon Wood dubbed it "the most influential pamphlet in the early constitution-making period." The North Carolina legislature requested Adams's writings, which he sent to John Penn, a fellow congressman. Penn served in the North Carolina convention that December, which switched from a unicameral model to one of checks and balances. Consulting Adams's pamphlet, New York followed suit in April 1777. See North Carolina Constitution of 1776, Declaration of Rights, Section IV; New York Constitution of 1777, Sections II–III; Massachusetts Constitution of 1780, Frame of Government, Chapter I, Section I, Article II; J. Adams, "Autobiography," 508; Nevins, *American States,* 178–81; Wood, *Creation of the American Republic,* 150–61, 203–22, 558–59, 576–77; Williams, "State Constitutions of the Founding Decade," 561–74; Kruman, *Between Authority and Liberty,* 109–30; W. Adams, *First American Constitutions,* 88–90, 254–73.

56. War pressed the issue. British troops threatened Philadelphia's storehouses and armories, but Pennsylvania's weak Executive Council, scattered around the state, was unable to meet to move the provisions. The state's newly formed Republican Party, long opponents of the 1776 Pennsylvania Constitution, printed a host of pamphlets decrying the new government. Drawing on Whig arguments, they asserted that the dominance of a single branch of government was tyranny. For the quote by "Associator"—probably James Wil-

son or Benjamin Rush—see Tocqueville, *Democracy in America,* 85–86; Wood, *Creation of the American Republic,* 233–37; Nelson, *Royalist Revolution,* 164, 313n72. See also Selsam, *Pennsylvania Constitution of 1776,* 205–46; Brunhouse, *Counter-Revolution in Pennsylvania,* 27–38; Nash, *Unknown American Revolution,* 277–80.

57. These cases brought backlash. In response to *Rutgers,* the *New York Packet* attacked the act of constitutional review by judges "who are independent of the people," a claim that Richard Dobbs Spaight repeated in North Carolina in response to *Bayard.* And after Rhode Island judges affirmed merchants' right to refuse paper money, the state legislature interrogated and reprimanded these judges, replacing all but one with paper-money advocates the following term. See *Commonwealth v. Caton,* 8 Va. (4 Call.) 5 (1782), originally reported as the *Case of the Prisoners, Bayard v. Singleton,* 1 NC (1 Mar.) 42 (1787); 1776 Constitution of Virginia, Section 3; Dougherty, *Power of Federal Judiciary over Legislation,* 28–34; Wood, *Creation of the American Republic,* 457–67; Treanor, "Case of the Prisoners," 491–515.

58. Adams accepted the Whig writer James Harrington's claim that "Power always follows Property." As Adams put it, "very few Men, who have no Property, have any Judgment of their own. They talk and vote as they are directed by Some Man of Property, who has attached their Minds to his Interest." Further, a broad franchise "tends to confound and destroy all Distinctions, and prostrate all Ranks, to one common Levell," undoing the careful class balance established under tripartite Whig government. Adams therefore sought a broad and equitable distribution of property as a precondition for a broad franchise. Lax constitutional and statutory voting requirements in Adams's Massachusetts and in New Hampshire, Connecticut, and Rhode Island allowed roughly two-thirds to three-fourths of each state's free male population to vote. Vermont's 1777 constitution, unrecognized by the Congress, was the only one to eschew any property requirements. J. Adams, "Letter to James Sullivan, May 26, 1776," 375–78; Kruman, *Between Authority and Liberty,* 87–98, 315–27; W. Adams, *First American Constitutions,* 196–205, 320; Nash, *Unknown American Revolution,* 284–88.

59. After Hardwick, Blandford, and Boothbay town meetings requested abolition and equal rights for Blacks, Massachusetts's 1780 constitutional convention considered banning slavery but instead settled on a broad due process clause promising liberty to "every individual of the society." Consequently, in 1781, Anthony Vassall of Cambridge successfully petitioned the Massachusetts legislature for reparations from his loyalist owner's seized property. Several years later, an elderly Medford slave named Belinda followed his example, drafting a legislative petition. In *Brom and Bett v. Ashley,* a Berkshire County, Massachusetts, municipal court ruled that the 1780 constitution freed specifically the slaves Brom and Mum Bett. Chief Justice William Cushing of the Supreme Judicial Court finally settled the issue in a series of cases leading to *Jennison,* interpreting the state's due process clause to free all Massachusetts slaves, which the legislature affirmed. The *Jennison* decision was not recorded or read outside Massachusetts until mentioned in a separate 1867 decision, which referenced the case as *Commonwealth v. Jennison,* Rec. 1783, fol. 85. Moore, *Notes on the History of Slavery in Massachusetts,* 51; O'Brien, "Did the Jennison Case Outlaw Slavery in Massachusetts?," 219–38, 240n60; Wiecek, "Somerset," 117; Lutz, "State Constitutional Pedigree of the U.S. Bill

of Rights"; Kruman, *Between Authority and Liberty,* 37, 106–7; W. Adams, *First American Constitutions,* 181–83; Menschel, "Abolition without Deliverance," 184n3; Kramer, *People Themselves,* 269n26; Horwitz, "Historiography of the People Themselves," 816; Nash, *Unknown American Revolution,* 124–25; Finkenbine, "Belinda's Petition," 99–104; Ablavsky, "Making Indians 'White,'" 1501–2.

60. The Connecticut legislature manumitted enslaved Black patriot servicemen and in 1784 passed the Gradual Abolition Act, freeing children of slaves after twenty-five years of indentured servitude. The recorded enslaved population then dwindled from 5,000 in 1775 to 310 in 1810, though formal abolition did not come to Connecticut until 1848. Rhode Island manumitted slaves serving in the Continental army in 1778, the following year prohibited the sale of an enslaved person without his or her consent, and in 1784 freed all children of slaves. The number of slaves decreased from 4,373 in 1775 to just over a hundred slaves by 1810. Zilversmit, *First Emancipation,* 105–8; L. Horton, "From Class to Race in Early America," 639; Menschel, "Abolition without Deliverance," 183.

61. My archival research suggests John Dickinson had drafted a similar bill for gradual emancipation in Pennsylvania in 1776, stating that every "Negro or Mulatto shall be and is hereby declared to be free and to all intents and purposes," given that the slave had reached the age of eighteen or twenty-one. The Pennsylvania legislature again considered banning slave importation in 1778, and the Executive Council debated abolition the following year. The 1780 statute freed slaves after seven to twenty-eight years of indenture and, even so, was nearly repealed months after passage. A 1788 amendment freed slaves entering the state. In 1780, the *New Jersey Gazette* reprinted the Pennsylvania act, and the New Jersey legislature heard three antislavery petitions. But the state constitution lacked equality and due process clauses, and the legislature's proslavery faction killed the proposals, instead passing a 1785 nonimportation bill with some grounds for manumission. At New York's 1776 convention, Gouverneur Morris struck a proposal to "dispense the blessings of freedom to all mankind," instead deferring to "future Legislatures of the State of New-York, to take the most effective measures, consistent with the public safety, and the private property of individuals, for abolishing domestic slavery with the same." The rephrased measure passed thirty-one to five two days later. In 1781, the legislature manumitted slaves who served in the armed forces, and in 1785, it rejected an immediate abolition proposal by Aaron Burr, instead emancipating only the children of slaves and additionally forbidding the Black vote. Leading the state Council of Revision, Robert Livingston rejected the bill for violating the 1777 constitution's equality clause. Following a 1788 manumission statute and agitation by John Jay and the state Manumission Society, in 1799 the legislature freed all male children of slaves after twenty-eight years of indenture and females after twenty-five, leading slaveholders to sell off their slaves rather than free them. Delaware's 1776 constitution prohibited slave importation and freed any imported slaves on their arrival, granting the state's slave owners a monopoly on the local slave trade. Maryland allowed broader manumission, but the 1776 constitution denied slaves the due process right to life, liberty, and property. See *Mahoney v. Ashton,* 4 H. & Mc H. 295, 1799 WL 397 (Md. Gen. Ct. 1799); Delaware Constitution of 1776, Article 26; Maryland Constitution of 1776, Article XXI; R. R. Logan collection of John Dickinson papers, Series 1. b. Political, 1774–1808, Box 3, Folder 19, Historical

Society of Pennsylvania, Philadelphia; "Journal of the Provincial Convention," 887–89; Zilversmit, *First Emancipation,* 125–26, 139–46, 152–53; McManus, *History of Negro Slavery in New York,* 161–79; Wiecek, "Somerset," 128; Kaminski, *Necessary Evil?,* 31–32; L. Horton, "From Class to Race in Early America," 639; Nash, *Unknown American Revolution,* 323–27.

62. In *Robin v. Hardaway,* twelve Virginia petitioners won their freedom by establishing that they were descended from Native American women who were free under a 1691 statute. The precedent was largely forgotten, but in at least three cases between 1787 and 1793, the state Supreme Court of Appeals again used this statute to free Native American petitioners who established matrilineal Native American descent. In 1806, Native American slaves set to be transported from Virginia sued for their freedom in *Hudgins v. Wrights,* claiming that as Native Americans, they were legally "persons perfectly *white*" and hence free. Wythe granted their freedom on due process grounds, but St. George Tucker of the state supreme court held that this was a mere statutory right—much like modern Native American citizenship under the 1924 Indian Citizenship Act. He added that judges could judge Native American descent by physiological appearance, often in ways that excluded Blacks from making such matrilineal freedom appeals, cementing Black chattel slavery. Further, in 1795, the legislature forbade the state's abolitionist groups from representing slaves outside their local court district, and in 1806, outlawed freedom suits by illegally imported slaves who had resided in Virginia for a year. Under a 1782 law, some slaves could also sue owners who had reneged on promises of manumission, though such suits were now difficult. See *Robin v. Hardaway,* 1 Jeff. 109 (Va. Gen. Ct. 1772); *Hannah v. Davis* (1787); *Jenkins v. Tom* (1792); *Coleman v. Dick & Pat* (1793); *Hudgins v. Wrights,* 11 Va. (1 Hen. 8c M.) 134, 139 (1806); North Carolina Constitution of 1776, Article XII; South Carolina Constitution of 1778, Article XLI; McColley, *Slavery and Jeffersonian Virginia,* 163–67; Wiecek, "Somerset," 123–24; Countryman, *American Revolution,* 165, 239–40; Nicholls, "Squint of Freedom," 50–57; W. Adams, *First American Constitutions,* 183–84; Finkelman, *Slavery and the Founders,* 31–32; Nash, *Unknown American Revolution,* 327–29; Gutzman, *Virginia's American Revolution,* 27; Ablavsky, "Making Indians 'White,'" 1487–94, 1501–5.

63. McColley, *Slavery and Jeffersonian Virginia,* 164–67; Maier, *American Scripture,* 265n33; Nicholls, "Squint of Freedom," 51, 54–55; W. Adams, *First American Constitutions,* 178–80; Finkelman, *Slavery and the Founders,* 22–32.

64. Pennsylvania, Maryland, North Carolina, and Georgia adopted in full or part Delaware's claim to "sole exclusive and inherent Right of governing and regulating the internal Police." New York and Massachusetts also drafted similar clauses. The Articles almost exactly imitated Massachusetts's sovereignty clause. Note that the original, rejected draft of the Articles that John Dickinson reported to the Continental Congress on July 12, 1776, read, "Each Colony shall retain and enjoy as much of its present Laws, Rights and Customs, as it may think fit, and reserves to itself the sole and exclusive Regulation and Government of its internal police, in all matters that shall not interfere with the Articles of this Confederation," potentially allowing national intervention in state police powers. Congress faced the additional burden of weighing and rejecting statehood appeals from the frontier republics of Westsylvania, Vermont, and Kentucky. See 1776 Delaware Dec-

laration of Rights, Section 4; 1776 North Carolina Declaration of Rights, Section II; Massachusetts Constitution of 1780, Part I, Article IV; Articles of Confederation, Articles II and XIII; R. R. Logan collection of John Dickinson papers: Series 1. b. Political, 1774–1808, Box 3, Folders 20–21, and Box 4, Folder 22, Historical Society of Pennsylvania, Philadelphia; W. Ford, *Journals of the Continental Congress,* 5:547.

65. Gouverneur Morris, a veteran of New York's 1776 convention, explained, "the federal compact may be altered by *a majority of* [convention delegates]; in like manner as the Constitution of a particular state may be altered by a majority of the people of the state." See May 30 and 31 convention debates in Farrand, *Records,* 2:92. Williams, citing at least five other scholars, estimates that a third to a half of the federal delegates had already framed state constitutions. Farrand, 2:476, 486; Williams, "Experience Must Be Our Only Guide"; Williams, "State Constitutions of the Founding Decade," 542–43.

66. Madison expounded his frustration with the Pennsylvania model in *Federalist* 48 and Wilson in his lectures on law. George Clymer, another opponent of Pennsylvania's unicameralism, served with them at the convention. South Carolina's Pierce Butler also argued for the "distribution of the powers into different bodies." Dickinson, "Letter IV, April 19, 1788," 181–82; Farrand, *Records,* 1:30–34, 2:278, 3:595; Wood, *Creation of the American Republic,* 604; Hamilton, Madison, and Jay, *Federalist,* 243–44.

67. Pennsylvania issued a symbolic dissent to the measure, probably out of deference to Franklin, the framer of Pennsylvania's unicameral legislature. As Robert Williams explains, "One of the earliest—and most resolute—decisions of the Convention was in favor of bicameralism. . . . There was no real controversy over this point." Note also that models for bicameralism came mostly from the state constitutions, with delegates only mentioning the British Parliament twice during the debates of May 30 and 31. Farrand, *Records,* 1:46n3, 48–49, 52, 54–55, 58; Williams, "State Constitutions of the Founding Decade," 577.

68. Wilson's objection to Patterson's New Jersey plan exactly echoed his concerns with Pennsylvania: "The government is implemented in an improper manner—legislative Authority single—executive divided. . . . It provides not effectively for the true Ends of Government. The legislature and executive Power are too feeble and dependent—They and the judicial Power are too confined." See James Wilson Papers (#0721), Box 1, Volumes 2–4, Folder 2, pp. 58–59, Historical Society of Pennsylvania, Philadelphia. See also Farrand, *Records,* 1:242, 404–7, 515; W. Adams, *First American Constitutions,* 295–96; Robertson, *Constitution and America's Destiny,* 40–45.

69. Even references to classical and English Whig executives mixed with lessons from the states. Note also that delegates rejected New York's and Massachusetts's direct gubernatorial elections. Farrand, *Records,* 1:96–97; W. Adams, *First American Constitutions,* 289, 293–95; Robertson, *Constitution and America's Destiny,* 152–57; Beeman, *Penguin Guide to the United States Constitution,* 157–58.

70. New York and Vermont constitutions allowed a similarly independent council, and on August 15, Wilson suggested modeling the national council on the Pennsylvania one. Farrand, *Records,* 1:21, 97–98, 110–11, 2:74–75, 299–300; Wood, *Creation of the American Republic,* 462–63; Treanor, "Judicial Review before 'Marbury,'" 496–97, 554–57.

71. In early August, Gouverneur Morris and James Madison argued that a freehold requirement would grant the vote to small, independent farmers, while the tradesmen Gorham of Boston and Franklin of Philadelphia replied that this rule unfairly disenfranchised city dwellers. See U.S. Constitution, Article I, Section 2, Clause I, and Section 4, Clause I; Farrand, *Records,* 1:48–50, 132–38, 2:130, 216; Keyssar, *Right to Vote,* 21–24; Lutz, "Political Participation in Eighteenth-Century America," 20–21; Beaumont, *Civic Constitution,* 89–91.

72. But note that Dickinson and John Langdon broke with Northerners, arguing to nationalize abolition. John Rutledge recorded the Southern threat of defection. Farrand, *Records,* 1:476, 486, 2:369–73.

73. Note also that on July 17, Roger Sherman proposed a clause prohibiting federal interference "with the Government of the individual states in any matters of internal police which respect the Govt. of such states only, and wherein the General welfare of the U. States is not concerned." Southerners, favoring broad national powers to protect slavery, defeated this provision and a similar one, which seemed merely weak "parchment barriers." For added security, on June 11, Rutledge and Pierce Butler proposed that legislative representation remain proportionate to property in slaves, following some state models. Undeterred, on August 21, Luther Martin deemed slavery "inconsistent with the principles of the revolution and dishonorable to the American character to have such a feature in the Constitution." Four days later, Madison agreed that he "thought it wrong to admit in the Constitution the idea that there could be property in men. . . . Slaves are not like merchandise, consumed &c." Rutledge, representing South Carolina's robust slave-importation business, answered that "Religion & humanity had nothing to do with this question." See U.S. Constitution, Article I, Section 9, Clause 1; Farrand, *Records,* 2:25, 364, 370, 629–30; McColley, *Slavery and Jeffersonian Virginia,* 167; Countryman, *American Revolution,* 189–91; Finkelman, *Slavery and the Founders,* 11; Robertson, *Constitution and America's Destiny,* 177–81; Graber, *Dred Scott and the Problem of Constitutional Evil,* 101–6; Robertson, *Original Compromise,* 178–205.

74. Farrand, *Records,* 2:370.

75. In anticipation of the ratifying conventions, on November 19, 1787, the *Boston Gazette* reprinted a column arguing for ratifying by convention Pennsylvania's 1776 constitution, as did the *Maryland Gazette* of Baltimore on December 21, 1787. See U.S. Constitution, Article IV, Section 4; Farrand, *Records,* 2:88–93; "*Boston Gazette,* 19 November," 274–76; Hamilton, Madison, and Jay, *Federalist,* 183, 237–40, 426; W. Adams, *First American Constitutions.*

76. Virginia, Pennsylvania, Delaware, Maryland, North Carolina, Massachusetts, New Hampshire, and Vermont had bills of rights, Rhode Island and Connecticut kept their charters, and New Jersey, Georgia, New York, and South Carolina lacked bills. See Hamilton, Madison, and Jay, *Federalist,* 404–26; Farrand, *Records,* 1:493, 2:376, 587–88; Dumbauld, "State Precedents for the Bill of Rights"; Wood, *Creation of the American Republic;* Williams, "Experience Must Be Our Only Guide"; Lutz, "State Constitutional Pedigree of the U.S. Bill of Rights," 28; Kramer, *People Themselves,* 269n26; Beeman, *Penguin Guide to the United States Constitution,* 162.

77. See Hamilton, Madison, and Jay, *Federalist,* 240–45; Wilson and McKean, *Commen-*

taries on the Constitution of the United States of America, 41–44; Elliot, *Debates in the Several State Conventions,* 622; Bernstein and Agel, *Amending America,* 31–33; Kyvig, *Explicit and Authentic Acts,* 90–93.
78. Lutz, "State Constitutional Pedigree of the U.S. Bill of Rights," 20–29, 39–40; Bernstein and Agel, *Amending America,* 33–44; Dumbauld, "State Precedents for the Bill of Rights," 335–40.
79. Kyvig, *Explicit and Authentic Acts,* 99–109.
80. For canonical readings of the Connecticut Compromise, see Riker, "Heresthetics of Constitution-Making"; Lee, *Sizing up the Senate;* Robertson, *Constitution and America's Destiny;* Robertson, *Original Compromise;* Beeman, *Penguin Guide to the United States Constitution.* Bilder warns against overreliance on the unreliable *Notes* and, by extension, Farrand's *Records.* See Bilder, *Madison's Hand.* A handful of historians debate the states' influence on the federal Constitution. Regrettably, these insightful histories neither venture a broader causal story nor speculate beyond the founding era. See W. Adams, *First American Constitutions;* Kruman, *Between Authority and Liberty;* Lutz, "State Constitutional Pedigree of the U.S. Bill of Rights"; Miller, *Rise and Fall of Democracy in Early America;* Nash, *Unknown American Revolution;* Onuf, "State Politics and Republican Virtue"; Wood, *Creation of the American Republic;* Wood, "Foreword."
81. Winchester, *Plain Political Catechism,* 11–12, 59–62.

Chapter 3. Antebellum Consensus, 1792–1849

1. A 1796 schoolbook instructed that "no riots, mobs, nor tumultuous proceedings are necessary" to change the Constitution, with "a vast majority of the enlightened citizens of these states, examining, approving, and consenting to it." David E. Kyvig concludes, "Contributing to the limited use of amendment during the first half of the nineteenth century was a widespread, though hardly universal, feeling that once the Bill of Rights had been added, the Constitution provided an adequate structure of government." Nevertheless, after the disputed presidential election of 1800, Jeffersonians considered scrapping the Constitution through a second convention, and Federalists at the 1814–15 Hartford Convention considered New England secession or fundamental constitutional redesign via eight amendments. Winchester, *Plain Political Catechism,* 11–12, 59–62; Fiske, *Critical Period of American History,* 390; Wilentz, *Chants Democratic,* 87; Caplan, *Constitutional Brinksmanship,* 42–46; Kammen, *Machine That Would Go of Itself,* 14–15, 45–48, 52; Kyvig, *Explicit and Authentic Acts,* 110, 120–21; Jefferson, "Letter to Samuel Kercheval, July 12, 1816."
2. McCormick, "Political Development and the Second Party System"; Sundquist, *Dynamics of the Party System;* Skowronek, *Politics Presidents Make;* Whittington, *Political Foundations of Judicial Supremacy,* 33–34, 56–61, 75; Whittington, "Judicial Review of Congress."
3. The 1777 New York Constitution, for example, did not allow amendment, presaging the 1821 New York Constitution's failure to provide a mechanism for calling future conventions. And elites often passed legally dubious reforms and vetoed legitimate popular referenda, so that, according to James Dealey, only eight of the eighteen states replacing

their constitutions between 1828 and 1860 followed the constitutionally sanctioned procedure for calling a convention. As Donald Lutz summarizes, "The first state constitutions were not used legalistically the way Americans use constitutions today. . . . Political conflicts were not susceptible to resolutions on the basis of the precise wording of a constitution." Later Jacksonian framers formalized higher amendment barriers to prevent legislative practices that contributed to the Panic of 1837, as explained in this chapter. Paine, *Rights of Man,* 297; Dealey, *Growth of American State Constitutions,* 41–50; Parkinson, "Antebellum State Constitution-Making," 1–13; Tarr, *Understanding State Constitutions,* 102–5; Henretta, "Rise of 'Democratic-Republicanism,'" 61–63; Lutz, "Political Participation in Eighteenth-Century America," 21; Dinan, *State Constitutional Politics.*

4. *Chisholm v. Georgia,* 2 U.S. 419, 457 (1793) stripped states' sovereign immunity, but was soon overruled by the Eleventh Amendment, granting states sovereign immunity from private suits by citizens of other states. This did little to clarify the extent of state economic powers.

5. Jeffersonians opposed a national bank that could muscle out state banks, for as Jefferson explained, "To take a single step beyond the boundaries thus specifically drawn around the powers of Congress, is to take possession of a boundless field of power, no longer susceptible to any definition. The incorporation of a bank, and the powers assumed by this bill, have not, in my opinion, been delegated to the United States, by the Constitution." Therefore, in the winter of 1793–94, the Senate debated three proposed amendments excluding bankers from Congress. The rechartering of the Bank of the United States brought eight proposals on congressional authority to establish a bank between 1813 and 1821. Jefferson, "Opinion on the Constitutionality of a National Bank," 198; Ames, *Proposed Amendments,* 29–30; Goodman, "First American Party System," 63–85; Aldrich, *Why Parties?,* 70–83.

6. Hofstadter, *Idea of a Party System,* 168–71; Lomazoff, "Turning (into) 'The Great Regulating Wheel,'" 4–14.

7. For example, in *Calder,* Justice Samuel Chase had held the federal Supreme Court "has no jurisdiction to determine that any law of any state Legislature, contrary to the Constitution of such state, is void. . . . The courts of Connecticut are the proper tribunals to decide, whether laws, contrary to the constitution thereof, are void." But also note that in *Martin,* the Federalist Joseph Story ruled that the Constitution granted the federal courts appellate jurisdiction over civil cases originating in the state courts, to the frustration of Virginia judge Spencer Roane. Five years later in *Cohens,* Marshall rejected Roane's claim to sole jurisdiction over state criminal cases, arguing that the Cohens's appeal concerned federal law. See *Calder v. Bull,* 3 U.S. 386, 392–93 (1798); *Martin v. Hunter's Lessee,* 14 U.S. 304 (1816); *Cohens v. Virginia,* 19 U.S. 264 (1821).

8. In *McCulloch,* Marshall again interpreted "the constitutional powers of the national government liberally" to uphold Madison's rechartering of the National Bank as a means to "effectuate [the Constitution's] great objects" of national economic development. As Keith Whittington notes, "*McCulloch* was decidedly activist, but this activism was directed against the states on behalf of the national constitutional regime." Jefferson had

predicted as much, noting that a federal "court may encroach on the jurisdiction of the state courts. It may. But there will be a power, to wit, Congress, to watch & restrain them." Lowrie's attack on *McCulloch,* the Court, and the National Bank, made on behalf of the Pennsylvania legislature, used distinctly Jeffersonian language: "In proportion as the capital of a moneyed institution is increased, its branches extended, and its direction removed from the body of the people, so also will be increased its power and inclination to do evil and to tyrannize." See *McCulloch v. Maryland,* 17 U.S. 316, 386 (1819); *Osborn v. Bank of the United States,* 22 U.S. 738 (1824); Jefferson, "Letter to James Madison, June 20, 1787," 285; *Debates and Proceedings in the Congress of the United States: Sixteenth Congress, First Session,* 70; Ames, *Proposed Amendments,* 255–57; B. Hammond, "Bank Cases," 30–33; Whittington, *Political Foundations of Judicial Supremacy,* 111–12.
9. Ames, *Proposed Amendments,* 255–58.
10. *Worcester v. Georgia,* 31 U.S. (6 Pet.) 515 (1832); *Congressional Globe: Twenty-Third Congress, Second Session,* 150; Ames, *Proposed Amendments,* 250, 257; B. Hammond, *Banks and Politics in America,* 326–457.
11. In upholding the state charter in *Willson,* Marshall affirmed a suit brought by the dam company against Thompson Willson, who disassembled part of the dam while piloting a sloop under a federal shipping license granted under Congress's commerce powers. See *Willson v. Black-Bird Creek Marsh Co.,* 27 U.S. (2 Pet.) 245 (1829); *Barron v. Baltimore,* 32 U.S. (7 Pet.) 243 (1833); McCloskey and Levinson, *American Supreme Court,* 23–30, 50–52; Whittington, *Political Foundations of Judicial Supremacy,* 31–33, 107–14; Laska, *Tennessee State Constitution,* 7.
12. In *Charles River Bridge,* the Charles River Bridge Company claimed that in forming a competing company, the Massachusetts legislature violated the Charles River Bridge Company's original charter and according federal Contract Clause rights. But Taney asserted that the charter never granted exclusive rights and so could not constrain the legislature. *Briscoe* was more remarkable for circumventing the federal Constitution's stipulation that the states not issue credit. See *Charles River Bridge v. Warren Bridge,* 36 U.S. 420 (1837); *Mayor of New York v. Miln,* 36 U.S. 102 (1837); *Briscoe v. Bank of Commonwealth of Kentucky,* 36 U.S. 257 (1837); *Bank of Augusta v. Earle,* 38 U.S. 519 (1839); U.S. Constitution, Article I, Section 10; B. Hammond, *Banks and Politics in America,* 563–72.
13. The Michigan Constitution of 1835 stipulated only that an act of incorporation be approved by two-thirds of both legislative houses. But in Tennessee, a rash of special legislation led delegates to the state's 1834 convention to forbid legislators from suspending any general law for the benefit of a private party and from granting immunities to any citizen that could not apply to all citizens. See Michigan Constitution of 1835, Article III, Section 43; B. Hammond, *Banks and Politics in America,* 451–53; Laska, *Tennessee State Constitution,* 9; Fino, *Michigan State Constitution,* 1–8; Steinglass and Scarselli, *Ohio State Constitution,* 16–17.
14. B. Hammond, *Banks and Politics in America,* 451–99; Steinglass and Scarselli, *Ohio State Constitution,* 16–17.
15. The one exception is Missouri's 1820 constitution, which included only two regulations.

16. For example, in 1846, Iowa's framers required that corporate and bank charters be approved by voters, last no more than twenty years, and be subject to legislative repeal and forbade the chartering of banks to print money. See Florida Constitution of 1839, Article VI, Section 3, and Article XIII, Sections 1–14; Iowa Constitution of 1846, Article I, Section 12, Article IX, Sections 5–8, 10–11, 13, Article X, Sections 1–3; California Constitution of 1849, Article IV, Sections 33–36, Article VIII, and Article XI, Section 10; Oregon Constitution of 1857, Article I, Section 19, Article XI, Section 1–10; Minnesota Constitution of 1857, Article VIII; Kansas's Lecompton Constitution of 1857, Article XII, Sections 1–7, Article IX, Section 3–4; D'Alemberte, *Florida State Constitution*, 1–5; Grodin, Massey, and Cunningham, *California State Constitution*, 1–9; Stark, *Iowa State Constitution*, 1–5.
17. New York passed no direct taxes between 1826 and 1842 but through loans financed an elaborate public works system, including the Erie Canal. The state soon exhausted its treasury and credit, and New Yorkers voted overwhelmingly for the 1846 convention that scrapped all but eleven of the previous constitution's clauses, building an elaborate system of constitutional checks on legislators, adding provisions keeping legislators from granting special charters or incurring debt without public approval, forcing legislators to repay canal debt, and creating an independent Canal Board to oversee future projects. An 1846 amendment to Arkansas's 1836 constitution forbade the incorporation of new banks, and in 1847, Maine legislators passed an amendment limiting the state's authority to take on debt. On state banking and finance amendments generally, see Dinan, *State Constitutional Politics*, 159–71. See Indiana Constitution of 1816, Article I, Section 17, and Article X, Section 1; Maine Constitution of 1819, Article IX, Section 1, amendment of 1847; Michigan Constitution of 1835, Article III, Section 43, the New York Constitution of 1846, Article V, Section 5, Article VII; Arkansas Constitution of 1836, Article I, amendment of 1846; Michigan Constitution of 1850, Articles XIV–XV; Indiana Constitution of 1851, Article I, Section 22, Article XI, Section 1–7, 11–13, Article X, Section 5–6; Tinkle, *Maine State Constitution*, 7; Goss, *Arkansas State Constitution*, 1–3.
18. For example, in 1835, Tennessee instituted judicial elections to check the legislature, and after local road and turnpike projects failed, Kentucky delegates required that the legislature submit to voters all nonemergency loans over $500,000. But note that Dove and Young find that for 1841–84, lower-specificity state constitutions were less likely to be associated with state default. See New York Constitution of 1846, Article III, Section 2; Laska, *Tennessee State Constitution*, 7–9; Ireland, *Kentucky State Constitution*, 6–8; Gallie, *Ordered Liberty*, 9–116; Dinan, *American State Constitutional Tradition*, 67–76; Dove and Young, "US State Constitutional Entrenchment and Default."
19. Debtors' protections were the oldest and most common debt regulation. Wisconsin's 1846 constitutional convention, for example, proposed preventing the seizure of debtors' homes and banning banks outright, but voters rejected the document. Two years later, voters instead approved a constitution forbidding imprisonment for debt but allowing lenders to seize debtors' homes, limited by the "privilege of the debtor to enjoy the necessary comforts of life." Kentucky's 1850 document was the lone post-1837 antebellum constitution not to regulate banks. See Wisconsin Constitution of 1848, Article I, Sec-

tions 16–17. In 1852, Wisconsin voters approved a referendum instituting banks within the state but subject to careful regulation. Stark, *Wisconsin State Constitution,* 4–8.

20. As the panic spread in March 1837, a select congressional committee proposed prohibiting the states from incorporating a bank to issue paper notes. The amendment failed, as did similar amendments proposed by Representative Rice Garland of Louisiana and James Buchanan—neither drawing floor debate—and another proposed by an 1840 select committee. Van Buren, "Fourth Annual Message to Congress," 1149; Ames, *Proposed Amendments,* 250–58; *Congressional Globe: Twenty-Fifth Congress, Second Session,* 311; *Congressional Globe: Twenty-Sixth Congress, First Session,* 224–25.

21. At the federal convention, Madison proposed making this balance explicit by representing slaves in one house but not the other, but the measure failed; and so the Northwest Ordinance and North Carolina Cession Act filled this role as quasi-constitutional statutes, the latter aiming for the permanence of a constitutional amendment, declaring, "*Provided always* that no regulations made or to be made by Congress shall tend to emancipate Slaves." Farrand, *Records,* 1:486–87; Lynd, "Compromise of 1787," 225–33, 243–50; Onuf, *Origins of the Federal Republic,* 169–71; Finkelman, *Slavery and the Founders,* 8–22, 37–39; Graber, *Dred Scott and the Problem of Constitutional Evil,* 9–16, 102–3.

22. "In the Northwestern Territory," Harper argued, "the regulation forbidding slavery was a very proper one, as the people inhabiting that part of the country were from parts where slavery did not prevail." But to extend abolition to Mississippi would unwisely strike "at the habits and customs of the people" of the Mississippi Territory. *Debates and Proceedings in the Congress of the United States: Fifth Congress, Second Session,* 1306–11; Ames, *Proposed Amendments,* 45–46; Fehrenbacher, *Slaveholding Republic,* 256–58; J. Hammond, *Slavery, Freedom, and Expansion,* 11–29; Hartley, *Failed Attempts to Amend the Constitution,* 25–26.

23. For example, the Federalist senator James Hillhouse of Connecticut sought to reduce Southern seats in Congress by abolishing the domestic and international slave trade within the Louisiana Territory and emancipating male slaves at the latest at age twenty-two and females at nineteen. Federalists Timothy Pickering and John Quincy Adams rallied with Democratic-Republican Southerners to defeat the latter provision. The importation prohibition stood, provoking an angry, seditious petition from Louisiana slaveholders, and so Southerners led Congress to let these antislavery provisions expire the following year. An 1811 attempt by the Massachusetts Federalist Josiah Quincy to block Louisiana statehood also failed. *Debates and Proceedings in the Congress of the United States: Eighth Congress, First Session,* 238–44; Finkelman, "Evading the Ordinance," 30–33; Finkelman, *Slavery and the Founders,* 40, 60–72; Skowronek, *Politics Presidents Make,* 78–79; Fehrenbacher, *Slaveholding Republic,* 260–61; Levinson and Sparrow, introduction to *Louisiana Purchase,* 9–13; Graber, *Dred Scott and the Problem of Constitutional Evil,* 118–19; J. Hammond, *Slavery, Freedom, and Expansion,* 3, 30–58, 103–13.

24. Subsequent presidents enforced the clause in the District of Columbia and the territories and requested fugitives' return from Spanish Florida, Mexico, Canada, and some Native American tribes but did not interfere with the states' enforcement. Similarly, in 1801,

Northern representatives defeated a proposed amendment to the act fining employers who hired Blacks who did not carry a certificate of freedom. In 1817, a bill to compel Northern governors and judges to enforce the act passed the House and Senate but died during reconciliation. Fehrenbacher, *Slaveholding Republic*, 205–14; Finkelman, *Slavery and the Founders*, 81–104.

25. In New England, initially only Vermont constitutionally abolished slavery, while other New England legislatures and courts extended state constitutional due process liberties to all persons, including slaves. New York and Pennsylvania passed personal liberty laws protecting the legal rights of free Blacks and punishing slave catchers who seized freemen, as did the new states of Ohio and Indiana. Courts in Virginia, the Carolinas, and Georgia still largely refused to extend constitutional rights to slaves and free Blacks, and in 1832, the Virginia legislature defeated a gradual emancipation proposal. See Vermont Constitution of 1793, Chapter 1, Section 1; Rhode Island Constitution of 1842, Article I, Section 4; the failed "Landholder's Constitution" of 1842, Article I, Section 19; Graber, *Dred Scott and the Problem of Constitutional Evil*, 128.

26. Old Northwest states upheld national bisectionalism while preserving limited slavery within their borders. The Ohio Constitution declared, "no alteration of this constitution shall ever take place so as to introduce slavery or involuntary servitude into this State," but allowed indentured servitude for Black apprentices and forbade Blacks from voting, officeholding, military service, and legal testimony against whites. The Indiana Constitution also allowed continued indenture of existing servants and forbade Blacks from militia service. The state supreme court twice upheld the ban on slavery, and slaveholders fled west. In 1800, 5.3 percent of Indianans and 45.3 percent of Indianan Blacks were enslaved. By 1820, the proportion decreased to 1 percent and 13.3 percent, respectively. The state's 1851 constitution consequently forbade Blacks from immigrating and fined resident Blacks for engaging in contracts, using profits from these fines to pay Blacks to leave the state. The Illinois Constitution of 1818 legalized Black indenture and granted slaveholders a seven-year grace period before slavery was expressly abolished and allowed the indenture of servants' children. James Talmadge unsuccessfully rallied thirty-three Northern House members against Illinois's admission to the Union but was defeated by the moderate House majority. Ultimately an 1845 Illinois Supreme Court decision, *Jarrot v. Jarrot*, 2 Gilman 1 (1845), abolished slavery, affirmed by the 1848 Illinois constitutional convention, which also outlawed immigration of free and enslaved Black people. See Ohio Constitution of 1802, Article VII, Section 5, and Article VIII, Section 2; Indiana Constitution of 1816, Article VII, Article VIII, Section 1, and Article IX, Section 7; Illinois Constitution of 1818, Article VI, Sections 1–3; Illinois Constitution of 1848, Article XIII, Section 16, and Article XIV; Indiana Constitution of 1851, Article XIII; *State v. Lasselle*, 1 Blackf. (Ind.) 122 (1821); *In re Mary Clark, a Woman of Color*, 1 Blackf. (Ind.) 122 (1822); Robinson, *Slavery in the Structure of American Politics*, 404; Finkelman, *Imperfect Union*, 150–55; Finkelman, *Slavery and the Founders*, 38–39, 58–80, 208n6, 221; McLauchlan, *Indiana State Constitution*, 1–5; Fehrenbacher, *Slaveholding Republic*, 264; Steinglass and Scarselli, *Ohio State Constitution*, 1–13; J. Hammond, *Slavery, Freedom, and Expansion*, 76–95, 113–23.

27. Kentucky's second convention, in 1799, renewed the 1792 slavery provision and ex-

pressly disenfranchised "negroes, mulattoes, and Indians." Louisiana's 1812 convention entrenched the state's planter class with property and tax requirements on voting and officeholding. Tennessee, however, enfranchised freeholders, including Blacks. See Kentucky Constitution of 1792, Article IX; Kentucky Constitution of 1799, Article II, Section 8; Tennessee Constitution of 1796, Article I, Section 26, and Article III, Section 1; Louisiana Constitution of 1812, Article II, Section 8, and Article III, Section 4; Mississippi Constitution of 1817, Article V, Section 6, and Article VI; Robinson, *Slavery in the Structure of American Politics*, 385–86, 404; Laska, *Tennessee State Constitution*, 2–7; Hargrave, *Louisiana State Constitution*, 2–3; Winkle, *Mississippi State Constitution*, 2–5; Ireland, *Kentucky State Constitution*, 1–5; J. Hammond, *Slavery, Freedom, and Expansion*, 1–8.

28. Under the 1800 Harrison Land Act, the federal government helped incoming settlers finance Missouri land purchases, attracting middling slaveholders who could not buy expensive Southeastern land. Later slaveholders came to the territory after Illinois banned slavery in 1818.

29. Tallmadge argued that the Constitution's Guarantee Clause, requiring republican government in all states, forbade slavery. For the Livermore amendment, see *Debates and Proceedings in the Congress of the United States: Fifteenth Congress, First Session*, 1675–76. See also Fehrenbacher, *Slaveholding Republic*, 263; Graber, *Dred Scott and the Problem of Constitutional Evil*, 120–23; Mason, *Slavery and Politics*, 177–212; J. Hammond, *Slavery, Freedom, and Expansion*, 3, 55–75, 150–67.

30. During the Missouri crisis, Congressman Rufus King cited Article IV, Section 3, to argue that Congress's authority over the territories extended to regulating slavery, and John W. Taylor argued that the Nonimportation Clause of Article I, Section 9, allowed Congress to prohibit slave importation into the territories. Congress could also refuse statehood to noncompliant territories. After the Crisis, Congress refused to intervene and rebuffed Northern state legislatures' petitions to abolish territorial slavery, including Ohio's early request in 1824. *Debates and Proceedings in the Congress of the United States: Sixteenth Congress, First Session*, 952; Dealey, *Growth of American State Constitutions*, 50; Fehrenbacher, *Slaveholding Republic*, 264; Graber, *Dred Scott and the Problem of Constitutional Evil*, 123–25.

31. Congress delayed Arkansas's statehood petition until paired with Michigan, admitting the former under an 1836 constitution that largely forbade emancipation and Black voting and legislative officeholding, and charged the legislature with controlling the slave trade. Florida's constitution, framed two years later, also prohibited legislators from emancipating slaves, allowing them to control the influx of free and enslaved people of color into the state, though Congress did not admit Florida until 1845, paired with Iowa. Wisconsin soon joined, balancing the 1845 admission of Texas. Texans forbade legislators from emancipating slaves without compensation or blocking their importation. However, the 1845 constitution also prohibited legislators from stripping slaves' rights to jury trial and obligated slaveholders to feed and clothe their slaves. Over a dozen Southern constitutions promised humane treatment of slaves, though these clauses were mere parchment barriers. In contrast, Oregon's 1843 and 1845 Organic Laws and subsequent territorial legislation prohibited slavery and Black immigration, under punishment of

whipping. By the ratification of Mississippi's 1831 constitution, nearly all Southern states constitutionally recognized slavery. See Arkansas Constitution of 1836, Article II, Section 21, Article IV, Sections 2, 4, 6, 25, Article IX, Section 1; Texas Constitution of 1845, Article III, Sections 1–3; Oregon Organic Law of 1843, Article I, Section 4; Oregon Organic Law of 1845, Article I, Section 4; Florida Constitution of 1839, Article XVI, Sections 1–3; the proposed Wisconsin Constitution of 1846, Article XVI, Section 2; the ratified Wisconsin Constitution of 1848, Article I, Section 2; and appendix C; D'Alemberte, *Florida State Constitution*, 1–5; Grodin, Massey, and Cunningham, *California State Constitution*, 1–9; Goss, *Arkansas State Constitution*, 1–9; Schuman, "Creation of the Oregon Constitution," 611–17; Stark, *Iowa State Constitution*, 1–5; Herron, *Framing the Solid South*, 51–52.

32. Starting in 1832, the Democratic Party required that all presidential and vice presidential candidates claim two-thirds of convention delegates to receive the party's nomination, requiring interregional compromise between delegates. Three years later, Jackson ordered the federal post to impound abolitionist printing and refused Texas's 1836 statehood petition until it was paired with a free state's. And in 1835, free-state Democratic congressmen joined their slave-state counterparts in instituting a gag rule to table antislavery petitions. Free-state Democrats voted for the measure sixty-one to fourteen and voted seventy-five to five for a separate resolution preventing interference with slavery in the District of Columbia. Free-state Whigs, however, voted against the gag rule forty-three to one, pointing to an early split between antislavery and "cotton" Whigs. *Debates and Proceedings in the Congress of the United States: Twenty-Fourth Congress, First Session*, 665; Ames, *Proposed Amendments*, 193; Sundquist, *Dynamics of the Party System*, 50–55; Fehrenbacher, *Slaveholding Republic*, 266; Graber, *Dred Scott and the Problem of Constitutional Evil*, 12–13, 91–93, 102–3, 115–26.

33. Adams declared, "Power always follows Property," such that the propertyless were not sufficiently independent to vote, a position he elaborated at Massachusetts's 1821 constitutional convention. In 1776, Jefferson proposed granting many Virginian males fifty acres, hoping that a propertied electorate would think and vote independently, and a generation later, endorsed an 1816 movement to reform the Virginia Constitution to grant universal white male suffrage. J. Adams, "Letter to James Sullivan, May 26, 1776," 375–78; Keyssar, *Right to Vote*, 11, 27, 30; Hamilton, Madison, and Jay, *Federalist*, 256.

34. The former were Massachusetts, Virginia, New York, Maryland, South Carolina; and the latter, New Hampshire, Pennsylvania, New Jersey, Georgia. In Connecticut, a preliminary election then narrowed the field by a third, from which a second election selected a representative. In 1800, John Nicholas proposed a national amendment for House election by district. Similar district proposals came in 1802 and 1813, with three later amendments passing the Senate before failing in the House. Ames, *Proposed Amendments*, 28–29, 56–58, 80–84, 113.

35. Patrician delegates to New York's 1776 constitutional convention restricted the vote for state assemblymen to those who held twenty pounds in freehold or rented a tenement valued at forty shillings, enfranchising only 70.7 percent of the heads of families and 60 percent of white males. By 1821, only 78 percent of adult male New Yorkers could vote for assemblymen and only 39 percent for the governor or senators. Adult males with at

least a hundred pounds in freehold—only 28.9 percent of the total—could vote for state senators or governor. Similarly, a muster of one thousand Shenandoah County, Virginia, militiamen found that seven hundred lacked the vote. In Loudon County to the north, one thousand of twelve hundred were disenfranchised. See New York Constitution of 1777, Articles VII and X; Cheyney, *Anti-Rent Agitation in the State of New York;* McKinley, *Suffrage Franchise,* 284–92; Gallie, *Ordered Liberty,* 90–94; Kruman, *Between Authority and Liberty,* 87–90; Keyssar, *Right to Vote,* 12–19, 34–37, 228; W. Adams, *First American Constitutions,* 196–205; Nash, *Unknown American Revolution,* 284–88; Henretta, "Rise of 'Democratic-Republicanism,'" 37–39.

36. Congressional acts authorizing Ohio's and Indiana's first constitutional conventions allowed white male taxpayers with a year of residence to vote for state convention delegates. Congress abandoned these taxpaying requirements for convention elections in Illinois in 1818, Michigan in 1835, and Wisconsin in 1846. Note also that in some states, framers held that militia service qualified men to vote. Framers in Delaware, South Carolina, and Michigan also reduced residency requirements on the franchise, and after Pennsylvania Whigs passed an 1836 Registry Act to temper the Democratic vote, Democrats halved residency requirements at the state's 1837 constitutional convention, hoping to attract new immigrant voters. See Kentucky Constitution of 1792, Article I, Section 11; Kentucky Constitution of 1799, Article II, Section 8; Tennessee Constitution of 1796, Article III, Section 1; Indiana Constitution of 1816, Article VI, Section 1; Alabama Constitution of 1819, Article III, Section 5; McCormick, "New Perspectives on Jacksonian Politics," 297–98; R. Smith, *Civic Ideals,* 171; Ireland, *Kentucky State Constitution,* 1–5; Keyssar, *Right to Vote,* 30, 37–39; Henretta, "Rise of 'Democratic-Republicanism,'" 59.

37. Between 1800 and 1806, Democratic-Republicans captured from Federalists both houses of the legislature in New York (1800–1802), Pennsylvania (1801), New Jersey (1801–1802), New Hampshire (1805), and Massachusetts (1806); held both houses in Maryland (1800–1801) and Rhode Island (1801); and swept unicameral Vermont (1802). Connecticut (1817–1818) and Delaware (1822) soon followed. Connecticut's Jeffersonian Toleration Party, for example, captured the lower house in 1817 and the upper house the following year, amending the constitution to exempt taxpayers and militiamen from property qualifications on the vote. See Connecticut Constitution of 1818, Article I, Sections 3–4, Article VI, Section 2; Goodman, "First American Party System," 65–81; W. Horton, *Connecticut State Constitution,* 5–14; Dubin, *Party Affiliations in the State Legislatures,* 33–34; Graham, *South Carolina State Constitution,* 13–16.

38. Attacking the property requirement, Van Buren captured the nation's spirit: "in none of [the Southern] Constitutions, nor in those of any state in the Union, except North Carolina, was such a provision as that proposed by the amendment to be found. In the Constitution of the Union, too, which has been in operation long enough to test the correctness and soundness of its principles, there was no excessive freehold representation." For Van Buren, free labor guaranteed the material independence that qualified one to vote. This disqualified those who did not own their labor—women, slaves, and perhaps Native Americans and aliens. The convention kept the freehold qualification for Blacks, and so the vote would go only to white men, "who have wives and children to protect and support." Van Buren also opposed enfranchising highway workers, whom he thought too

deferential to their wealthy employers and "not prepared for universal suffrage." See New York Constitution of 1821, Article II, Section 1; Carter and Stone, *Proceedings and Debates,* 256–57; R. Smith, *Civic Ideals,* 172; Tarr, *Understanding State Constitutions,* 103; Keyssar, *Right to Vote,* 45; Henretta, "Rise of 'Democratic-Republicanism,'" 56–58.

39. For example, Delaware eliminated constitutional property qualifications in 1792 and Maryland in 1802. Massachusetts repealed property restrictions over John Adams's protestation in 1821, and Democrats enfranchised North Carolina's landless poor in 1850. Louisiana's 1845 convention unseated the French planter class and scrapped property and taxpaying requirements to extend the vote to all adults over twenty-one with two years of state residency, reapportioned the legislature, and increased the number of elected offices. When the Connecticut convention of 1818 replaced the state's outmoded colonial charter and broadened the franchise, it also provided for annual elections, legislative amendment and election of judges, and amendment by referendum. See Delaware Constitution of 1792, Article IV, Section 1; Maryland Constitution of 1776, Article II, amendment of 1802; Connecticut Constitution of 1818, Article 6 and Article 11, Section 1; Louisiana Constitution of 1845, Title II, Articles 8 and 10. For full data on state constitutional repeal measures, see Keyssar, *Right to Vote,* 29–32, 50–52, 271, 330–35. See also J. Adams, "Letter to James Madison, June 17, 1817," 267–68; Carter and Stone, *Proceedings and Debates of the Convention of 1821,* 278; Dealey, *Growth of American State Constitutions,* 42–46; Sturm, "Development of American State Constitutions," 63–66; Hargrave, *Louisiana State Constitution,* 1–5; R. Smith, *Civic Ideals,* 172; Tarr, *Understanding State Constitutions,* 102–5.

40. The New York labor movement, as Sean Wilentz writes, "had been reclaimed by more conventional politicians; after 1832 the consolidation of a new brand of establishment politics, under the aegis of the Democrats and the emerging Whigs, would preclude the rise of anything like the Working Men's movement for twenty years." Contrast this to Europe, where exclusion of urban laborers prompted the organization of workingmen's parties. American franchise expansion coincided with race- and gender-based restrictions. At New York's 1846 convention, John Kennedy declared that the franchise was "not a natural right" but "a privilege, a franchise, a civil right," conditioned on "mature age and sex." Framers in some states asserted that even adult wage-earning Blacks, Native Americans, and immigrants lacked the mental and moral capacities for citizenship or the vote. For example, delegates to Maine's 1819 convention excluded some Native Americans from the state polity and vote but included free Blacks in both. New York, Massachusetts, Connecticut, Vermont, Maryland, and Virginia repealed universal suffrage for citizen suffrage and excluded aliens, as did every new state constitution drafted between 1800 and 1840, save Illinois's. Free Blacks lost the vote in Connecticut, North Carolina, and Tennessee in 1835, in Pennsylvania in 1839, and in New Jersey in 1844; in 1807, New Jersey repealed the nation's only provision to allow female suffrage. By 1860, only the New England states, save Connecticut, still allowed free Blacks to vote without qualification. Jacksonians were more meticulous in restricting citizenship to white males than were Whigs. See Maine Constitution of 1819, Article II, Section 1; Pennsylvania Constitution of 1839, Article III, Section 1; North Carolina Constitution of 1819, Article I,

Section 3, amendment of 1835; Tennessee Constitution of 1835, Article IV, Section 1; New Jersey Constitution of 1844, Article II, Section 1; Crosswell and Sutton, *Debates and Proceedings in the New York Convention*, 783; Wilentz, *Chants Democratic*, 213; R. Smith, *Civic Ideals*, 165–242; Tarr, *Understanding State Constitutions*, 105–7; Scalia, *America's Jeffersonian Experiment*, 58–62; Keyssar, *Right to Vote*, 32–33, 44–48; Henretta, "Rise of 'Democratic-Republicanism,'" 52–55.

41. The legislature first rejected an 1817 call and offered in February 1821 to call a convention but refused to address the suffrage issue, so Providence voters defeated the proposition. Three years later, voters approved a convention; but delegates were selected under the standing malapportionment scheme, and they maintained malapportionment and suffrage restrictions and even scrapped the clause enfranchising the sons of freemen. Voters rejected this proposed 1824 constitution. Five years later, the legislature rejected an appeal by Providence residents for suffrage expansion. And an 1834 convention dissolved for lack of quorum, leaving apportionment and suffrage laws untouched. Mowry, *Dorr War*, 28–38; Dealey, *Growth of American State Constitutions*, 42, 49–50; Wiecek, "Peculiar Conservatism," 241; Tarr, *Understanding State Constitutions*, 102; Keyssar, *Right to Vote*, 71–76, 333.

42. See *Luther v. Borden*, 48 U.S. 1 (1849); Rhode Island Constitution of 1843, Article II, Section 1; Tyler, "Letter to Samuel King, May 7, 1842," 2146–47; Mowry, *Dorr War*, 268; Wiecek, "Peculiar Conservatism," 240–45; Keyssar, *Right to Vote*, 70–76, 333; Conley and Flanders, *Rhode Island State Constitution*; Chaput, *People's Martyr*, 119–81.

43. I am not claiming that franchise expansion alone prevented local tumult but rather that most states expanded the franchise and found relative political stability. From my passing survey of the Oxford Commentaries on the State Constitutions of the United States, between 1800 and 1850, prolonged rioting, militia mobilizing, or extralegal constitutional agitation by free males occurred in seven states: Rhode Island, Maryland, New York, Pennsylvania, Texas, New Mexico, and California. The latter three granted broad suffrage to white males but faced domestic turmoil during their split from Mexico. Note also that Virginia, Louisiana, and North Carolina bucked the national trend, maintaining franchise restrictions and malapportionment with little trouble. Jameson, *Treatise on Constitutional Conventions*, 216; Egle and Ritner, "Buckshot War"; Dealey, *Growth of American State Constitutions*, 49; McCormick, "Political Development and the Second Party System," 134–47, 154–66; Gallie, *New York State Constitution*, 1–14; Gallie, *Ordered Liberty*, 9–116.

44. Ames's summary mentions no antebellum proposals for a suffrage amendment, nor does Kyvig's study, which asserts that the antebellum Congress avoided the suffrage issue. Ames, *Proposed Amendments*; Kyvig, *Explicit and Authentic Acts*, 386–87.

45. Following Congress's 1842 Apportionment Act, Georgia, Mississippi, Missouri, and New Hampshire continued to use at-large elections. Holst, *Constitutional and Political History*, 336–40; Ames, *Proposed Amendments*, 56–58; Mast, "History of Single-Member Districts"; Vile, *Encyclopedia of Constitutional Amendments*, 547–64.

46. *Congressional Globe: Twenty-First Congress: First Session*, 8.

47. Stanwood, *History of Presidential Elections*, 74–100; Ames, *Proposed Amendments*, 21, 82, 85–88, 106–7, 112, 122, 339–43.

Chapter 4. State Reconstruction, 1850–1877

1. The 1850–77 yearly federal amendment proposal rate exceeded the 1792–1877 yearly mean in 1860–61, 1864–69, 1872–73, and 1876–77 and by at least a standard deviation in 1860–61, 1864, 1866, and 1869.
2. The 1850–77 yearly state constitutional proposal rate exceeded the 1792–1877 yearly mean by at least a standard deviation for 1850–51, 1857, 1861, 1864–65, 1868, and 1875 and exceeded the 1792–1877 yearly mean, even when weighted by the increasing number of states, by at least a standard deviation in 1850–51, 1857, 1861, 1864–65, and 1868.
3. Sundquist, *Dynamics of the Party System;* Dubin, *Party Affiliations in the State Legislatures,* 10.
4. Further, some states failed to specify a revision procedure, and dozens of nineteenth-century state constitutions were drafted or revised without explicit legal authority, including many Confederate state constitutions. See Herron, *Framing the Solid South,* 92.
5. On the federal courts' role in the 1850s slavery crisis, see *Prigg v. Pennsylvania,* 41 U.S. 539 (1842); *Dred Scott v. Sandford,* 60 U.S. 393 (1857); Graber, "Nonmajoritarian Difficulty," 45–61. On Lincoln, see Skowronek, *Politics Presidents Make.* See also Garrison, "Letter to Samuel J. May, July 17, 1845," 303.
6. In mentioning the "Constitution," "Congress," "White House," and "Supreme Court," this chapter refers to the Union institutions and not their Confederate counterparts, unless otherwise noted.
7. Note also that these amendment counts are minimums, as they do not include amendments that do not match the search terms but may still be relevant to the topic. For example, in 1850, David Disney proposed an amendment protecting the local governments' sovereignty. Although not explicit, this amendment was intended to protect slavery. Ames, *Proposed Amendments,* 353.
8. By 1850, New York had a population of roughly three million and thirty-six Electoral College votes; Pennsylvania and Ohio had roughly two million each and twenty-six and twenty-three votes, respectively; and Virginia, the largest slave state, had just over a million inhabitants and only seventeen votes. Garrison, "Letter to the Editor of the London Patriot, August 6, 1833," 248–49; Sundquist, *Dynamics of the Party System,* 50–65; Silbey, *American Political Nation,* 125–40; Grodin, Massey, and Cunningham, *California State Constitution,* 3–9; R. Smith, *Civic Ideals,* 246–49; Fehrenbacher, *Slaveholding Republic,* 266–68, 271–73; Graber, *Dred Scott and the Problem of Constitutional Evil,* 126–35; Aldrich, *Why Parties?,* 132–33.
9. Calhoun specified that the North controlled "the two elements which constitute the federal government: a majority of States, and a majority of their population, estimated in federal numbers. Whatever section concentrates the two in itself possesses the control of the entire government." Calhoun, "Speech on the Slavery Question," 544–46; Herron, *Framing the Solid South,* 8.
10. With the stipulation that a legal challenge to these regulations could be appealed to the U.S. Supreme Court.
11. Similar to Clingman's claims, a May 24, 1850, letter from the Academy of Natural Sciences of Philadelphia to the Senate Committee on Territories promised that the Southwestern territories held "mines of the precious metals and of other valuable mineral pro-

ductions ... [and] valuable woods and other vegetable productions." Note that in this August 31, 1850, speech, Clingman opposed the 1850 Compromise. McClernand advocated the Compromise for the sake of Union, rather than abolition. He had opposed the Wilmot Proviso, fearing it would divide the nation. Also note that some proslavery Whigs, seeing California as inhospitable to slavery, worried that splitting the state would yield two free states, and thus they joined antislavery Northerners in backing the Compromise. See the Record SEN 31A-H22 Senate Committee on Territories, Center for Legislative Archives, National Archives and Record Administration; *Congressional Globe: Thirty-First Congress, First Session,* vol. 21, part 2, 1698, 1700; Sundquist, *Dynamics of the Party System,* 68–70; Graber, *Dred Scott and the Problem of Constitutional Evil,* 151–53.

12. As the historian Donald Fehrenbacher concludes, the "enigma of Cass' popular sovereignty—which confusingly translated into either Calhoun's constitutional position effectively protecting slavery in the territories up until statehood *or* a possible instrument to kill slavery during the territorial stage well before any application for statehood—was built into the very structure of the settlement." Fehrenbacher, *Slaveholding Republic,* 268–73.

13. In 1850, Representative John Daniel of North Carolina proposed an amendment to ban the abolition of slavery. In 1858, an amendment was proposed to recognize the right to own slaves in the territories. Representative David Disney of Ohio also proposed a pair of 1850 amendments asserting "that the people of every community have an inherent right to form their own domestic laws and to establish their own local government when they do not conflict with the Constitution." This would have cemented popular sovereignty in the federal Constitution. *Congressional Globe: Thirty-First Congress, First Session,* vol. 21, part 1, 228, 276, 697; *Congressional Globe: Thirty-First Congress, First Session,* vol. 21, part 2, 1349; Ames, *Proposed Amendments,* 192.

14. Southern legislatures also cited the 1850 Compromise, which expanded states' authority over slavery, to silence local abolitionist petitions. The Maryland legislature resolved "that Congress has no power under the Constitution to interfere with or control the domestic institutions of the several States, and that such States are the proper and sole judges of every thing appertaining to their own affairs," to the exclusion of the "abolitionists and others ... [whose petitions] are calculated to lead to the most alarming and dangerous consequences." These resolutions were submitted to the Virginia governor in 1844. Other states later referred the same text to the House Committee on Territories, and the Democratic Party incorporated this text into its national platform in 1856. State of Virginia, *Journal of the House of Delegates of Virginia,* 66; Schamel et al., *Guide to the Records of the United States House of Representatives,* 189.

15. In 1808, the New York legislature specified harsh penalties for such slave catchers, and Ohio followed suit seven years later. Pennsylvania in 1826 passed a law punishing warrantless private seizures of slaves and constraining the authority of state sheriffs and magistrates to enforce the federal Fugitive Slave Act of 1793. Indiana's 1816 and 1824 personal liberty laws guaranteed alleged fugitives a jury hearing. In contrast, Louisiana's antebellum territorial governor William C. C. Claiborne had coerced Mexico to agree to return slaves who fled to Texas. See U.S. Constitution, Article IV, Section 2, Clause 3;

Emerson, "Fugitive Slave Law," 867; Maltz, "Slavery, Federalism, and the Structure of the Constitution," 471; Fehrenbacher, *Slaveholding Republic,* 205–19, 261; Finkelman, *Slavery and the Founders,* 81–104; Graber, *Dred Scott and the Problem of Constitutional Evil,* 84.

16. In *Aves,* the Boston Female Anti-Slavery Society requested a writ of habeas corpus to inquire about Aves's right to hold Med, a six-year-old enslaved person visiting from New Orleans. Massachusetts Supreme Court Chief Justice Lemuel Shaw held that "all persons coming within the limits of a state, become subject to all its municipal laws, civil and criminal, and entitled to the privileges which those laws confer; that this rule applies as well to blacks as whites." Citing *Somerset,* Shaw noted that slavery regulation was a matter of local positive law, so that the Massachusetts Constitution's equality clause allowed Med to refuse to return to Louisiana, though it did not preempt the federal Fugitive Slave Clause or the 1793 Fugitive Slave Act, precluding freedom suits by fugitives. See *Commonwealth v. Aves,* 35 Mass. (18 Pick.) 193 (1836). Note the Massachusetts Supreme Court precedents for *Aves* in *Commonwealth v. Griffith,* 19 Mass. 11, 2 Pick. 22 (1823), holding that federal officers could seize a fugitive without producing a warrant, and in *In re Francisco,* 9 Am. Jur. 490 (1833), in which Shaw offered freedom to an enslaved boy brought to Massachusetts. See also Connecticut's *Jackson v. Bulloch,* 12 Conn. 43 (1837), in which Chief Justice Thomas Williams extended state constitutional due process liberty to slaves but also noted that the equality provision in the state's bill of rights was "limited to those who are parties to the social compact thus formed. Slaves cannot be said to be parties to that compact, or be represented in it." Wiecek, "Somerset," 132–33; Finkelman, *Imperfect Union,* 101–30; W. Horton, *Connecticut State Constitution,* 21; Wong, *Neither Fugitive nor Free,* 183–239.

17. In *Groves,* slaveholders asked the Court to strike down Mississippi's constitutional prohibition on interstate slave sales on Commerce Clause grounds. Rather than alienate Southerners by voiding state-level slave law, Thompson, joined by the antislavery Justice John McClean, held that the clause had not been enforced and so could not be overturned for conflicting with the Commerce Clause. McClean added, "The power over slavery belongs to the states respectively. It is local in its character, and in its effects; and the transfer or sale of slaves cannot be separated from this power." Taney's concurrence agreed that "the power over this subject is exclusively with the several states, . . . [which] cannot be controlled by Congress, either by virtue of its power to regulate commerce or by virtue of any power conferred by the Constitution of the United States." See *Groves v. Slaughter,* 40 U.S. (15 Pet.) 449, 503–8 (1841); Mississippi Constitution of 1832, Article IX, Section 2; Maltz, "Slavery, Federalism, and the Structure of the Constitution," 471–73; R. Smith, *Civic Ideals,* 259–60.

18. *Prigg* partly enlarged national powers. In the decision, Story declared, "it cannot be that the state legislatures have a right to interfere and, as it were, by way of complement to the legislation of Congress, to prescribe additional regulations and what they may deem auxiliary provisions for the same purpose." Taney felt that free states were obligated to aid slaveholders in recapturing their fugitives and added that Congress could force state officials to aid in this recapture. See *Prigg v. Pennsylvania,* 41 U.S. 615–16, 617–18, 626–34, 670–72 (1842); Finkelman, "*Prigg v. Pennsylvania* and Northern State Courts,"

19–20; Graber, *Dred Scott and the Problem of Constitutional Evil,* 18. For scholarly accounts affirming how *Prigg* left enforcement to the states, see N. Rosenberg, "Personal Liberty Laws and Sectional Crisis," 27–28; Finkelman, "*Prigg v. Pennsylvania* and Northern State Courts," 14–15; Finkelman, *Imperfect Union,* 132; Maltz, "Slavery, Federalism, and the Structure of the Constitution," 473–80; Finkelman, "Story Telling on the Supreme Court"; Finkelman, *Slavery and the Founders,* 91.

19. The 1850 act mandated that federal marshals capture alleged fugitive slaves, receiving two dollars for capturing a slave and one for a freeman, and allowed federal commissioners or their appointees to rally bystanders as a *posse comitatus* and recapture fugitives. Commissioners could also judge an alleged fugitive's case without hearing testimony from the fugitive. Ames, *Proposed Amendments,* 193; R. Smith, *Civic Ideals,* 261–63; Fehrenbacher, *Slaveholding Republic,* 225–32.

20. In *Strader,* Taney rejected the states' authority to override "duties and obligations imposed on them, by the Constitution of the United States," including the duty to return fugitives. *Strader v. Graham,* 51 U.S. 82, 93–94 (1851); Wiecek, "Somerset," 137–38; R. Smith, *Civic Ideals,* 203–4, 246–53, 260.

21. As Mark Graber writes, "The various materials for making constitutional arguments before the Civil War were, unsurprisingly, as conflicted about slavery as was the general polity. What Americans needed—and what constitutional law had no capacity to provide—was the political consensus necessary for a decisive choice to be made between the more egalitarian and more racist strands of the antebellum American constitutional tradition." Graber, *Dred Scott and the Problem of Constitutional Evil,* 86.

22. New Mexico's 1846 Organic Law distinguished between free and unfree male citizens. While Bretting and Garcia suggest that the document led to "the articulation of an unequivocal antislavery provision," I could not find such a provision. Chuck Smith makes no reference to such a clause in his history of the state. But note that slavery was affirmed by statute in Utah in 1852 and New Mexico in 1859. And in April 1860, thirty-two settlers of the New Mexico Territory met in Tucson to draft an implicitly proslavery constitution for the separatist provisional government of Arizona, though the government never formed. See Organic Law of the Territory of New Mexico Territory of 1846, Article III, Sections 4, 6, and 8; New Mexico Constitution of 1849, Article II, Sections 3, 4, 6, 8; New Mexico Constitution of 1850, Article I, Declaration of Rights, Section 1; C. Smith, *New Mexico State Constitution,* 2–5; Fehrenbacher, *Slaveholding Republic,* 273, 280; Graber, *Dred Scott and the Problem of Constitutional Evil,* 43; Bretting and Garcia, "New Mexico's Constitution," 745; R. Larson, *New Mexico's Quest for Statehood,* 13–40.

23. The original California draft did not mention slavery, but delegate W. E. Shannon imported Section 23 of the 1846 Iowa Constitution, banning slavery. Oregon's 1843 and 1845 Organic Laws also banned slavery, and legislative statutes penned by California's Morton McCarver threatened whipping for any African American, free or slave, who attempted to enter the territory. Of the sixty delegates to Oregon's 1857 constitutional convention, roughly forty-five were Democrats, and twenty-seven hailed from slave states, submitting to voters proposed clauses establishing slavery and prohibiting Black immigration. Voters approved the constitution and the clause limiting Black immigration but rejected the proslavery clause 7,727 to 2,645. Oregonians also excluded Black,

mixed-race, and Chinese citizens from owning property, working mining claims, entering contracts, bringing lawsuits, and voting. Oregon, they hoped, would have no Black citizens, free or slave. See California Constitution of 1849, Article I, Section 18; Oregon Organic Law of 1843, Article I, Section 4; Oregon Organic Law of 1845, Article I, Section 4; Oregon Constitution of 1857, Article I, Section 35, Article II, Section 6, Article XIV, Miscellaneous, Section 8, and Article XVII, Schedule, Section 4; Browne, *Debates in the Convention of California,* 182–83, 420–21; D. Johnson, *Founding the Far West,* 114–15, 127–37, 178–81, 278–79; Grodin, Massey, and Cunningham, *California State Constitution,* 3–9; Schuman, "Creation of the Oregon Constitution," 611–17; R. Smith, *Civic Ideals,* 254–55; Leichter, "Oregon's Constitution," 756–80; Lloyd, "1849 California Constitution," 717–18, 723–24.

24. See Iowa Constitution of 1846, Article II, Section 23; Iowa Constitution of 1857, Article I, Section 23; Wisconsin Constitution of 1848, Article I, Section 2, Article III, Section 1, Clause 4; Illinois Constitution of 1848, Article XIII, Section 16; Michigan Constitution of 1850, Article XVIII, Section 11; Indiana Constitution of 1851, Article I, Section 37; Stark, *Wisconsin State Constitution,* 4–8; Stark, *Iowa State Constitution,* 65–66; Zumbrunnen, "Wisconsin," 472–73.

25. While a paralyzed Congress mulled the 1857 proposal, Kansas voters installed a free-state majority in their legislature, which called a convention in Leavenworth to revise the original antislavery constitution. The nation's eyes now on Kansas, a divided Congress ignored the contentious Leavenworth proposal. Kansans then made a fourth and final constitution. The 1859 Wyandotte Convention adopted the old constitution's abolition clause but tabled divisive provisions integrating public schools and abrogating the Fugitive Slave Act and reserved suffrage to whites, clearing the U.S. Senate two years later. The Republican supermajority in Kansas's 1859 convention drafted the state's boundaries and institutions to exclude Democrats, who boycotted the proposed document. It passed anyway, handing the state to Republicans for almost a century. See Kansas's Topeka Constitution of 1855, Article I, Sections 6 and 21; Kansas's Lecompton Constitution of 1857, Article VII, Sections 2–4, and Article XV, Schedule, Section 14; Kansas's Leavenworth Constitution of 1857, Article I, Section 6; Kansas's Wyandot Constitution of 1859, Article I, Section 6, and Article V, Section 1; Heller, *Kansas State Constitution,* 3–8; Freehling, "Louisiana Purchase and the Coming of the Civil War," 77; Graber, *Dred Scott and the Problem of Constitutional Evil,* 40–41, 164; Heller and Schumaker, "Kansas Constitution," 490–91, 496–97.

26. Of the twenty-six state constitutions proposed in these years, only three expressly recognizing slavery were ratified: Virginia (1850), Kentucky (1850), and Maryland (1851). In 1852, Louisiana ratified a new constitution that did not expressly recognize slavery. Sundquist, *Dynamics of the Party System,* 74–98; Fehrenbacher, *Slaveholding Republic,* 272–80; Graber, *Dred Scott and the Problem of Constitutional Evil,* 40, 154–59; Mason, *Slavery and Politics in the Early American Republic,* 213–19; Aldrich, *Why Parties?,* 138–59. On the petitions, see Record HR 33A—G23.11, 24.1–6 House of Representatives Committee on the Territories, Center for Legislative Archives, National Archives and Record Administration. The records seem not to include petitions from the free states

of Pennsylvania, Iowa, and California. They include petitions from Delaware and a single petition from North Carolina, both slave states.

27. In 1846, the New York Court of Oyer and Terminer cited *Prigg* in releasing an enslaved person seized under Georgia law in New York, adding that the federal Full Faith and Credit Clause did not require New York officials to enforce the law of slave states. The Pennsylvania legislature similarly responded to *Prigg* by passing an 1847 act preventing state jailers and judges from detaining an alleged fugitive. When the slave catcher Martin C. Auld cited the Fugitive Slave Clause and *Prigg* to appeal his conviction under the 1847 law for capturing Alexander Burns, Justice Frederick Watts of the Court of Quarter Sessions of Cumberland County held that Burns, born free in Pennsylvania, could not be considered a slave and that *Prigg* thus could not override Pennsylvania's liberty law. To Watts, residency or birth under a state's laws trumped federal law. See *In re George Kirk*, 1 Parker Cr. R. (N.Y.) 67 (1846); *Commonwealth v. Auld*, 4 Pa. L.J. (Pa.) 515 (1850); *In re Lewis Pierce*, 1 W. Legal Observer (Pa.) 14 (1849); *Kauffman v. Oliver*, 10 Pa. St. 514 (1849). Both *Lewis* and *Kauffman* followed the same tack as *Commonwealth v. Aves*, citing *Somerset* to uphold local regulation of slavery. Also see *Passmore Williamson's Case*, 26 Pa. St. 9 (1855); Giddings, "Pacificus," 415–19; Seward, *In the Supreme Court of the United States*, 33; Finkelman, *Imperfect Union*, 131–45; Fehrenbacher, *Slaveholding Republic*, 221–25, 412–3n58; R. Smith, *Civic Ideals*, 261.

28. John Greenleaf Whittier echoed Douglass's sentiment: "So far as that law is concerned, I am a nullifier. By no act or countenance or consent of mine shall that law be enforced in *Massachusetts*." In 1854, Bostonians mobbed federal marshals to free the alleged fugitive Anthony Burns, and the following year, the state legislature passed a comprehensive personal liberty law. Still unsatisfied, Worcester citizens rallied to a disunion convention in 1857. However, in *Ex parte Bushnell, Ex Parte Langston*, 9 Ohio St. 77 (1859), the Ohio courts cited the 1850 Fugitive Slave Act to uphold the detention of Langston and Bushnell, abolitionists who had allegedly aided fugitives' escape. See *Hone v. Ammons*, 14 Ill. 29 (1852); *Anderson v. Poindexter*, 6 Ohio St. 623 (1857); 1843 Rhode Island Constitution, Article I, Section 4; Iowa Constitution of 1846, Article I, Section 23; Illinois Constitution of 1848, Article XIII, Section 16; Indiana Constitution of 1851, Article II, Section 37; Michigan Constitution of XVIII, Section 11; Wisconsin Constitution of 1848, Article I, Section 2; Whittier, "Letter to 'The Bay State,' October 4th, 1850," 113–14; Douglass, "Fugitive Slave Law," 72; Houston, "Another Nullification Crisis," 254n3, 256–71; Finkelman, "*Prigg v. Pennsylvania* and Northern State Courts"; Finkelman, *Imperfect Union*, 130–31, 177–78; N. Rosenberg, "Personal Liberty Laws and Sectional Crisis," 25–34; Pease and Pease, "Confrontation and Abolition in the 1850s," 923–37.

29. Smith held the "respective states and the people thereof were the source from which the federal government has derived all its powers, and remain sovereign and independent only in so far as they have delegated or relinquished powers and attributes incident to complete sovereignty." Justice Edward Whiton affirmed this ruling, holding that the state's liberty protections overrode the Fugitive Slave Act. The third justice, Samuel Crawford, rejected not only the act's legitimacy but also his own authority to void the act. See *In re*

Booth and Rycraft, 3 Wis. 157–58, 190–95 (1855); Finkelman, *"Prigg v. Pennsylvania* and Northern State Courts," 22; Finkelman, *Slavery in the Courtroom,* 119–23; Maltz, "Slavery, Federalism, and the Structure of the Constitution," 494–95; R. Smith, *Civic Ideals,* 262–63; H. Baker, *Rescue of Joshua Glover,* 112–34.

30. See *Ableman v. Booth,* 62 U.S. 506 (1859); Buchanan, *Message from the President,* 6–7; Toombs, "Letter to E.B. Pullin and Others, December 13, 1860," 519–22; N. Rosenberg, "Personal Liberty Laws and Sectional Crisis," 40–43; Wiecek, "Somerset," 137; Finkelman, *Imperfect Union,* 181–225.

31. Representatives Henry L. Dawes and John A. Bingham moved to block Oregon's admission to the Union for violating the federal Guarantee and Privileges and Immunities Clauses, but the state was nevertheless admitted under the unmodified 1857 constitution. *Congressional Globe: Thirty-Fifth Congress, Second Session,* 1:974–75, 984; Finkelman, *Slavery in the Courtroom,* 154; Maltz, "Slavery, Federalism, and the Structure of the Constitution," 484.

32. Massachusetts Chief Justice Lemuel Shaw ruled against Benjamin Roberts's appeal for integration under the Massachusetts Constitution's equality clause, asserting that states could stratify citizenship and could segregate schools by gender or class as long as facilities were equal in quality. The state's Free Soil Party eventually captured the legislature and repealed the law in 1855, but *Roberts* stood as a precedent for racial segregation of public institutions. Blacks held the franchise in Maine, Vermont, New Hampshire, Massachusetts, and Rhode Island, as well as in New York, though with a prohibitive qualification of $250 in freehold estate. See the Massachusetts Declaration of Rights, Article I; *Roberts v. City of Boston,* 59 Mass. (5 Cush.) 198 (1850); Kettner, *Development of American Citizenship,* 323–24; R. Smith, *Civic Ideals,* 215–20, 253–57; Fehrenbacher, *Constitutions and Constitutionalism,* 26–27; Foner, *Short History of Reconstruction,* 43.

33. In Connecticut, Prudence Crandall appealed a Connecticut statute banning her charity school for Blacks on the grounds that the statute violated the federal Privileges and Immunities Clause rights of her out-of-state students. But the state's Chief Justice David Daggett replied in *Crandall v. State of Connecticut,* 10 Conn. 339 (1834), that these students never held birthright citizenship, voiding their claims against the statute. The Connecticut Supreme Court of Errors dodged the issue by later reversing Daggett on a factual technicality, in *Colchester v. Lyme,* 13 Conn. 274 (1834). Pennsylvania's Chief Justice John B. Gibson revived Connecticut's arguments against Black citizenship in *Hobbs v. Fogg,* 6 Watts 533 (1837), distinguishing between Blacks' freedom from slavery and the full complement of political rights belonging to a freeman. Deep South courts were more direct—a Mississippi court cited Daggett in a pair of 1859 cases constraining Black citizenship rights. See *Shaw v. Brown,* 35 Miss. 246, 320 (1858); *Heirn v. Bridault,* 37 Miss. 224 (1859); and *Mitchell v. Wells,* 37 Miss. 260 (1859). Kentucky, Virginia, Alabama, and Louisiana courts granted birthright citizenship only to the children of slaves in the process of gaining their freedom, with Louisiana adding that long-term residence in a free territory freed a plaintiff not born in a slave state or territory. Tennessee's Chief Justice John Catron similarly declared that the states' Blacks held inferior citizenship status to whites in *Fisher's Negroes v. Dabs,* 14 Tenn., 6 Yerger 119–31 (1834). North Carolina, which in *State v. Manuel,* 25 Devereaux & Battle's Law 20 (1838), gave

birthright citizenship to free and manumitted Blacks from the state, reversed this for partial citizenship in *State v. Newsome,* 5 Iredell 250–54 (1844), and *State v. Jowers,* 11 Iredell 555 (1850). Kettner, *Development of American Citizenship,* 316–24; R. Smith, *Civic Ideals,* 255–58.

34. In 1833, John Emerson transported Dred Scott, born an enslaved person probably in Virginia, to the free state of Illinois and territory of Wisconsin, where Scott lived as a free servant before Emerson took him to the slave state of Missouri. After Emerson's death, his widow sued to possess Scott, which the Missouri Supreme Court granted in *Scott v. Emerson,* 15 Mo. 576 (1852), citing *Strader v. Graham* to establish that slavery "reattached" on reentering a slave state or territory. The court thus denied that Illinois's and Wisconsin's liberty laws, or Massachusetts's precedent of *Commonwealth v. Aves,* held any force over slaves in Missouri. Emerson's widow then transferred Scott to her brother, John Sanford of New York, whom Scott sued for freedom, now in federal courts under interstate jurisdiction. The federal district court not only affirmed Scott's enslavement under the Missouri Supreme Court's ruling but also held that it had jurisdiction to hear slaves' appeals, opening the federal courts as a venue for slaves, as federal citizens, to challenge Southern and fugitive slave laws, upending the 1850 Compromise. The request for a federal decision on territorial slavery came from Senator Judah P. Benjamin of Louisiana, backed by Cass, Douglas, and James Buchanan. Fehrenbacher, *Slaveholding Republic,* 280–81.

35. Taney did not defer all citizenship regulation to the states but instead asserted that the state and federal governments could not interfere with each other's citizenship law and additionally allowed Congress to continue regulating the territories to prepare them for statehood, so long as this did not extend to regulating slavery. Against Taney, Justice Benjamin Curtis's dissent cited early state constitutional provisions and cases granting Black Americans citizenship rights. See *Dred Scott v. Sandford,* 60 U.S. 405–6, 430–53 (1857); R. Smith, *Civic Ideals,* 265–68; Graber, *Dred Scott and the Problem of Constitutional Evil,* 20.

36. Though the federal Fifth Amendment did not bind the states, Taney's opinion might have encouraged appeals to a right to property in slaves under state constitutional due process protections. Taney also read the Importation Clause to affirm a right to property in slaves. See *Dred Scott,* 60 U.S. 411; Wiecek, "Somerset," 138; Maltz, "Slavery, Federalism, and the Structure of the Constitution," 480–88; R. Smith, *Civic Ideals,* 263–71; Fehrenbacher, *Dred Scott Case;* Fehrenbacher, *Slaveholding Republic,* 281–83; Graber, *Dred Scott and the Problem of Constitutional Evil,* 18–20.

37. Similarly, Northerners' objection to the 1850 Fugitive Slave Act was not primarily over Blacks' maltreatment but rather that the act overrode Northern personal liberty laws and forced Northerners to assist in recapturing fugitives. Many Northerners were content with stripping Blacks' rights, so long as it was on Northern whites' terms. See *Ableman v. Booth,* 62 U.S. 506 (1859); N. Rosenberg, "Personal Liberty Laws and Sectional Crisis," 36; Finkelman, *Slavery in the Courtroom,* 119–23; Maltz, "Slavery, Federalism, and the Structure of the Constitution," 488–89; Fehrenbacher, *Slaveholding Republic,* 239–40, 281–83, 290.

38. John Crittenden suggested allowing popular sovereignty and prohibiting uncompensated

emancipation; Stephen Douglas proposed protecting the interstate slave trade; Jefferson Davis offered an amendment recognizing a right to property in slaves; and Thomas Corwin sought to keep the federal government from interfering with slavery within an existing state. The Corwin Amendment, initially backed by Lincoln, was ratified by only three states. In separate proposals, Thomas Florence and Garrett Davis recognized Taney's *Dred Scott* ruling against Black federal citizenship. See Buchanan, *Message from the President*, 6–7; Toombs, "Letter to E. B. Pullin and Others, December 13, 1860," 519–22; Ames, *Proposed Amendments*, 194–95; Livingston, *Federalism and Constitutional Change*, 203; N. Rosenberg, "Personal Liberty Laws and Sectional Crisis," 40–43; Caplan, *Constitutional Brinksmanship*, 55; Vile, *Encyclopedia of Constitutional Amendments*, 75–76, 426.

39. Note also that in 1862 Lincoln proposed to Congress a scheme for gradual compensated emancipation by 1900. Ames, *Proposed Amendments*, 211; Dealey, *Growth of American State Constitutions*, 56–60; Caplan, *Constitutional Brinksmanship*, 55–56; Vile, *Encyclopedia of Constitutional Amendments*, 426.

40. Mississippi, North Carolina, Tennessee, and Virginia rejected proposed constitutions, retaining or amending existing ones, while Louisiana's 1861 constitution was essentially identical to its predecessor. Many state constitutions opened with the state's secession ordinance. For example, Florida's held that "all political connection between [Florida] and the government of said States ought to be and the same is hereby totally annulled and said Union of States dissolved, and the State of Florida is hereby declared a sovereign and independent Nation." See Florida Constitution of 1861, Ordinance of Secession. See Dealey, *Growth of American State Constitutions*, 60; Herron, *Framing the Solid South*, 73–98.

41. See Louisiana Constitution of 1864, Title I, Articles 1–2, Title III, Article 7, Title IX, Article 135, and Title XI; Arkansas Constitution of 1864, Article V; Lincoln's March 6, 1862, Message to Congress; Dealey, *Growth of American State Constitutions*, 61–62; Foner, *Short History of Reconstruction*, 21–23; Laska, *Tennessee State Constitution*, 12–14; Hargrave, *Louisiana State Constitution*, 7–8; Goss, *Arkansas State Constitution*, 4–6; Gossett, "Louisiana Experience," 311–12; Niles, "Change and Continuity in Arkansas Politics," 254.

42. In 1861, two-thirds of Virginia's western state legislators voted unsuccessfully against Confederate secession. Reconvening weeks later, they drafted an independent constitution affirming the federal Constitution's supremacy. Far westerners moved to immediately abolish slavery, but proslavery delegates defeated the measure. Senator Charles Sumner then blocked statehood for West Virginia until abolition was restored. A handful of loyalist Virginians meeting in Alexandria the following year drafted another antislavery Virginia constitution, though this one never saw ratification. Congress also forced the new Nevada Territory to draft a constitution, including clauses rejecting slavery and Mormonism, though suffrage was reserved to whites and subject to a poll tax. Similarly, Black residents were disenfranchised in Louisiana and Maryland. See West Virginia Constitution of 1863, Article I, Section 1, and Article XI, Section 7; Maryland Constitution of 1864, Declaration of Rights, Article 24, Article III, Section 43, and Article VIII; Nevada Constitution of 1864, Preliminary Ordinance, and Article II, Sections 1 and 7;

Foner, *Short History of Reconstruction*, 18–19; Bastress, *West Virginia State Constitution*, 10–15; DiClerico, "West Virginia Constitution," 216–20; Herron, *Framing the Solid South*, 95–96.

43. On the House floor on June 13, 1864, Ohio Democrat Samuel Cox declared that the Union was a compact that Southern states could exit and reenter without losing sovereignty and attendant rights and police powers. New York's Fernando Wood argued the same on May 3. However, the following day, George Boutwell of Massachusetts replied that the Southern states, in exiting the Union, had legally dissolved. The radical Pennsylvanian Thaddeus Stevens asserted that the ex-Confederate states ought to be treated as conquered alien territories. *Congressional Globe: Thirty-Eighth Congress, First Session*, 2075, 2078–80, 2102–3, 2917–18; Foner, *Short History of Reconstruction*, 30–34.

44. In May 1864, Ohio Democrat George Pendleton summarized the radical Republican Party as "revolutionary": "It seeks to use [legislative] powers to destroy the Government, to change its form, to change its spirit. It seeks under the forms of law to make a new Government, a new Union, to ingraft upon it new principles, new theories. . . . It is in rebellion against the Constitution." The other four failed amendments concerned Confederate war debt, congressional representation, suffrage, and selection of presidential electors. *Congressional Globe: Thirty-Eighth Congress, First Session*, 2105; Ames, *Proposed Amendments*, 23.

45. *Congressional Globe: Thirty-Eighth Congress, First Session*, 1419–24; Ames, *Proposed Amendments*, 212–18; Zuckert, "Completing the Constitution"; Kyvig, *Explicit and Authentic Acts*, 159–61; R. Smith, *Civic Ideals*, 282–83; Belz, *New Birth of Freedom*, 126, 140; Tsesis, *Thirteenth Amendment and American Freedom*, 37–48.

46. The Wade-Davis Bill proclaimed Black equality and prohibited high-ranking ex-Confederate officeholders and soldiers from electing or serving as delegates but delayed a state's convention until a majority of whites proclaimed loyalty to the federal Constitution. During later debates over the bill, Pennsylvania's William Kelley declared that the defeated Confederate states were now territories awaiting federal recognition and thus were unnecessary for ratifying the Thirteenth Amendment under Article V. But Representative Fernando Wood, citing Jefferson and Madison's compact theory, replied that the Southern states were "distinct political communities with their own State constitutions and forms of government deriving authority from the people," existing with or without federal recognition. Since the Southern states still existed and had voluntarily reentered the Union, the Thirteenth Amendment required their ratification. In turn, the states would need new constitutions. When the House passed the Thirteenth Amendment on January 31, 1865, Alexander Coffroth of Pennsylvania affirmed that the amendment would need the support of the ex-Confederate states. That summer, Johnson and his secretary of state, William Seward, agreed that ratification required the Southern states, which the Supreme Court affirmed in declaring that the Union was "composed of indestructible states," in *Texas v. White*, 74 U.S. 700, 700 (1869). *Congressional Globe: Thirty-Eighth Congress, First Session*, 2075, 2078–80, 2105–7; *Congressional Globe: Thirty-Eighth Congress, Second Session*, 523; Vorenberg, *Final Freedom*, 227–33; Foner, *Short History of Reconstruction*, 28–29.

47. For example, in May 1864, Representative William Allison warned that without land and education, Southern Blacks would face "a system of wages-slavery as much to be deplored as chattel-slavery. This class [of former slaveholders] will seek to take advantage of the ignorant slave suddenly made free, and will require of him excessive labor, with inadequate compensation." Allison noted that the Freedmen's Bureau might aid former slaves, but the bureau still could not constitutionally interfere in the states' authority over Black education, marriage, citizenship, and suffrage. *Congressional Globe: Thirty-Eighth Congress, First Session*, 2115.
48. *Congressional Globe: Thirty-Eighth Congress, First Session*, 1246; Chase, "Letter to Abraham Lincoln, April 11, 1865," 428.
49. Note that the Georgia Constitution disenfranchised Blacks, the Florida Constitution excluded Blacks from voting or serving in office or on juries, and the Alabama Constitution prohibited interracial marriage. For abolition clauses, see appendix C. See also Alabama Constitution of 1865, Article I, Section 34, and Article IV, Section 31; Georgia Constitution of 1865, Article I, Section 20, and Article II, Section 5; Florida Constitution of 1864, Article XVI, Sections 1–3; Salokar, "Florida," 271–72; Herron, *Framing the Solid South*, 49, 129–36; Louisiana Constitutional Convention, *Debates in the Convention*, 189.
50. Note, however, that between March and June 1866, Northern congressmen proposed ten amendments prohibiting compensation. *Congressional Globe: Thirty-Eighth Congress, Second Session*, 523–25.
51. At least thirty of the thirty-six states had already emancipated slaves by state constitutional provision, statute, or judicial ruling, and framers in the remaining six states were pushing for constitutional abolition clauses in tandem with the federal amendment. For example, Mississippi's governor William Sharkey used the amendment's impending ratification to coax his state's convention to abolish slavery, though state legislators deemed the federal amendment redundant to the state's abolition clause. Delaware's legislature rejected the amendment, as did Kentucky's, fearing congressional overreach under the second clause. Legislators in Ohio and Indiana expressed the same worry. See appendix C; Winkle, *Mississippi State Constitution*, 7–9; Ackerman, *We the People*, 2:141–44; Vorenberg, *Final Freedom*, 212, 216–20, 228.
52. David Kyvig calls the amendment's second section, allowing congressional enforcement, "a dramatic intrusion into state authority." The section concerned some congressmen and South Carolina, Florida, Alabama, Louisiana, and Mississippi legislators, who ratified the amendment on President Johnson and Secretary Seward's promise that the amendment's second section would not enfranchise Blacks. As Michael Zuckert affirms, save for the radical Republicans, the amendment's framers probably intended the section to apply only to enforcing abolition, a concern made largely redundant by existing state clauses. Similarly, sections 12 and 13 of the Wade-Davis Bill, also drafted by the Thirty-Eighth Congress, limited Congress to freeing any Blacks who might have been unconstitutionally reenslaved. Fess, *Ratification of the Constitution and Amendments*, 4; TenBroek, *Equal under Law*; Zuckert, "Completing the Constitution," 272–73; Kyvig, *Explicit and Authentic Acts*, 156; Vorenberg, *Final Freedom*, 216–33; Tsesis, *Thirteenth Amendment and American Freedom*, 39–40, 48.
53. Senator Lyman Trumbull copied his proposed abolition clause, including the provision

allowing slavery "as a punishment for crime whereof the party shall have been duly convicted," from the Missouri Compromise bill and the Northwest Ordinance. Most Old Northwest states, including Indiana, Ohio, Michigan, Minnesota, and Wisconsin, also took the convict slavery clause from the Ordinance, though Illinois closed the loophole in 1848. On April 8, 1864, Charles Sumner tried redacting Trumbull's provision, but Trumbull pushed the Senate to pass the full amendment with little attention to the rider. See *Congressional Globe: Thirty-Eighth Congress, First Session*, 1487–88; Robinson, *Slavery in the Structure of American Politics*, 381–84; Kyvig, *Explicit and Authentic Acts*, 160–61; Belz, *New Birth of Freedom*, 115; Fehrenbacher, *Slaveholding Republic*, 254–55; Finkelman, *Slavery and the Founders*, 37–51; Raghunath, "Promise the Nation Cannot Keep," 419–21.

54. Following the amendment's ratification, every ex-Confederate state included a similar punishment clause. Reflecting on the clause, Representative John Farnsworth lamented, "we find those states now reducing these men again to slavery as punishment for crime, and declaring every little petty offense the Black man may commit that he shall be sold into bondage." See appendix C; *Congressional Globe: Thirty-Ninth Congress, First Session*, 383.

55. The act granted federal citizenship to all "persons born in the United States," including Blacks; let federal courts remove Thirteenth Amendment litigation from the state courts; and excluded from citizenship Native Americans who were not taxed and those others who were subject to a foreign power. Foner, *Short History of Reconstruction*, 86–100; Kyvig, *Explicit and Authentic Acts*, 163–64; Vorenberg, *Final Freedom*, 227; Valelly, *Two Reconstructions*, 26–28.

56. As Eric Foner concludes, the act "honored the traditional presumption that the primary responsibility for law enforcement lay with the states." *Congressional Globe: Thirty-Ninth Congress, First Session*, 1756–57; McPherson, "Majority Report of the Joint Committee on Reconstruction," 89; Foner, *Short History of Reconstruction*, 108–14; R. Smith, *Civic Ideals*, 305–8.

57. Stevens reported the Fourteenth Amendment on April 30, 1866. Under the amendment's second section, states disenfranchising adult males in federal elections would lose seats in Congress and the Electoral College, backed by congressional enforcement. Reverdy Johnson, the committee's lone Democratic senator, unsuccessfully attempted to redact the amendment's Privileges or Immunities Clause. See *Congressional Globe: Thirty-Ninth Congress, First Session*, 14; Ames, *Proposed Amendments*, 23, 219–26, 247–50, 371–73.

58. Suffragettes like Elizabeth Cady Stanton and Susan B. Anthony opposed the measure, the first ratified to explicitly condone an all-male franchise, but were largely ignored. Representative James Brooks's proposed amendment granting the franchise regardless of sex failed in 1869. McPherson, "Majority Report of the Joint Committee on Reconstruction," 88; *Congressional Globe: Fortieth Congress, Third Session*, 561.

59. In floor debates in 1871, John Bingham, one of the amendment's authors, suggested that he intended the amendment's first section to incorporate the full Bill of Rights against the states. However, other Republicans argued that the amendment only applied temporarily to noncompliant states, muddling the extent to which framers intended to strong-arm the

states. Kyvig, *Explicit and Authentic Acts,* 165–70; Foner, *Short History of Reconstruction,* 114–17; R. Smith, *Civic Ideals,* 310–11; Beaumont, *Civic Constitution,* 159.

60. Sumner held, "There is no clause which gives to Congress such supreme power over the States as that [Guarantee] clause." Republican representative John Broomall of Pennsylvania voiced the opposition. *Congressional Globe: Thirty-Ninth Congress, Second Session,* 350–51; *Congressional Globe: Fortieth Congress, First Session,* 614; Dealey, *Growth of American State Constitutions,* 63–66; Kyvig, *Explicit and Authentic Acts,* 170–75; Ackerman, *We the People,* 2:110–13; Valelly, *Two Reconstructions,* 30–32, 41–44.

61. When Georgians refused to ratify the Fourteenth Amendment in late 1866, army officers repudiated the state's 1865 constitution and arranged the election of Northerners to the state's 1867 constitutional convention. Mississippi established citizenship for all residents and race-blind public schooling, as did Alabama. Congress also forced an 1868 convention in North Carolina, staffed in large part by Blacks and Northerners, which declared equality between men and provided for public schooling, with no provision for segregation, though an 1876 amendment required that "the children of the white race and the children of the colored race shall be taught in separate public schools, but there shall be no discrimination made in favor of, or to the prejudice of, either race." Virginia's 1869 convention also guaranteed the equal protection of the laws and free public education. See Arkansas Constitution of 1864, Article VIII, Section 1; Arkansas Constitution of 1868, Article I, Section 3, and Article VII, Sections 2 and 5; Georgia Constitution of 1868, Article I, Section 2, Article II, Section 2, and Article VI, Section 1; Louisiana Constitution of 1868, Title I, Articles 2 and 13, Title VI, Articles 98 and 100, and Title VII, Article 135; Louisiana Constitution of 1879, Article 23; Mississippi Constitution of 1869, Article VII, Section 3 and Article VIII; North Carolina Constitution of 1868, Article I, Section 1, and Article IX; Virginia Constitution of 1870, Article I, Section 20, and Article VIII, Section 1; D'Alemberte, *Florida State Constitution,* 6–7; Hargrave, *Louisiana State Constitution,* 8–9; Goss, *Arkansas State Constitution,* 6–7; Hill, *Georgia State Constitution,* 7–10; Hill and Hill, "Georgia," 290–91; Tarr, *Understanding State Constitutions,* 97; Niles, "Change and Continuity in Arkansas Politics," 254–55; Salokar, "Florida," 272; Williams, *Law of American State Constitutions,* 91.

62. While Virginia's 1776 equality clause held "that all men are by nature equally free and independent," the state's stronger 1870 equal protection clause made this an enforceable citizenship right, holding "that all citizens of the state are hereby declared to possess equal civil and political rights and public privileges." But note that the U.S. Supreme Court struck down federal and state loyalty oaths in *Cummings v. Missouri,* 71 U.S. 277 (1867), that some Southerners understood universal manhood suffrage under their constitutions to enfranchise ex-Confederates, and that many state legislators unconstitutionally segregated schools by statute. See Georgia Constitution of 1865, Article II, Section 5; Georgia Constitution of 1868, Article I, Section 2; Alabama Constitution of 1867, Article I, Section 2; Virginia Constitution of 1870, Article I, Section 20; Foner, *Short History of Reconstruction,* 43–44; Hill, *Georgia State Constitution,* 7–10; Tarr, *Understanding State Constitutions,* 107; Williams, *Law of American State Constitutions,* 91.

63. Lincoln claimed in his July 4, 1861, address to Congress that the Declaration's "mutual

pledge" of union created the states: "The Union, and not [the states] separately, procured independence, and their liberty. . . . The Union is older than any of the states and, in fact, it created them as States. . . . Not one of them ever had a state constitution independent of the Union." Since the states did not predate the Union, they could not have compacted to form it and could not revoke or modify it. Though note, per appendix B, that four states drafted constitutions before the Declaration, and these were not, as Lincoln claimed, fully "dependent on, and preparatory to, coming into the Union." See Louisiana Constitution of 1868, Title I, Articles 2 and 13; North Carolina Constitution of 1868, Article I, Sections 4–5; Lincoln, "Message to Congress," 309–10.

64. See appendix C.
65. Note that these Southern states were the exception, as other states had already disenfranchised Blacks. In 1865, only six states in the Union, five of them in New England, allowed Blacks to vote, leaving only 6 percent of the nation's Black population enfranchised. Congress, which considered amendments disenfranchising Blacks in 1861, initially showed little interest in enfranchising Blacks through the Fourteenth Amendment's section 2 or, per Sumner, the Guarantee Clause and the Thirteenth Amendment's section 2 and/or through ten proposals to enfranchise Blacks in 1866. Congress did use the Territories Clause to propose enfranchising Montana Blacks and enfranchised Blacks in the District of Columbia under the District Clause. See U.S. Constitution, Article I, Section 8, Clause 17; Ames, *Proposed Amendments,* 226–35; Kyvig, *Explicit and Authentic Acts,* 159, 176–81; Beaumont, *Civic Constitution,* 159.
66. Between the passage of the Military Reconstruction Act in March 1867 and the end of 1868, every Southern state revised its suffrage laws, except Texas, which had in 1866. Referenda in Connecticut, Minnesota, Wisconsin, the Colorado Territory, and the District of Columbia in 1865 showed Republican support for enfranchising Blacks. Minnesotans in 1868 and Michiganders in 1869 passed amendments removing the stipulation that voters be white. But voters in the Democratic strongholds of Ohio and New Jersey refused reforms enfranchising Blacks in 1867, and racial disenfranchisement survived in Kansas until 1918 and Oregon until 1926. Loyalist Kentucky avoided constitutional reconstruction and thus only enfranchised Blacks, subject to a poll tax, with the Fifteenth Amendment's passage. Delaware refused ratification, Maryland instituted a prohibitively high property qualification for Blacks in 1870, and Missouri voters defeated an 1868 amendment enfranchising Blacks only to accept the Fifteenth Amendment two years later. West Virginia's radical Republicans passed an 1866 state amendment disenfranchising ex-Confederates, while the moderate Republican governor William Stevenson urged ratifying the Fifteenth Amendment to restore the ex-Confederate vote. After Democrats then swept state elections, ex-Confederates held a second constitutional convention, forbidding loyalty oath requirements and nearly disenfranchising Blacks. To study the Fifteenth Amendment without corresponding state constitutionalism is to misunderstand the amendment's application. See appendix C; Tennessee Constitution of 1870, Article IV, Section 1; West Virginia Constitution of 1872, Article III, Section 11, Article IV, Section 5, and Article VI, Section 43; Tennessee Constitutional Convention, *Proceedings of the Convention of Tennessee of 1870,* 303; Loeb, *Constitutions and Constitutional Conventions in Missouri,* 20; Laska, *Tennessee State Constitution,* 14–18; Bastress,

West Virginia State Constitution, 15–21; Kyvig, *Explicit and Authentic Acts,* 173–78; Ireland, *Kentucky State Constitution,* 8; Allen, "Framing Government for a Frontier Commonwealth," 522; DiClerico, "West Virginia Constitution," 216–20; Houghton, "Michigan," 444; Heller and Schumaker, "Kansas Constitution," 498; Leichter, "Oregon's Constitution," 760; Herron, *Framing the Solid South,* 154–84.

67. For example, David Kyvig asserts, "Defense of states' rights remained a concern in many quarters during the effort to devise new constitutional provisions. Once the new amendments were ratified, they were interpreted in ways that preserved state power even at the expense of [Blacks'] civil rights." Kyvig, *Explicit and Authentic Acts,* 155. See also Ackerman, *We the People,* vol. 2.

68. Sherwin, "Sex Discrimination and State Constitutions," 119.

Chapter 5. Progressive Experimentation, 1878–1931

1. The incomplete NBER–University of Maryland State Constitutions Project data include nearly two thousand ratified state amendments for 1878–1931, and Rohlfing estimates the states proposed roughly twenty-five hundred amendments and ratified fifteen hundred between 1900 and 1935. Rohlfing, "Amendment and Revision of State Constitutions"; Sturm, "Development of American State Constitutions," 66–71.

2. The 1912 Socialist Party platform, for example, proposed lowering Article V ratification requirements to a majority of voters in a majority of states. Ames, *Proposed Amendments,* 301–4; Burgess, *Political Science and Comparative Constitutional Law;* Musmanno, *Proposed Amendments,* 212–15; *Congressional Record: Sixty-Second Congress, Second Session,* 9850; Grimes, *Democracy and the Amendments to the Constitution,* 65–66; Vile, *Rewriting the United States Constitution,* 30–32.

3. McCloskey and Levinson, *American Supreme Court.*

4. Holst, *Constitutional and Political History;* Lowell, "Responsibilities of American Lawyers"; Bryce, *American Commonwealth;* Ashley, "Constitution Worship"; Ames, *Proposed Amendments;* Corwin, "Worship of the Constitution"; Kammen, *Machine That Would Go of Itself.*

5. To avoid tilting the sample of national issues toward those on the congressional record of amendments, I also address labor and tax law, main issues before the Supreme Court, even though these issues were outside the top-four most common amendment topics.

6. *Congressional Record: Fifty-Third Congress, Second Session,* 6711; *Congressional Record: Fifty-Third Congress, Third Session,* 411–15; Seligman, *Income Tax,* 493–590; Ratner, *Taxation and Democracy in America,* 145–214; Weisman, *Great Tax Wars,* 93–172.

7. See *Hylton v. United States,* 3 U.S. 171 (1796); *Pollock v. Farmers Loan and Trust* I and II, 157–58 U.S. 429, 685, 695 (1895); *United States v. E. C. Knight Co.,* 156 U.S. 1 (1895).

8. As Harlan put it, "The serious aspect of the present decision is that, by a new interpretation of the Constitution, it so ties the hands of the legislative branch of the government that, without an amendment of that instrument, or unless this court at some future time should return to the old theory of the Constitution, Congress cannot subject [income] to

taxation." See *Pollock v. Farmers Loan and Trust* I and II, 157–58 U.S. 429, 685, 695 (1895); Ames, *Proposed Amendments,* 245–46; Musmanno, *Proposed Amendments,* 161–63, 171, 210–15; Ratner, *Taxation and Democracy in America,* 145–214; Grimes, *Democracy and the Amendments to the Constitution,* 66–74; Kyvig, *Explicit and Authentic Acts,* 194–208; Weisman, *Great Tax Wars,* 93–172; Einhorn, "Look Away Dixieland."

9. For assessors' quotes and figures, see Alabama Auditor Report of 1883, in Kinsman, "Income Tax in the Commonwealths of the United States," 82; Kinsman, "Present Period of Income Tax Activity," 296–300. See also Mehrotra, *Making the Modern American Fiscal State,* 194–96; Dinan, *State Constitutional Politics,* 173–76.

10. See *Pollock v. Farmers Loan and Trust* II, 158 U.S. 629 (1895); Bryce, *American Commonwealth,* 524; Seligman, "Income Tax in the American Colonies and States," 239–42; Newcomer, "Separation of State and Local Revenues," 9–11; Seligman, *Income Tax,* 399–414; Mehrotra, *Making the Modern American Fiscal State,* 185–91.

11. Figures and quote from Kinsman, "Present Period of Income Tax Activity," 296–303.

12. Nevada Constitutional Convention, *Debates and Proceedings,* 225.

13. In *People ex rel. Thomas v. Scott,* 12 P. 608 (1897), the state's supreme court affirmed that the Colorado Constitution of 1876, Article X, Section 11, placed a maximum property tax of four mills on the dollar. See also Colorado Tax Commission, *Colorado Tax Commission Report,* 9–11. Other states maintained old tax uniformity clauses. See, for example, Ohio Constitution of 1851, Article XII, Section 2; Oregon Constitution of 1857, Article IX, Section 1; Tarr, *Understanding State Constitutions,* 119.

14. The U.S. Supreme Court had recently upheld a similar railroad regulation law in *Munn v. Illinois* 94 U.S. 113 (1877). See California Constitution of 1878, Article XIII, Section 10; Utah Constitution of 1896, Article XIII, Section 12; Oklahoma Constitution of 1907, Article X, Section 12; Plehn, "Plan for Tax Reform in California," 1–2; Scheiber, "Race, Radicalism, and Reform," 59–62; D. Johnson, *Founding the Far West,* 250–58; Bridges, *Democratic Beginnings,* 52–55, 66, 84; Dinan, *State Constitutional Politics,* 219–20.

15. Arkansas was probably the only old Confederacy state not to institute an income tax before the Sixteenth Amendment. Note also that some small farmers felt that locally elected assessors would be more lenient. See Texas Constitution of 1845, Article VII, Section 27, and Constitution of 1876, Article VIII, Section 1; Louisiana Constitution of 1845, Title VI, Article 127, and Constitution of 1868, Title VI, Article 118; North Carolina Constitution of 1868, Article V, Section 4; Virginia Constitution of 1870, Article X, Section 4; Tennessee Constitution of 1870, Article II, Section 28; South Carolina Constitution of 1895, Article X, Section 1; Virginian Constitution of 1902, Article XIII, Section 170; Kinsman, "Income Tax in the Commonwealths of the United States," 100–109; Kinsman, "Present Period of Income Tax Activity," 304–6; Seligman, "Progressive Taxation in Theory and Practice," 104–9; Seligman, *Income Tax,* 414–18; Penniman, *State Income Taxation,* 2; Hyman, *Anti-Redeemers,* 114–19; Dinan, *State Constitutional Politics,* 219–20.

16. Lyons, "Wisconsin Income Tax," 86. See also *State ex rel. Bolens vs. Frear; Winding v. Frear,* 148 Wis. 456 (1914); Wisconsin Constitution of 1848, Article VIII, Section 1; Wisconsin State Tax Commission, *Report,* 72; Seligman, *Income Tax,* 419–28; Kennan, "Wisconsin Income Tax"; Lyons, "Wisconsin Income Tax," 83–85; Stark, *Wisconsin*

State Constitution, 16–17, 155–56; Mehrotra, *Making the Modern American Fiscal State,* 228–41.

17. Colorado Tax Commission, *Colorado Tax Commission Report,* 10–11; Special Tax Commission of the State of New York, *Report,* 49–51.
18. Kinsman explained in 1909, "while over forty state tax commissions were appointed prior to 1895, only seven treated the income tax, but during the short period since that date, six have considered it." He also noted, "The current movement is not due to the success of the tax in any state, but rather the spirit of reform now sweeping the country." R. Ely, "Reforms in Taxation," 136; National Tax Association, *Addresses and Proceedings;* Kinsman, "Present Period of Income Tax Activity," 296, 303, 306; Newcomer, "Separation of State and Local Revenues," 180; Ketcham, "Sixteenth Amendment," 7–8; Mehrotra, *Making the Modern American Fiscal State,* 188–89.
19. Figures from Newcomer, "Separation of State and Local Revenues in the United States," 177. Stanley and Mehrotra show that special property tax revenue increased in this period, keeping total property tax revenue stable at roughly 66 percent, declining to 57 percent in 1932, while between 1903 and 1913, the general property tax declined from 44 percent to 38 percent of total state revenue, with inheritance taxes growing from 4 percent to 7 percent and the income tax remaining well below 1 percent. This exceptionally low income tax revenue distinguished the income tax from other state taxes—while states might want to protect, for example, their existing lucrative sales taxes from a potential competing federal sales tax, prior to the Sixteenth Amendment, the state income tax produced almost no revenue, and so a federal tax and accompanying federal enforcement could only aid, and not harm, state income tax receipts. See R. Stanley, *Dimensions of Law in the Service of Order,* 203–9; Weisman, *Great Tax Wars;* Mehrotra, *Making the Modern American Fiscal State,* 191–93; Dinan, *State Constitutional Politics,* 217–22.
20. Anselm McLaurin proposed explicitly authorizing a graduated income tax, as did Joseph Bailey, who also sought ratification by state convention, though neither proposal carried. House skirmishes were minor. New York's Sereno Payne intended the amendment as a limited wartime emergency measure, while Samuel McCall of Massachusetts feared it would become an overreaching tool for social control and redistribution. *Congressional Record: Sixty-First Congress, First Session,* 1570, 3138, 3377, 3974, 4108, 4390–94, 4438–40; *Congressional Record: Sixty-Second Congress, Second Session,* 9687; Seligman, *Income Tax,* 590–92; Blakey and Blakey, *Federal Income Tax,* 60–64.
21. The following accounts focus almost exclusively on Congress and the White House: Musmanno, *Proposed Amendments,* 212–15; Blakey and Blakey, *Federal Income Tax,* 60–64; Paul, *Taxation in the United States,* 90–99; Ratner, *American Taxation,* 265–320; Grimes, *Democracy and the Amendments to the Constitution,* 73–74; J. Witte, *Politics and Development of the Federal Income Tax,* 74–76; Bernstein and Agel, *Amending America,* 121–22; Kyvig, *Explicit and Authentic Acts,* 200–208; Weisman, *Great Tax Wars,* 207–36; Pollack, *War, Revenue, and State Building,* 242–46; Einhorn, "Look Away Dixieland," 790–91; *Congressional Record: Sixty-First Congress, Second Session,* 2245.
22. Still, some Southern legislators, particularly in Virginia, opposed the amendment as an affront to states' rights, and the South as a whole lagged in ratification. *Congressional*

Record: Sixty-First Congress, Second Session, 1694–99, 2245–47; Blakey and Blakey, *Federal Income Tax*, 64–71; Ratner, *American Taxation*, 304–7; Weisman, *Great Tax Wars*, 237–65; Einhorn, "Look Away Dixieland," 292–96.

23. Penniman, *State Income Taxation*, 230–36.
24. Income taxes passed in Mississippi in 1912; Connecticut, Oklahoma, and Virginia in 1915; New York, Delaware, and Missouri in 1917; North Dakota in 1919; North Carolina in 1921; South Carolina in 1922; and New Hampshire and Tennessee in 1923.
25. Specifically, Nebraskans approved a 1920 amendment allowing taxation of intangible property, including income. See Massachusetts Constitution of 1780, Article XLVI; Ohio Constitution of 1851, Article XII, Section 8; Nebraska Constitution of 1875, Article IX, Section 1; South Dakota Constitution of 1889, Article XI, Section 2; Arizona Constitution of 1912, Article IX, Section 12; Louisiana Constitution of 1921, Article X, Section 1; Brownlee, *Progressivism and Economic Growth*, 42–43.
26. Currently, Alaska, Florida, Nevada, South Dakota, Texas, Washington, and Wyoming do not tax individual income at all. It is also worth noting that between 1910 and 1930, about a dozen amendments modified property tax uniformity clauses to lessen burdens on rural real estate owners. See *Santee Mills etc. v. Query*, 122 S.C. 158, 115 S.E. 202 (1922); *Featherston v. Norman*, 170 Ga. 370, 153 S.E. 58 (1930); Indiana Constitution of 1851, Article X, Section 8; Kansas Constitution of 1861, Article XI, Section 2; West Virginia Constitution of 1872; Colorado Constitution of 1876, Article X, Section 17, Article X, Section 1; Montana Constitution of 1889, Article XII, Section 1a; Utah Constitution of 1896, Article XIII, Section 3; Alabama Constitution of 1901, Article XII, Section 213; Penniman, *State Income Taxation*, 2–8, 247–48; Dinan, *State Constitutional Politics*, 219–25.
27. Admittedly, state provisions differed from the federal amendment, which redistributed regional wealth from the Northeast to the South and West, expanded congressional finance powers, and replenished federal reserves. But the similarities were greater. Like state reforms, the amendment aimed to alleviate wealth inequality and rebuild government revenues after the economic downturn of 1907. From the Wisconsin tax, the national tax borrowed expert, impartial tax assessors and collectors. Robert Stanley agrees that the "legal environment of the states into which the [amendment] resolution had been sent played a more significant role in calming the fears in the center over the potential radicalism of progressive taxation." R. Stanley, *Dimensions of Law in the Service of Order*, 203; Weisman, *Great Tax Wars*; I. Martin, *Rich People's Movements*; Mehrotra, *Making the Modern American Fiscal State*, 240–41; Einhorn, "Look Away Dixieland."
28. G. Smith, "Has the American Senate Decayed?," 468; Haynes, *Election of Senators*, 39–42.
29. See also Ames, *Proposed Amendments*, 60–63; Haynes, *Election of Senators*, 36–70, 100–105; Musmanno, *Proposed Amendments*, 215–19; Grimes, *Democracy and the Amendments to the Constitution*, 74–76; Caplan, *Constitutional Brinksmanship*, 61–62; Kyvig, *Explicit and Authentic Acts*, 208–10; Schiller and Stewart, *Electing the Senate*.
30. Of the 752 Senate elections held between 1871 and 1913, only 19 failed to select a candidate, suggesting that grave concerns among legislators, academics, and the public ex-

ceeded the actual harm done. Schiller and Stewart, *Electing the Senate,* 16–17; Merriam, *Primary Elections.* For the Washington legislature's resolution, see Haynes, *Election of Senators,* 38–39, 65–70, 159.

31. In California, Nevada, and Illinois, voters overwhelmingly approved their state legislature's popular election petitions to Congress. Petition figures from Haynes, *Election of Senators,* 38–39, 65–70, 100–129; Haynes, *Senate of the United States,* 85–96; Rossum, *Federalism, the Supreme Court, and the Seventeenth Amendment,* 180–81.

32. The Mississippi legislature required primary elections in 1902, but many Southern states did not, instead allowing political parties, not bound by the Equal Protection Clause, to run all-white primaries. Note also that nationally, Senate primaries actually occurred in only 43 of the 121 elections in which they were authorized. See Nebraska Constitution of 1875, Article XVI, Section 312; Schiller and Stewart, *Electing the Senate,* 116.

33. See Oregon Constitution of 1859, Article IV, Section 1.

34. New York's Senate also reported on the Oregon experiment. For the report and quote by Geer, see State of New York, *Documents of the Senate,* 44. See also Barnett, "Forestalling the Direct Primary in Oregon"; Haynes, *Election of Senators,* 130–52; Haynes, *Senate of the United States,* 96–106; W. Wilson, "Letter to George H. Haynes, March 27, 1911."

35. Scholars agree on when states instituted their primaries but disagree on when these laws were implemented. For example, in 1908 Charles Merriam counted twelve states with advisory senatorial primaries, while a 1907 Senate report counted eight. Romero and Schiller and Stewart agree Lapinski presents the most accurate and recent data, which is largely supported by data from Rossum. This book therefore uses the Lapinski data as presented in Schiller and Stewart. For another recent account, see Engstrom and Kernell. See U.S. Senate, *Abstract of Laws Relating to the Election of United States Senators;* Merriam, *Primary Elections,* 273–88; Musmanno, *Proposed Amendments,* 217–20; Hoebeke, *Road to Mass Democracy,* 133; Rossum, *Federalism, the Supreme Court, and the Seventeenth Amendment,* 209n49; Engstrom and Kernell, "Effects of Presidential Elections"; Lapinski, "Direct Election"; Romero, "Impact of Direct Election"; Schiller and Stewart, *Electing the Senate,* 111–16.

36. States coordinated their petitions—as a 1901 Pennsylvania petition reminded Congress, in total twenty-seven states had requested an amendment in some form. In total, between 1890 and 1905, thirty-one states across the country sent Congress ninety-three petitions asking Congress to propose an amendment. Twenty-six petitions came from the Midwest, twenty-two from the South, forty-three from the West, and two from the staid Northeast. Heyburn speculated that reformers wanted the "constitutional convention so that they can get into the Constitution the recognition of [their] radical demands. . . . All the old bitterness of the race question would have to be thrashed out in such a convention. . . . The restriction that insures equal representation in this body would be wiped out, as would every other provision." The Socialist Party had indeed called for abolition of the Senate in its 1908 platform. *Congressional Record: Fifty-Seventh Congress, First Session,* 2617; *Congressional Record: Sixty-First Congress, Third Session,* 2770–72; Haynes, *Election of Senators,* 38–39, 65–70, 120–25, 159; Rossum, *Federalism, the Supreme Court, and the Seventeenth Amendment,* 181–82.

37. Owen added, "Only nine States . . . have failed to definitely act in favor of the election or selection of Senators by direct vote of the people, and even in these States the tendency of the people is strongly manifested toward such selection of Senators." Senator Augustus Bacon of Georgia also praised the direct election as an anticorruption measure. U.S. Senate, *Abstract of Laws Relating to the Election of United States Senators; Congressional Record: Sixty-First Congress, Second Session*, 5824–30, 7109–21; *Congressional Record: Sixty-First Congress, Third Session*, 2771; Hoebeke, *Road to Mass Democracy*, 150; Bybee, "Ulysses at the Mast," 527–28; R. Harrison, *Congress, Progressive Reform, and the New American State*, 156–91; Romero, "Impact of Direct Election," 281.
38. *Congressional Record: Sixty-First Congress, Third Session*, 3307; Haynes, *Election of Senators*, 116–20, 250; Musmanno, *Proposed Amendments*, 217–19; Grimes, *Democracy and the Amendments to the Constitution*, 76–82; Caplan, *Constitutional Brinksmanship*, 62–65; Kyvig, *Explicit and Authentic Acts*, 211–13; Harrison, *Congress, Progressive Reform, and the New American State*, 184–85.
39. The Democratic Party, the National Grange, and the American Federation of Labor adopted a popular election plank at the turn of the century, though it failed nearly ten to one at the 1908 Republican Convention. For a summary of these accounts, see, for example, Zywicki, "Senators and Special Interests," 1015–26; Bybee, "Ulysses at the Mast," 536–47.
40. Prior to 1913, Arizona, Nebraska, and Ohio constitutionally guaranteed the popular vote in senatorial elections. Zywicki suggests that Oregon and Nevada did so as well, though I found no record of this. About a dozen states revised their constitutions after the Seventeenth Amendment's ratification. Between 1898 and 1912, the citizen initiative was constitutionally recognized in thirteen states: South Dakota (1898), Utah (1900), Oregon (1902), Oklahoma (1907), Michigan (1908), Missouri (1908), Arkansas (1910), California (1911), Arizona (1912), Colorado (1912), Nebraska (1912), Nevada (1912), and Ohio (1912). Direct election was also instituted in all these states between 1898 and 1912, seven under the Oregon system. See Nebraska Constitution of 1875, Article XVI, Section 312; Arizona Constitution of 1912, Article VII, Sections 9–10; Ohio Constitution of 1851, Article V, Section 7 (via a 1913 amendment); Haynes, *Election of Senators*, 120–29; Rossum, *Federalism, the Supreme Court, and the Seventeenth Amendment*, 181; Hoebeke, *Road to Mass Democracy*, 133; Dinan, *State Constitutional Politics*, 16–19; Zywicki, "Beyond the Shell and Husk of History," 191–92.
41. Prior to the amendment proposals, women had held the full franchise only in New Jersey until 1807 under an oversight under the state's constitution, though widows and divorcees might hold limited legal rights in many states. Elsewhere women were explicitly disenfranchised under the state constitutions.
42. Phillips, "Speech of Wendell Phillips, May 9, 1865," 78; *Congressional Globe: Thirty-Ninth Congress, Second Session*, 350–51; Ames, *Proposed Amendments*, 237–38; Musmanno, *Proposed Amendments*, 246–47; DuBois, *Feminism and Suffrage*, 53–104.
43. Stone declared that she favored a universal franchise but added, "I believe that the safety of the government would be more promoted by the admission of woman as an element of restoration and harmony than the negro." Note also that the *Minor* decision held that the Privileges and Immunities Clause did not protect the voting rights of citizens, includ-

ing women, and so was a loss for suffragettes who had attempted to vote in 1872 on these grounds. Anthony held that "the American Association is trying the popular-vote method. The National Association is trying the constitutional method. . . . As the two methods do not conflict, and what is done in the several states tells on the nation, and what is done by congress reacts again on the states, it must be a good thing to keep up both kinds of agitation." See *Bradwell v. State of Illinois*, 83 U.S. 130 (1873); *Minor v. Happersett*, 88 U.S. 162, 172, 175, 178 (1875); *Congressional Globe: Fortieth Congress, Third Session*, 561, 708, 828; Stanton, Anthony, and Gage, *History of Woman Suffrage*, 2: 66, 350, 382–84, 930; Flexner, *Century of Struggle*, 145–58, 176–78; DuBois, *Feminism and Suffrage*, 162–202; Kyvig, *Explicit and Authentic Acts*, 226–28; Keyssar, *Right to Vote*, 139–49; Beaumont, *Civic Constitution*, 178–82; Teele, *Forging the Franchise*, 93–97.

44. The "lower orders of foreigners now crowding our shores" had proved "the most hostile to the equality of women," Anthony had added elsewhere. Stanton, Anthony, and Gage, *History of Woman Suffrage*, 2: 353–54; Stanton, Anthony, and Gage, *History of Woman Suffrage*, vol. 3, 66; "Senator Farwell on Woman Suffrage"; *Congressional Record: Forty-Ninth Congress, Second Session*, 33–38, 986; U.S. Senate, *Report of the Senate Select Committee on Woman Suffrage*, 4–5, 19–20; Flexner, *Century of Struggle*, 176–78; Keyssar, *Right to Vote*, 149–50; McConnaughy, *Woman Suffrage Movement in America*, 230–38.

45. *Congressional Globe: Thirty-Ninth Congress, First Session*, 350–51; Pennsylvania Constitutional Convention, *Debates of the Convention*, 553; Stanton, Anthony, and Gage, *History of Woman Suffrage*, vol. 3, 697; North Dakota Constitutional Convention, *Proceedings and Debates*, 34–41, 277; Musmanno, *Proposed Amendments*, 243–44; Morgan, *Suffragists and Democrats*, 17–18; Flexner, *Century of Struggle*, 159–81; Keyssar, *Right to Vote*, 150–58.

46. Anthony quoted in Catt and Shuler, *Woman Suffrage and Politics*, 227.

47. Anthony and Harper, *History of Woman Suffrage*, vol. 4, 218–19; Catt and Shuler, *Woman Suffrage and Politics*, 107; Flexner, *Century of Struggle*, 228–31; Keyssar, *Right to Vote*, 365–66.

48. Harper, *History of Woman Suffrage*, vol. 5, 270–73; Catt and Shuler, *Woman Suffrage and Politics*, 227.

49. Specifically, the Supreme Court had refused to review *Scown v. Szarnecki*, 261 Ill. 205 (1914), the case challenging the Illinois law. See also U.S. Senate, *Report of the Senate Select Committee on Woman Suffrage*, 20; Catt, "Why the Federal Amendment?," 10–11; Flexner, *Century of Struggle*, 262–70; Kyvig, *Explicit and Authentic Acts*, 228–30; Keyssar, *Right to Vote*, 164–70.

50. At the 1902 meeting, the NAWSA's Stanton argued for literacy tests, and the following NAWSA convention allowed Southern chapters to exclude Black women, continuing the NWSA's and AWSA's commitment to native-born, upper-middle-class white women. Morgan, *Suffragists and Democrats*, 84–99; Flexner, *Century of Struggle*, 271–77; L. Ford, "Alice Paul and the Triumph of Militancy"; Keyssar, *Right to Vote*, 161.

51. McCormick quoted in Morgan, *Suffragists and Democrats*, 91–92. See also Flexner, *Century of Struggle*, 271–85; Kyvig, *Explicit and Authentic Acts*, 230–33; Keyssar, *Right to Vote*, 166.

52. Hymowitz and Weissman, *History of Women in America,* 280.
53. For Catt's plan and quotes, see Flexner, *Century of Struggle,* 286–92. See also Kraditor, *Ideas of the Woman Suffrage Movement,* 231–48; Morgan, *Suffragists and Democrats,* 89–90, 97–99; Fowler, "Carrie Chapman Catt, Strategist."
54. This proportion includes states passing any form of enfranchisement, local or federal.
55. Harper, *History of Woman Suffrage,* 5:542–43; Musmanno, *Proposed Amendments,* 247–48; Keyssar, *Right to Vote,* 170–74; Flexner, *Century of Struggle,* 292–301, 326; McConnaughy, *Woman Suffrage Movement in America,* 207–30; Teele, *Forging the Franchise,* 105.
56. See *Williams v. Mississippi,* 170 U.S. 213 (1898); U.S. House, *Report of the House Judiciary Committee,* 8; *Congressional Record: Sixty-Sixth Congress, First Session,* 80–86, 563, 620–21, 635; Harper, *History of Woman Suffrage,* vol. 5, 763; Musmanno, *Proposed Amendments,* 251–53; Morgan, *Suffragists and Democrats,* 117–43; Flexner, *Century of Struggle,* 301–3, 319–28; McConnaughy, *Woman Suffrage Movement in America,* 238–50.
57. Morgan, *Suffragists and Democrats,* 144–53; Flexner, *Century of Struggle,* 328–37; Kyvig, *Unintended Consequences of Constitutional Amendment,* 236–39.
58. For conventional stories of the amendment's passage, see Grimes, *Democracy and the Amendments to the Constitution,* 90–97. As noted in Congress, the Nineteenth Amendment was nearly identical in wording to Anthony's 1877 amendment proposal but was far less radical than the 1877 proposal, as it, unlike the 1877 proposal, complemented state reform. *Congressional Record: Sixty-Sixth Congress, First Session,* 83; Catt and Shuler, *Woman Suffrage and Politics,* 230.
59. The 1850s saw only statutory bans. As a delegate to the 1850 Michigan constitutional convention explained, "We should only embrace general principles. We should not define the sale and use of ardent spirits to be a crime. . . . What may be considered proper now, may be deemed immoral hereafter; and what may be thought wrong in our day, may be esteemed proper in the next generation." Some convention delegates nevertheless regulated liquor sale licenses and proposed broader bans. See Michigan Constitutional Convention, *Proceedings and Debates,* 187; Colvin, *Prohibition in the United States,* 29–48; Dinan, *American State Constitutional Tradition,* 256–68.
60. Bittenbender, *National Prohibitory Amendment Guide,* 28; Musmanno, *Proposed Amendments,* 226–28; Hamm, *Shaping the Eighteenth Amendment,* 18–31.
61. *Mugler v. Kansas,* 123 U.S. 623 (1887), held that prohibition under state police powers trumped due process and takings appeals by a Kansas brewer. See also *Bowman v. Chicago & Northwestern Ry. Co.,* 125 U.S. 465 (1888); *Leisy v. Hardin,* 135 U.S. 100, 123–125 (1890); Woman's Christian Temperance Union, *Minutes,* 58; Musmanno, *Proposed Amendments,* 228–30; Hamm, *Shaping the Eighteenth Amendment,* 63–65; J. Ely, "Railroad System Has Burst through State Limits," 958.
62. See *In re Rahrer,* 140 U.S. 545 (1891); *Congressional Record: Fifty-First Congress, First Session,* 5325–26; *Congressional Record: Sixty-Second Congress, Third Session,* 828; Ames, *Proposed Amendments,* 272–73; Musmanno, *Proposed Amendments,* 225–33; Grimes, *Democracy and the Amendments to the Constitution,* 82–84; Kyvig, *Explicit and Authentic Acts,* 218–21; Hamm, *Shaping the Eighteenth Amendment,* 78–88.

63. Data on state-level prohibition from Beienburg, *Prohibition, the Constitution, and States' Rights,* checked against Colvin, *Prohibition in the United States,* 135–44, 202–27, 435; Cashman, *Prohibition.* This section lists states by the year they first adopted prohibition, post-1880. South Dakota repealed (1896) and reimplemented (1916) prohibition, as did Alabama (1911 and 1915), while Iowa repealed without reimplementation (1916). Blocker, *Retreat from Reform,* 68–198, esp. 85–94, 102–11; Bordin, *Woman and Temperance,* 52–71, 117–40.

64. The Kansas WCTU independently developed the state amendment strategy in 1879, though Foster, who was more skeptical of the Prohibition Party, perfected it in Iowa three years later. In 1901, WCTU president Lillian M. N. Stevens joined the Anti-Saloon League's National Executive Committee in a show of goodwill. For six amendments that passed in the 1880s, see Maine Constitution of 1820, Article XXVI; Rhode Island Constitution of 1843, Article 5; Iowa Constitution of 1857, Article I, Section 26; Kansas Constitution of 1861, Article XV, Section 10; North Dakota Constitution of 1889, Article XX; South Dakota Constitution of 1889, Article XXIV. Four states constitutionalized the local option. See Texas Constitution of 1876, Article XVI, Section 20; Florida Constitution of 1885, Article XIX; Kentucky Constitution of 1891, Section 61; Delaware Constitution of 1897, Article XIII, Sections 1–3; "Battle Shifts to the City," 9; Richardson, *Liquor Problem,* 126; Blocker, *Retreat from Reform,* 68–198; Blocker, *American Temperance Movements,* 85–94, 102–11; Bordin, *Woman and Temperance,* 52–71, 117–40; Kyvig, *Explicit and Authentic Acts,* 219; Dinan, *American State Constitutional Tradition,* 256–70; Dinan, *State Constitutional Politics,* 238–41; Beienburg, *Prohibition, the Constitution, and States' Rights,* 37.

65. See Maine Constitution of 1819; Ohio Constitution of 1851, Article XV, Section 9; Oklahoma Constitution of 1907, Article I, Section 7; Blocker, *Retreat from Reform,* 105–7; Tinkle, *Maine State Constitution,* 10; Steedman, "Demagogues and the Demon Drink."

66. See Maine Constitution of 1819, amendment of 1885; Ohio Constitution of 1851, Article XV, Section 9; Oklahoma Constitution of 1907, Article I, Section 7; Anti-Saloon League of America, *Proceedings,* 30–31; Odegard, *Pressure Politics,* 130–32; Blocker, *Retreat from Reform,* 214–34; Blocker, *American Temperance Movements,* 105–7; Tinkle, *Maine State Constitution,* 10; J. Ely, "Railroad System Has Burst through State Limits," 959.

67. "Near-Dry States"; Anti-Saloon League of America, "Make the Map All White"; "Wet and Dry Map"; Kerr, *Organized for Prohibition,* 115–22, 147–50; Blocker, *American Temperance Movements,* 105–7; Dando, "Map Proves It."

68. Grimes, *Democracy and the Amendments to the Constitution,* 82–90; Blocker, *American Temperance Movements,* 111–19; Bernstein and Agel, *Amending America,* 173; McGirr, *War on Alcohol,* 3–6; Beienburg, *Prohibition, the Constitution, and States' Rights,* 27–30.

69. See Arizona Constitution of 1912, Article XXIII, Section 1; Colorado Constitution of 1876, Article XXII, Section 1; Oregon Constitution of 1857, Article XXXIX, Section 36; P. Baker, "Next and Final Step," 4; Richardson, *Liquor Problem,* 128–29; Kerr, *Organized for Prohibition,* 139–59, 187–94; Blocker, *American Temperance Movements,* 111–19; Kyvig, *Explicit and Authentic Acts,* 220–21; McGirr, *War on Alcohol,* 22–23; Beienburg, *Prohibition, the Constitution, and States' Rights,* 37–38.

70. See *Clark Distilling Co. v. Western Maryland Railway Co.,* 242 U.S. 311 (1917); Colvin,

Prohibition in the United States, 435; Dinan, *State Constitutional Politics*, 238–41; Beienburg, *Prohibition, the Constitution, and States' Rights*, 33–34.

71. This states'-rights language had precedent in an 1889 Senate Education and Labor Committee report, citing the "prayers of multitudes of the people," which advocated passing an amendment and leaving ratification to the states, "the only tribunal which can enlarge that jurisdiction [of fundamental law]." Note also that post-amendment state-level dry reform was entirely statutory, affirming the Volstead Act. Webb and Volstead quoted in *Meriwether v. State*, 87 So. (Miss.) 411, 413 (1921). See also U.S. Senate, *Report of the Senate Education and Labor Committee; Congressional Record: Sixty-Fifth Congress, First Session*, 5552; *Congressional Record: Sixty-Sixth Congress, First Session*, 562; Caplan, *Constitutional Brinksmanship*, 85–90; Kyvig, *Explicit and Authentic Acts*, 224–26; Beienburg, *Prohibition, the Constitution, and States' Rights*, 35–36, 43, 51–54, 70–102, 265n86.

72. For example, Missouri, a wet state and brewing hub, constitutionally forbade legislators from ratifying any federal amendment impairing "local self-government." Missouri legislators nevertheless ignored this clause, ratifying the Eighteenth Amendment and passing concurrent legislation, approved by voters, to back Volstead enforcement. See Missouri Constitution of 1875, Article II, Section 3; Beienburg, *Prohibition, the Constitution, and States' Rights*, 70–100.

73. See Colorado Constitution of 1876, Article XVIII, Section 5; Colvin, *Prohibition in the United States*, 374–75, 400–409; Blocker, *American Temperance Movements*, 116; McGirr, *War on Alcohol*, 21–22; Beienburg, *Prohibition, the Constitution, and States' Rights*, 40–42.

74. Wets were unconvinced by the Supreme Court's prohibition on double jeopardy for violators in *United States v. Lanza*, 260 U.S. 377 (1922). See Beienburg, *Prohibition, the Constitution, and States' Rights*, 100–119, 131–33.

75. Musmanno, *Proposed Amendments*, 237–42; Beienburg, *Prohibition, the Constitution, and States' Rights*, 144–48.

76. Curran quoted in Beienburg, *Prohibition, the Constitution, and States' Rights*, 150. See also Beienburg, 149–88.

77. Association Against the Prohibition Amendment, *Report*, 7; Kerr, *Organized for Prohibition*, 211–42; Blocker, *American Temperance Movements*, 123–25; Kyvig, *Explicit and Authentic Acts*, 275–79; Okrent, *Last Call*, 300–310; Beienburg, *Prohibition, the Constitution, and States' Rights*, 169–75.

78. Note that wets, constrained by the Supremacy Clause, could not reform state constitutions to directly nullify the Eighteenth Amendment but instead used nonenforcement to a similar quasi-constitutional effect. Repeal data from Beienburg, *Prohibition, the Constitution, and States' Rights*. This count includes Maryland, which never passed concurrent enforcement, and California, which legislatively reversed a repeal referendum. Curran quoted in "Asserts 24 States Now Favor Repeal"; Vose, *Constitutional Change*, 105–10; Kyvig, *Explicit and Authentic Acts*, 280–82; Beienburg, *Prohibition, the Constitution, and States' Rights*, 196–228.

79. The Seventy-Second Congress heard roughly a hundred repeal amendments exempting home-brewed and low-alcohol-by-volume products or calling a repeal referendum, in-

cluding sixty-five repealing the Eighteenth Amendment. State data from Beienburg, *Prohibition, the Constitution, and States' Rights*. *Congressional Record: Seventy-Second Congress, First Session*, 5923, 4509, 4517; Musmanno, *Proposed Amendments*, 237–42; Vose, *Constitutional Change*, 110–21; Grimes, *Democracy and the Amendments to the Constitution*, 109–13; Blocker, *American Temperance Movements*, 126–29; Caplan, *Constitutional Brinksmanship*, 66; Bernstein and Agel, *Amending America*, 176–77; Kyvig, *Explicit and Authentic Acts*, 275–88; Okrent, *Last Call*, 239–41; Beienburg, *Prohibition, the Constitution, and States' Rights*, 190, 213–40.
80. Grant, "Seventh Annual Message to Congress," 175, 180; *Congressional Record: Forty-Fourth Congress, First Session*, 5580, 5587; *Congressional Record: Forty-Fourth Congress, Second Session*, 205, 5245–46, 5318–19; Larson, "Blaine Amendment"; DeForrest, "Overview and Evaluation," 565–76; Green, *Bible, the School, and the Constitution*, 179–223; Hartley, *Failed Attempts to Amend the Constitution*, 83–84.
81. See New Hampshire Constitution of 1784, Part II, Article 83; Minnesota Constitution of 1858, Article VIII, Section 3; Nevada Constitution of 1864, Article XI, Section 10; Colorado Constitution of 1876, Article IX, Section 7. Note that the Nevada amendment passed the legislature in 1877 but was not approved by voters until three years later. For a thorough discussion and count of the clauses, see Dinan, *American State Constitutional Tradition*, 231–37; Dinan, *State Constitutional Politics*, 75–79. See also Ames, *Proposed Amendments*, 278; Larson, "Blaine Amendment"; Kyvig, *Explicit and Authentic Acts*, 189; Viteritti, "Blaine's Wake"; DeForrest, "Overview and Evaluation," 576–601; Thomas, "Rights of Conscience and State School Systems"; Green, "Blaine Amendment Reconsidered"; Green, *Bible, the School, and the Constitution;* Hartley, *Failed Attempts to Amend the Constitution*, 83–84.
82. Note also that between 1906 and 1916, twenty-six states called for a national constitutional convention banning polygamy. See *Reynolds v. United States*, 98 U.S. 145 (1879); Grant, "Seventh Annual Message to Congress," 175, 180; *Congressional Record: Fifty-Sixth Congress, First Session*, 4861–63; Ames, *Proposed Amendments*, 272–78; Musmanno, *Proposed Amendments*, 132, 182–83; Caplan, *Constitutional Brinksmanship*, 66; Kyvig, *Explicit and Authentic Acts*, 189–96; Hartley, *Failed Attempts to Amend the Constitution*, 83–84.
83. Idaho prohibited polygamist voting. See Montana Constitution of 1889, Article III, Section 4; Idaho Constitution of 1890, Article VI, Section 3; Utah Constitution of 1896, Article III, Section 1; Oklahoma Constitution of 1907, Article I, Section 2; New Mexico Constitution of 1911, Article XXI, Section 1; Arizona Constitution of 1912, Article XX, Section 2.
84. Considering the same amendment, Representative Dorsey Shackleford added, "When it is proposed to take from the States their power to regulate offenses over which they now have jurisdiction and control by giving Congress the power to legislate on the offenses connected with adultery I must oppose it. I think it a bad precedent to establish." *Congressional Record: Fifty-Sixth Congress, First Session*, 175, 180, 4862–63. See also Kyvig, *Explicit and Authentic Acts*, 190–91.
85. See Mississippi Constitution of 1890, Article VIII, Section 206, Article XII, Sections 242–45; Alabama Constitutional Convention, *Journal of the Proceedings*, 527, 538; Key,

Southern Politics in State and Nation; Hall and Ely, *Uncertain Tradition;* Hyman, *Anti-Redeemers;* Perman, *Struggle for Mastery;* Valelly, *Two Reconstructions;* Dinan, *American State Constitutional Tradition;* Herron, *Framing the Solid South,* 189–225.

86. With one exception, all of these amendments were sponsored by a few Southerners, mainly in the House—Oscar Underwood of Alabama, William W. Kitchin of North Carolina, and Thomas Hardwick of Georgia together proposed twenty-three of these amendments. See *Slaughterhouse Cases,* 83 U.S. 36 (1873); *Civil Rights Cases,* 109 U.S. 3 (1883); *Plessy v. Ferguson,* 163 U.S. 537 (1896); *Williams v. Mississippi,* 170 U.S. 213 (1898); *Giles v. Harris,* 189 U.S. 482, 488; Mississippi Constitution of 1890, Article XII, Section 241; Alabama Constitution, Article VIII, Sections 180–88; *Congressional Record: Sixty-Third Congress, Second Session,* 5097; National Association for the Advancement of Colored People, *Annual Reports,* 29; Musmanno, *Proposed Amendments,* 207–10.

87. *Holden v. Hardy,* 169 U.S. 366 (1898); *Atkin v. Kansas,* 191 U.S. 207 (1903); *Muller v. Oregon,* 208 U.S. 412 (1908); *Employers' Liability Cases,* 207 U.S. 463 (1908); *Second Employers' Liability Case,* 223 U.S. 1 (1912); *Sturges & Burn Mfg. Co. v. Beauchamp,* 231 U.S. 325 (1913); *Bunting v. Oregon,* 243 U.S. 426 (1917); Bortz, "Special Study #1"; Skocpol, *Protecting Soldiers and Mothers,* 373–479.

88. Connelly quoted in Bridges, "Managing the Periphery," 121–22. See *Lochner v. New York,* 198 U.S. 45 (1905); *Adkins v. Children's Hospital,* 261 U.S. 525 (1923); Ohio Constitution of 1912, Article II, Section 34, amendment of 1912; Nebraska Constitution of 1875, Article XV, Section 8, amendment of 1920; Colorado Constitution of 1876, Article XVI, Section 2; California Constitution of 1879, Article XX, Section 17½, amendment of 1914; North Dakota Constitution of 1889, Article XVII, Section 209; Wyoming Constitution of 1889, Article XIX, Section 2; Idaho Constitution of 1890, Article XIII, Section 4; Utah Constitution of 1896, Article XVI, Section 3, amendment of 1981, and Section 8, amendment of 1933; Oklahoma Constitution of 1907, Article XXIII, Section 3; Michigan Constitution of 1908, Article V, Section 29, amendment of 1920; New Mexico Constitution of 1911, Article XX, Section 10; Arizona Constitution of 1912, Article XVIII, Section 2, amendment of 1972; Louisiana Constitution of 1921, Article IV, Section 7; Massachusetts Constitutional Convention, *Debates,* 738–39; Bortz, "Special Study #1"; Vose, *Constitutional Change,* 182–86; Urofsky, "State Courts and Protective Legislation"; Kens, "Source of a Myth"; Zackin, *Looking for Rights in All the Wrong Places,* 106–45; Dinan, *American State Constitutional Tradition,* 125–30, 188, 190, 194, 376–78; Dinan, *State Constitutional Politics,* 201–3.

89. See *Hammer v. Dagenhart,* 247 U.S. 251 (1918); *Bailey v. Drexel Furniture Co.,* 250 U.S. 20 (1922); and American Federation of Labor, *Report of Proceedings,* 242; *Congressional Record: Sixty-Eighth Congress, First Session,* 7171; Kammen, *Machine That Would Go of Itself,* 260–61, 317; Caplan, *Constitutional Brinksmanship,* 101–4; Bernstein and Agel, *Amending America,* 179–81; Skocpol, *Protecting Soldiers and Mothers,* 480–524; Kyvig, *Explicit and Authentic Acts,* 253–56.

90. The Georgia legislature is quoted in Kyvig, *Explicit and Authentic Acts,* 257–61.

91. Walsh quoted in Kyvig, 268; Sheppard and Fisher quoted in Okrent, *Last Call,* 330; *Congressional Record: Seventy-Second Congress, First Session,* 4514; Kyvig, *Explicit and Authentic Acts,* 221.

Chapter 6. Welfare States, 1932–1979

1. Eskridge and Ferejohn, "Super-Statutes"; McCloskey and Levinson, *American Supreme Court,* 91–147; Ackerman, *We the People,* vol. 3.
2. *Book of the States* state amendment data counts 3,767 ratified amendments for 1950–79 and 5,267 proposed amendments for 1960–79. NBER–University of Maryland State Constitutions Project data count 6,329 ratified amendments for 1932–79. Sturm, *Thirty Years of State Constitution-Making;* Sturm, "Development of American State Constitutions," 68–86; Advisory Commission on Intergovernmental Relations, *Question of State Government Capability,* 35–44; Tarr, *Understanding State Constitutions,* 135–37.
3. Roosevelt, "Fireside Chat, March 9, 1937," 93; Kyvig, *Explicit and Authentic Acts,* 289–314.
4. Roosevelt, "Fireside Chat, March 9, 1937," 9; Grey, "Constitution as Scripture"; Kammen, *Machine That Would Go of Itself;* May, "Constitutional Amendment and Revision Revisited," 168; Kyvig, *Explicit and Authentic Acts,* 258; Ackerman, *We the People,* 2:271; Cushman, *Rethinking the New Deal Court;* Eskridge and Ferejohn, "Super-Statutes"; Levinson, *Our Undemocratic Constitution;* Levinson, *Framed;* Magliocca, "Court-Packing and the Child Labor Amendment"; McCloskey and Levinson, *American Supreme Court;* Leuchtenburg, *Supreme Court Reborn.*
5. For the Brandeis quotes, see Schlesinger, *Age of Roosevelt,* vol. 3, 220, 280. See also *Home Building & Loan Association v. Blaisdell,* 290 U.S. 398, 399 (1934); *Nebbia v. New York,* 291 U.S. 502 (1934); *A.L.A. Schechter Poultry Co. v. U.S.,* 295 U.S. 495 (1935); Hardy, "Taxation and Tax-Exempt Securities"; Brandeis, "Letter to Norman Hapgood, August 2, 1935," 556; Roosevelt, "209th Press Conference, May 31, 1935," 221; Lent, "Origin and Survival of Tax-Exempt Securities"; Schlesinger, *Age of Roosevelt,* vol. 3, 385–408; Ott and Meltzer, "Issues in the Tax Treatment of State and Local Securities"; Badger, *New Deal,* 11–65; Gely and Spiller, "Political Economy of Supreme Court Constitutional Decisions"; Ackerman, *We the People,* 2:279–93.
6. See New York Constitution of 1894, Article I, Section 19, amendment of 1913; *Ives v. South Buffalo Railway,* 201 N.Y. 271 (1911); Sterett, *Public Pensions,* 131–38; Zackin, *Looking for Rights in All the Wrong Places,* 111; Dinan, *American State Constitutional Tradition,* 194–95, 377n60; Dinan, *State Constitutional Politics,* 193–98.
7. Montana's clause excluded farm and livestock workers, while New York's applied only to public workers. Still, New York's revised constitution established "a concrete social obligation which no court may ever misread," according to the delegate Edward F. Corsi. See Montana Constitution of 1889, Article XVIII, Section 4, amendment of 1936; New York Constitution of 1938, Article I, Section 17; New York Constitutional Convention, *Revised Record,* 2126; Zackin, *Looking for Rights in All the Wrong Places,* 112–43; Dinan, *American State Constitutional Tradition,* 94, 377n52; Dinan, *State Constitutional Politics,* 198–201.
8. See New York Constitution, Article I, Sections 16–18; Tarr, *Understanding State Constitutions,* 148–50; Dinan, *American State Constitutional Tradition,* 195–204; Dinan, *State Constitutional Politics,* 204–5.
9. As Clement Vose concludes, by the passage of the Fair Labor Standards Act, nearly half the states had already regulated wages: "before Roosevelt was elected in November and

took office in March 1933, there was a stirring in the states akin to the federal programs he came to sponsor in the years from 1933 to 1938." See New York Constitution of 1894, Article I, Section 16; Utah Constitution of 1895, Article XVI, Section 1, and Section 8, amendment of 1933; Vose, *Constitutional Change,* 179–239; Gallie, *New York State Constitution,* 63–65; Katz, *In the Shadow of the Poorhouse,* 191–95; Zackin, *Looking for Rights in All the Wrong Places,* 110–13, 119–20; Vile, *Encyclopedia of Constitutional Amendments,* 313–14; Dinan, *State Constitutional Politics,* 201–3. For a general account and lists of workers' protections in the state constitutions, see Zackin, *Looking for Rights in All the Wrong Places,* 106–45; Dinan, *American State Constitutional Tradition,* 188–95; Dinan, *State Constitutional Politics,* 190–205.

10. At least sixteen states constitutionally require poverty relief. See Montana Constitution of 1889, Article X, Section 5; Braveman, "Children, Poverty, and State Constitutions," 595–604; Neuborne, "State Constitutions and the Evolution of Positive Rights," 893–96; A. Cohen, "More Myths of Parity," 634–45; Tarr, *Understanding State Constitutions,* 148–50; Hershkoff, "Rights and Freedoms under the State Constitution"; Hershkoff, "Welfare Devolution and State Constitutions"; Hershkoff, "Positive Rights and the Evolution of State Constitutions"; Sterett, *Public Pensions,* 75–104; Dinan, *American State Constitutional Tradition,* 48–49, 211–12.

11. Congressman William B. Wilson introduced the first national pension plan in 1909, William Sirovich proposed scrapping state old-age pension programs for a single national program in 1927, and William Connery and Clarence Dill did the same in 1932, with the latter bill dying in committee. See Ohio Constitution of 1851, Article VII, Section 1; Missouri Constitution of 1875, Article III, Section 38a, amendments of 1916 and 1932; California Constitution of 1879, Article IV, Section 22, amendments of 1920 and 1928; Louisiana Constitution of 1921, Article XVIII, Section 5; Pennsylvania Constitution of 1873, Article III, Section 18, amendment of 1933; *Lucas v. State,* 75 Oh. St. 114 (1906); *State v. Edmonson,* 95 Ohio 351 (1913); Bortz, "Special Study #1"; L. Moore, "Mothers' Pensions," 113–91; Leff, "Consensus for Reform," 405; Braveman, "Children, Poverty, and State Constitutions," 608; Skocpol, *Protecting Soldiers and Mothers,* 154–59, 424–79; Mettler, "Dividing Social Citizenship by Gender," 7–9; Sterett, *Public Pensions,* 105–66; I. Martin, *Rich People's Movements,* 27–28, 38–40; Dinan, *State Constitutional Politics,* 205–11.

12. Patterson, *New Deal and States,* 26–49; Leff, "Consensus for Reform," 402; Mink, "Welfare Reform in Historical Perspective"; Cauthen and Amenta, "Not for Widows Only," 436; Sterett, *Public Pensions,* 129–38.

13. Parker, "Experience under State Old-Age Pension Laws"; J. Brown, *Public Relief,* 26–27; Bortz, "Special Study #1"; Cauthen and Amenta, "Not for Widows Only," 434; Katz, *In the Shadow of the Poorhouse,* 208–17; Sterett, *Public Pensions,* 129–38; Dinan, *State Constitutional Politics,* 208–11.

14. Andrews, "Prospects for Unemployment Compensation Laws"; Whiting, *Final Statistical Report,* 26; E. Witte, "Development of Unemployment Compensation"; Schlesinger, *Age of Roosevelt,* 2:314; Bortz, "Special Study #1"; Katz, *In the Shadow of the Poorhouse,* 195–200.

15. Perkins quoted in Schlesinger, *Age of Roosevelt,* 2:305. Schlesinger agreed that the na-

tional bill "left ample room for local experimentation in the Brandeis tradition." See *Florida v. Mellon,* 273 U.S. 12 (1927); Committee on Economic Security, *Report;* Whiting, *Final Statistical Report,* 26; E. Witte, "Development of Unemployment Compensation"; E. Witte, "Twenty Years of Social Security"; Altmeyer, *Formative Years of Social Security,* 11–12; Schlesinger, *Age of Roosevelt,* 2:282–315; Bortz, "Special Study #1"; W. Cohen, "Development of the Social Security Act of 1935," 400n136; Caplan, *Constitutional Brinksmanship,* 67–68; Katz, *In the Shadow of the Poorhouse,* 234–45; Kyvig, *Explicit and Authentic Acts,* 289–91, 296–301; Ackerman, *We the People,* 2:293–311; Vile, *Encyclopedia of Constitutional Amendments,* 9, 313–14, 457–58; Hartley, *Failed Attempts to Amend the Constitution,* 48–60.

16. As Leff concludes, "the rudimentary measures instituted between 1911 and 1919 had already forged one of the major contributions of the social-justice movement to the New Deal's formulation of the welfare state." Specifically, according to Cauthen and Amenta, "ADC was more likely to be enacted as a federal-state matching program rather than a national program because mothers' pensions already existed at the state level." Like the SSA, the Agricultural Adjustment Act, the Federal Emergency Relief Administration, the Civil Works Administration, and the Works Progress Administration funded existing state programs. See Pennsylvania Constitution of 1873, Article III, Section 18, amendment of 1933; Missouri Constitution of 1875, Article III, Section 38, amendment of 1932; Roosevelt, "Message to Congress, June 8, 1934," 4; Committee on Economic Security, *Report;* Committee on Economic Security, *Social Security in America,* 231; E. Witte, "Development of Unemployment Compensation"; Altmeyer, *Formative Years of Social Security,* 29–42; Patterson, *New Deal and States,* 74–101; Leff, "Consensus for Reform," 402; W. Cohen, "Development of the Social Security Act of 1935"; Mink, "Welfare Reform in Historical Perspective"; Cauthen and Amenta, "Not for Widows Only," 434–36; Lieberman and Lapinski, "American Federalism, Race and the Administration of Welfare"; Beienburg, "Neither Nullification nor Nationalism"; Beienburg, *Prohibition, the Constitution, and States' Rights.*

17. Note also that in 1939, Congress amended the SSA to replace the cooperative state-federal program under Title I with direct federal payments under the Old-Age and Survivors Insurance program. See *In re Interrogatories of the Governor,* 99 Colo. 591 (1937); Colorado Constitution of 1876, Article XXIV, Section 1, amendment of 1936; New York Constitution of 1894, Article VII, Section 8, Article XVII, Sections 1, 3, 4, and Article XVIII, Section 1; California Constitution of 1879, Article XXV, amendment of 1948; Parker, "Experience under State Old-Age Pension Laws in 1932"; E. Witte, "Are Old Age Pensions Worth Their Cost?," 7; J. Brown, *Public Relief,* 328–31; Bortz, "Special Study #1"; Dinan, *State Constitutional Politics,* 208–11.

18. See *Morehead v. New York ex rel. Tipaldo,* 298 U.S. 587 (1936); *U.S. v. Butler,* 297 U.S. 1 (1936); Brandeis, "Letter to Norman Hapgood, August 2, 1935"; Schlesinger, *Age of Roosevelt,* 2:282–315; Caplan, *Constitutional Brinksmanship,* 67–68; Kyvig, *Explicit and Authentic Acts,* 289–91, 296–301; Ackerman, *We the People,* 2:293–311; Sterett, *Public Pensions,* 160–66; Vile, *Encyclopedia of Constitutional Amendments,* 9, 313–14, 457–58; Hartley, *Failed Attempts to Amend the Constitution,* 48–60.

19. Though Cushman emphasizes continuity in Court decisions. Cushman, *Rethinking the New Deal Court.*
20. In *Helvering v. Davis,* 301 U.S. 619, 645 (1937), Cardozo noted, "A system of old age pensions has special dangers of its own if put in force in one state and rejected in another." See *West Coast Hotel v. Parrish,* 300 U.S. 379 (1937); *National Labor Relations Board v. Jones & Laughlin Steel Corporation,* 301 U.S. 1 (1937); *Carmichael v. Southern Coal & Coke Co.,* 301 U.S. 495, 496–97, 514 (1937); *Steward Machine Co. v. Davis,* 301 U.S. 548, 582–83, 587–88 (1937); *United States v. Carolene Products Company,* 304 U.S. 144, 148 (1938); *Helvering v. Gerhardt,* 304 U.S. 405 (1938); *U.S. v. Darby Lumber Co.,* 312 U.S. 100 (1941); *Wickard v. Filburn,* 317 U.S. 111 (1942); Roosevelt, "Message to Congress, February 5, 1937," 59; Schlesinger, *Age of Roosevelt,* 3:468–96; Kyvig, *Explicit and Authentic Acts,* 289–314; Ackerman, *We the People,* 2:312–66; Cushman, *Rethinking the New Deal Court,* 9–44; White, *Constitution and the New Deal,* 167–236; McCloskey and Levinson, *American Supreme Court,* 108–20; Whittington, "State Constitutional Law in the New Deal Period," 1141–50.
21. Sterett adds that by "the time Congress enacted the Social Security Act of 1935, much of the legal groundwork concerning why spending for individuals benefited the public had been laid in the states." Urofsky also gives a nicely nuanced view of state labor regulation: "Rather than as bastions of reaction, most state courts could be fairly characterized as upholders of the best common-law tradition, attempting to meet the new social and economic conditions of the country. In doing so they did not embrace one doctrine to the exclusion of others but, in most instances, balanced legal doctrines, contract and police power, and, again in most instances, deferred to legislative judgment in policy matters." Urofsky, "State Courts and Protective Legislation," 91; Sterett, *Public Pensions,* 4, 15, 176–78.
22. Ackerman, for example, tells us, "Having killed off Article Five amendments, the Court filled the gap it created with a series of landmark opinions." Leuchtenburg, *Supreme Court Reborn,* 163–79; Ackerman, *We the People,* 2:359; McCloskey and Levinson, *American Supreme Court,* 108–20. For critiques of these accounts, see White, *Constitution and the New Deal.*
23. Fourteen states passed right-to-work laws alongside the passage of the 1947 Taft-Hartley Act, including five by constitutional amendment. Galvin notes a pattern of national labor law preempting subnational innovation, channeling subnational reform instead toward employment law. Galvin, "From Labor Law to Employment Law." See also *Dandridge v. Williams,* 397 U.S. 471 (1970); Urofsky, "State Courts and Protective Legislation," 91; Mettler, "Dividing Social Citizenship by Gender," 11; Howard, "American Welfare State, or States?"; Eskridge and Ferejohn, "Super-Statutes"; Ackerman, *We the People,* 2:255–420; Hartley, *Failed Attempts to Amend the Constitution,* 121–24; Dinan, *State Constitutional Politics,* 248–50.
24. See *Williams v. Mississippi,* 170 U.S. 213 (1898); *Giles v. Harris,* 189 U.S. 475 (1903); *James v. Bowman,* 190 U.S. 127 (1903); *Giles v. Teasley,* 193 U.S. 146 (1904); *Breedlove v. Suttles,* 302 U.S. 277 (1937); Mississippi Constitution of 1868, Article VIII, Section 7; Mississippi Constitution of 1890, Article XII, Section 243; Woodward, *Origins of the*

New South, 335–37; Ogden, *Poll Tax in the South,* 1–31; J. Kousser, *Shaping of Southern Politics,* 45–82; Kyvig, *Explicit and Authentic Acts,* 350–52; Lawson, *Black Ballots,* 1–22; Keyssar, *Right to Vote,* 64–138, 189–90, 334–35, 340–55; Valelly, *Two Reconstructions,* 121–48, 163–64; Ellis, "Cost of the Vote," 1041–47; Ackerman, *We the People,* vol. 3, 85–88; Hartley, *Failed Attempts to Amend the Constitution,* 78–80, 202n278; Herron, *Framing the Solid South,* 192–93.

25. *Baker v. Carr,* 369 U.S. 186 (1962); *Wesberry v. Sanders,* 376 U.S. 1 (1964); *Reynolds v. Sims,* 377 U.S. 533 (1964).

26. Kyvig, for example, agrees that these amendments "represented a focused response to a particular problem of government rather than a broad declaration of fundamental principle." See also Vile: "Most amendments ratified over the course of the last sixty years have dealt with minor structural features of the Constitution." See *Brown v. Board of Education of Topeka I,* 347 U.S. 483 (1954); Vile, *Rewriting the United States Constitution,* 7; Kyvig, *Explicit and Authentic Acts,* 349; Valelly, *Two Reconstructions;* G. Rosenberg, *Hollow Hope;* Ackerman, *We the People,* 3:8–9.

27. Quoted in Ackerman, *We the People,* 3:354n10.

28. Southern Conference on Human Welfare resolution quoted in Sitkoff, *New Deal for Blacks,* 100; Truman quoted in Frederickson, *Dixiecrat Revolt,* 39.

29. For Southern opposition to federal bans, see Strom Thurmond: "If Congress can use this law to establish the power to deal with the right of the American people to vote, it can establish a form of Federal suffrage.... The States would thus lose their effective voice in the national legislative halls as they did in Reconstruction Days when ballot boxes were surrounded by Federal bayonet." Thurmond, "President Truman's So-Called Civil Rights Program," 3–4. Also see Louisiana attorney general Jack P. F. Gremillion's testimony before the House Judiciary Committee on the 1957 civil rights bill: "This legislation is unnecessary because of the fact that, insofar as Louisiana is concerned, there has not been any deprivation of civil rights regardless of any minority group.... The poll tax was wiped off our books in 1934." U.S. House, *Civil Rights Hearings,* 989. See North Carolina Constitution of 1868, Article VI, Section 4, amendment of 1920; Tennessee Constitution of 1870, Article II, Section 4, amendment of 1953; Arkansas Constitution of 1874, amendment of 1944; South Carolina Constitution of 1896, Article XI, Section 6, amendment of 1951; Louisiana Constitution of 1921, Article VIII, Section 2, amendment of 1940; *Pirtle v. Brown et al., Judges of Election, et al.,* 314 U.S. 621 (1941); *Biggs v. Beeler,* 173 S.W.2d 144 (Tenn. 1943); Brewer, "Poll Tax and Poll Taxers"; Strong, "American Government and Politics"; Kallenbach, "Constitutional Aspects of Federal Anti-Poll Tax Legislation"; Key, *Southern Politics in State and Nation,* 578–618; Ogden, *Poll Tax in the South,* 178–280; Bunche, *Political Status of the Negro,* 328–83; Sitkoff, *New Deal for Blacks,* 128–38; Kyvig, *Explicit and Authentic Acts,* 355; Lawson, *Black Ballots,* 55–85, 103, 125; Keyssar, *Right to Vote,* 182–84, 422n21, 423n39; Frederickson, *Dixiecrat Revolt,* 2, 36–39, 77–78, 88–89, 105–6; K. Johnson, *Reforming Jim Crow,* 91–115; McMahon, *Reconsidering Roosevelt on Race,* 121, 126–27, 144–50, 156–59, 248n57.

30. But note that Louisiana's Edwin Willis, Texas's Bruce Alger, and South Carolina's William Dorn condemned the amendment as redundant to prior state reforms. See Arkansas

Constitution of 1874, Article III, Section 1, amendment 1920, amendment of 1963; *Congressional Record: Eighty-Sixth Congress, Second Session,* 849–50; *Congressional Record: Eighty-Seventh Congress, Second Session,* 17654–70; Grimes, *Democracy and the Amendments to the Constitution,* 130–36; Bernstein and Agel, *Amending America,* 136–38; Kyvig, *Explicit and Authentic Acts,* 350–57; Keyssar, *Right to Vote,* 207, 422n21; Ackerman, *We the People,* 3: 88–92; Hartley, *Failed Attempts to Amend the Constitution,* 79–81.

31. Hartley notes that in *Harper,* Justice Arthur Goldberg convinced the Court that the amendment required overturning *Breedlove.* Ackerman, however, holds that "it was the statute, not the amendment that inaugurated the constitutional revolution." But also note that Ackerman mentions state reform in passing. See *Harper v. Virginia Board of Elections,* 383 U.S. 663, 666 n.4 (1966); Bernstein and Agel, *Amending America,* 136–38; Keyssar, *Right to Vote,* 218–21; Ackerman, *We the People,* 3: 84–88; Hartley, *Failed Attempts to Amend the Constitution,* 81–82; Schickler, *Racial Realignment.*
32. See *Nixon v. Herndon,* 273 U.S. 536 (1937); *Nixon v. Condon,* 186 U.S. 73 (1932); *Grovey v. Townsend,* 295 U.S. 45 (1935); *Smith v. Allwright,* 321 U.S. 649 (1944); J. Kousser, *Shaping of Southern Politics,* 72–82; Lawson, *Black Ballots,* 23–54; Keyssar, *Right to Vote,* 197–202; Valelly, *Two Reconstructions,* 149–63.
33. Key, *Southern Politics in State and Nation,* 555–77; Matthews and Prothro, "Political Factors and Negro Voter Registration," 358; Lawson, *Black Ballots,* 87–88, 374n3; Stanley, *Voter Mobilization and the Politics of Race,* 85–99.
34. See *Katzenbach v. Morgan,* 384 U.S. 641 (1966); *Gaston County v. U.S.,* 395 U.S. 285 (1969); *Oregon v. Mitchell,* 400 U.S. 112 (1970); *Dunn v. Blumstein,* 405 U.S. 330 (1972); Lawson, *Black Ballots,* 290–95; Keyssar, *Right to Vote,* 114–18, 221–23, 340–45.
35. Commission on Intergovernmental Relations, *Report,* 37; Dixon, *Democratic Representation,* 261–89; Tarr, *Understanding State Constitutions,* 144–47.
36. Oberst, "Genesis of the Three States-Rights Amendments"; *Congressional Record: Ninetieth Congress, First Session,* 9342, 10110; Dixon, *Democratic Representation,* 385–435; Caplan, *Constitutional Brinksmanship,* 73–75; Kyvig, *Explicit and Authentic Acts,* 370–76; Keyssar, *Right to Vote,* 230–33; Ross, "Attacks on the Warren Court," 529–610; Hartley, *Failed Attempts to Amend the Constitution,* 103–6.
37. For redistricting commission clauses from the 1960s and 1970s, see Maine Constitution of 1820, Article IV, Part III, Section 1A, amendment of 1975; Colorado Constitution of 1876, Article V, Section 48, amendment of 1974; Missouri Constitution of 1945, Article III, Sections 2, 7, amendment of 1966; New Jersey Constitution of 1948, Article IV, Section 3, amendment of 1966; Hawaii Constitution of 1959, Article III, Section 4, amendment of 1968; Michigan Constitution of 1964, Article IV, Section 6; Pennsylvania Constitution of 1968, Article II, Section 17; Montana Constitution of 1973, Article V, Section 14. For a list of state equal-population apportionment clauses and companion state cases, see Gardner, "Representation without Party," 895n43, 929–34. See also Dixon, *Democratic Representation,* 290–384; Dixon and Hatheway, "Seminal Issue in State Constitutional Revision"; Hardy, Heslop, and Anderson, introduction to *Reapportionment Politics;* Grofman and Handley, "Impact of the Voting Rights Act"; Dinan, *American State Constitutional Tradition,* 172–82; Dinan, *State Constitutional Politics,* 64–68.

38. Amendment data from the *Book of the States*. See Michigan Constitution of 1964, Article IV, Section 52; Connecticut Constitution of 1964, Article I, Section 20; Florida Constitution of 1968, Article I, Section 2; Advisory Commission on Intergovernmental Relations, *Question of State Government Capability,* 35–44; Tarr, "Explaining State Constitutional Change."
39. Javits reiterated the redundancy of Dirksen's amendment proposals: "Since these measures were offered, however, the entire character of the problem has been altered drastically. Forty State legislatures have already been reapportioned or will complete reapportionment by the next election. Seven States are under court order and the remaining three are in the courts now." Pell similarly noted, "more than 40 States have already complied with the Supreme Court decision." See *Kirkpatrick v. Presiler,* 394 U.S. 526 (1969); *Mahan v. Howell,* 410 U.S. 315 (1973); *Congressional Record: Eighty-Ninth Congress, Second Session,* 3831–32, 5155–58, 8567–79; *Congressional Record: Ninetieth Congress, First Session,* 7551–52, 7573–74, 9342–43, 10109–15; P. Martin, "Application Clause of Article Five," 624–26; Vose, *Constitutional Change,* 352–54; Caplan, *Constitutional Brinksmanship,* 75–78; Kyvig, *Explicit and Authentic Acts,* 376–79; Hartley, *Failed Attempts to Amend the Constitution,* 106–8.
40. Alaska and Hawaii used voting ages of nineteen and twenty, respectively. See Massachusetts Constitution of 1780, Article C, amendments of 1970 and 1972; New Hampshire Constitution of 1792, Part I, Article XI, amendment of 1976; Maine Constitution of 1819, Article II, Section 1, amendments of 1970 and 1971; Minnesota Constitution of 1857, Article VII, Section 1, amendment of 1970; Nevada Constitution of 1864, Article II, Section 1, amendment of 1971; Georgia Constitution of 1877, Article II, Section 1, amendment of 1945; Nebraska Constitution of 1875, Article III, Section 8, amendments of 1970 and 1972; Montana Constitution of 1889, Article IX, Section 2, amendment of 1970; Mississippi Constitution of 1890, Article XII, Section 241, amendment of 1972; Kentucky Constitution of 1891, Suffrage Article, Section 145, amendment of 1955; South Carolina Constitution of 1895, Article II, Section 4, amendment of 1972; Oklahoma Constitution of 1907, Article III, Section 1, amendment of 1971; Missouri Constitution of 1945, Article VIII, Section 2, amendment of 1974; Alaska Constitution of 1959, Article V, Section 1, amendment of 1970; Hawaii Constitution of 1959, Article II, Section 1; North Carolina Constitution of 1971, Article VI, Section 1, amendment of 1972; Montana Constitution of 1972, Article IV, Section 2; *Oregon v. Mitchell,* 400 U.S. 112 (1970); Council of State Governments, *Book of the States;* Neale, "Eighteen-Year-Old Vote"; Ballotpedia, "Voting Age"; Kyvig, *Explicit and Authentic Acts,* 363–68.
41. The 1921 Wisconsin act forbade gender discrimination "unless such constructions will deny to females the special protection and privileges which they now enjoy for the general welfare." Similarly, Paul told the Massachusetts NWP chair, "be very certain that none of the legislation which you introduce in any way disturbs any protective legislation that may have been passed in your state." Quoted in Cott, *Grounding of Modern Feminism,* 121.
42. "National Amendment Is the Permanent Way," 4; Matthews, "Federal Amendment Avoids Referendum Campaigns," 5.
43. Similarly, surveying state protections, the League of Women Voters member Mrs. Wil-

liam J. Carson told the House Judiciary Committee, "The States should be left free to study the question and to make up their own minds. . . . The States have the right to do their own experimenting." Carson quoted in U.S. House, *Equal Rights Amendment to the Constitution,* 24–25; Park quoted in Cott, *Grounding of Modern Feminism,* 74–82, 117–42; Walsh quoted in Kyvig, *Explicit and Authentic Acts,* 254–55, 394–400. See also *Textile Worker* 11 (1923): 684; Geidel, "National Woman's Party"; S. Becker, *Origins of the Equal Rights Amendment,* 15–111; Cott, "Feminist Politics in the 1920s"; Steiner, *Constitutional Inequality,* 7–10; Mansbridge, *Why We Lost the ERA,* 8–9; Berry, *Why ERA Failed,* 56–58; Freeman, "Social Revolution and the Equal Rights Amendment," 145–47; Hartley, *Failed Attempts to Amend the Constitution,* 15–16.

44. Miller quoted in U.S. Senate, *Equal Rights Amendment,* 146; Roosevelt statement quoted in *Congressional Record: Seventy-Ninth Congress, Second Session,* 9399–9401.
45. President's Commission on the Status of Women, *American Women,* 35–48.
46. Between 1966 and 1971, ten states ruled that the 1964 Civil Rights Act's Title VII superseded state protective laws, eight states repealed gender-specific working-hour laws, and six modified them. Brown et al., "Equal Rights Amendment," 922–28; Berry, *Why ERA Failed,* 65.
47. Echoing Eleanor Roosevelt, AFL president William Green memorialized Congress: "We have consistently fought for State and Federal legislation giving special protection for women. . . . The equal-rights amendment will wipe out all such protective laws." Referring to traditional gender differences "ordained by Nature and God," Orrice Murdock took a conservative tack: "States have done a good job in legislatively treating the difference between men and women. . . . I am unwilling, in the name of equality of rights under the Federal Constitution, to repeal all those protections." Dissenting against the ERA in 1971, David W. Dennis similarly held, "I see no good reason why Congress, or the Legislatures of the several States, should not retain full power to enact reasonable legislation to safeguard the health and safety of the people, including that reasonably designed to protect the health and safety of women." U.S. House, *Report to the House Judiciary Committee,* 5–6; U.S. Senate, *Report to the Senate Judiciary Committee;* Freeman, "Social Revolution and the Equal Rights Amendment," 147–48; Grimes, *Democracy and the Amendments to the Constitution,* 147–53; Steiner, *Constitutional Inequality,* 7–25; Mansbridge, *Why We Lost the ERA,* 8–13, 36–44; Berry, *Why ERA Failed,* 58–64; C. Harrison, *On Account of Sex;* Bernstein and Agel, *Amending America,* 140–42; Kyvig, *Explicit and Authentic Acts,* 397–408; Hartley, *Failed Attempts to Amend the Constitution,* 16–24.
48. See *Rosenfeld v. Southern Pacific Co.,* 444 F2d. 1219 (1971); Berry, *Why ERA Failed,* 64–67; Boles, *Politics of the Equal Rights Amendment,* 61–66, 72–78.
49. See *Reed v. Reed,* 404 U.S. 71 (1971); *Roe v. Wade,* 410 U.S. 113 (1973); *Frontiero v. Richardson,* 411 U.S. 677 (1973); *Craig v. Boren,* 429 U.S. 190 (1976); Grimes, *Democracy and the Amendments to the Constitution,* 153; Mansbridge, *Why We Lost the ERA,* 12–14; Freeman, "Social Revolution and the Equal Rights Amendment," 148; Bernstein and Agel, *Amending America,* 142–43; Soule and Olzak, "When Do Movements Matter?"; Hartley, *Failed Attempts to Amend the Constitution,* 40–46.
50. Boles, *Politics of the Equal Rights Amendment;* Steiner, *Constitutional Inequality,* 26–51,

75–95; Mansbridge, *Why We Lost the ERA;* Berry, *Why ERA Failed;* Freeman, "Social Revolution and the Equal Rights Amendment"; Kyvig, *Explicit and Authentic Acts,* 407–19.
51. Illinois Constitutional Convention, *Record of Proceedings,* 3669. For the first three provisions, see California Constitution of 1879, Article XX, Section 18; Wyoming Constitution of 1889, Article I, Section 3; Utah Constitution of 1896, Article IV, Section 1. Frontier California and Wyoming included clauses to encourage female settlement, and Utah, to dispel congressional anxieties of female subjugation through polygamy.
52. Schermerhorn quoted in Lear, "You'll Probably Think I'm Stupid," 31.
53. See also Maryland Constitution of 1867, Declaration of Rights, Article XLVI; Texas Constitution of 1876, Article I, Section 3a, amendment of 1972; Washington Constitution of 1889, Article XXXI, Section 1, amendment of 1972; New Mexico Constitution of 1911, Article II, Section 18, amendment of 1972; Pennsylvania Constitution of 1968, Article I, Section 28, amendment of 1971; Illinois Constitution of 1970, Article I, Sections 17–18; Virginia Constitution of 1971, Article I, Section 11; *Jacobson v. Lenhart,* 30 Ill. 2d. 225, 195 N.E.2d 638 (1964); *People v. Ellis,* 57 Ill. 2d 127, 311 N.E.2d 98 (1974). In addition to the twenty-two explicit clauses, the New Jersey Constitution of 1947, Article I, Section 5, and Article X, Section 4, jointly forbid gender discrimination. Advances have since been piecemeal. Rhode Island added an ERA in 1986, as did Iowa and Florida in 1998 and Oregon in 2014, yielding twenty-two state constitutional equal rights provisions. Several decades after state ERA adoption, Baldez, Epstein, and Martin confirm that judges in ERA states are more likely to impose strict scrutiny against legal gender distinctions. See Lear, "You'll Probably Think I'm Stupid," 112; Driscoll and Rouse, "Through a Glass Darkly"; Gokel, "One Small Word," 956; Munns, "Iowans to Vote on State ERA"; Fleming, "ERA Showdown in Maine"; Proebsting, "Washington's Equal Rights Amendment"; Williams, "Equality Guarantees," 1212–14; Steiner, *Constitutional Inequality,* 65; Mansbridge, *Why We Lost the ERA,* 14; Marquez, "Comparable Worth and the Maryland ERA"; Kilgarlin and Tarver, "Equal Rights Amendment," 1546–49; Gladstone, "Equal Rights Amendments"; Brigance, "Equal Rights Amendment"; Hartley, *Failed Attempts to Amend the Constitution,* 82–83, 159–60; Dinan, *State Constitutional Politics,* 81–84; Schlafly, "Effect of ERAs in State Constitutions," 4; Baldez, Epstein, and Martin, "Does the U.S. Constitution Need an Equal Rights Amendment?"
54. Schlafly, "Effect of ERAs in State Constitutions," 4; Berry, *Why ERA Failed,* 90–100.
55. Schermerhorn quoted in Lear, "You'll Probably Think I'm Stupid," 31. Judges interpreted state constitutional equality provisions to require strict scrutiny in California, Colorado, Connecticut, Hawaii, Illinois, Massachusetts, Maryland, New Mexico, Pennsylvania, Texas, and Washington (note that all of these states ratified the federal ERA); intermediate scrutiny in Montana; and minimal scrutiny in Utah, Louisiana, and Virginia. They did not specify standards in Alaska, New Hampshire, and Wyoming. Some state ERAs applied only to state action, and even so, some legislators still did not repeal suspect statutory gender distinctions. These lists by state are derived from Berry, but for a discussion, with some disagreement, of standards and linked cases by state, see U.S. House, *Equal Rights Amendments Extension,* 248; Treadwell and Page, "Equal Rights

Provisions"; Driscoll and Rouse, "Through a Glass Darkly"; Boles, *Politics of the Equal Rights Amendment,* 85, 142–80; Tarr and Porter, "Gender Equality and Judicial Federalism"; Avner, "Some Observations on State Equal Rights Amendments," 145; Steiner, *Constitutional Inequality,* 89–90; Berry, *Why ERA Failed,* 90–100; Gammie, "State ERAs"; Linton, "State Equal Rights Amendments"; Tarr, *Understanding State Constitutions,* 13, 47, 201–5.

56. Some federal ERA proponents pointed to state measures. Recounting opponents' predictions of coed bathrooms and same-sex marriage, Congresswoman Liz Holtzman noted, "Governors of five states, where ERA has not only been ratified but put into the state constitution, have stated that not one of these allegations has come true." Note also that Nevada, Illinois, and Virginia ratified after the 1982 deadline. U.S. House, *Equal Rights Amendments Extension,* 175, 254, 363, 373–77; U.S. Senate, *Equal Rights Amendment Extension,* 331–32, 401, 427–28, 491–94; *Congressional Record: Ninety-Fifth Congress, Second Session,* 26260, 34283, 34306. For arguments supporting Nevada's, Illinois's, and Virginia's delayed ratification, see Held, Herndon, and Stager, "Equal Rights Amendment." On Congress's authority over deadlines, see *Dillon v. Gloss,* 256 U.S. 368 (1921); *Coleman v. Miller,* 307 U.S. 433 (1939).

57. Hatch asked Henry Hyde whether the proposed federal ERA endorsed abortion; Hyde replied, "I believe that because the arguments have already been made in court based on State ERAs that they do grant that right." See Massachusetts Constitution of 1780, Part I, Article I, amendment of 1976; Hawaii Constitution of 1950, Article I, Section 3, amendment of 1972; Connecticut Constitution of 1965, Article I, Section 20, amendment of 1974; *Fisher v. Commonwealth Dept. of Public Welfare,* 509 Pa. 164 (1985); U.S. Senate, *Impact of the Equal Rights Amendment,* 45–46, 83–87, 116, 263–64, 441–42, 511–12, 625–33, 657–58, 663; U.S. House, *Equal Rights Amendment,* 6–7, 22–25, 231–32, 317–18, 416–57, 699–714; Berry, *Why ERA Failed,* 70–85, 101–20; Kyvig, *Explicit and Authentic Acts,* 415–19.

58. Treadwell and Page, "Equal Rights Provisions"; Driscoll and Rouse, "Through a Glass Darkly"; Boles, *Politics of the Equal Rights Amendment,* 85, 162, 172; Tarr and Porter, "Gender Equality and Judicial Federalism"; Avner, "Some Observations on State Equal Rights Amendments"; Sherwin, "Sex Discrimination and State Constitutions"; Williams, "Equality Guarantees in State Constitutional Law," 1212–14; Berry, *Why ERA Failed,* 90–100; Gammie, "State ERAs"; Linton, "State Equal Rights Amendments"; Wharton, "State Equal Rights Amendments Revisited."

59. Boles, *Politics of the Equal Rights Amendment;* S. Becker, *Origins of the Equal Rights Amendment;* Steiner, *Constitutional Inequality;* Mansbridge, *Why We Lost the ERA;* Freeman, "Social Revolution and the Equal Rights Amendment"; Harrison, *On Account of Sex;* Kyvig, *Explicit and Authentic Acts,* 407–19.

60. Ackerman, *We the People,* 3:311.

Chapter 7. Contemporary Constitutionalism, 1980–2020

1. Hamilton, Madison, and Jay, *Federalist,* 246; Kyvig, *Explicit and Authentic Acts,* 349, 426–60; Ackerman, *We the People,* 2:84–88; Strauss, "Irrelevance of Constitutional

Amendments," 1459; Latham, "Historical Amendability of the American Constitution"; Huq, "Function of Article V"; Clymer, "Dale Bumpers." Though on Court activism, also note Keck, *Most Activist Supreme Court in History.* For the Madison veneration quote, see Hamilton, Madison, and Jay, *Federalist,* 246.
2. Quoted in Peters and Avery, "Oklahoma's Statutory Constitution," 575.
3. Quoted in Benjamin and Gais, "Constitutional Conventionphobia," 70. See also Dinan, "Political Dynamics"; Tarr, "Explaining State Constitutional Change"; Levinson and Blake, "When Americans Think about Constitutional Reform"; Williams, "Evolving State Constitutional Processes"; Benjamin, "Amending Clause in the New York Constitution."
4. Brennan, "State Constitutions and the Protection of Individual Rights"; Linde, "First Things First"; Cain and Noll, "Malleable Constitutions"; Williams, *Law of American State Constitutions,* 113–234; Dinan, "State Constitutional Amendments."
5. See *Engel v. Vitale,* 370 U.S. 421 (1962); *Bowsher v. Synar,* 478 U.S. 714 (1986); *Texas v. Johnson,* 491 U.S. 397 (1989); *Clinton v. City of New York,* 524 U.S. 417 (1998); Condray and Conlan, "Article V Conventions and American Federalism."
6. Currently fifteen states impose term limits. See *U.S. Term Limits, Inc. v. Thornton,* 514 U.S. 779 (1995); T. Kousser, *Term Limits,* 3–12; National Conference of State Legislatures, *Term-Limited States.*
7. Federal courts comprehensively addressed these issues, perhaps also obviating congressional amendment. Dinan, *State Constitutional Politics,* 138–43, 155–59, 225–31, 242–44.
8. Reagan, "State of the Union Address, February 4, 1986"; Fisher and Devins, "Can the States' Item Veto Be Transferred to the President?"; Moe, *Prospects for the Item Veto;* Alm and Evers, "Item Veto and State Government Expenditures"; Proposed Constitutional Amendments to Balance the Federal Budget, 83, 137, 1057, 1501; U.S. House, *Item Veto;* Savage, *Balanced Budgets and American Politics,* 198–236; "Balanced Budget Amendment Fails in House."
9. Note that these amendment counts are nonexclusive, and many individual amendment proposals included balanced-budget, tax-cap, and line-item-veto provisions. See *Bowsher v. Synar;* Bernstein and Agel, *Amending America,* 181–87; Kyvig, *Explicit and Authentic Acts,* 426–47; McGirr, *Suburban Warriors;* Lassiter, *Silent Majority;* Vile, *Encyclopedia of Constitutional Amendments,* 37–38; Hartley, *Failed Attempts to Amend the Constitution,* 181–87; MacLean, *Democracy in Chains.*
10. Dinan also explains that there is some academic disagreement whether to class debt-limit clauses as balanced-budget provisions, so the count of thirty-five balanced-budget clauses is probably modest. See Rhode Island Constitution of 1843, Article IV, Section 13; Indiana Constitution of 1851, Article I, Section 5; Nevada Constitution of 1864, Article XI, Section 3, amendment of 1989; Maryland Constitution of 1867, Article III, Section 52, amendment of 1974; Tennessee Constitution of 1870, Article II, Section 24, amendment of 1978; West Virginia Constitution of 1872, Article X, Section 4; Illinois Constitution of 1970, Article VIII, Section 2; North Carolina Constitution of 1971, Article III, Section 5, amendment of 1977; Hawaii Constitution of 1959, Article VII, Section 5, amendment of 1978; Virginia Constitution of 1871, Article X, Section 7, amendment of 1984; Rhode Island Constitution of 1986, Article VI, Section 16; Briffault, "State and Local Finance,"

211–17; Hou and Smith, "Do State Balanced Budget Requirements Matter?," 30–42; Dinan, *State Constitutional Politics,* 171–73; National Conference of State Legislatures, *State Balanced Budget Provisions.*

11. Note that Isaac Martin casts the California tax revolt as moderate homeowners' effort to protect tax exemptions. Note also that Congress in 1971 considered a narrowly tailored amendment requiring a national referendum on war declarations. See Nevada Constitution of 1864, Article IV, Section 18, amendment of 1996; Tennessee Constitution of 1870, Article II, Section 24, amendment of 1978; California Constitution of 1879, Article XIII, A and B, amendments of 1978 and 1979; Oklahoma Constitution of 1907, Article V, Section 33, amendment of 1992; Arizona Constitution of 1912, Article 9, Section 22, amendment of 1992; Missouri Constitution of 1945, Article X, Section 16, amendment of 1980; Hawaii Constitution of 1959, Article VII, Section 9, amendment of 1978; Michigan Constitution of 1963, Article IX, Section 26, amendment of 1978; Tarr, *Understanding State Constitutions,* 156–60; Dinan, *State Constitutional Politics,* 177–84; Dinan, "Policy Provisions in State Constitutions," 184–85; Lowery and Sigelman, "Understanding the Tax Revolt"; Mullins and Wallin, "Tax and Expenditure Limitations"; Sears and Citrin, *Tax Revolt,* 19–72; I. Martin, *Permanent Tax Revolt,* 115–18; O'Sullivan, Sexton, and Sheffrin, *Property Taxes and Tax Revolts,* 1–14; Rabushka and Ryan, *Tax Revolt,* 144, 185–94; Mikesell, "Path of the Tax Revolt."
12. See Colorado Constitution of 1876, Article X, Section 20, amendment of 1992; Bollenbacher, "Two Sides of Colorado," 603–8; Briffault, "State and Local Finance," 217–21; General Accounting Office, *Balanced Budget Requirements;* James and Wallis, "Tax and Spending Limits in Colorado"; D. Smith, "Populist Entrepreneur"; O'Sullivan, Sexton, and Sheffrin, *Property Taxes and Tax Revolts.*
13. Dinan, *American State Constitutional Tradition,* 113–23, 337–38n99, 338–39n102; Dinan, *State Constitutional Politics,* 60–64.
14. See *Nordlinger v. Hahn,* 505 U.S. 1 (1992); *Clinton v. City of New York;* Vile, *Encyclopedia of Constitutional Amendments,* 368–70, 456; Kyvig, *Explicit and Authentic Acts,* 443–47.
15. Dinan, *State Constitutional Politics,* 97–100, 134–38.
16. Winchester, *Plain Political Catechism,* 1796; Kammen, *Machine That Would Go of Itself,* 72–73.

BIBLIOGRAPHY

Ablavsky, Gregory. "Making Indians 'White': The Judicial Abolition of Native Slavery in Revolutionary Virginia and Its Racial Legacy." *University of Pennsylvania Law Review* 159, no. 5 (April 1, 2011): 1457–1531.

Ackerman, Bruce. "Storrs Lectures: Discovering the Constitution." *Faculty Scholarship Series,* Yale Law School, January 1, 1984.

———. *We the People.* Vol. 1, *Foundations.* Cambridge, MA: Harvard University Press, 1993.

———. *We the People.* Vol. 2, *Transformations.* Cambridge, MA: Harvard University Press, 1998.

———. *We the People.* Vol. 3, *The Civil Rights Revolution.* Cambridge, MA: Harvard University Press, 2014.

Adams, John. "Autobiography." In *The Works of John Adams, Second President of the United States: With a Life of the Author, Notes and Illustrations,* edited by Charles Francis Adams, vol. 2, 503–18, and vol. 3, 1–93. Boston: Little, Brown, 1850.

———. "Diary." In *The Works of John Adams, Second President of the United States: With a Life of the Author, Notes and Illustrations,* edited by Charles Francis Adams, vol. 2, 94–128. Boston: Little, Brown, 1850.

———. "Letter to James Madison, June 17, 1817." In *The Works of John Adams, Second President of the United States: With a Life of the Author, Notes and Illustrations,* edited by Charles Francis Adams, vol. 10, 267–69. Boston: Little, Brown, 1856.

———. "Letter to James Sullivan, May 26, 1776." In *The Works of John Adams, Second President of the United States: With a Life of the Author, Notes and Illustrations,* edited by Charles Francis Adams, vol. 9, 375–79. Boston: Little, Brown, 1854.

———. "Letter to John Taylor, April 9, 1814." In *The Works of John Adams, Second President of the United States: With a Life of the Author, Notes and Illustrations,* edited by Charles Francis Adams, vol. 10, 94–97. Boston: Little, Brown, 1856.

———. "Letter to Joseph Palmer, September 26, 1774." In *The Works of John Adams, Sec-*

ond President of the United States: With a Life of the Author, Notes and Illustrations, edited by Charles Francis Adams, vol. 1, 154–56. Boston: Little, Brown, 1856.

———. "Letter to Patrick Henry, June 3, 1776." In *The Works of John Adams, Second President of the United States: With a Life of the Author, Notes and Illustrations*, edited by Charles Francis Adams, vol. 9, 386–89. Boston: Little, Brown, 1854.

———. "Letter to Richard Henry Lee, November 15, 1775." In *The Works of John Adams, Second President of the United States: With a Life of the Author, Notes and Illustrations*, edited by Charles Francis Adams, vol. 4, 185–89. Boston: Little, Brown, 1856.

———. "Letter to Timothy Pickering, August 6, 1822." In *The Works of John Adams, Second President of the United States: With a Life of the Author, Notes and Illustrations*, edited by Charles Francis Adams, vol. 2, 512–15. Boston: Little, Brown, 1850.

———. "Letter to William Tudor, March 29, 1817." In *The Works of John Adams, Second President of the United States: With a Life of the Author, Notes and Illustrations*, edited by Charles Francis Adams, vol. 10, 244–50. Boston: Little, Brown, 1856.

———. "Thoughts on Government." In *The Works of John Adams, Second President of the United States: With a Life of the Author, Notes and Illustrations*, edited by Charles Francis Adams, vol. 4, 193–201. Boston: Little, Brown, 1856.

Adams, Willi Paul. *The First American Constitutions: Republican Ideology and the Making of the State Constitutions in the Revolutionary Era.* Lanham, MD: Rowman and Littlefield, 2001.

Advisory Commission on Intergovernmental Relations. *The Question of State Government Capability.* Washington, DC: Advisory Commission on Intergovernmental Relations, January 1985.

Alabama Constitutional Convention. *Journal of the Proceedings of the Constitutional Convention of the State of Alabama.* Montgomery, AL: Brown, 1901.

Albert, Richard. *Constitutional Amendments: Making, Breaking, and Changing Constitutions.* Oxford: Oxford University Press, 2019.

Aldrich, John Herbert. *Why Parties? A Second Look.* Chicago: University of Chicago Press, 2011.

Allen, Barbara. "Framing Government for a Frontier Commonwealth: The Minnesota Constitution(s)." In *The Constitutionalism of American States*, edited by George E. Connor and Christopher W. Hammons, 163–82. Columbia: University of Missouri Press, 2008.

Alm, James, and Mark Evers. "The Item Veto and State Government Expenditures." *Public Choice* 68, no. 1/3 (1991): 1–15.

Altmeyer, Arthur J. *Formative Years of Social Security.* Madison: University of Wisconsin Press, 1966.

American Federation of Labor. *Report of Proceedings of the Forty-First Annual Convention of the American Federation of Labor.* Washington, DC: Law Reporter Printing, 1921.

Ames, Herman Vandenburg. *The Proposed Amendments to the Constitution of the United States during the First Century of Its History.* Washington, DC: Government Printing Office, 1897.

Andrews, John B. "Prospects for Unemployment Compensation Laws." *The Annals of the American Academy of Political and Social Science* 170, no. 1 (November 1, 1933): 88–92.

Anthony, Susan Brownell, and Ida Husted Harper, eds. *History of Woman Suffrage.* Vol. 4, *1883–1900.* Indianapolis: Hollenbeck, 1902.

Anti-Saloon League of America. "Make the Map All White by Constitutional Amendment: Thirty-Six States Can Do It." Westerville, OH: Anti-Saloon League of America, 1914. University of Virginia Special Collections.

———. *Proceedings of the Fourteenth National Convention of the Anti-Saloon League of America.* Westerville, OH: Anti-Saloon League of America, 1911.

Ashley, James Mitchell. "Constitution Worship." In *Public Opinion: A Comprehensive Summary of the Press throughout the World on All Important Current Topics,* vol. 19. New York: Public Opinion Company, 1895.

"Asserts 24 States Now Favor Repeal." *New York Times,* January 12, 1932.

Association Against the Prohibition Amendment. *Report to the Directors, Members and Friends of the Association Against the Prohibition Amendment.* Association Against the Prohibition Amendment, 1928.

Avner, Judith. "Some Observations on State Equal Rights Amendments." *Yale Law & Policy Review* 3, no. 1 (1984): 144–67.

Badger, Anthony J. *The New Deal: The Depression Years, 1933–1940.* New Haven, CT: Hill and Wang, 1989.

Bailyn, Bernard. *The Ideological Origins of the American Revolution.* Cambridge, MA: Harvard University Press, 1967.

Baker, H. Robert. *The Rescue of Joshua Glover: A Fugitive Slave, the Constitution, and the Coming of the Civil War.* Athens: Ohio University Press, 2007.

Baker, Purley. "The Next and Final Step." *American Issue,* June 1913.

"Balanced Budget Amendment Fails in House." In *CQ Almanac 1982,* 391–94. Washington, DC: Congressional Quarterly, 1983.

Baldez, Lisa, Lee Epstein, and Andrew D. Martin. "Does the U.S. Constitution Need an Equal Rights Amendment?" *Journal of Legal Studies* 35, no. 1 (2006): 243–83.

Ballotpedia. "Voting Age." Accessed May 4, 2020. http://ballotpedia.org /Voting_age.

Bannon, Alicia, and Laila Robbins. "The Nation's Top State Courts Face a Crisis of Legitimacy." *New York Times,* July 23, 2019.

Barnett, James D. "Forestalling the Direct Primary in Oregon." *Political Science Quarterly* 27, no. 4 (1912): 648–68.

Bastress, Robert M. *The West Virginia State Constitution: A Reference Guide.* Westport, CT: Greenwood, 1995.

"Battle Shifts to the City, The." *American Issue,* January 1, 1910.

Beaumont, Elizabeth. *The Civic Constitution: Civic Visions and Struggles in the Path toward Constitutional Democracy.* Oxford: Oxford University Press, 2013.

Becker, Carl Lotus. *The Declaration of Independence: A Study in the History of Political Ideas.* New York: Harcourt, Brace, 1922.

Becker, Susan D. *The Origins of the Equal Rights Amendment: American Feminism between the Wars.* Westport, CT: Greenwood, 1981.

Beeman, Richard. *The Penguin Guide to the United States Constitution: A Fully Annotated Declaration of Independence, U.S. Constitution and Amendments, and Selections from "The Federalist Papers."* New York: Penguin, 2010.

Beienburg, Sean. "Neither Nullification nor Nationalism: The Battle for the States' Rights Middle Ground during Prohibition." *American Political Thought* 7, no. 2 (March 1, 2018): 271–303.

———. *Prohibition, the Constitution, and States' Rights*. Chicago: University of Chicago Press, 2019.

Belz, Herman. *A New Birth of Freedom: The Republican Party and Freedmen's Rights, 1861 to 1866*. New York: Fordham University Press, 2000.

Benjamin, Gerald. "The Amending Clause in the New York Constitution and Conventionphobia." *Pace Law Review* 38, no. 1 (2018): 14–27.

Benjamin, Gerald, and Thomas Gais. "Constitutional Conventionphobia." *Hofstra Law and Policy Symposium* 1 (1996): 53–78.

Berkowitz, Daniel, and Karen Clay. "American Civil Law Origins: Implications for State Constitutions." *American Law and Economics Review* 7, no. 1 (April 1, 2005): 62–84.

Bernstein, Richard B., and Jerome Agel. *Amending America: If We Love the Constitution So Much, Why Do We Keep Trying to Change It?* New York: Random House, 1993.

Berry, Mary Frances. *Why ERA Failed: Politics, Women's Rights, and the Amending Process of the Constitution*. Bloomington: Indiana University Press, 1986.

Besso, Michael. "Constitutional Amendment Procedures and the Informal Political Construction of Constitutions." *Journal of Politics* 67, no. 1 (2005): 69–87.

Bilder, Mary Sarah. *Madison's Hand: Revising the Constitutional Convention*. Cambridge, MA: Harvard University Press, 2015.

Bittenbender, Ada. *The National Prohibitory Amendment Guide*. Chicago: Woman's Temperance Publication Association, 1889.

Blakey, Roy G., and Gladys C. Blakey. *The Federal Income Tax*. New York: Longmans, Green, 1940.

Bland, Richard. "An Inquiry into the Rights of the British Colonies." In *Tracts of the American Revolution, 1763–1776*, edited by Merrill Jensen, 108–27. Indianapolis: Bobbs-Merrill, 1967.

Blocker, Jack S. *American Temperance Movements: Cycles of Reform*. Boston: Twayne, 1988.

———. *Retreat from Reform: The Prohibition Movement in the United States, 1890–1913*. Westport, CT: Praeger, 1976.

Boles, Janet K. *The Politics of the Equal Rights Amendment: Conflict and the Decision Process*. New York: Addison-Wesley Longman, 1979.

Bollenbacher, Vicky. "Two Sides of Colorado, Amplified through Constitutional Redesign." In *The Constitutionalism of American States*, edited by George E. Connor and Christopher W. Hammons, 595–609. Columbia: University of Missouri Press, 2008.

Bordin, Ruth. *Woman and Temperance: The Quest for Power and Liberty, 1873–1900*. New Brunswick, NJ: Rutgers University Press, 1990.

Bortz, Abe. "Special Study #1: Lecture on the History of Social Security." Social Security Administration Historian's Office, n.d.

"*Boston Gazette,* 19 November." In *The Documentary History of the Ratification of the Constitution,* edited by John P. Kaminski, Gaspare J. Saladino, Richard Leffler, Charles H. Schoenleber, and Margaret A. Hogan, vol. 4, 274–76. Charlottesville: University of Virginia Press, 2009.

Boyd, Julian P. "Editorial Note: The Declaration of Independence." In *The Papers of Thomas Jefferson,* vol. 1, *1760–1776,* edited by Julian P. Boyd, 413–17. Princeton, NJ: Princeton University Press, 1950.

———. "Editorial Note: The Virginia Constitution." In *The Papers of Thomas Jefferson,* vol. 1, *1760–1776,* edited by Julian P. Boyd, 329–37. Princeton, NJ: Princeton University Press, 1950.

Brandeis, Louis D. "Letter to Norman Hapgood, August 2, 1935." In *Letters of Louis D. Brandeis,* edited by Melvin I. Urofsky and David W. Levy, vol. 5, 556. Albany: SUNY Press, 1978.

Branning, Rosalind L. *Pennsylvania Constitutional Development.* Pittsburgh: University of Pittsburgh Press, 2004.

Braveman, Daan. "Children, Poverty, and State Constitutions." *Emory Law Journal* 38 (1989): 577–614.

Braxton, Carter. "An Address to the Convention of the Colony and Ancient Dominion of Virginia, on the Subject of Government in General, and Recommending a Particular Form to Their Consideration." In *The Founders' Constitution: Major Themes,* edited by Philip B. Kurland and Ralph Lerner, 670–72. Indianapolis: Liberty Fund, 1987.

Brennan, William J., Jr. "State Constitutions and the Protection of Individual Rights." *Harvard Law Review* 90, no. 3 (January 1, 1977): 489–504.

Bretting, John, and F. Chris Garcia. "New Mexico's Constitution: Promoting Pluralism in La Tierra Encantada." In *The Constitutionalism of American States,* edited by George E. Connor and Christopher W. Hammons, 743–55. Columbia: University of Missouri Press, 2008.

Brewer, William M. "The Poll Tax and Poll Taxers." *Journal of Negro History* 29, no. 3 (1944): 260–99.

Bridges, Amy. *Democratic Beginnings: Founding the Western States.* Lawrence: University Press of Kansas, 2015.

———. "Managing the Periphery in the Gilded Age: Writing Constitutions for the Western States." *Studies in American Political Development* 22, no. 1 (March 2008): 32–58.

Briffault, Richard. "State and Local Finance." In *State Constitutions for the Twenty-First Century: The Agenda of State Constitutional Reform,* edited by G. Alan Tarr and Robert F. Williams, vol. 3, 211–40. Albany: SUNY Press, 2006.

Brigance, Linda. "Equal Rights Amendment." In *Encyclopedia of American Social Movements,* edited by Immanuel Ness, 373–77. London: Routledge, 2015.

Brown, Adam R., and Jeremy C. Pope. "Measuring and Manipulating Constitutional Evaluations in the States: Legitimacy Versus Veneration." *American Politics Research,* June 4, 2018, 1532673X18776626.

Brown, Barbara, Thomas Emerson, Gail Falk, and Ann Freedman. "The Equal Rights Amendment: A Constitutional Basis for Equal Rights for Women." *Yale Law Journal* 80, no. 5 (1971): 871–986.

Brown, Josephine Chapin. *Public Relief, 1929–1939.* New York: Holt, 1940.

Browne, John Ross. *Report of the Debates in the Convention of California, on the Formation of the State Constitution, 1849.* Washington, DC: Printed by John T. Towers, 1850.

Brownlee, Elliot W. *Progressivism and Economic Growth: The Wisconsin Income Tax, 1911–1929.* Port Washington, NY: Kennikat, 1974.

Brunhouse, Robert Levere. *The Counter-Revolution in Pennsylvania, 1776–1790.* Harrisburg: Pennsylvania Historical Commission, 1942.

Bryce, James. *The American Commonwealth.* Vol. 1. London: Macmillan, 1888.

Buchanan, James. *Message from the President of the United States to the Two Houses of Congress at the Commencement of the Second Session of the Thirty-Sixth Congress.* Washington, DC: George W. Bowman, 1860.

Bunche, Ralph J. *The Political Status of the Negro in the Age of FDR.* Chicago: University of Chicago Press, 1973.

Burgess, John William. *Political Science and Comparative Constitutional Law: Sovereignty and Liberty.* Boston: Ginn and Company, 1902.

Burgess, Michael, and G. Alan Tarr. "Introduction: Sub-national Constitutionalism and Constitutional Development." In *Constitutional Dynamics in Federal Systems: Sub-national Perspectives,* edited by Michael Burgess and G. Alan Tarr, 3–39. Montreal: McGill-Queen's Press, 2012.

Burke, Edmund. "Speech on Conciliation with America." In *The Works of the Right Honorable Edmund Burke: With a Biographical and Critical Introduction by Henry Rogers,* edited by Henry Rogers, vol. 1, 181–206. London: Henry G. Bohn, 1834.

Burnham, Walter Dean. *Critical Elections: And the Mainsprings of American Politics.* New York: Norton, 1970.

Bybee, Jay. "Ulysses at the Mast: Democracy, Federalism, and the Sirens' Song of the Seventeenth Amendment." *Northwestern University Law Review* 91, no. 2 (1997): 500–572.

Cain, Bruce E., and Roger G. Noll. "Malleable Constitutions: Reflections on State Constitutional Reform Symposium: What, If Anything, Do We Know about Constitutional Design: Constitutional Change." *Texas Law Review* 87, no. 7 (2009): 1517–44.

Calhoun, John Caldwell. "Speech on the Slavery Question, Delivered in the Senate, March 4, 1850." In *Speeches of John C. Calhoun Delivered in the House of Representatives and in the Senate of the United States,* edited by Richard Kenner Crallé, vol. 4, 542–74. New York: D. Appleton, 1850.

Caplan, Russell L. *Constitutional Brinksmanship: Amending the Constitution by National Convention.* New York: Oxford University Press, 1988.

Carleton, Mark T. "Elitism Sustained: The Louisiana Constitution of 1974." *Tulane Law Review* 54 (1980): 560–88.

Carmines, Edward G., and James A. Stimson. *Issue Evolution: Race and the Transformation of American Politics.* Princeton, NJ: Princeton University Press, 1989.

Carter, John W. "Religion and State Constitution Making." Washington, DC: Catholic University of America, 2009.

Carter, Nathaniel Hazeltine, and William Leete Stone. *Reports of the Proceedings and Debates of the Convention of 1821, Assembled for the Purpose of Amending the Constitution of the State of New York.* Albany, NY: E. and E. Hosford, 1821.

Cashman, Sean Dennis. *Prohibition: The Lie of the Land.* New York: Macmillan, 1981.

Catt, Carrie Chapman. "Why the Federal Amendment?" In *Woman Suffrage by Federal Constitutional Amendment,* edited by Carrie Chapman Catt, 1–11. New York: National Woman Suffrage Publishing, 1917.

Catt, Carrie Chapman, and Nettie Rogers Shuler. *Woman Suffrage and Politics: The Inner Story of the Suffrage Movement.* New York: Charles Scribner's Sons, 1923.
Cauthen, Nancy K., and Edwin Amenta. "Not for Widows Only: Institutional Politics and the Formative Years of Aid to Dependent Children." *American Sociological Review* 61, no. 3 (1996): 427–48.
Cayton, Adam. "Why Are Some Institutions Replaced While Others Persist? Evidence from State Constitutions." *State Politics & Policy Quarterly,* July 22, 2015, 1532440015594663.
Chaput, Erik J. *The People's Martyr: Thomas Wilson Dorr and His 1842 Rhode Island Rebellion.* Lawrence: University Press of Kansas, 2013.
Chase, Salmon P. "Letter to Abraham Lincoln, April 11, 1865." In *Official Records of the Union and Confederate Armies,* vol. 48. Washington, DC: Government Printing Office, 1895.
Cheyney, Edward Potts. *The Anti-Rent Agitation in the State of New York, 1839–1846.* Philadelphia: Porter and Coates, 1887.
Clymer, Adam. "Dale Bumpers, Liberal Stalwart of Arkansas Politics, Dies at 90." *New York Times,* January 2, 2016.
Cohen, Adam S. "More Myths of Parity: State Court Forums and Constitutional Actions for the Right to Shelter." *Emory Law Journal* 38 (1989): 615–60.
Cohen, Wilbur J. "The Development of the Social Security Act of 1935: Reflections Some Fifty Years Later." *Minnesota Law Review,* no. 2 (1984): 379–408.
Colorado Tax Commission. *Colorado Tax Commission Report to the Thirteenth Colorado General Assembly.* Washington, DC: Colorado Tax Commission, 1901.
Colvin, David Leigh. *Prohibition in the United States: A History of the Prohibition Party and of the Prohibition Movement.* New York: George H. Doran, 1926.
Commission on Intergovernmental Relations. *Commission on Intergovernmental Relations Report to the President.* Washington, DC: Commission on Intergovernmental Relations, 1955.
Committee on Economic Security. *Committee on Economic Security Report to the President.* Washington, DC: Committee on Economic Security, January 15, 1935.
———. *Social Security in America: The Factual Background of the Social Security Act as Summarized from Staff Reports to the Committee on Economic Security.* Washington, DC: Government Printing Office, 1937.
Condray, Patrick M., and Timothy J. Conlan. "Article V Conventions and American Federalism: Contemporary Politics in Historical Perspective." *Publius: The Journal of Federalism* 49, no. 3 (July 1, 2019): 515–39.
Congressional Globe: Twenty-First Congress: First Session. Washington, DC: Gales and Seaton, 1830.
Congressional Globe: Twenty-Third Congress, Second Session. Washington, DC: John C. Rives, 1835.
Congressional Globe: Twenty-Fifth Congress, Second Session. Washington, DC: Blair and Rives, 1838.
Congressional Globe: Twenty-Sixth Congress, First Session. Washington, DC: Blair and Rives, 1840.
Congressional Globe: Thirty-First Congress, First Session. Washington, DC: John C. Rives, 1850.

Congressional Globe: Thirty-Fifth Congress, Second Session. Washington, DC: John C. Rives, 1859.
Congressional Globe: Thirty-Eighth Congress, First Session. Washington, DC: John C. Rives, 1864.
Congressional Globe: Thirty-Eighth Congress, Second Session. Washington, DC: F. & J. Rives, 1865.
Congressional Globe: Thirty-Ninth Congress, First Session. Washington, DC: F. & J. Rives, 1866.
Congressional Globe: Thirty-Ninth Congress, Second Session. Washington, DC: F. & J. Rives, 1867.
Congressional Globe: Fortieth Congress, First Session. Washington, DC: F. & J. Rives, 1867.
Congressional Globe: Fortieth Congress, Third Session. Washington, DC: F. & J. Rives and George A. Bailey, 1869.
Congressional Record: Forty-Fourth Congress, First Session. Washington, DC: Government Printing Office, 1876.
Congressional Record: Forty-Fourth Congress, Second Session. Washington, DC: Government Printing Office, 1876.
Congressional Record: Forty-Ninth Congress, Second Session. Washington, DC: Government Printing Office, 1887.
Congressional Record: Fifty-First Congress, First Session. Washington, DC: Government Printing Office, 1889.
Congressional Record: Fifty-Third Congress, Second Session. Washington, DC: Government Printing Office, 1894.
Congressional Record: Fifty-Third Congress, Third Session. Washington, DC: Government Printing Office, 1894.
Congressional Record: Fifty-Sixth Congress, First Session. Washington, DC: Government Printing Office, 1900.
Congressional Record: Fifty-Seventh Congress, First Session. Washington, DC: Government Printing Office, 1902.
Congressional Record: Sixty-First Congress, First Session. Washington, DC: Government Printing Office, 1909.
Congressional Record: Sixty-First Congress, Second Session. Washington, DC: Government Printing Office, 1910.
Congressional Record: Sixty-First Congress, Third Session. Washington, DC: Government Printing Office, 1911.
Congressional Record: Sixty-Second Congress, Second Session. Washington, DC: Government Printing Office, 1912.
Congressional Record: Sixty-Second Congress, Third Session. Washington, DC: Government Printing Office, 1913.
Congressional Record: Sixty-Third Congress, Second Session. Washington, DC: Government Printing Office, 1914.
Congressional Record: Sixty-Fifth Congress, First Session. Washington, DC: Government Printing Office, 1917.

Congressional Record: Sixty-Sixth Congress, First Session. Washington, DC: Government Printing Office, 1919.
Congressional Record: Sixty-Eighth Congress, First Session. Washington, DC: Government Printing Office, 1924.
Congressional Record: Seventy-Second Congress, First Session. Washington, DC: Government Printing Office, 1932.
Congressional Record: Seventy-Ninth Congress, Second Session. Washington, DC: Government Printing Office, 1946.
Congressional Record: Eighty-Sixth Congress, Second Session. Washington, DC: Government Printing Office, 1960.
Congressional Record: Eighty-Seventh Congress, Second Session. Washington, DC: Government Printing Office, 1962.
Congressional Record: Eighty-Ninth Congress, Second Session. Washington, DC: Government Printing Office, 1966.
Congressional Record: Ninetieth Congress, First Session. Washington, DC: Government Printing Office, 1967.
Congressional Record: Ninety-Fifth Congress, Second Session. Washington, DC: Government Printing Office, 1978.
Conley, Patrick T., and Robert Flanders. *The Rhode Island State Constitution: A Reference Guide.* Westport, CT: Greenwood, 2007.
Connor, George E., and Christopher W. Hammond, eds. *The Constitutionalism of American States.* Columbia: University of Missouri Press, 2008.
Corwin, Edward S. "Worship of the Constitution." *Constitutional Review* 4 (1920): 3–10.
Cott, Nancy F. "Feminist Politics in the 1920s: The National Woman's Party." *Journal of American History* 71, no. 1 (June 1, 1984): 43–68.
———. *The Grounding of Modern Feminism.* New Haven, CT: Yale University Press, 1987.
Council of State Governments. *The Book of the States.* Lexington, KY: Council of State Governments, 2019.
Countryman, Edward. *The American Revolution.* New York: Macmillan, 1985.
Crosswell, Sherman, and R. Sutton. *Debates and Proceedings in the New-York State Convention, for the Revision of the Constitution.* Albany, NY: Albany Argus, 1846.
Cushman, Barry. *Rethinking the New Deal Court: The Structure of a Constitutional Revolution.* New York: Oxford University Press, 1998.
Dahl, Robert Alan. "Decision-Making in a Democracy: The Supreme Court as a National Policy-Maker." *Journal of Public Law* 6 (1957): 279–95.
———. *How Democratic Is the American Constitution?* New Haven, CT: Yale University Press, 2003.
D'Alemberte, Talbot. *The Florida State Constitution: A Reference Guide.* New York: Greenwood, 1991.
Dando, Christina Elizabeth. "'The Map Proves It': Map Use by the American Woman Suffrage Movement." *Cartographica: The International Journal for Geographic Information and Geovisualization,* November 1, 2010, 221–40.
Dealey, James Quayle. *Growth of American State Constitutions from 1776 to the End of the Year 1914.* Boston: Ginn, 1915.

Debates and Proceedings in the Congress of the United States: Fifth Congress, Second Session. Washington, DC: Gales and Seaton, 1851.

Debates and Proceedings in the Congress of the United States: Eighth Congress, First Session. Washington, DC: Gales and Seaton, 1852.

Debates and Proceedings in the Congress of the United States: Fifteenth Congress, First Session. Washington, DC: Gales and Seaton, 1854.

Debates and Proceedings in the Congress of the United States: Sixteenth Congress, First Session. Washington, DC: Gales and Seaton, 1855.

Debates and Proceedings in the Congress of the United States: Twenty-Fourth Congress, First Session. Washington, DC: Gales and Seaton, 1836.

De Figueiredo, Rui J. P., Jr., and Barry R. Weingast. "Self-Enforcing Federalism." *Journal of Law, Economics & Organization* 21, no. 1 (April 2005): 103–35.

DeForrest, Mark Edward. "An Overview and Evaluation of State Blaine Amendments: Origins, Scope, and First Amendment Concerns." *Harvard Journal of Law & Public Policy* 26 (2003): 551–626.

Dickinson, John. "Letter IV, April 19, 1788." In *Pamphlets on the Constitution of the United States: Published during Its Discussion by the People, 1787–1788,* edited by Paul Leicester Ford, 181–87. Brooklyn, NY, 1888.

———. "Letters from a Farmer in Pennsylvania to the Inhabitants of the British Colonies." In *Tracts of the American Revolution, 1763–1776,* edited by Merrill Jensen, 127–63. Indianapolis: Bobbs-Merrill, 1967.

DiClerico, Robert E. "The West Virginia Constitution: Securing the Popular Interest." In *The Constitutionalism of American States,* edited by George E. Connor and Christopher W. Hammons, 216–34. Columbia: University of Missouri Press, 2008.

Dinan, John J. *The American State Constitutional Tradition.* Lawrence: University Press of Kansas, 2006.

———. "Court-Constraining Amendments and the State Constitutional Tradition." *Rutgers Law Journal* 38 (2007): 983.

———. "Policy Provisions in State Constitutions: The Standards and Practice of State Constitution-Making in the Post–Baker v. Carr Era." *Wayne Law Review* 60 (2014): 155–201.

———. "The Political Dynamics of Mandatory State Constitutional Convention Referendums: Lessons from the 2000s Regarding Obstacles and Pathways to Their Passage." *Montana Law Review* 71 (2010): 395–432.

———. "State Constitutional Amendments and Individual Rights in the Twenty-First Century." *Albany Law Review* 76 (2013): 2105–40.

———. *State Constitutional Politics: Governing by Amendment in the American States.* Chicago: University of Chicago Press, 2018.

Dixon, Robert, Jr. *Democratic Representation: Reapportionment in Law and Politics.* London: Oxford University Press, 1968.

Dixon, Robert, Jr., and Gordon Hatheway. "The Seminal Issue in State Constitutional Revision: Reapportionment Method and Standards." *William & Mary Law Review* 10, no. 4 (May 1, 1969): 888.

Dixon, Rosalind, and Richard Holden. "Constitutional Amendment Rules: The Denominator

Problem." In *Comparative Constitutional Design,* edited by Tom Ginsburg, 195–218. Cambridge: Cambridge University Press, 2012.

Dodd, W. F. "Judicial Control over the Amendment of State Constitutions." *Columbia Law Review* 10, no. 7 (November 1, 1910): 618–38.

Dougherty, John Hampden. *Power of Federal Judiciary over Legislation: Its Origin, the Power to Set Aside Laws, Boundaries of the Power, Judicial Independence, Existing Evils and Remedies.* New York: G. P. Putnam's Sons, 1912.

Douglass, Frederick. "The Fugitive Slave Law." In *The Essential Douglass: Selected Writings and Speeches,* edited by Nicholas Buccola, 72–75. Indianapolis: Hackett, 2016.

Dove, John A., and Andrew T. Young. "US State Constitutional Entrenchment and Default in the 19th Century." *Journal of Institutional Economics* 15, no. 6 (December 2019): 963–82.

Driscoll, Dawn-Marie, and Barbara J. Rouse. "Through a Glass Darkly: A Look at State Equal Rights Amendments Symposium—Aspects of Federalism." *Suffolk University Law Review* 12, no. 5 (1978): 1282–1311.

Dubin, Michael J. *Party Affiliations in the State Legislatures: A Year by Year Summary, 1796–2006.* Jefferson, NC: McFarland, 2007.

DuBois, Ellen Carol. *Feminism and Suffrage: The Emergence of an Independent Women's Movement in America, 1848–1869.* Ithaca, NY: Cornell University Press, 1989.

Dulany, Daniel. "Considerations on the Propriety of Imposing Taxes in the British Colonies, for the Purpose of Raising a Revenue, by Act of Parliament." In *Tracts of the American Revolution, 1763–1776,* edited by Merrill Jensen, 94–107. Indianapolis: Bobbs-Merrill, 1967.

Dumbauld, Edward. "State Precedents for the Bill of Rights." *Journal of Public Law* 7 (1958): 323–44.

Egle, William Henry, and Joseph Ritner. "The Buckshot War." *Pennsylvania Magazine of History and Biography* 23, no. 2 (1899): 137–56.

Einhorn, Robin L. "Look Away Dixieland: The South and the Federal Income Tax Symposium." *Northwestern University Law Review* 108 (2014): 773–98.

Elazar, Daniel J. *American Federalism: A View from the States.* New York: Crowell, 1972.

———. "From the Editor of Publius: State Constitutional Design in the United States and Other Federal Systems." *Publius* 12, no. 1 (January 1, 1982): 1–10.

———. "The Principles and Traditions Underlying State Constitutions." *Publius* 12, no. 1 (January 1, 1982): 11–25.

Elkins, Zachary, Tom Ginsburg, and James Melton. *The Endurance of National Constitutions.* Cambridge: Cambridge University Press, 2009.

Elliot, Jonathan. *The Debates in the Several State Conventions on the Adoption of the Federal Constitution.* Philadelphia: J. B. Lippincott, 1891.

Ellis, Atiba R. "The Cost of the Vote: Poll Taxes, Voter Identification Laws, and the Price of Democracy." *Denver University Law Review* 86, no. 3 (2009): 1023–68.

Ely, James W., Jr. "The Railroad System Has Burst through State Limits: Railroads and Interstate Commerce, 1830–1920." *Arkansas Law Review* 55 (2003): 933.

Ely, Richard T. "Reforms in Taxation." In *Public Opinion,* vol. 30, 136. New York: Public Opinion, 1901.

Emerson, Ralph Waldo. "The Fugitive Slave Law." In *The Selected Writings of Ralph Waldo Emerson,* edited by Brooks Atkinson, 861–76. New York: Modern Library, 1950.

Engstrom, Erik J., and Samuel Kernell. "The Effects of Presidential Elections on Party Control of the Senate under Indirect and Direct Elections." Paper presented at the History of Congress conference, University of California, San Diego, December 5–6, 2003.

Eskridge, William N., Jr., and John Ferejohn. "Super-Statutes." *Duke Law Journal* 50 (2001): 1215–76.

Farrand, Max, ed. *The Records of the Federal Convention of 1787.* 3 vols. New Haven, CT: Yale University Press, 1911.

Fehrenbacher, Don E. *Constitutions and Constitutionalism in the Slaveholding South.* Athens: University of Georgia Press, 1989.

———. *The Dred Scott Case: Its Significance in American Law and Politics.* New York: Oxford University Press, 2001.

———. *The Slaveholding Republic: An Account of the United States Governments Relations to Slavery.* Edited by Ward M. McAfee. New York: Oxford University Press, 2001.

Fess, Simeon Davison. *Ratification of the Constitution and Amendments by the States.* Senate Document 240. Washington, DC: Government Printing Office, 1931.

Finkelman, Paul. "Evading the Ordinance: The Persistence of Bondage in Indiana and Illinois." *Journal of the Early Republic* 9, no. 1 (1989): 21–51.

———. *An Imperfect Union: Slavery, Federalism, and Comity.* Chapel Hill: University of North Carolina Press, 1981.

———. "*Prigg v. Pennsylvania* and Northern State Courts: Anti-Slavery Use of a Pro-Slavery Decision." *Civil War History* 25, no. 1 (1979): 5–35.

———. *Slavery in the Courtroom: An Annotated Bibliography of American Cases.* Washington, DC: Library of Congress, 1985.

———. *Slavery and the Founders: Race and Liberty in the Age of Jefferson.* Armonk, NY: M. E. Sharpe, 2001.

———. "Story Telling on the Supreme Court: *Prigg v. Pennsylvania* and Justice Joseph Story's Judicial Nationalism." *Supreme Court Review* 1994: 247–94.

Finkenbine, Roy E. "Belinda's Petition: Reparations for Slavery in Revolutionary Massachusetts." *William and Mary Quarterly,* 3rd ser., 64, no. 1 (January 1, 2007): 95–104.

Fino, Susan P. *The Michigan State Constitution: A Reference Guide.* Westport, CT: Greenwood, 1996.

Fisher, Louis, and Neal Devins. "How Successfully Can the States' Item Veto Be Transferred to the President?" *Georgetown Law Journal* 75 (1986): 159–97.

Fiske, John. *The Critical Period of American History, 1783–1789.* Boston: Houghton, Mifflin, 1892.

Fleming, Jon. "ERA Showdown in Maine." United Press International, November 2, 1984.

Flexner, Eleanor. *Century of Struggle: The Woman's Rights Movement in the United States.* Cambridge, MA: Harvard University Press, 1959.

Foner, Eric. *A Short History of Reconstruction.* New York: Harper and Row, 1990.

Ford, Linda G. "Alice Paul and the Triumph of Militancy." In *One Woman, One Vote: Rediscovering the Women's Suffrage Movement,* edited by Marjorie Spruill Wheeler, 277–94. Troutdale, OR: NewSage, 1995.

Ford, Paul Leicester. "The Adoption of the Pennsylvania Constitution of 1776." *Political Science Quarterly* 10, no. 3 (September 1, 1895): 426–59.
Ford, Worthington Chauncey, ed. *Journals of the Continental Congress: 1774–1789*. Vols. 1–5. Washington, DC: U.S. Government Printing Office, 1904–6.
Fowler, Robert B. "Carrie Chapman Catt, Strategist." In *One Woman, One Vote: Rediscovering the Women's Suffrage Movement,* edited by Marjorie Spruill Wheeler, 295–314. Troutdale, OR: NewSage, 1995.
Frederickson, Kari. *Dixiecrat Revolt and the End of the Solid South, 1932–1968*. Chapel Hill: University of North Carolina Press, 2001.
Freehling, William W. "The Louisiana Purchase and the Coming of the Civil War." In *The Louisiana Purchase and American Expansion, 1803–1898,* edited by Sanford Levinson and Bartholomew Sparrow, 69–82. Lanham, MD: Rowman and Littlefield, 2005.
Freeman, Jo. "The Origins of the Women's Liberation Movement." *American Journal of Sociology* 78, no. 4 (1973): 792–811.
———. "Social Revolution and the Equal Rights Amendment." *Sociological Forum* 3, no. 1 (1988): 145–52.
Friedman, Lawrence M. "The Endurance of State Constitutions: Preliminary Thoughts on the New Hampshire Constitution." *Wayne Law Review* 60, no. 1 (2013): 203–18.
———. "State Constitutions in Historical Perspective." *Annals of the American Academy of Political and Social Science* 496 (March 1, 1988): 33–42.
Fritz, Christian G. "Alternative Visions of American Constitutionalism: Popular Sovereignty and the Early American Constitutional Debate." SSRN Scholarly Paper. Rochester, NY: Social Science Research Network, 1997. http://papers.ssrn.com/abstract=1447962.
———. *American Sovereigns: The People and America's Constitutional Tradition before the Civil War.* Cambridge: Cambridge University Press, 2007.
Gallie, Peter J. *The New York State Constitution: A Reference Guide.* New York: Greenwood, 1991.
———. *Ordered Liberty: A Constitutional History of New York.* New York: Fordham University Press, 1995.
Galvin, Daniel J. "From Labor Law to Employment Law: The Changing Politics of Workers' Rights." *Studies in American Political Development* 33, no. 1 (2019): 50–86.
Gammie, Beth. "State ERAs: Problems and Possibilities Note." *University of Illinois Law Review* 1989, no. 4 (1989): 1123–60.
Gardner, James A. "Representation without Party: Lessons from State Constitutional Attempts to Control Gerrymandering." *Rutgers Law Journal* 37, no. 4 (2006): 881–970.
Garrison, William Lloyd. "Letter to the Editor of the London Patriot, August 6, 1833." In *The Letters of William Lloyd Garrison: I Will Be Heard, 1822–1835,* edited by Walter McIntosh Merrill, vol. 1, 248. Cambridge, MA: Harvard University Press, 1971.
———. "Letter to Samuel J. May, July 17, 1845." In *Letters of William Lloyd Garrison: 1841–1849,* edited by Walter McIntosh Merrill, vol. 3, 128. Cambridge, MA: Harvard University Press, 1973.
Geidel, Peter. "The National Woman's Party and the Origins of the Equal Rights Amendment, 1920–1923." *Historian* 42, no. 4 (1980): 557–82.
Gely, Rafael, and Pablo Spiller. "The Political Economy of Supreme Court Constitutional

Decisions: The Case of Roosevelt's Court Packing Plan." Working Paper Series on the Political Economy of Institutions, Bureau of Economic and Business Research, May 1989.

General Accounting Office. *Balanced Budget Requirements: State Experiences and Implications for the Federal Government.* Washington, DC: General Accounting Office, March 26, 1993.

Giddings, Joshua R. "Pacificus: The Rights and Privileges of the Several States in Regard to Slavery." In *The Life of Joshua R. Giddings,* edited by George Washington Julian, 415–62. Chicago: A. C. McClurg, 1892.

Gillman, Howard, and Mark A. Graber. *The Complete American Constitutionalism,* vol. 1, *Introduction and the Colonial Era.* Oxford: Oxford University Press, 2015.

Gladstone, Leslie W. "Equal Rights Amendments: State Provisions." Congressional Research Service, August 23, 2004.

Gokel, Ruth L. "One Small Word: Sexual Equality through the State Constitution Symposium on the Proposed Revisions to the Florida Constitution." *Florida State University Law Review* 6, no. 3 (1978): 947–82.

Goodman, Paul. "The First American Party System." In *The American Party System: Stages of Political Development,* edited by William N. Chambers and Walter Dean Burnham, 56–71. New York: Oxford University Press, 1967.

Goss, Kay Collett. *The Arkansas State Constitution: A Reference Guide.* Westport, CT: Greenwood, 1993.

Gossett, Amy. "The Louisiana Experience: Culture, Clashes, and Codification." In *The Constitutionalism of American States,* edited by George E. Connor and Christopher W. Hammons, 302–16. Columbia: University of Missouri Press, 2008.

Graber, Mark A. *Dred Scott and the Problem of Constitutional Evil.* Cambridge: Cambridge University Press, 2006.

———. "The Nonmajoritarian Difficulty: Legislative Deference to the Judiciary." *Studies in American Political Development* 7, no. 1 (1993): 35–73.

Graham, Cole Blease. *The South Carolina State Constitution: A Reference Guide.* Westport, CT: Greenwood, 2007.

Grant, Ulysses. "Seventh Annual Message to Congress." In *Congressional Record: Forty-Fourth Congress, First Session,* vol. 4, 175–81. Washington, DC: Government Printing Office, 1876.

Green, Steven Keith. *The Bible, the School, and the Constitution: The Clash That Shaped Modern Church-State Doctrine.* New York: Oxford University Press, 2012.

———. "The Blaine Amendment Reconsidered." *American Journal of Legal History* 36, no. 1 (January 1, 1992): 38–69.

Greene, Jack P. *The Constitutional Origins of the American Revolution.* Cambridge: Cambridge University Press, 2011.

———. *Negotiated Authorities: Essays in Colonial Political and Constitutional History.* Charlottesville: University of Virginia Press, 1994.

Grey, Thomas C. "The Constitution as Scripture." *Stanford Law Review* 37, no. 1 (1984): 1–25.

Grimes, Alan. *Democracy and the Amendments to the Constitution.* Lexington, MA: Lexington Books, 1978.

Grodin, Joseph R., Calvin R. Massey, and Richard B. Cunningham. *The California State Constitution: A Reference Guide.* Westport, CT: Greenwood, 1993.

Grofman, Bernard, and Lisa Handley. "The Impact of the Voting Rights Act on Black Representation in Southern State Legislatures." *Legislative Studies Quarterly* 16, no. 1 (1991): 111–28.

Guerra, Darren Patrick. *Perfecting the Constitution: The Case for the Article V Amendment Process.* Lexington, MA: Lexington Books, 2013.

Gutzman, Kevin R. C. *Virginia's American Revolution: From Dominion to Republic, 1776–1840.* Lexington, MA: Lexington Books, 2007.

Haffenden, Philip S. "The Crown and the Colonial Charters, 1675–1688: Part II." *William and Mary Quarterly,* 3rd ser., 15, no. 4 (October 1, 1958): 452–66.

Hale, Matthew. *The History of the Common Law of England and an Analysis of the Civil Part of the Law.* 6th ed. London: Butterworth, 1820.

Hall, Kermit. "Mostly Anchor and Little Sail: The Evolution of American State Constitutions." In *Toward a Usable Past: Liberty under State Constitutions,* edited by Paul Finkelman and Stephen E. Gottlieb, 388–418. Athens: University of Georgia Press, 2009.

Hall, Kermit, and James W. Ely Jr. *An Uncertain Tradition: Constitutionalism and the History of the South.* Athens: University of Georgia Press, 1989.

Hamilton, Alexander, James Madison, and John Jay. *The Federalist: With Letters of Brutus.* Edited by Terence Ball. New York: Cambridge University Press, 2003.

Hamm, Richard F. *Shaping the Eighteenth Amendment: Temperance Reform, Legal Culture, and the Polity, 1880–1920.* Chapel Hill: University of North Carolina Press, 1995.

Hammond, Bray. "The Bank Cases." In *Quarrels That Have Shaped the Constitution,* edited by John A. Garraty, 30–48. New York: Harper and Row, 1964.

———. *Banks and Politics in America: From the Revolution to the Civil War.* Princeton, NJ: Princeton University Press, 1957.

Hammond, John Craig. *Slavery, Freedom, and Expansion in the Early American West.* Charlottesville: University of Virginia Press, 2007.

Hardy, C. O. "Taxation and Tax-Exempt Securities." *Proceedings of the Annual Conference on Taxation under the Auspices of the National Tax Association* 18 (1925): 222–41.

Hardy, Leroy Clyde, Alan Heslop, and Stuart Anderson. Introduction to *Reapportionment Politics: The History of Redistricting in the 50 States,* 17–25. Beverly Hills, CA: Sage, 1981.

Hargrave, Lee. *The Louisiana State Constitution: A Reference Guide.* New York: Greenwood, 1991.

Harper, Ida Husted, ed. *History of Woman Suffrage.* Vol. 5, *1900–1920.* New York: J. J. Little and Ives, 1922.

Harrison, Cynthia. *On Account of Sex: The Politics of Women's Issues.* Berkeley: University of California Press, 1989.

Harrison, Robert. *Congress, Progressive Reform, and the New American State.* Cambridge: Cambridge University Press, 2004.

Hartley, Roger C. *How Failed Attempts to Amend the Constitution Mobilize Political Change.* Nashville, TN: Vanderbilt University Press, 2017.

Haynes, George Henry. *The Election of Senators.* New York: Holt, 1912.

———. *The Senate of the United States: Its History and Practice.* Vol. 1. New York: Russell and Russell, 1938.

Held, Allison, Sheryl Herndon, and Danielle Stager. "The Equal Rights Amendment: Why the ERA Remains Legally Viable and Properly before the States." *William & Mary Journal of Race, Gender, and Social Justice* 3, no. 1 (April 1, 1997): 113.

Heller, Francis Howard. *The Kansas State Constitution: A Reference Guide.* Westport, CT: Greenwood, 1992.

Heller, Francis Howard, and Paul D. Schumaker. "The Kansas Constitution: Conservative Politics through Republican Dominance." In *The Constitutionalism of American States,* edited by George E. Connor and Christopher W. Hammons, 490–508. Columbia: University of Missouri Press, 2008.

Henretta, James A. "The Rise of 'Democratic-Republicanism': Political Rights in New York and the Several States, 1800–1915." In *Toward a Usable Past: Liberty under State Constitutions,* edited by Paul Finkelman and Stephen E. Gottlieb, 50–90. Athens: University of Georgia Press, 2009.

Herron, Paul E. *Framing the Solid South: The State Constitutional Conventions of Secession, Reconstruction and Redemption: 1860–1902.* Lawrence: University Press of Kansas, 2017.

Hershkoff, Helen. "Positive Rights and the Evolution of State Constitutions." *Rutgers Law Journal* 33 (2002): 799.

———. "Rights and Freedoms under the State Constitution: A New Deal for Welfare Rights." *Touro Law Review* 13 (1997): 631.

———. "Welfare Devolution and State Constitutions." *Fordham Law Review* 67, no. 4 (1999): 1403–33.

Hershkoff, Helen, and Stephen Loffredo. "State Courts and Constitutional Socio-economic Rights: Exploring the Underutilization Thesis." *Penn State Law Review* 115 (2011): 923.

Hill, Melvin B. *The Georgia State Constitution: A Reference Guide.* Westport, CT: Greenwood, 1994.

Hill, Melvin B., and Laverne Williamson Hill. "Georgia: Tectonic Plates Shifting." In *The Constitutionalism of American States,* edited by George E. Connor and Christopher W. Hammons, 287–301. Columbia: University of Missouri Press, 2008.

Hirschl, Ran. "'Juristocracy'—Political, Not Juridical." *Good Society* 13, no. 3 (2004): 6–11.

———. *Towards Juristocracy: The Origins and Consequences of the New Constitutionalism.* Cambridge, MA: Harvard University Press, 2009.

Hoebeke, C. H. *The Road to Mass Democracy: Original Intent and the Seventeenth Amendment.* New Brunswick, NJ: Transaction, 1995.

Hofstadter, Richard. *The Idea of a Party System: The Rise of Legitimate Opposition in the United States, 1780–1840.* Berkeley: University of California Press, 1969.

Holst, Hermann Von. *The Constitutional and Political History of the United States.* Vol. 2. Translated by John Lalor. Chicago: Callaghan, 1888.

Horton, Lois E. "From Class to Race in Early America: Northern Post-Emancipation Racial Reconstruction." *Journal of the Early Republic* 19, no. 4 (December 1, 1999): 629–49.

Horton, Wesley W. *The Connecticut State Constitution: A Reference Guide.* Westport, CT: Greenwood, 1993.

Horwitz, Morton J. "A Historiography of the People Themselves and Popular Constitutionalism." *Chicago-Kent Law Review* 81 (2006): 813–24.
Hou, Yilin, and Daniel L. Smith. "Do State Balanced Budget Requirements Matter? Testing Two Explanatory Frameworks." *Public Choice* 145, no. 1 (October 1, 2010): 57–79.
Houghton, David. "Michigan: Four Constitutions, Four New Beginnings." In *The Constitutionalism of American States,* edited by George E. Connor and Christopher W. Hammons, 432–46. Columbia: University of Missouri Press, 2008.
Houston, Horace K. "Another Nullification Crisis: Vermont's 1850 Habeas Corpus Law." *New England Quarterly* 77, no. 2 (2004): 252–72.
Howard, Christopher. "The American Welfare State, or States?" *Political Research Quarterly* 52, no. 2 (1999): 421–42.
Huq, Aziz Z. "The Function of Article V." *University of Pennsylvania Law Review* 162 (2014): 1165–1236.
Hutson, James H. *Pennsylvania Politics, 1746–1770: The Movement for Royal Government and Its Consequences.* Princeton, NJ: Princeton University Press, 1972.
Hyman, Michael R. *The Anti-Redeemers: Hill-Country Political Dissenters in the Lower South from Redemption to Populism.* Baton Rouge: Louisiana State University Press, 1990.
Hymowitz, Carol, and Michaele Weissman. *A History of Women in America: From Founding Mothers to Feminists—How Women Shaped the Life and Culture of America.* New York: Random House, 2011.
Illinois Constitutional Convention. *Record of Proceedings of the Sixth Illinois Constitutional Convention.* Springfield, IL: John W. Lewis, 1972.
Ireland, Robert F. *The Kentucky State Constitution: A Reference Guide.* Westport, CT: Greenwood, 1999.
Jacobsohn, Gary. "Constitutional Identity." *Review of Politics* 68, no. 3 (June 2006): 361–97.
———. *Constitutional Identity.* Cambridge, MA: Harvard University Press, 2010.
———. "Rights and American Constitutional Identity." *Polity* 43, no. 4 (October 2011): 409–31.
James, Franklin J., and Allan Wallis. "Tax and Spending Limits in Colorado." *Public Budgeting & Finance* 24, no. 4 (Winter 2004): 16–33.
Jameson, John Alexander. *A Treatise on Constitutional Conventions: Their History, Powers, and Modes of Proceeding.* Chicago: Callaghan, 1887.
Jefferson, Thomas. "Composition Draft of That Part of the Declaration of Independence containing the Charges against the Crown." In *The Papers of Thomas Jefferson,* vol. 1, *1760–1776,* edited by Julian P. Boyd, 417–20. Princeton, NJ: Princeton University Press, 1950.
———. "Fragment of the Composition Draft of the Declaration of Independence." In *The Papers of Thomas Jefferson,* vol. 1, *1760–1776,* edited by Julian P. Boyd, 420–23. Princeton, NJ: Princeton University Press, 1950.
———. "Letter to Augustus B. Woodward, April 3, 1825." In *The Works of Thomas Jefferson,* edited by Paul Leicester Ford, vol. 12, 407–8. New York: G. P. Putnam's Sons, 1904.
———. "Letter to Henry Lee, May 8, 1825." In *The Works of Thomas Jefferson,* edited by Paul Leicester Ford, vol. 12, 408–9. New York: G. P. Putnam's Sons, 1905.

———. "Letter to James Madison, June 20, 1787." In *The Works of Thomas Jefferson*, edited by Paul Leicester Ford, vol. 5, 283–90. New York: G. P. Putnam's Sons, 1904.

———. "Letter to Samuel Kercheval, July 12, 1816." Jefferson Quotes & Family Letters, Papers of Thomas Jefferson: Retirement Series. http://tjrs.monticello.org/letter/1384.

———. "Notes of Proceedings in the Continental Congress, 7 June to 1 August 1776." In *The Papers of Thomas Jefferson*, vol. 1, *1760–1776*, edited by Julian P. Boyd, 309–29. Princeton, NJ: Princeton University Press, 1950.

———. "Opinion on the Constitutionality of a National Bank." In *The Works of Thomas Jefferson*, edited by Henry Augustine Washington, vol. 6, 197–204. New York: John C. Riker, 1904.

Jensen, Merrill. "Introduction: The Pamphlet Writers and Their Times." In *Tracts of the American Revolution, 1763–1776*, xiii–lxxi. Indianapolis: Bobbs-Merrill, 1967.

Johnson, David Alan. *Founding the Far West: California, Oregon, and Nevada, 1840–1890*. Berkeley: University of California Press, 1992.

Johnson, Kimberley. *Reforming Jim Crow: Southern Politics and State in the Age before Brown*. Oxford: Oxford University Press, 2010.

Jordan, Winthrop D. "Enslavement of Negroes in America to 1700." In *Colonial America: Essays in Politics and Social Development*, edited by Stanley Nider Katz, 229–70. Boston: Little, Brown, 1976.

"Journal of the Provincial Convention." In *Journals of the Provincial Congress, Provincial Convention, Committee of Safety and Council of Safety of the State of New-York 1775–1776–1777*, Vol. 1. Albany, NY: Thurlow Weed, 1842.

Kallenbach, Joseph E. "Constitutional Aspects of Federal Anti–Poll Tax Legislation." *Michigan Law Review* 45, no. 6 (1947): 717–32.

Kaminski, John P. *A Necessary Evil? Slavery and the Debate over the Constitution*. Lanham, MD: Rowman and Littlefield, 1995.

Kammen, Michael G. *A Machine That Would Go of Itself: The Constitution in American Culture*. New York: St. Martin's, 1986.

Katz, Michael B. *In the Shadow of the Poorhouse: A Social History of Welfare in America*. New York: Basic Books, 1996.

Kaye, Judith S. "State Courts at the Dawn of a New Century: Common Law Courts Reading Statutes and Constitutions." *New York University Law Review* 70, no. 1 (1995): 1–35.

Keck, Thomas M. *The Most Activist Supreme Court in History: The Road to Modern Judicial Conservatism*. Chicago: University of Chicago Press, 2004.

Kennan, Kossuth Kent. "The Wisconsin Income Tax." *Annals of the American Academy of Political and Social Science* 59, no. 1 (May 1, 1915): 65–76.

Kens, Paul. "The Source of a Myth: Police Powers of the States and Laissez Faire Constitutionalism, 1900–1937." *American Journal of Legal History* 35, no. 1 (1991): 70–98.

Kerr, K. Austin. *Organized for Prohibition: A New History of the Anti-Saloon League*. New Haven, CT: Yale University Press, 1985.

Ketcham, Earle Hoyt. "The Sixteenth Amendment." PhD diss., University of Illinois, 1924.

Kettl, Donald. *The Divided States of America: Why Federalism Doesn't Work*. Princeton, NJ: Princeton University Press, 2020.

Kettner, James H. *The Development of American Citizenship, 1608–1870.* Chapel Hill: University of North Carolina Press, 1978.
Key, V. O. *American State Politics: An Introduction.* New York: Knopf, 1956.
———. "Secular Realignment and the Party System." *Journal of Politics* 21, no. 2 (May 1959): 198–210.
———. *Southern Politics in State and Nation.* New York: Vintage Books, 1949.
———. "A Theory of Critical Elections." *Journal of Politics* 17, no. 1 (February 1955): 3–18.
Keyssar, Alexander. *The Right to Vote: The Contested History of Democracy in the United States.* New York: Basic Books, 2000.
Kilgarlin, William Wayne, and Banks Tarver. "Equal Rights Amendment: Governmental Action and Individual Liberty." *Texas Law Review* 68, no. 7 (1990): 1545–72.
Kinsman, Delos O. "The Income Tax in the Commonwealths of the United States." *Publications of the American Economic Association* 4, no. 4 (1903): 1–128.
———. "The Present Period of Income Tax Activity in the American States." *Quarterly Journal of Economics* 23 (1909): 296–306.
Kogan, Vladimir. "The Irony of Comprehensive State Constitutional Reform." *Rutgers Law Journal* 41, no. 4 (2010): 881–906.
Kousser, J. Morgan. *The Shaping of Southern Politics: Suffrage Restriction and the Establishment of the One-Party South, 1880–1910.* New Haven, CT: Yale University Press, 1974.
Kousser, Thad. *Term Limits and the Dismantling of State Legislative Professionalism.* Cambridge: Cambridge University Press, 2005.
Kraditor, Aileen S. *The Ideas of the Woman Suffrage Movement, 1890–1920.* New York: Norton, 1965.
Kramer, Larry D. *The People Themselves: Popular Constitutionalism and Judicial Review.* Oxford: Oxford University Press, 2004.
Kruman, Marc W. *Between Authority and Liberty: State Constitution-Making in Revolutionary America.* Chapel Hill: University of North Carolina Press, 1997.
Kyvig, David E. *Explicit and Authentic Acts: Amending the U.S. Constitution, 1776–1995.* Lawrence: University Press of Kansas, 1996.
———. *Unintended Consequences of Constitutional Amendment.* Athens: University of Georgia Press, 2000.
Lapinski, John S. "Direct Election and the Emergence of the Modern Senate." 2004. https://www.researchgate.net/publication/241648960_Direct_Election_and_the_Emergence_of_the_Modern_Senate.
Larson, Edward J. "The 'Blaine Amendment' in State Constitutions." In *The School-Choice Controversy: What Is Constitutional?*, edited by James W. Skillen, 35–50. Grand Rapids, MI: Baker Books, 1993.
Larson, Robert W. *New Mexico's Quest for Statehood, 1846–1912.* Albuquerque: University of New Mexico Press, 2013.
Laska, Lewis L. *The Tennessee State Constitution: A Reference Guide.* New York: Greenwood, 1990.

Lassiter, Matthew D. *The Silent Majority: Suburban Politics in the Sunbelt South.* Princeton, NJ: Princeton University Press, 2006.

Latham, Darren R. "The Historical Amendability of the American Constitution: Speculations on an Empirical Problematic." *American University Law Review* 55 (2005): 145–266.

Lawson, Steven F. *Black Ballots: Voting Rights in the South, 1944–1969.* New York: Columbia University Press, 1976.

Lear, Martha Weinman. "'You'll Probably Think I'm Stupid.'" *New York Times Magazine,* April 11, 1976.

Lee, Frances E. *Sizing Up the Senate: The Unequal Consequences of Equal Representation.* Chicago: University of Chicago Press, 1999.

Leedham, Charles. *Our Changing Constitution.* New York: Dodd, Mead, 1964.

Leff, Mark H. "Consensus for Reform: The Mothers'-Pension Movement in the Progressive Era." *Social Service Review* 47, no. 3 (September 1, 1973): 397–417.

Leichter, Howard. "Oregon's Constitution: A Political Richter Scale." In *The Constitutionalism of American States,* edited by George E. Connor and Christopher W. Hammons, 756–70. Columbia: University of Missouri Press, 2008.

Lent, George E. "The Origin and Survival of Tax-Exempt Securities." *National Tax Journal* 12, no. 4 (1959): 301–17.

Leuchtenburg, William E. *The Supreme Court Reborn: The Constitutional Revolution in the Age of Roosevelt.* New York: Oxford University Press, 1996.

Levinson, Sanford V. *Framed: America's 51 Constitutions and the Crisis of Governance.* Oxford: Oxford University Press, 2012.

———. *Our Undemocratic Constitution: Where the Constitution Goes Wrong (And How We the People Can Correct It).* Oxford: Oxford University Press, 2006.

———. "Pledging Faith in the Civil Religion; or, Would You Sign the Constitution 1787: The Constitution in Perspective." *William and Mary Law Review* 29 (1988): 113–44.

Levinson, Sanford V., and William D. Blake. "When Americans Think about Constitutional Reform: Some Data and Reflections." *Ohio State Law Journal* 77, no. 2 (2016): 211–36.

Levinson, Sanford V., and Bartholomew Sparrow. Introduction to *The Louisiana Purchase and American Expansion, 1803–1898,* edited by Sanford Levinson and Bartholomew Sparrow, 1–18. Lanham, MD: Rowman and Littlefield, 2005.

Lieberman, Robert C., and John S. Lapinski. "American Federalism, Race and the Administration of Welfare." *British Journal of Political Science* 31, no. 2 (2001): 303–29.

Lincoln, Abraham. "Message to Congress in Special Session, July 4, 1861." In *Abraham Lincoln: Selected Speeches and Writings,* 246–61. New York: Library of America, 1989.

Linde, Hans A. "First Things First: Rediscovering the States' Bills of Rights." *University of Baltimore Law Review* 9 (1980): 379.

Lindquist, Stefanie A., and Pamela C. Corley. "National Policy Preferences and Judicial Review of State Statutes at the United States Supreme Court." *Publius: The Journal of Federalism* 43, no. 2 (April 1, 2013): 151–78.

Linton, Paul Benjamin. "State Equal Rights Amendments: Making a Difference or Making a Statement Emerging Issues in State Constitutional Law." *Temple Law Review* 70, no. 3 (1997): 907–44.

Livingston, William S. *Federalism and Constitutional Change.* Oxford: Oxford University Press, 1956.

Lloyd, Gordon. "The 1849 California Constitution: An Extraordinary Achievement by Dedicated, Ordinary People." In *The Constitutionalism of American States,* edited by George E. Connor and Christopher W. Hammons, 714–27. Columbia: University of Missouri Press, 2008.

Loeb, Isidor. *Constitutions and Constitutional Conventions in Missouri.* Columbia: State Historical Society of Missouri, 1920.

Lomazoff, Eric. "Turning (into) 'The Great Regulating Wheel': The Conversion of the Bank of the United States, 1791–1811." *Studies in American Political Development* 26 (2012): 1–23.

Louisiana Constitutional Convention. *Debates in the Convention for the Revision and Amendment of the Constitution of the State of Louisiana.* New Orleans: W. R. Fish, 1864.

Lovejoy, David S. "Rights Imply Equality: The Case against Admiralty Jurisdiction in America, 1764–1776." *William and Mary Quarterly,* 3rd ser., 16, no. 4 (October 1, 1959): 460–84.

Lowell, A. Lawrence. "The Responsibilities of American Lawyers." *Harvard Law Review* 1, no. 5 (1887): 232–40.

Lowery, David, and Lee Sigelman. "Understanding the Tax Revolt: Eight Explanations." *American Political Science Review* 75, no. 4 (1981): 963–74.

Lutz, Donald S. "Political Participation in Eighteenth-Century America." In *Toward a Usable Past: Liberty under State Constitutions,* edited by Paul Finkelman and Stephen E. Gottlieb, 19–49. Athens: University of Georgia Press, 2009.

———. *Popular Consent and Popular Control: Whig Political Theory in the Early State Constitutions.* Baton Rouge: Louisiana State University Press, 1980.

———. "The Purposes of American State Constitutions." *Publius* 12, no. 1 (January 1, 1982): 27–44.

———. "The State Constitutional Pedigree of the U.S. Bill of Rights." *Publius* 22, no. 2 (March 20, 1992): 19–45.

———. "Toward a Theory of Constitutional Amendment." *American Political Science Review* 88, no. 2 (June 1, 1994): 355–70.

———. "The United States Constitution as an Incomplete Text." *Annals of the American Academy of Political and Social Science* 496 (March 1, 1988): 23–32.

Lynch, Michael J. "The Other Amendments: Constitutional Amendments That Failed." *Law Library Journal* 93 (2001): 303–10.

Lynd, Staughton. "The Compromise of 1787." *Political Science Quarterly* 81, no. 2 (1966): 225–50.

Lyons, Thomas E. "The Wisconsin Income Tax." In *Annals of the American Academy of Political and Social Science,* vol. 58, 77–86. Philadelphia: A. L. Hummel, 1915.

MacLean, Nancy. *Democracy in Chains: The Deep History of the Radical Right's Stealth Plan for America.* New York: Penguin, 2017.

Magliocca, Gerard N. "Court-Packing and the Child Labor Amendment." *Constitutional Commentary* 27 (2011): 455.

Maier, Pauline. *American Scripture: Making the Declaration of Independence.* New York: Knopf Doubleday, 1997.

———. "Popular Uprisings and Civil Authority in Eighteenth-Century America." In *Colonial America: Essays in Politics and Social Development,* edited by Stanley Nider Katz, 423–51. Boston: Little, Brown, 1976.

Maltz, Earl M. "Slavery, Federalism, and the Structure of the Constitution." *American Journal of Legal History* 36, no. 4 (1992): 466–98.

Mansbridge, Jane. *Why We Lost the ERA.* Chicago: University of Chicago Press, 1986.

Margolick, David. "State Judges Are Shaping Law That Goes Beyond the Supreme Court." *New York Times,* May 19, 1982.

Marquez, Awilda. "Comparable Worth and the Maryland ERA." *Maryland Law Review* 47, no. 4 (January 1, 1988): 1129–87.

Marshfield, Jonathan L. "Amendment Creep." *Michigan Law Review* 115 (2017): 215–76.

———. "Models of Substantial Constitutionalism." *Penn State Law Review* 115 (2011): 1151–98.

Martin, Isaac William. *The Permanent Tax Revolt: How the Property Tax Transformed American Politics.* Stanford, CA: Stanford University Press, 2008.

———. *Rich People's Movements: Grassroots Campaigns to Untax the One Percent.* New York: Oxford University Press, 2013.

Martin, Philip L. "The Application Clause of Article Five." *Political Science Quarterly* 85, no. 4 (1970): 616–28.

Mason, Matthew. *Slavery and Politics in the Early American Republic.* Chapel Hill: University of North Carolina Press, 2006.

Massachusetts Constitutional Convention. *Debates in the Massachusetts Constitutional Convention, 1917–1918.* Vol. 2. Boston: Wright and Potter, 1918.

Mast, Tory. "The History of Single-Member Districts for Congress: Seeking Fair Representation Before Full Representation." Voting and Democracy Report. Fair Vote Program for Representative Government, 1995.

Matthews, Burnita Shelton. "A Federal Amendment Avoids Referendum Campaigns." *Equal Rights,* December 29, 2019.

Matthews, Donald R., and James W. Prothro. "Political Factors and Negro Voter Registration in the South." *American Political Science Review* 57, no. 2 (1963): 355–67.

May, Janice C. "Constitutional Amendment and Revision Revisited." *Publius* 17, no. 1 (January 1, 1987): 153–79.

Mayhew, David R. *Electoral Realignments: A Critique of an American Genre.* New Haven, CT: Yale University Press, 2002.

McCloskey, Robert G., and Sanford Levinson. *The American Supreme Court.* Chicago: University of Chicago Press, 2004.

McColley, Robert. *Slavery and Jeffersonian Virginia.* Urbana: University of Illinois Press, 1964.

McConnaughy, C. M. *The Woman Suffrage Movement in America: A Reassessment.* Cambridge: Cambridge University Press, 2013.

McConville, Brendan. *The King's Three Faces: The Rise and Fall of Royal America, 1688–1776.* Chapel Hill: University of North Carolina Press, 2007.

McCormick, Richard P. "New Perspectives on Jacksonian Politics." *American Historical Review* 65, no. 2 (January 1, 1960): 288–301.

———. "Political Development and the Second Party System." In *The American Party System: Stages of Political Development*, edited by William N. Chambers and Walter Dean Burnham, 90–116. New York: Oxford University Press, 1967.

McGirr, Lisa. *Suburban Warriors: The Origins of the New American Right.* Princeton, NJ: Princeton University Press, 2002.

———. *The War on Alcohol: Prohibition and the Rise of the American State.* New York: Norton, 2015.

McKinley, Albert Edward. *The Suffrage Franchise in the Thirteen English Colonies in America.* Philadelphia: University of Pennsylvania Press, 1905.

McLauchlan, William P. *The Indiana State Constitution: A Reference Guide.* Westport, CT: Greenwood, 1996.

McMahon, Kevin J. *Reconsidering Roosevelt on Race: How the Presidency Paved the Road to Brown.* Chicago: University of Chicago Press, 2003.

McManus, Edgar J. *A History of Negro Slavery in New York.* Syracuse, NY: Syracuse University Press, 1970.

McPherson, Edward, ed. "Majority Report of the Joint Committee on Reconstruction." In *A Political Manual for 1866: Including a Classified Summary of the Important Executive, Legislative, and Politico-Military Facts of the Period.* Washington, DC: Philp and Solomons, 1866.

Mehrotra, Ajay K. *Making the Modern American Fiscal State: Law, Politics, and the Rise of Progressive Taxation, 1877–1929.* Cambridge: Cambridge University Press, 2013.

Menschel, David. "Abolition without Deliverance: The Law of Connecticut Slavery, 1784–1848." *Yale Law Journal* 111, no. 1 (October 1, 2001): 183–222.

Merriam, Charles Edward. *Primary Elections: A Study of the History and Tendencies of Primary Election Legislation.* Chicago: University of Chicago Press, 1908.

Mettler, Suzanne. "Dividing Social Citizenship by Gender: The Implementation of Unemployment Insurance and Aid to Dependent Children, 1935–1950." *Studies in American Political Development* 12, no. 2 (October 1998): 303–42.

Michigan Constitutional Convention. *Report of the Proceedings and Debates in the Convention to Revise the Constitution of the State of Michigan.* Lansing, MI: R. W. Ingals, 1850.

Mikesell, John L. "The Path of the Tax Revolt: Statewide Expenditure and Tax Control Referenda since Proposition 13." *State & Local Government Review* 18, no. 1 (1986): 5–12.

Milkis, Sidney M., and Daniel J. Tichenor. *Rivalry and Reform: Presidents, Social Movements, and the Transformation of American Politics.* Chicago: University of Chicago Press, 2018.

Miller, Joshua. *The Rise and Fall of Democracy in Early America, 1630–1789: The Legacy for Contemporary Politics.* University Park: Pennsylvania State University Press, 1999.

Mink, Gwendolyn. "Welfare Reform in Historical Perspective." *Social Justice* 21, no. 1 (1994): 114–31.

Moe, Ronald C. *Prospects for the Item Veto at the Federal Level: Lessons from the States.* Washington, DC: National Academy of Public Administration, 1988.

Moore, George Henry. *Notes on the History of Slavery in Massachusetts.* New York: D. Appleton, 1866.

Moore, Libba Gage. "Mothers' Pensions: The Origins of the Relationship between Women and the Welfare State." Ph.D. diss., University of Massachusetts, Amherst, 1986.

Morgan, David. *Suffragists and Democrats: The Politics of Woman Suffrage in America.* East Lansing: Michigan State University Press, 1972.

Mowry, Arthur May. *The Dorr War; or, The Constitutional Struggle in Rhode Island.* Providence, RI: Preston and Rounds, 1901.

Mullins, Daniel R., and Bruce A. Wallin. "Tax and Expenditure Limitations: Introduction and Overview." *Public Budgeting & Finance* 24, no. 4 (2004): 2–15.

Munns, Rogers. "Iowans to Vote on State ERA." Associated Press, October 13, 1980.

Musmanno, Michael Angelo. *Proposed Amendments to the Constitution.* Westport, CT: Greenwood, 1978.

Nash, Gary B. *The Unknown American Revolution: The Unruly Birth of Democracy and the Struggle to Create America.* New York: Penguin, 2006.

"National Amendment Is the Permanent Way of Establishing Equal Rights, A." *Equal Rights,* December 15, 1923.

National Association for the Advancement of Colored People. *Annual Reports of the National Association for the Advancement of Colored People for 1917 and 1918.* New York: National Association for the Advancement of Colored People, January 1919.

National Conference of State Legislatures. *State Balanced Budget Provisions.* Washington, DC: National Conference of State Legislatures, October 2010.

———. *The Term-Limited States.* Washington, DC: National Conference of State Legislatures, March 13, 2015.

National Tax Association. *Addresses and Proceedings of the National Tax Association National Conference, 1907.* New York: Macmillan, 1908.

Neale, Thomas H. "The Eighteen-Year-Old Vote: The Twenty-Sixth Amendment and Subsequent Voting Rates of Newly Enfranchised Age Groups." Report. Congressional Research Service, May 20, 1983.

"Near-Dry States, The." *American Issue,* March 6, 1910.

Nelson, Eric. *The Royalist Revolution: Monarchy and the American Founding.* Cambridge, MA: Harvard University Press, 2014.

Neuborne, Burt. "State Constitutions and the Evolution of Positive Rights." *Rutgers Law Journal* 20, no. 4 (1989): 881–902.

Nevada Constitutional Convention. *Debates and Proceedings in the Constitutional Convention of the State of Nevada.* San Francisco: Frank Eastman, 1866.

Nevins, Allan. *The American States: During and after the Revolution, 1775–1789.* New York: Macmillan, 1927.

Newcomer, Mabel. "Separation of State and Local Revenues in the United States." dissertation, Columbia University, 1917.

New York Constitutional Convention. *Revised Record of the Constitutional Convention of the State of New York, 1938.* Albany, NY: J. B. Lyon, 1938.

Nicholls, Michael L. "'The Squint of Freedom': African-American Freedom Suits in Postrevolutionary Virginia." *Slavery & Abolition* 20 (August 1, 1999): 47–62.

Niles, Franklyn C. "Change and Continuity in Arkansas Politics after the 1874 Arkansas State Constitutional Convention." In *The Constitutionalism of American States,* edited by

George E. Connor and Christopher W. Hammons, 251–68. Columbia: University of Missouri Press, 2008.

North Dakota Constitutional Convention. *Official Report of the Proceedings and Debates of the First Constitutional Convention of North Dakota.* Bismarck, ND: Tribune, 1889.

Novkov, Julie. "Bringing the States Back In: Understanding Legal Subordination and Identity through Political Development." *Polity* 40, no. 1 (2008): 24–48.

Oberst, Paul. "Genesis of the Three States-Rights Amendments of 1963." *Notre Dame Law Review* 39, no. 6 (1964): 16.

O'Brien, William. "Did the Jennison Case Outlaw Slavery in Massachusetts?" *William and Mary Quarterly,* 3rd ser., 17, no. 2 (April 1, 1960): 219–41.

Odegard, Peter H. *Pressure Politics: The Story of the Anti-Saloon League.* New York: Octagon Books, 1966.

Ogden, Frederic D. *The Poll Tax in the South.* Tuscaloosa: University of Alabama Press, 1958.

Okrent, Daniel. *Last Call: The Rise and Fall of Prohibition.* New York: Simon and Schuster, 2010.

Oldfield, John R. *Popular Politics and British Anti-Slavery: The Mobilisation of Public Opinion against the Slave Trade, 1787–1807.* Manchester, UK: Manchester University Press, 1995.

Onuf, Peter S. *The Origins of the Federal Republic: Jurisdictional Controversies in the United States, 1775–1787.* Philadelphia: University of Pennsylvania Press, 1983.

———. "State Politics and Republican Virtue: Religion, Education, and Morality in Early American Federalism." In *Toward a Usable Past: Liberty under State Constitutions,* edited by Paul Finkelman and Stephen E. Gottlieb, 91–116. Athens: University of Georgia Press, 2009.

Orfield, Lester B. *The Amending of the Federal Constitution.* Ann Arbor: University of Michigan Press, 1942.

O'Sullivan, Arthur, Terri A. Sexton, and Steven M. Sheffrin. *Property Taxes and Tax Revolts: The Legacy of Proposition 13.* Cambridge: Cambridge University Press, 1995.

Ott, David Jackson, and Allan H. Meltzer. "Issues in the Tax Treatment of State and Local Securities." Washington, DC: Brookings Institution, 1963.

Paine, Thomas. *Common Sense.* In *"Common Sense," "The Rights of Man" and Other Essential Writings of Thomas Paine,* 23–74. New York: Meridian, 1969.

———. *The Rights of Man.* In *"Common Sense," "The Rights of Man" and Other Essential Writings of Thomas Paine,* 121–287. New York: Meridian, 1969.

Parker, Florence. "Experience under State Old-Age Pension Laws in 1932." *Monthly Labor Review* 37, no. 2 (1933): 251–61.

Parkinson, George. "Antebellum State Constitution-Making: Retention, Circumvention, Revision." PhD diss., University of Wisconsin–Madison, 1972.

Patterson, James T. *The New Deal and States: Federalism in Transition.* Princeton, NJ: Princeton University Press, 1969.

Paul, Randolph E. *Taxation in the United States.* Boston: Little, Brown, 1954.

Pease, Jane H., and William H. Pease. "Confrontation and Abolition in the 1850s." *Journal of American History* 58, no. 4 (March 1, 1972): 923–37.

Penniman, Clara. *State Income Taxation.* Baltimore: Johns Hopkins University Press, 1980.
Pennsylvania Constitutional Convention. *Debates of the Convention to Amend the Constitution of Pennsylvania, 1872–3.* Harrisburg, PA: Benjamin Singerly, 1873.
Perman, Michael. *Struggle for Mastery: Disfranchisement in the South, 1888–1908.* Chapel Hill: University of North Carolina Press, 2001.
Perry, H. W. *Deciding to Decide: Agenda Setting in the United States Supreme Court.* Cambridge, MA: Harvard University Press, 2009.
Peters, Ronald M., and Michael K. Avery. "Oklahoma's Statutory Constitution." In *The Constitutionalism of American States,* edited by George E. Connor and Christopher W. Hammons, 565–70. Columbia: University of Missouri Press, 2008.
Phillips, Wendell. "Speech of Wendell Phillips, May 9, 1865." *Liberator,* May 19, 1865.
Pierson, Paul. *Politics in Time: History, Institutions, and Social Analysis.* Princeton, NJ: Princeton University Press, 2004.
Plehn, Carl C. "The Plan for Tax Reform in California." Paper presented at the annual convention of the Bankers' Association of California, Oakland, CA, May 18, 1905.
Pollack, Sheldon D. *War, Revenue, and State Building: Financing the Development of the American State.* Ithaca, NY: Cornell University Press, 2009.
Pope, James Gray. "An Approach to State Constitutional Interpretation." *Rutgers Law Journal* 24 (1993): 985–1008.
President's Commission on the Status of Women. *American Women: Report of the President's Commission on the Status of Women.* Washington, DC: President's Commission on the Status of Women, October 11, 1963.
Proebsting, Patricia L. "Washington's Equal Rights Amendment: It Says What It Means and It Means What It Says Symposium: The Washington Constitution: Comment." *University of Puget Sound Law Review* 8, no. 2 (1985): 461–84.
Proposed Constitutional Amendments to Balance the Federal Budget, Pub. L. No. 103-92 (1994).
"Provincial Conference." In *The Proceedings Relative to Calling the Conventions of 1776 and 1790: The Minutes of the Convention That Formed the Present Constitution of Pennsylvania, Together with the Charter to William Penn, the Constitutions of 1776 and 1790, and a View of the Proceedings of the Convention of 1776, and the Council of Censors.* Harrisburg, PA: John S. Wiestling, 1825.
Rabushka, Alvin, and Pauline Ryan. *The Tax Revolt.* Stanford, CA: Hoover Institution Press, 1982.
Raghunath, Raja. "A Promise the Nation Cannot Keep: What Prevents the Application of the Thirteenth Amendment in Prison." *William & Mary Bill of Rights Journal* 18 (2010): 395–444.
Ratner, Sidney. *American Taxation: Its History as a Social Force in Democracy.* New York: Norton, 1942.
———. *Taxation and Democracy in America.* New York: John Wiley and Sons, 1967.
Reagan, Ronald. "State of the Union Address, February 4, 1986." Miller Center. Accessed December 20, 2019. http://millercenter.org/the-presidency/presidential-speeches/february-4-1986-state-union-address.
Richardson, Norman Egbert. *The Liquor Problem.* New York: Association Press, 1915.

Riker, William H. "The Heresthetics of Constitution-Making: The Presidency in 1787, with Comments on Determinism and Rational Choice." *American Political Science Review* 78, no. 1 (March 1, 1984): 1–16.

Robertson, David Brian. *The Constitution and America's Destiny.* Cambridge: Cambridge University Press, 2005.

———. *The Original Compromise: What the Constitution's Framers Were Really Thinking.* New York: Oxford University Press, 2013.

Robinson, Donald L. *Slavery in the Structure of American Politics, 1765–1820.* New York: Harcourt Brace Jovanovich, 1971.

Rogin, Michael. "The Two Declarations of American Independence." *Representations* 55 (July 1, 1996): 13–30.

Rohlfing, Charles C. "Amendment and Revision of State Constitutions." *Annals of the American Academy of Political and Social Science* 181 (1935): 180–87.

Romero, Francine Sanders. "The Impact of Direct Election on Reform Votes in the U.S. Senate." *Social Science Quarterly* 88, no. 3 (2007): 816–29.

Roosevelt, Franklin Delano. "Fireside Chat, March 9, 1937." In *FDR's Fireside Chats,* edited by Russell D. Buhite and David W. Levy, 83–95. Norman: University of Oklahoma Press, 1992.

———. "Message to Congress, June 8, 1934." In *Congressional Series of United States Public Documents,* 1–4. Washington, DC: Government Printing Office, 1934.

———. "Message to Congress, February 5, 1937." In *The Public Papers and Addresses of Franklin D. Roosevelt,* edited by Samuel Rosenman, vol. 4, 51–65. New York: Macmillan, 1941.

———. "209th Press Conference, May 31, 1935." In *The Public Papers and Addresses of Franklin D. Roosevelt,* edited by Samuel Rosenman, 200–222. New York: Random House, 1938.

Rosenberg, Gerald N. *The Hollow Hope: Can Courts Bring about Social Change?* 2nd ed. Chicago: University of Chicago Press, 2008.

Rosenberg, Norman L. "Personal Liberty Laws and Sectional Crisis: 1850–1861." *Civil War History* 17, no. 1 (1971): 25–44.

Ross, William G. "Attacks on the Warren Court by State Officials: A Case Study of Why Court-Curbing Movements Fail." *Buffalo Law Review* 50, no. 2 (2002): 483–612.

Rossum, Ralph A. *Federalism, the Supreme Court, and the Seventeenth Amendment: The Irony of Constitutional Democracy.* Lexington, MA: Lexington Books, 2001.

Roznai, Yaniv. *Unconstitutional Constitutional Amendments: The Limits of Amendment Powers.* Oxford: Oxford University Press, 2017.

Salokar, Rebecca Mae. "Florida: Defining and Redefining Citizenship and Community." In *The Constitutionalism of American States,* edited by George E. Connor and Christopher W. Hammons, 269–86. Columbia: University of Missouri Press, 2008.

Savage, James. *Balanced Budgets and American Politics.* Ithaca, NY: Cornell University Press, 1988.

Scalia, Laura J. *America's Jeffersonian Experiment: Remaking State Constitutions, 1820–1850.* DeKalb: Northern Illinois University Press, 1999.

Schamel, Charles E., Mary Rephlo, Rodney Ross, David Kepley, Robert W. Coren, and

James Gregory Bradsher, eds. *Guide to the Records of the United States House of Representatives at the National Archives, 1789–1989*. Washington, DC: National Archives and Records Administration, 1989.

Schapiro, Robert A. "Identity and Interpretation in State Constitutional Law." *Virginia Law Review* 84, no. 3 (April 1, 1998): 389–457.

Schattschneider, Elmer Eric. *The Semi-Sovereign People: A Realist's View of Democracy in America*. New York: Holt, Rinehart, and Winston, 1975.

Scheiber, Harry N. "Race, Radicalism, and Reform: Historical Perspective on the 1879 California Constitution." *Hastings Constitutional Law Quarterly* 17 (1990): 35.

Schickler, Eric. *Racial Realignment: The Transformation of American Liberalism, 1932–1965*. Princeton, NJ: Princeton University Press, 2016.

Schiller, Wendy J., and Charles Stewart. *Electing the Senate: Indirect Democracy before the Seventeenth Amendment*. Princeton, NJ: Princeton University Press, 2014.

Schlafly, Phyllis. "The Effect of ERAs in State Constitutions." *Phyllis Schlafly Report*, August 1979.

Schlesinger, Arthur M. *The Age of Roosevelt*. Vol. 2, *The Coming of the New Deal*. Boston: Houghton Mifflin, 1958.

———. *The Age of Roosevelt*. Vol. 3, *The Politics of Upheaval*. Boston: Houghton Mifflin, 1960.

Schuman, David. "The Creation of the Oregon Constitution." *Oregon Law Review* 74 (1995): 611–42.

Sears, David O., and Jack Citrin. *Tax Revolt: Something for Nothing in California*. Cambridge, MA: Harvard University Press, 1985.

Seligman, Edwin R. A. *The Income Tax: A Study of the History, Theory, and Practice of Income Taxation at Home and Abroad*. New York: Macmillan, 1914.

———. "The Income Tax in the American Colonies and States." *Political Science Quarterly* 10, no. 2 (1895): 221–47.

———. "Progressive Taxation in Theory and Practice, 2nd ed." *Publications of the American Economic Association,* 3rd ser., 9 (1908): 562–896.

Selsam, J. Paul. *The Pennsylvania Constitution of 1776: A Study in Revolutionary Democracy*. Philadelphia: University of Pennsylvania Press, 1936.

Selsam, J. Paul, and Joseph G. Rayback. "French Comment on the Pennsylvania Constitution of 1776." *Pennsylvania Magazine of History and Biography* 76, no. 3 (July 1, 1952): 311–25.

"Senator Farwell on Woman Suffrage." *Chicago Daily Tribune,* May 8, 1887.

Seward, William Henry. *In the Supreme Court of the United States: John Van Zandt, Ad Sectum Wharton Jones: Argument for the Defendant*. Albany, NY: Weed and Parsons, 1847.

Shaeffer, John N. "Public Consideration of the 1776 Pennsylvania Constitution." *Pennsylvania Magazine of History and Biography* 98, no. 4 (October 1, 1974): 415–37.

Sherwin, Elizabeth A. "Sex Discrimination and State Constitutions: State Pathways through Federal Roadblocks Note." *New York University Review of Law & Social Change* 13, no. 1 (1985): 115–48.

Silbey, Joel H. *The American Political Nation, 1838–1893*. Stanford, CA: Stanford University Press, 1991.

Sitkoff, Harvard. *A New Deal for Blacks: The Emergence of Civil Rights as a National Issue.* New York: Oxford University Press, 1978.

Skocpol, Theda. *Protecting Soldiers and Mothers.* Cambridge, MA: Harvard University Press, 1995.

Skowronek, Stephen. *The Politics Presidents Make: Leadership from John Adams to George Bush.* Cambridge, MA: Harvard University Press, 1993.

Smith, Chuck. *The New Mexico State Constitution: A Reference Guide.* Westport, CT: Greenwood, 1996.

Smith, Daniel A. "Populist Entrepreneur: Douglass Bruce and the Tax and Government Limitation Movement in Colorado, 1986–1992." *Great Plains Research* 6, no. 2 (1996): 269–94.

Smith, Goldwin. "Has the American Senate Decayed?" *Saturday Review of Politics, Literature, Science and Art,* May 9, 1896.

Smith, Rogers M. *Civic Ideals: Conflicting Visions of Citizenship in U.S. History.* New Haven, CT: Yale University Press, 1997.

Sosin, Jack M. *English America and the Revolution of Sixteen Eighty-Eight: Royal Administration and the Structure of Provincial Government.* Lincoln: University of Nebraska Press, 1985.

Soule, Sarah A., and Susan Olzak. "When Do Movements Matter? The Politics of Contingency and the Equal Rights Amendment." *American Sociological Review* 69, no. 4 (2004): 473–97.

Special Tax Commission of the State of New York. *Report of the Special Tax Commission of the State of New York.* Albany, NY: J. B. Lyon, January 15, 1907.

Stanley, Harold Watkins. *Voter Mobilization and the Politics of Race: The South and Universal Suffrage, 1952–1984.* New York: Praeger, 1987.

Stanley, Robert. *Dimensions of Law in the Service of Order: Origins of the Federal Income Tax, 1861–1913.* New York: Oxford University Press, 1993.

Stanton, Elizabeth Cady, Susan B. Anthony, and Matilda Joslyn Gage, eds. *History of Woman Suffrage.* Vol. 2, *1861–1876.* New York: Fowler and Wells, 1882.

———, eds. *History of Woman Suffrage.* Vol. 3, *1876–1885.* Rochester, NY: Charles Mann, 1886.

Stanwood, Edward. *A History of Presidential Elections.* Boston: J. R. Osgood, 1884.

Stark, Jack. *The Iowa State Constitution: A Reference Guide.* Westport, CT: Greenwood, 1998.

———. *The Wisconsin State Constitution: A Reference Guide.* Westport, CT: Greenwood, 1997.

State of New York. *Documents of the Senate of the State of New York: One Hundred and Twenty-Seventh Session.* Vol. 20. Albany, NY: Oliver A. Quayle, 1904.

State of Virginia. *Journal of the House of Delegates of Virginia.* Richmond, VA: Samuel Sheperd, 1844.

Steedman, Marek D. "Demagogues and the Demon Drink: Newspapers and the Revival of Prohibition in Georgia." In *Statebuilding from the Margins: Between Reconstruction and the New Deal,* edited by Carol Nackenoff and Julie Novkov, 65–94. Philadelphia: University of Pennsylvania Press, 2014.

Steiner, Gilbert. *Constitutional Inequality: The Political Fortunes of the Equal Rights Amendment.* Washington, DC: Brookings Institution Press, 1985.

Steinglass, Steven H., and Gino J. Scarselli. *The Ohio State Constitution: A Reference Guide.* Westport, CT: Greenwood, 2004.

Stephanopoulos, Nicholas, and Mila Versteeg. "The Contours of Constitutional Approval." SSRN Scholarly Paper. Rochester, NY: Social Science Research Network, August 18, 2015. http://papers.ssrn.com/abstract=2646773.

Sterett, Susan Marie. *Public Pensions: Gender and Civic Service in the States, 1850–1937.* Ithaca, NY: Cornell University Press, 2003.

Stohler, Stephan. "Slavery and Just Compensation in American Constitutionalism." *Law & Social Inquiry* 44, no. 1 (2019): 102–35. https://doi.org/10.1111/lsi.12351.

Strauss, David. "The Irrelevance of Constitutional Amendments." *Harvard Law Review* 114 (2001): 1457.

Strong, Donald S. "American Government and Politics: The Poll Tax: The Case of Texas." *American Political Science Review* 38, no. 4 (1944): 693–709.

Sturm, Albert L. "The Development of American State Constitutions." *Publius* 12, no. 1 (January 1, 1982): 57–98.

———. *Methods of State Constitutional Reform.* Ann Arbor: University of Michigan Press, 1954.

———. *Thirty Years of State Constitution-Making, 1938–1968: With an Epilogue: Developments during 1969.* New York: National Municipal League, 1970.

Sundquist, James L. *Dynamics of the Party System: Alignment and Realignment of Political Parties in the United States.* Washington, DC: Brookings Institution Press, 1983.

Sutton, Jeffrey S. *51 Imperfect Solutions: States and the Making of American Constitutional Law.* New York: Oxford University Press, 2018.

Tarr, G. Alan. "Explaining State Constitutional Change." *Wayne Law Review* 60, no. 1 (2015): 9–30.

———. "Explaining Sub-national Constitutional Space." *Penn State Law Review* 115 (2011): 1133–49.

———. *Understanding State Constitutions.* Princeton, NJ: Princeton University Press, 1998.

Tarr, G. Alan, and Mary Cornelia Porter. "Gender Equality and Judicial Federalism: The Role of State Appellate Courts." *Hastings Constitutional Law Quarterly* 9, no. 4 (1982): 919–74.

Teele, Dawn Langan. *Forging the Franchise: The Political Origins of the Women's Vote.* Princeton, NJ: Princeton University Press, 2018.

TenBroek, Jacobus. *Equal under Law: The Antislavery Origins of the Fourteenth Amendment.* New York: Collier Books, 1965.

Tennessee Constitutional Convention. *Journal of the Proceedings of the Convention of Delegates Elected by the People of Tennessee, to Amend, Revise, or Form and Make a New Constitution, for the State, 1870.* Nashville, TN: Jones Purvis, 1870.

Textile Worker: Official Journal of the United Textile Workers of America 11 (1923).

Thayer, Theodore. *Pennsylvania Politics and the Growth of Democracy: 1740–1776.* Harrisburg: Pennsylvania Historical and Museum Commission, 1953.

Thomas, James. "Rights of Conscience and State School Systems in Nineteenth-Century America." In *Toward a Usable Past: Liberty Under State Constitutions,* edited by Paul Finkelman and Stephen E. Gottlieb, 117–47. Athens: University of Georgia Press, 2009.

Thorpe, Francis Newton. *The Federal and State Constitutions: Colonial Charters, and Other Organic Laws of the States, Territories, and Colonies, Now or Heretofore Forming the United States of America.* 7 vols. Washington, DC: Government Printing Office, 1909.

———. "Recent Constitution-Making in the United States." *Annals of the American Academy of Political and Social Science* 2, no. 2 (November 1, 1891): 1–57.

Thurmond, Strom. "President Truman's So-Called Civil Rights Program." Columbia, SC, March 17, 1948.

Tinkle, Marshall J. *The Maine State Constitution: A Reference Guide.* Westport, CT: Greenwood, 1992.

Tocqueville, Alexis de. *Democracy in America.* Edited by Jacob Peter Mayer. Translated by George Lawrence. New York: HarperCollins, 2006.

Toombs, Robert Augustus. "Letter to E. B. Pullin and Others, December 13, 1860." In *The Correspondence of Robert Toombs, Alexander H. Stephens, and Howell Cobb,* edited by Ulrich B. Phillips, 519. Washington, DC: Government Printing Office, 1913.

Treadwell, Lujuana Wolfe, and Nancy Wallace Page. "Equal Rights Provisions: The Experience under State Constitutions Comments." *California Law Review* 65, no. 5 (1977): 1086–1112.

Treanor, William Michael. "Case of the Prisoners and the Origins of Judicial Review." *University of Pennsylvania Law Review* 143 (1994): 491–570.

———. "Judicial Review before 'Marbury.'" *Stanford Law Review* 58, no. 2 (November 1, 2005): 455–562.

Tsesis, Alexander. *The Thirteenth Amendment and American Freedom: A Legal History.* New York: NYU Press, 2004.

Tushnet, Mark. *Taking the Constitution Away from the Courts.* Princeton, NJ: Princeton University Press, 2000.

Tyler, John. "Letter to Samuel King, May 7, 1842." In *A Compilation of the Messages and Papers of the Presidents: Prepared under the Direction of the Joint Committee on Printing, of the House and Senate, Pursuant to an Act of the Fifty-Second Congress of the United States,* vol. 5, 2146–47. New York: Bureau of National Literature, 1897.

Unger, Harlow Giles. *Lion of Liberty: Patrick Henry and the Call to a New Nation.* Cambridge, MA: Da Capo, 2011.

Urofsky, Melvin I. "State Courts and Protective Legislation during the Progressive Era: A Reevaluation." *Journal of American History* 72, no. 1 (1985): 63–91.

U.S. House. *Civil Rights Hearings before House Judiciary Subcommittee No. 5, House of Representatives Committee on the Judiciary.* 1957.

———. *Equal Rights Amendment: Hearings before the Subcommittee on Civil and Constitutional Rights of the House Judiciary Committee.* 1983.

———. *Equal Rights Amendment to the Constitution: Hearings before the House Judiciary Committee, Pub. L. No. 13.* 1932.

———. *Equal Rights Amendments Extension: Hearings before the Subcommittee on Civil and Constitutional Rights of the House Judiciary Committee.* 1977.

———. *Item Veto: State Experience and Its Application to the Federal Situation.* Committee on Rules, Ninety-Ninth Congress, Second Session. Washington, DC: U.S. Government Printing Office, 1986.

———. *Report of the House Judiciary Committee.* Sixty-Fourth Congress, Second Session, January 10, 1917.

———. *Report to the House Judiciary Committee.* Ninety-Second Congress, First Session, July 14, 1971.

U.S. Senate. *Abstract of Laws Relating to the Election of United States Senators.* Senate Doc. No. 393, Fifty-Ninth Congress, Second Session, 1907.

———. *Equal Rights Amendment: Hearing before a Subcommittee of the Senate Judiciary Committee.* 1945.

———. *Equal Rights Amendment Extension: Hearings before the Subcommittee on the Constitution of the Senate Judiciary Committee.* 1978.

———. *The Impact of the Equal Rights Amendment: Hearings before the Subcommittee on the Constitution of the Senate Judiciary Committee.* 1983.

———. *Report of the Senate Education and Labor Committee.* Fiftieth Congress, First Session, March 2, 1889.

———. *Report of the Senate Select Committee on Woman Suffrage.* Forty-Ninth Congress, First Session, February 2, 1886.

———. *Report to the Senate Judiciary Committee.* Ninety-Second Congress, First Session, March 14, 1971.

Valelly, Richard M. *The Two Reconstructions: The Struggle for Black Enfranchisement.* Chicago: University of Chicago Press, 2004.

Van Buren, Martin. "Fourth Annual Message to Congress." In *The Addresses and Messages of the Presidents of the United States, Inaugural, Annual, and Special, from 1789 to 1846,* edited by Edwin Williams, 1140–57. New York: Edward Walker, 1847.

Versteeg, Mila, and Emily Zackin. "Constitutions Unentrenched: Toward an Alternative Theory of Constitutional Design." *American Political Science Review* 110, no. 4 (November 2016): 657–74.

Vile, John R. *The Constitutional Amending Process in American Political Thought.* New York: Praeger, 1992.

———. *Encyclopedia of Constitutional Amendments, Proposed Amendments, and Amending Issues, 1789–2015.* 4th ed. 2 vols. Santa Barbara, CA: ABC-CLIO, 2015.

———. *Rewriting the United States Constitution: An Examination of Proposals from Reconstruction to the Present.* New York: Praeger, 1991.

Viteritti, Joseph P. "Blaine's Wake: School Choice, the First Amendment, and State Constitutional Law." *Harvard Journal of Law & Public Policy* 21 (1998): 657–718.

Vorenberg, Michael. *Final Freedom: The Civil War, the Abolition of Slavery, and the Thirteenth Amendment.* Cambridge: Cambridge University Press, 2001.

Vose, Clement E. *Constitutional Change: Amendment Politics and Supreme Court Litigation since 1900.* Lexington, MA: Lexington Books, 1972.

Wallis, John. "The NBER–Maryland State Constitutions Project." Accessed December 2019. www.stateconstitutions.umd.edu.

Wax, Darold D. "Negro Import Duties in Colonial Virginia: A Study of British Commercial Policy and Local Public Policy." *Virginia Magazine of History and Biography* 79, no. 1 (1971): 29–44.

Weisman, Steven R. *The Great Tax Wars: Lincoln to Wilson—The Fierce Battles over Money and Power That Transformed the Nation.* New York: Simon and Schuster, 2002.

"Wet and Dry Map, The." 1916. Persuasive Maps: PJ Mode Collection, Cornell University Library, Ithaca, NY.

Wharton, Linda J. "State Equal Rights Amendments Revisited: Evaluating Their Effectiveness in Advancing Protection against Sex Discrimination." *Rutgers Law Journal* 36, no. 4 (2005): 1201–94.

White, G. Edward. *The Constitution and the New Deal.* Cambridge, MA: Harvard University Press, 2000.

Whiting, Theodore E. *Final Statistical Report of the Federal Emergency Relief Administration.* Washington, DC: Government Printing Office, 1942.

Whittier, John Greenleaf. "Letter to 'The Bay State,' October 4th, 1850." In *Whittier Correspondence from the Oak Knoll Collections, 1830–1892,* edited by John Albree, 113–14. Salem, MA: Essex Book and Print Club, 1911.

Whittington, Keith E. "Judicial Review of Congress before the Civil War." *Georgetown Law Journal* 97, no. 5 (2009): 1257–1332.

———. *Political Foundations of Judicial Supremacy: The Presidency, the Supreme Court, and Constitutional Leadership in U.S. History.* Princeton, NJ: Princeton University Press, 2007.

———. "State Constitutional Law in the New Deal Period." *Rutgers Law Journal* 67 (2015): 1141–68.

Wiecek, William M. "'A Peculiar Conservatism' and the Dorr Rebellion: Constitutional Clash in Jacksonian America." *American Journal of Legal History* 22, no. 3 (July 1, 1978): 237–53.

———. "Somerset: Lord Mansfield and the Legitimacy of Slavery in the Anglo-American World." *University of Chicago Law Review* 42, no. 1 (October 1, 1974): 86–146.

Wilentz, Sean. *Chants Democratic: New York City and the Rise of the American Working Class, 1788–1850.* New York: Oxford University Press, 1984.

Williams, Robert F. "Are State Constitutional Conventions Things of the Past? The Increasing Role of the Constitutional Commission in State Constitutional Change." *Hofstra Law and Policy Symposium* 1 (1996): 1–26.

———. "Equality Guarantees in State Constitutional Law." *Texas Law Review* 63, nos. 6–7 (1985): 1195–1224.

———. "Evolving State Constitutional Processes of Adoption, Revision, and Amendment: The Path Ahead." *Arkansas Law Review* 69, no. 2 (2017): 553–78.

———. "Experience Must Be Our Only Guide: The State Constitutional Experience of the Framers of the Federal Constitution." *Hastings Constitutional Law Quarterly* 15 (1988): 403.

———. *The Law of American State Constitutions.* Oxford: Oxford University Press, 2009.

———. *The New Jersey State Constitution.* New York: Oxford University Press, 2012.

———. "The State Constitutions of the Founding Decade: Pennsylvania's Radical 1776 Constitution and Its Influences on American Constitutionalism." *Temple Law Review* 62 (1989): 541.

Wilson, James. *The Substance of a Speech Delivered by James Wilson, Esq.: Explanatory of the General Principles of the Proposed Fœderal Constitution; . . . in the Convention of the State of Pennsylvania, . . . 24 Nov. 1787.* Philadelphia: Thomas Bradford, 1787.

Wilson, James, and Thomas McKean. *Commentaries on the Constitution of the United States of America.* London: T. Lloyd, 1792.

Wilson, Woodrow. *Constitutional Government in the United States.* New York: Columbia University Press, 1908.

———. "Letter to George H. Haynes, March 27, 1911." In *The Senate of the United States: Its History and Practice,* 104–5. New York: Russell and Russell, 1938.

Winchester, Elhanan. *A Plain Political Catechism: Intended for the Use of Schools, in the United States of America: Wherein the Great Principles of Liberty, and of the Federal Government, Are Laid Down and Explained, by Way of Question and Answer. Made Level to the Lowest Capacities.* Greenfield, MA: T. Dickman, 1796.

Winkle, John W. *The Mississippi State Constitution: A Reference Guide.* Westport, CT: Greenwood, 1993.

Wisconsin State Tax Commission. *Report of the Wisconsin State Tax Commission.* Madison: Wisconsin State Tax Commission, 1899.

Witte, Edwin. "Are Old Age Pensions Worth Their Cost?" *American Labor Legislation Review* 26, no. 1 (1936): 7–14.

———. "Development of Unemployment Compensation." *Yale Law Journal* 55, no. 1 (1945): 21–52.

———. "Twenty Years of Social Security." *Social Security Bulletin,* 1955.

Witte, John F. *The Politics and Development of the Federal Income Tax.* Madison: University of Wisconsin Press, 1986.

Woman's Christian Temperance Union. *Minutes of the National Woman's Christian Temperance Union, Fourteenth Annual Meeting.* Chicago: Woman's Temperance Publication Association, 1888.

Wong, Edlie L. *Neither Fugitive nor Free: Atlantic Slavery, Freedom Suits, and the Legal Culture of Travel.* New York: NYU Press, 2009.

Wood, Gordon S. *The Creation of the American Republic, 1776–1787.* New York: Norton, 1972.

———. "Foreword: State Constitution-Making in the American Revolution." *Rutgers Law Journal* 24 (1993): 911.

———. *The Radicalism of the American Revolution.* New York: Random House, 1992.

Woodward, Comer Vann. *Origins of the New South: 1877–1913.* Baton Rouge: Louisiana State University Press, 1951.

York, Neil L. "The First Continental Congress and the Problem of American Rights." *Pennsylvania Magazine of History and Biography* 122, no. 4 (October 1, 1998): 353–83.

Young, Thomas. "To the Inhabitants of Vermont, a Free and Independent State, Bounding on the River Connecticut and Lake Champlain, April 11, 1777." In *Vermont State Papers,* edited by William Slade, 76. Middlebury, VT: J. W. Copeland, 1777.

Zackin, Emily. *Looking for Rights in All the Wrong Places: Why State Constitutions Contain America's Positive Rights.* Princeton, NJ: Princeton University Press, 2013.

Zilversmit, Arthur. *The First Emancipation: The Abolition of Slavery in the North.* Chicago: University of Chicago Press, 1967.

Zuckert, Michael P. "Completing the Constitution: The Thirteenth Amendment." *Constitutional Commentary* 4 (1987): 259–84.

Zumbrunnen, John. "Wisconsin: Rejection, Ratification, and the Evolution of a People." In *The Constitutionalism of American States,* edited by George E. Connor and Christopher W. Hammons, 460–78. Columbia: University of Missouri Press, 2008.

Zywicki, Todd J. "Beyond the Shell and Husk of History: The History of the Seventeenth Amendment and Its Implications for Current Reform Proposals." *Cleveland State Law Review* 45 (1997): 165–234.

———. "Senators and Special Interests: A Public Choice Analysis of the Seventeenth Amendment." *Oregon Law Review* 73 (January 1, 1994): 1007–56.

INDEX

Figures and tables are indicated by "f" and "t" following page numbers.

Ableman v. Booth (1859), 80
abolition of slavery: in antebellum era, 49, 73, 250n26; in Civil War era, 69, 77; in colonial period, 26–27; compensation for emancipation, 81–85, 89, 190, 263–64nn38–39, 266n50; constitutional amendment, proposal of (1850), 257n13; Constitutional Convention (1787) and, 42–43, 244n72; emancipation at end of Civil War, 82, 83, 266n47; in first state constitutions, 38–39, 240n59; gag rule on antislavery petitions, 252n32; gradual emancipation laws, 39, 241nn60–61, 250n25; international slave trade, abolition of, 39, 43, 56, 249n24; nullification resolutions in Northern states, 78, 79; in Reconstruction-era constitutions, 82–83, 266n49, 266n51; in territories and new states, 75–77, 79. *See also* Thirteenth Amendment
abortion, 16, 181, 291n57
Ackerman, Bruce, 11, 12, 147, 159, 161, 164, 177, 180
Adams, John: drafting Declaration of Independence, role in, 32; drafting state constitutions, role in, 234n28; judicial review and, 38; Pennsylvania convention and, 36–37, 238–39nn52–53; Revolutionary role of, 30–33, 232–33nn20–23; slavery and, 235n36; suffrage and, 59, 240n58, 252n33, 254n39; *Thoughts on Government* (pamphlet), 30–31, 36–37, 238–39n53, 239n55

Adams, John Quincy, 58, 63, 249n23
Adams, Samuel, 232n17, 232n20
Adams, Willi Paul, 41
affirmative action, 183, 188
AFL-CIO, 160, 163, 166
Agassiz, Louis, 74
Agel, Jerome, 164
Agricultural Adjustment Act of 1933, 148, 157, 284n16
Aid to Dependent Children (ADC) program, 155–56, 160, 284n16
Aid to the Blind program, 152–53, 156
Alabama: Black citizenship and, 262n33, 266n52, 268n61; constitutional convention (1875), 139; constitutional convention (1901), 139–40; income tax and, 97, 104–5; length of state constitution, 222n12; pension law and, 157; poll taxes and, 163–65; prohibition and, 278n63; Reconstruction-era constitutions, 83, 84, 86–87, 266n49;

Alabama (*continued*)
  school segregation and, 268nn61–62; slavery and, 58, 73; suffrage and, 60, 165, 268n62; Thirteenth Amendment ratification and, 266n52
A.L.A. Schechter Poultry Co. v. United States (1935), 150, 157
Alaska, 129, 168–69, 180, 273n26, 288n40, 290n55
Aldrich, Nelson, 102–3, 105, 110
Alger, Bruce, 286n30
Allen, William, 96
Allison, William, 266n47
Altmeyer, Arthur J., 154–55, 158
Amenta, Edwin, 155
American Association for Labor Legislation, 154
American Bar Association, 166
American Civil Liberties Union, 166
American Equal Rights Association, 112–13
American Federation of Labor (AFL), 118, 141, 148, 150–51, 160, 162–63, 170, 275n39
American Woman Suffrage Association (AWSA), 22, 113, 115–16, 276n43, 276n50
Ames, Herman, 55, 63–64, 138
antebellum era (1792–1849), 20–21, 47–65, 190; bisectionalism constitutionalized at state level, 49, 54, 56–58, 65, 66, 190, 250n26; conflict decentralization in, 48–49; deference to state banking law, 20–21, 48, 51–54, 65, 190; deference to state election law, 48, 59–65, 190; deference to state slave law, 21, 48–49, 55–59, 65, 190; state as site of constitutional change during, 47; state constitutional slavery clauses (1776–1849), 213–19; topics of proposed federal amendments during, 15, 16f, 49, 50t
Anthony, Susan B., 112–14, 116, 119, 135, 267n58, 276nn43–44, 277n58
anticorruption measures. *See* corruption
antifederalists, 44–45
Anti-Saloon League, 125–33, 135–36, 278n64

Apportionment Act of 1842, 255n45
Arizona, 105, 117, 129, 134, 153, 186, 259n22, 275n40
Arkansas: banking law and, 248n17; citizen initiative and, 275n40; constitutional convention (1874), 139; income tax and, 105, 271n15; poll taxes and, 162, 163–64; prohibition and, 128–29; Reconstruction-era constitutions, 81, 83, 86; slavery abolition and, 58, 81; statehood and, 251n31; suffrage and, 122, 139; term limits and, 181; Thirteenth Amendment ratification and, 84
Arnall, Ellis, 163
Articles of Confederation (1781), 24, 40
Article V: in antebellum era, 62–64; as barrier to amendments, 4–8, 47–48, 89, 109, 146, 193, 224n25; circumvention of, 13, 16, 92; in Civil War era, 68, 80; congressional oversight and, 14; in contemporary era, 180, 187–89; efforts to amend Article V itself, failure of, 11; ERA ratification and, 173, 178; in Great Society era, 166–67; Madison on, 225n34; in New Deal era, 146–47, 150–51, 157, 160–61; in Progressive era, 91–93, 115, 118, 143, 191, 270n2; in Reconstruction era, 67; stability of Constitution insured by, 13, 189, 223n17; state constitutional reform as result of, 4, 189, 191; Thirteenth Amendment ratification and, 265n46. *See also* supermajority requirement to amend U.S. Constitution
Association Against the Prohibition Amendment (AAPA), 132–35
Atchison, David, 76
Atlanta race riot (1906), 127
Aves, Commonwealth v. (1836), 73, 258n16, 263n34

Bacon, Augustus, 275n37
Bailey, Joseph, 103, 272n20
Baker, Purley, 128–30
Baker v. Carr (1962), 166–67, 228n59
balanced-budget amendments, 3t, 3–4, 16, 23, 181, 184, 292nn9–10

INDEX

Baldwin, Abraham, 42
banking: deference to state banking law
  (1792–1849), 20–21, 48, 51–54, 65, 190;
  first Congress and, 45; state banks, charter
  of, 20, 49, 51, 53, 246n5; state constitu-
  tional amendments and, 54–55. *See also*
  National Bank
Bank of the United States. *See* National Bank
Barron v. Baltimore (1833), 53, 224n20
Bayard v. Singleton (1787), 38, 41, 240n57
Bayh, Birch, 169, 172, 183–84
Beaman, Fernando, 83
Benjamin, Judah P., 263n34
Bernstein, Richard, 164
Berry, Mary Frances, 175
bicameralism, 20, 36–38, 40–41, 43, 45,
  239n53, 239n55
Biddle, Francis, 162
Bill of Rights, 20, 43–45, 47, 53, 245n1;
  Fourteenth Amendment and, 267n59
bill of rights, state, 35–36, 86, 244n76
Bingham, John A., 262n31, 267n59
Bittenbender, Ada, 124, 126
Blacks. *See* abolition of slavery; citizenship;
  slavery; suffrage
Blackwell, Alice Stone, 116–17
Blackwell, Henry, 112–16
Blaine, James G., 137–38
Blaine, John J., 135
Blair, Henry W., 114, 118, 124–25
Blair, John, 41
Bland, Richard, 232n16
Blanton, Thomas, 121
Boles, Janet, 175
Book of the States, 17, 228n58, 229n63,
  282n2
Booth and Rycraft, In re (1854), 78
Borah, William, 110–11, 122, 131
Boston Female Anti-Slavery Society, 258n16
Boston Tea Party, 28
Botts, Charles T., 75–76
Bourne, Johnathan, 110
Boutwell, George, 265n43
Bowman v. Chicago & Nw. Ry. (1888), 124

Bradford, William, 33–34
Brandegee, Frank, 122
Brandeis, Elizabeth, 154
Brandeis, Louis, 5, 22, 145, 150, 154, 157–58
Braxton, Carter, 25, 37, 239n53
Breedlove v. Suttles (1937), 287n31
Brennan, William, 179–80
Briffault, Richard, 187
Briscoe v. Bank of Commonwealth of Ky.
  (1837), 53, 247n12
Brissot, Jacques Pierre, 238n50
Bristow, Joseph, 111
Britain, 26–31, 230n7; English Constitution,
  227n53. *See also specific monarchs*
British East India Company, 28
Britten, Frederick, 135
Brom and Bett v. Ashley (1780), 240n59
Brooks, James, 112–13, 267n58
Brooks, Preston, 76
Broomall, John, 112, 115, 268n60
Brown, Henry Billings, 96
Brown, John, 76
Brown, Norris, 103–4
Bruce, Douglass, 186
Bryan, George, 237–38nn46–47
Bryan, William Jennings, 96
Bryce, Lord James, 11, 90, 97–98
Buchanan, James, 78–80, 88, 155, 249n20,
  263n34
Budget and Impoundment Control Act of
  1974, 183
Bumper, Dale, 180
Burger Court, 16, 181
Burgess, John William, 11
Burke, Edmund, 26
Burnham, Walter Dean, 12
Burns, Alexander, 261nn27–28
Burns, Lucy, 118
Burr, Aaron, 51, 241n61
Bushnell, Ex parte (1859), 261n28
Butler, Pierce, 158, 243n66, 244n73

Calder v. Bull (1798), 246n7
Calhoun, John C., 48, 52, 71, 256n9

California: child labor and, 142; constitutional convention (1849), 54; corporation taxes and, 99; gender equality clauses and, 290n55; income tax and, 105; initiative and referendum, 185–87, 275n40; labor regulation and, 141–42; pension law and, 152–53; prohibition and, 129, 132–34, 279n78; Proposition 1 (1973), 185; Proposition 4 (1978), 185; Proposition 13 (1978), 185, 186; quantitative and qualitative effects of proposed constitutional revision in, 18; senatorial elections and, 274n31; slavery and, 69, 71–72, 75, 257n11, 259n23; suffrage and, 115–17, 255n43; tax-cap provisions and, 185–87, 293n11
Cameron, James, 237–38nn46–47
Cannon, James, 36, 237n46
canonical explanations of American constitutional development, 11–14
Cardozo, Benjamin, 157–58, 285n20
Carmichael v. Southern Coal & Coke Co. (1937), 157–59
Carolene Prods. Co., United States v. (1938), 158
Carter, Jimmy, 183
Carter, Landon, 231n16
Cass, Lewis, 71, 257n12, 263n34
Caton, Commonwealth v. (1782), 38, 41
Catt, Carrie Chapman, 92, 97, 118–19, 122–23, 136, 170–71
Cauthen, Nancy, 155
Cazabat, Alphonse, 83
Celler, Emanuel, 164, 169, 171–72
Charles River Bridge v. Warren Bridge (1837), 53, 247n12
Chase, Salmon P., 83
Chase, Samuel, 246n7
checks and balances, 20, 37, 40, 238–39n53. *See also* separation of powers
Cherrington, Ernest, 128–31, 133, 136
child labor, 93–94, 140–42, 143, 158
Child Labor Amendments (1920s), 22, 142–43, 146, 150–51, 157–58
Chisholm v. Georgia (1792), 246n4

Choate, Joseph H., 96
circumvention, 5, 13, 22, 189, 191
citizenship, 4, 21; to all persons born in United States, 267n55; Blacks and, 68–69, 74, 78–80, 82–87, 94, 190, 262–63n33, 263n35, 264n38, 267n55; in Progressive era, 15; proposed federal rights and amendments (1788–2020), 17*f*; in Reconstruction era, 15; suffrage and, 114
civil rights: constitutional amendments related to, 19, 69, 94, 161–62, 167; Jim Crow and, 139–40; New Deal and Great Society era and, 145
Civil Rights Act of 1866, 85, 267nn55–56
Civil Rights Act of 1964, 145, 147, 161; Title VII, 172, 177, 289n46
Civil Rights Cases (1883), 139
Civil War era (1850–1865), 66–80, 190; from federal deference to state divergence on slavery, 4, 69–75; secession of Southern states (formation of Confederacy), 80–81; state divergence and onset of war, 75–80
Civil Works Administration, 284n16
Claiborne, William C. C., 257n15
Clay, Henry, 63
Cleveland, Grover, 96, 106
Clingman, Thomas Lanier, 71–72, 256n11
Clinton, DeWitt, 60–61
Clinton, George, 51
Clymer, George, 237n46, 243n66
Coercive Acts (1774), 28, 35
Coffroth, Alexander, 83–84, 265n46
Cohens v. Virginia (1821), 246n7
Colchester v. Lyme (1834), 262n33
Coleman, Thomas, 139
colonial period and unrest, 26–30, 231n14
Colorado: Constitution (1876), 271n13; constitutional amendment process in, 222n10; gender equality clauses and, 290n55; income taxes and, 99, 101, 105; parochial schooling and, 137; pension law and, 156; prohibition and, 129, 132–34; property taxes and, 271n13; senatorial elections and, 109, 275n40; suffrage and,

115–17, 269n66; tax-cap provisions and, 186–87
Colquitt, Alfred, 125
Commerce Clause, 3, 128, 142, 161, 258n17
Commission on the Status of Women, 171
Committee of Five, 32–33, 234n29
Committee of the Whole, 31–32, 40, 238n52
Committee on Civil Rights, 162
Committee on Economic Security, 154–55, 159
Commons, John R., 154
Commonwealth v. See name of opposing party
Compromise of 1820, 79
Compromise of 1850, 21, 67, 69, 71–72, 75–76, 79, 88, 257n11, 257n14, 263n34
concurrent powers of state and federal governments, 2, 3; advantage of framing controversy for, 5, 221n3; banking and economic regulation, 51; in Civil War and Reconstruction eras, 68–69; in contemporary era, 181; election methods for federal offices, 59–60; income and, 101, 102; in Progressive era, 93–94; prohibition and, 279n72. *See also* preemption; Supremacy Clause
Confederate states, 69, 80–81, 256n4, 265n46. *See also* Civil War era; Southern states *for* secession; suffrage *for* disenfranchisement *of* ex-Confederates
conflict decentralization, 14–19; in America's formative years, 25; in antebellum era, 48–49, 62; in Civil War, 67–69; constitutional reform as result of, 2, 189; cyclical pattern of, 3*t*, 7–8, 190, 191, 192; in Great Society era, 148; in New Deal era, 148, 159; party realignment and, 7, 8, 192; paths for, 2, 192–93; preemption and, 3; in Progressive era, 91, 92, 94, 112; in Reconstruction era, 69
Congress, U.S., party division (1788–2020), 7*f*, 51. *See also* partisan realignment
Congress of Industrial Organizations (CIO), 148, 160, 162–63. *See also* AFL-CIO

Connecticut: Black citizenship and, 79, 262n33; charter of, 231n14, 236n40, 244n76; constitution (1818), 253n37, 254n39; constitutional convention (1965), 167; election of House representatives in, 252n34; frontier regulation and, 27; gender equality clauses and, 170, 176, 290n55; Gradual Abolition Act, 241n60; income tax and, 103, 273n24; Jeffersonians in, 253n37; legislative apportionment and, 167; minimum wage law and, 151; prohibition and, 132–33; slavery and, 39, 77, 78, 241n60; suffrage and, 60, 240n58, 254n39, 254n40, 269n66
Connecticut Compromise, 45, 245n80
Connelly, Patrick, 141
Connery, William, 283n11
constitutional convention, federal, as possibility, 11, 23, 111
Constitutional Convention (1787), 19, 20, 24, 190, 221n3, 230n4, 249n21; imitating state design, 25, 40–46, 242n64
constitutional conventions, state, 6, 193, 229n1; approval of call for, 222n11; in contemporary era, rare use of, 180; list by state (1776–2020), 195–210; in New Deal and Great Society era (1932–1979), 145, 166; number of, 14, 222n11; in Progressive era, 115; public approval of constitutions drafted by, 236n43; in Reconstruction era, 66, 68, 69, 81, 82–83, 86–87; structures of first conventions, 30–34; types of revision assemblies, 17, 18*t*, 228n59
contemporary era (1980–2020), 8, 179–88, 191–92; fiscal reform and, 3, 181–88; initiative and referendum processes, 180–81, 185–86; state constitutional conventions rarely used in, 180; term limits, 180, 181; topics of proposed amendments, 181, 182*t*
Continental Congress (1774), 24, 30, 232–33n20
Continental Congress (1776), 19, 24–25, 30, 40
Contracts Clause, 247n12

convergence: in cycle of conflict decentralization, 3*t*, 7–8, 192; federal response to state convergence, 4–5; female suffrage and, 112–23, 136; in Great Society era, 165, 168; income tax and, 94–106; judicial imitation of, 9; in New Deal era, 148, 177, 191; poll tax bans and, 10, 160–69, 193; in Progressive era, 22, 91–136; prohibition and, 123–36; providing resolution at state level to national issues, 189; in Reconstruction era, 21, 68–69, 81–89, 190, 191; senatorial elections and, 106–12; states providing experiments for federal reform through, 5, 14, 22
convict labor, 84, 267n53
Corcoran, Thomas, 150, 154
corruption, 53, 80, 97, 99, 107, 111, 118, 134, 275n37
Corwin, Thomas, 264n38
Corwin Amendment (1861), 264n38
Council of State Governments, 166
Cox, Nicholas, 138
Cox, Samuel, 265n43
Craig v. Boren (1976), 173
Crandall v. Connecticut (1834), 79, 262n33
Crawford, William, 63, 261n29
crime victims' rights, 188
Crittenden, John, 263–64n38
Cummings v. Missouri (1867), 268n62
Cummins, Albert, 103
Curran, Henry, 132–34
Curtis, Benjamin, 263n35
Curtis, Carl, 183
Curtis, Charles, 170–71
Cushing, William, 240n59
Cushman, Barry, 147

Daggett, David, 262n33
Dahl, Robert, 9, 11, 12, 13
Daniel, John, 257n13
Darby Lumber Co., United States v. (1941), 158
Davie, William, 41
Davis, Garrett, 82, 264n38

Davis, Jefferson, 264n38
Dawes, Henry L., 262n31
Dayton, William, 77
Declaration of Independence, 32–33, 74, 211–12, 234n27, 234n29, 234–35n31, 268–69n63
deference: in antebellum era, 48–49, 51–65, 190; banking law and, 20–21, 48, 51–55, 65, 190; in Civil War era, 69, 74; in contemporary era, 3–4, 181–88, 192; in cycle of conflict decentralization, 3*t*, 7–8, 192; distinguished from circumvention, 5; in drafting of U.S. Constitution, 20, 43; election law and, 48, 59–65; female suffrage and, 112–23, 135, 193; fiscal reform and, 3–4, 181–88; gender equality clauses and, 148, 169–78; government's passivity in, 3; income tax and, 94–106; judicial deference to states, 10; labor regulation and child labor law and, 136–43; poll tax bans and, 193; in Progressive era, 91–94, 97, 105, 112, 136–43, 191; prohibition and, 123–36; providing resolution at state level to national issues, 189; in Reagan era, 179; slavery, 20, 21, 55–59, 65, 68, 72, 74, 88; territorial slavery question and, 72, 88
Delany, Martin, 74
Delaware: banking law and, 51; bill of rights, state, 244n76; constitutional amendment process in, 34–35, 170, 222n10, 236n43; constitutional convention in, 236n40; enumeration of rights and, 242n64; first constitution of, 36; gradual emancipation law in, 39, 241n61; income tax and, 273n24; prohibition and, 128, 133; senatorial representation and, 107; slavery and, 32–33, 235n38; state constitutional convention delegate elections in, 34; suffrage and, 253n36, 254n39, 269n66; Thirteenth Amendment ratification and, 266n51
Democratic-Republicans: in antebellum era, 47–48, 57, 253n37; banking law and, 52–53; Monroe as presidential nominee

(1816) and, 63; slavery and, 249n23; supermajorities of, 224n27

Democrats: in antebellum era, 47–48; in contemporary era, 8, 180, 184; Equal Rights Amendment and, 171; Great Society, 146; New Deal, 146, 150–51, 157, 165; poll taxes and, 160–63; presidential nomination process, 252n32; in Progressive era, 90, 91, 94, 96, 103–4, 107–8, 125–26, 133–34, 137, 139; in Reconstruction era, 83–84; senatorial elections and, 275n39; states' rights and, 224n20, 257n14; suffrage issues and, 60, 117–18, 119–20, 253n36, 254nn39–40, 269n66; supermajorities of, 224n27

Dennis, David W., 289n47

devolution: in antebellum era, 48, 49, 53, 55, 59, 64, 74, 88; in Civil War era, 69; in Progressive era, 92, 97; relationship of state and federal constitutional reform through, 19; strategic use of, 3*t*, 3–4, 7; territorial slavery question and, 72, 76–77. *See also* deference; dictation

Dewey, Thomas, 163

Dickinson, John: abolition of slavery and, 241n61, 244n72; on compromise to enact U.S. Constitution, 45; Revolutionary role of, 28, 30, 231n13, 233n20, 233n25; on state constitutional drafting as guide for federal, 25, 242n64; on tripartite government, 40–41; unicameral legislature and, 35

dictation: in Civil War era, 190; congressional use of, 3, 4, 10, 81–89; in cycle of conflict decentralization, 7–8; judicial use of, 4; in New Deal era, 157, 165, 191; in Progressive era, 93, 94, 123, 132, 135–36; providing resolution at state level, 189–90; rare use of, 192; in Reconstruction era, 10, 69, 80–89, 190, 193; territorial slavery question and, 79, 80; voting age, lowering of, 4, 148, 169, 193

Dill, Clarence, 283n11

Dirksen, Everett, 166, 288n39

disenfranchisement. *See* suffrage

Disney, David, 256n7, 257n13

District Clause, 269n65

District of Columbia, 161, 249n24, 252n32, 269nn65–66

divergence, 7–8, 190, 192; in Civil War era, 4, 68, 75–80, 88, 190; federal response as active in, 4–5. *See also* dictation

Dorn, William, 286n30

Dorr, Thomas, 61–62

Douglas, Stephen A., 71–72, 76, 263n34, 264n38

Douglass, Frederick, 74, 78, 112–13, 261n28

Douglass, William O., 164

Dow, Neal, 93, 123, 131, 135–36

Drayton, William Henry, 37

Dred Scott v. Sandford (1857), 21, 66–68, 79, 85, 88, 190, 263nn34–36, 264n38

Duane, James, 30–31

DuBois, Fred, 109

due process clauses: in Reconstruction era, 85; slavery and, 38–39, 240n59, 250n25, 258n16

Dulany, Daniel, 28

Dunmore, Lord. *See* Murray, John

Dyer, Leonidas, 134

Eastland, James, 163–64

E. C. Knight Co., United States v. (1895), 91, 96–97

Edmunds, William, 137

education: parochial school funding, 136–38, 143; in Progressive era, 15, 93–94, 136–37; proposed federal rights and amendments (1788–2020), 17*f*; in Reconstruction era, 15, 21, 268n61

Edwards, Edward, 132

Eighteenth Amendment, 4, 22, 90, 121–22, 132–35, 143–44, 279n72, 279–80nn79–80

Eisenhower, Dwight, 166, 171

elections: in antebellum era, 20, 48, 59–65, 190; presidential, 93; primaries, 108, 165, 274n32, 274n35; in Progressive era, 15, 20, 21–22; proposed federal rights and amendments (1788–2020), 17*f*; in Reconstruction

elections (*continued*)
  era, 15, 20; reform amendments before Congress to standardize federal elections, 59, 62–63; senatorial, 91–94, 106–12, 110*f,* 143, 273–74n30; term limits, 16*f,* 23, 35, 52, 93, 180, 181, 292n6. *See also* suffrage
Elections Clause, 3, 59, 62
Electoral College: amendments to reform, 59, 63–64; balancing slave vs. free states, 56, 71, 75, 77, 256n8; female suffrage and, 117, 119–22; in Reconstruction era, 87, 267n57; state use of, 41–42
Elementary and Secondary Education Act of 1965, 161
elevation, 3*t,* 4–5, 7; relationship of state and federal constitutional reform through, 19. *See also* convergence; divergence
Eleventh Amendment, 47, 246n4
Eliot, Thomas H., 154
Elkins, Zachary, 11
Ellsworth, Oliver, 42–43
Ely, Richard T., 94, 97, 101
Emerson, Ralph Waldo, 73
England. *See* Britain
enumeration of rights, 17*f;* drafting of U.S. Constitution and, 43–44, 242–43n64, 244n73; first state constitutions and, 24, 25
Equal Pay Act of 1963, 172
equal protection, 21, 85, 139, 268nn61–62
Equal Protection Clause, 87, 89, 160–61, 274n32
Equal Rights Amendment (ERA), 23, 146, 148, 170–78, 191, 289n47, 290n53, 290–91nn55–57
Ervin, Sam, 167, 172
Eskridge, William, 147, 159
Esquivel-Quintana v. Sessions (2017), 224n21
Europe, suffrage in, 254n40
executive powers: dictation in Reconstruction era, 68–69, 80–81; in New Deal era, 147; proposed amendments of (1788–2020), 16*f;* U.S. Constitution drafting and, 41, 45. *See also* veto powers

experimentation by states. *See* state constitutional reform

Fair Labor Standards Act of 1938, 158, 282–83n9
Farnsworth, John, 267n54
federal constitutional amendment: agency in, 222n6; Constitutional Convention (1787) and, 24; desirability of, 221n2; destabilizing effects of, 16, 67, 225n54; difficulty to amend, 2, 10, 11; erroneous conclusions of mainstream accounts of, 11–14, 192–93; judicial role in, 9, 9*f,* 12, 13, 16, 192; proposed amendments of amendment process (1788–2020), 11, 16*f;* quantitative vs. qualitative effects, 15–19, 225n53; state amendments' effect on, 9, 9*f,* 10, 19–20, 20*f,* 189, 192, 193, 229n64; time limit on proposals, 11; topics of proposed amendments, 15–16, 16–17*f,* 229n62; topics of proposed amendments (1792–1849), 15, 49, 50*t;* topics of proposed amendments (1850–1877), 66, 68–69, 70*t,* 256n1; topics of proposed amendments (1878–1931), 15, 16*f,* 93–94, 95*t;* topics of proposed amendments (1932–1979), 15–16, 16*f,* 147–48, 149*t;* topics of proposed amendments (1980–2020), 15–16, 16*f,* 181, 182*t. See also* Article V; conflict decentralization; deference; supermajority requirement to amend U.S. Constitution; *specific Amendments by number*
federal convention of 1787. *See* Constitutional Convention (1787)
federal courts: certiorari denials, effect of, 9; dictation, use of, 4; gradualist approach of, 5, 8, 12, 13, 188, 189; imitation of majority positions among states, 9; national outcomes attributed to, 8–9, 9*f;* nonintervention periods of, 192; proposed structures and powers amendments (1788–2020), 16*f;* reliance on state constitutional reform, 9; in slavery crisis of 1850s, 256n5; state models for, 41–42; unelected judges, debate over, 9.

See also judicial review; Supreme Court, U.S.; *specific case names*
Federal Emergency Relief Act of 1934, 154
Federal Emergency Relief Administration, 284n16
Federal Estate Tax Act of 1926, 154
federalism, 49, 97, 156–58, 160, 191, 225n36; new judicial federalism, 176, 179
The Federalist, 43; No. 1, 24; No. 10, 222n8; No. 48, 243n66; No. 84, 44
Federalists, 48, 51–52, 56, 60, 245n1, 249n23
Federations of Women's Clubs, 152
Ferejohn, John, 147, 159
Fifteenth Amendment, 4, 10, 62, 66, 87–88, 113, 139–40, 164–65, 193, 269n66
Fifth Amendment, 79, 173, 263n36
Fillmore, Millard, 78
First Continental Congress. *See* Continental Congress (1774)
Fisher, Irving, 144
Fisher's Negroes v. Dabs (1834), 262n33
flag burning, 16, 181, 183, 187
Fletcher v. Peck (1810), 224n20
Florence, Thomas, 264n38
Florida: constitution (1839), 251n31; constitution (1968), 167; constitutional convention (1838–1939), 54; constitutional convention (1885–1886), 139; ERA ratification and, 175; gender equality clauses and, 290n53; income tax and, 273n26; initiative process to amend constitution in, 222n10; labor relations and, 152; prohibition and, 128; Reconstruction-era constitutions, 83, 84, 266n49; secession of, 264n40; slavery and, 73; suffrage and, 162, 163, 266n49, 266n52; Thirteenth Amendment ratification and, 266n52
Florida v. Mellon (1927), 154–55
Folsom, Jim, 163
Foster, J. Ellen, 124, 126, 278n64
Fourteenth Amendment, 4, 66, 86–87, 112, 139–40, 164, 173, 267n57, 268n61, 269n65
France, 238n50
franchise law. *See* suffrage

Francisco, In re (1833), 258n16
Frankfurter, Felix, 157
Franklin, Benjamin, 32, 237–38nn45–47, 243n67, 244n71
Freedmen's Bureau, 85, 266n47
Free Soilers, 71, 76–78, 262n32
Fremont, John C., 77
French and Indian War, 27
Frontiero v. Richardson (1973), 173
frontier regulation, 19, 20, 25, 26, 27, 31, 190; suffrage and, 20, 27, 33, 60
Frye, William, 125
Fugitive Slave Act of 1793, 57, 72–74, 257–58nn15–16
Fugitive Slave Act of 1850, 74, 77–78, 259n19, 260n25, 261nn28–29, 263n37
Fugitive Slave Clause, 42–43, 57, 72–74, 258n16, 261n27
fugitive slaves, 29, 39, 56–57, 68, 72–74, 88, 249–50n24, 258n16, 263n37. *See also* personal liberty laws
Full Faith and Credit Clause, 4, 261n27

gambling, 183, 188
Gann, Paul, 185–86
Garfield, James, 106
Garrett, Finis, 143
Garrison, William Lloyd, 48, 67, 69, 74
Geer, Theodore, 108
gender-equality clauses, 23, 148, 169–78, 191
George, James, 125
George III (British king), 29, 32, 234n27, 234n30, 235n35
Georgia: charter of, 230n5; child labor and, 143; constitutional amendment process in, 34–35, 236n43; constitutional convention (1776–1777), 236n40; constitutional convention (1877), 139; constitution modeled on Pennsylvania's, 36; enumeration of rights and, 242n63; Fourteenth Amendment ratification and, 268n61; income tax and, 104–5; legislative apportionment and, 167–68; no bill of rights, 244n76; poll taxes and, 163; prohibition and, 123, 127, 132;

Georgia (*continued*)
  Reconstruction-era constitutions, 81, 83, 84, 86–87, 266n49, 268n61; Revolutionary unrest in, 30, 235n31; slavery and, 73, 235n36, 250n25, 261n27; sovereign immunity and, 246n4; suffrage and, 38, 165; voting age, lowering of, 168
Gerry, Elbridge, 41
gerrymandering. *See* legislative apportionment
Gibbons v. Ogden (1824), 52, 224n20
Gibson, Henry R., 88
Giddings, Joshua, 77
Gilded Age constitutional provisions, 152
Giles v. Harris (1903), 140
Ginsburg, Tom, 11
Goldberg, Arthur, 287n31
Goldwater, Barry, 183
Gonzales v. Duenas-Alvare (2007), 224n21
Graber, Mark, 9
Gramm-Rudman-Hollings Act of 1985, 184
Grant, Ulysses, 137–38
Grassley, Chuck, 176
Great Depression, 22, 88, 105, 134, 148, 153, 183
Great Society era (1960s), 7, 22; Article V in, 166–67; civil rights and voting rights and, 145–47, 161, 164, 173, 191; conflict decentralization in, 148
Green, William, 289n47
Gremillion, Jack P. F., 286n30
Grenville, George, 27–28
Griffith, Commonwealth v. (1823), 258n16
Griffiths, Martha, 172
Grimes, Alan, 11
Groves v. Slaughter (1841), 73, 258n17
Guarantee Clause, 3, 43, 86, 112, 115, 251n29, 262n31, 268n60, 269n65
Guthrie, William D., 96

habeas corpus protection, 29, 77–78, 230n7, 258n16
Hale, Frederick, 121
Hale, Matthew, 227n53
Hamilton, Alexander, 24, 43–45, 51

Hamm, Richard, 125
Hammer v. Dagenhart (1918), 142
Hammond, John Craig, 56–57
Hancock, John, 44–45
Hanna, Mark, 107
Hansen, Alvin H., 154
Hardy, Rufus, 121
Harlan, John Marshall, 96, 270–71n8
Harper, Robert Goodloe, 56
Harper v. Virginia Bd. of Elections (1966), 9, 23, 164, 178, 192, 287n31
Harrington, James, 240n58
Harrison, Pat, 162
Harrison, William Henry, 56
Harrison Land Act of 1800, 251n28
Hartley, Roger, 164
Harvey, James, 115
Hatch, Orrin, 176, 184, 291n57
Haugen, Nils P., 100
Hawaii, 152, 168, 176, 185–86, 288n40, 290n55
Hawley, Albert, 99
Hayes, Rutherford, 90
Haynes, George H., 106–7, 109
Helvering v. Davis (1937), 157–59, 285n20
Helvering v. Gerhardt (1938), 158
Henry, Patrick, 28–29, 37, 40, 234n28, 238–39n53
Herrick, Anson, 84
Herrick, Ebenezer, 63
Herron, Paul, 83–84
Heyburn, Weldon, 109
Hillhouse, James, 249n23
Hirschl, Ran, 12
Hobbs v. Fogg (1837), 262n33
Hobson, Richmond, 129–30
Hobson-Sheppard amendment (1914), 129
Hoebke, C. H., 111
Holland, Spessard, 164
Holmes, Oliver Wendell, Jr., 223n20, 227n55
Holtzman, Liz, 291n56
Hoover, Herbert, 133
Hudgins v. Wrights (1806), 39, 242n62
Hughes, Charles Evans, 103–4

INDEX   341

Huq, Aziz, 15, 180
Hutchinson, Thomas, 29
Hyde, Henry, 291n57

Idaho, 105, 116–17, 129, 173, 280n83
Illinois: Black immigration and movement in, 79; budget clause and, 185; child labor laws and, 140–41; constitution (1848), 250n26; convict slavery and, 267n53; ERA ratification and, 175, 291n56; gender equality clauses and, 170, 290n55; income tax and, 104; initiative process to amend constitution in, 222n10; minimum wage law and, 151; pension law and, 152; primary elections and, 108; prohibition and, 132–33; senatorial elections and, 274n31; slavery and, 56, 57, 65, 76, 78, 250n26, 251n28, 263n34; suffrage and, 60, 115, 117, 119, 253n36, 254n40, 276n49
imitation of state policy. *See* convergence
immigration: disenfranchisement of immigrants, 60, 61; in Northern state populations in Civil War era, 71; prohibition and, 123, 127; westward movement and, 27
impeachment provisions, 35, 41, 52
Importation Clause, 263n36
income tax, 21–22, 191, 272n20; federal deference and state convergence, 90, 92–106, 143; state taxes, 97–105, 143, 272n19
Indiana: Black immigration and movement in, 79; budget clause and, 185; constitution (1851), 54; convict slavery and, 267n53; ERA ratification and, 173; income tax and, 98; pension law and, 153; primary elections and, 108; prohibition and, 123; slavery and, 56, 65, 76, 78, 250n26, 257n15; suffrage and, 60, 253n36; Thirteenth Amendment ratification and, 266n51
initiative and referendum processes, 91, 180–81, 185–86, 191, 193, 228n59, 275n40
Internal Revenue Bureau, 104
Iowa, 76, 78, 105, 175–76, 180, 248n16, 251n31, 259n23, 278n63, 290n53

Iredell, James, 38
item-veto provision, 23, 181, 187, 292n9

Jackson, Andrew, 21, 48–49, 52, 55, 63, 224n20, 252n32
Jacksonian era and Jacksonians, 7, 49, 55, 58, 64, 190, 246n3, 254n40
James I (British king), 26
James II (British king), 26, 231n14
Jarrot v. Jarrot (1845), 250n26
Jarvis, Howard, 185
Javits, Jacob, 164, 167–68, 288n39
Jay, John, 241n61
Jefferson, Thomas: Committee of Five and, 234n29; compact theory, 78, 87, 265n46; congressional system and, 239nn53–54; drafting Declaration of Independence, 32, 211–12; drafting Virginia constitution, 233–34nn26–27, 235n35; on federal vs. state court jurisdiction, 246–47n8; National Bank and, 51; reverence toward federal Constitution and, 48, 188; slavery and, 32–33, 235–36n39; suffrage and, 59, 252n33
Jeffersonian era and Jeffersonians, 5, 20, 49, 52, 56–60, 62, 190, 245n1, 246n5, 253n37
Jennison, Commonwealth v. (1783), 39, 240n59
Jim Crow laws, 3*t*, 5, 91, 94, 109–10, 122, 136, 139, 143, 164–65. *See also* poll taxes
Johnson, Andrew, 84–86, 106, 265n46, 266n52
Johnson, Lyndon, 164, 172. *See also* Great Society era
Johnson, Reverdy, 267n57
Jones, James McHall, 75
Jowers, State v. (1850), 263n33
judicial review: briefer national constitutions in combination with, 12; certiorari denials, effect of, 9; change in national outcomes due to, 9, 9*f,* 12, 13, 16, 192; deference to states, 9–10; imitating state convergence on a majority position, 9; state constitutional reform deterring at federal level, 189, 191;

judicial review (*continued*)
   state courts' powers of, 38; state models for federal system of, 41–42; topics of proposed amendments, common across eras, 229n62
Julian, George, 113

Kammen, Michael, 11, 13, 15
Kansas, 76, 105, 113, 116–17, 124, 140, 260n25, 269n66, 278n64
Kansas-Nebraska Act of 1854, 21, 67, 76–77, 88
Keating-Owen Act of 1916, 142
Kelley, William, 265n46
Kennedy, John (1846), 254n40
Kennedy, John F., 171
Kennedy, Robert, 167
Kentucky: Black citizenship and, 79, 262n33; constitution (1850), 248n18, 260n26; constitutional convention (1890–1891), 139; ERA ratification and, 173; income tax and, 100, 104–5; pension law and, 153; slavery and, 57, 65, 250–51n27; state debt, voter approval required for, 248n19; suffrage and, 60, 122, 269n66; Thirteenth Amendment ratification and, 266n51; voting age, lowering of, 168
Kenyon, William, 128
Kernan, Francis, 137
Kestenbaum Commission (1955), 166
Key, V. O., 8, 12
Keyssar, Alexander, 42, 62, 164
King, Rufus, 43, 251n30
Kinsman, Delos Oscar, 96–99, 100–101
Kramer, Larry, 9, 12
Ku Klux Klan, 139, 165
Kyvig, David E., 45, 138, 161, 180

labor and commerce: minimum wage laws, 81, 141–42, 151, 157; in New Deal era, 15, 22, 145, 148, 151–52, 191; in Progressive era, 21–22, 140–43, 151; proposed federal rights and amendments (1788–2020), 17*f*; in Reconstruction era, 21, 87; unemployment programs, 154, 158–59; women workers, regulation of, 141, 170; workers' compensation clauses, 151; working hours, regulation of, 87, 140–42, 151. *See also* child labor; slavery
La Follette, Robert, 100, 103, 142
La Guardia, Fiorello, 144
Langdon, John, 244n72
Langston, Ex parte (1859), 261n28
Latham, Darren, 15, 180
Laughlin, Gail, 169
League of Women Voters, 166, 170, 288–89n43
Lee, Richard Henry, 31–32, 37, 44, 233n25, 234n28, 238–39n53
Leedham, Charles, 11
Leff, Mark H., 153
Legare, Hugh, 79
legislative apportionment, 16, 20, 23, 42–43, 68, 147, 161, 165–66, 230–31n9, 239n54, 288n39
legislative sovereignty, 19, 24, 25, 26, 31–32, 33–40, 190
Leisy v. Hardin (1890), 124–25
Leopold, Alice K., 171
Leuchtenberg, William, 147, 159
Lever Act of 1917, 130
Levinson, Sanford, 11, 13
liberty laws. *See* personal liberty laws
Lincoln, Abraham, 21, 66–68, 78, 80–84, 88, 94, 264nn38–39, 268–69n63
Linde, Hans, 181
Line Item Veto Act of 1997, 184, 187
liquor laws. *See* prohibition
Little, Edward, 121
Livermore, Arthur, 58, 251n29
Livingston, Robert R., 29, 32, 241n61
Lochner v. New York (1905), 91, 141
Lodge, Henry Cabot, 139
Lodge Federal Elections Bill (1890), 125, 139
Long, Huey, 162
Louisiana: Black citizenship and, 262n33; child labor and, 142; constitution (1852),

260n26; constitutional convention (1864), 264n42; constitutional convention (1879), 139; constitutional convention (1898), 139; frequent constitutional revision in, 223n14; gender equality clauses and, 290n55; income tax and, 97, 99, 105; legislative apportionment and, 167; pension law and, 153; prohibition and, 134; Reconstruction-era constitutions, 81, 83, 86; secession of, 264n40; slavery and, 57, 65, 73, 249n23, 251n27, 257n15; suffrage and, 162, 165, 254n39, 255n43, 264n42; Thirteenth Amendment ratification and, 84, 266n52

Louisiana Territory, 56, 249n23

Lowrie, Walter, 52, 247n8

Ludlow, Louis, 171

Luther, Seth, 61

Luther v. Borden (1849), 223n20

Lutz, Donald, 45

Lyons, Thomas, 100–101

Maddox, John, 138

Madison, James: on Article V, 225n34; constitutional drafting and, 40–45, 221n3; *Federalist* 10, 222n8; *Federalist* 48, 243n66; National Bank and, 51; *Notes,* 45; on reverence toward federal Constitution, 48; slavery and, 244n73; suffrage and, 59, 244n71, 249n21

Madisonian system of institutional power-sharing, 12

Maine: debt limits and, 248n17; ERA ratification and, 173, 175; parochial school funding and, 137; pension law and, 153; prohibition and, 123–24, 127; slavery and, 56, 58, 78, 79; suffrage and, 113, 121, 254n40, 262n32; voting age, lowering of, 169

malapportionment. *See* legislative apportionment

Mansfield, Lord, 26, 230n7

Manuel, State v. (1838), 262–63n33

Marbury v. Madison (1803), 53

marijuana regulation, 183, 188

marriage, 15, 266n49; polygamy, 93–94, 138–39, 143, 191, 280nn82–84; same-sex marriage, 174–75, 183, 188

Marshall, John, 21, 51–53, 223–24n20, 246nn7–8, 247n11

Marshall Court, 47–48, 53, 64

Martin, Luther, 43, 244n73

Martin v. Hunter's Lessee (1816), 246n7

Maryland: bill of rights, state, 244n76; budget clause and, 185; charter of, 230n5; constitution (1851), 260n26; constitutional amendment process in, 236n43; enumeration of rights and, 242n64; ERA ratification and, 173; first constitution, 36; gender equality clauses and, 290n55; gradual emancipation law in, 39, 241n61; income tax and, 104–5; prohibition and, 132–33, 279n78; Reconstruction-era constitutions, 81, 83; Revolutionary unrest in, 30, 32, 234n28, 235n31; slavery and, 230n6, 257n14; state constitutional convention delegate elections in, 34; suffrage and, 254n39, 254n40, 255n43, 264n42, 269n66; Thirteenth Amendment ratification and, 84

Mason, George, 40, 43–44, 235n36; *Objections to the Proposed Federal Constitution,* 44

Massachusetts: bicameralism in, 37; bill of rights, state, 244n76; charter of, 231–32n16; constitution (1780), 234n28, 237n44; constraints on amendment, 35, 228n60; election of presidential electors and, 64; elections and, 243n69; equality clause and, 258n16, 262n32; first state constitutional convention, 25, 30, 35, 37, 236n43; freedom suits in, 39; frontier regulation and, 27; gender equality clauses and, 170, 290n55; income tax and, 97, 105; initiative process to amend constitution in, 222n10; legislative sovereignty in, 35; as model for other state constitutions, 25; pension law and, 153; primary elections and, 108; prohibition and, 132–33; Proposition 2½ (1980), 186; ratification of U.S. Constitution and, 44, 45;

Massachusetts (*continued*)
  Revolutionary unrest in, 29, 231n14, 235n31; slavery and, 77, 78, 240n59, 263n34; sovereignty clause, 242n64; suffrage and, 113, 116, 240n58, 254n39, 254n40; unemployment insurance and, 154; veto power of executive in, 41; voting age, lowering of, 169
Mathias, Charles, 184
Matlack, Timothy, 36, 237n46
Matthews, Burnita Shelton, 170
Mayhew, David, 8
Mayor of N.Y. v. Miln (1837), 53
McCall, Samuel, 272n20
McCarver, Morton, 75, 259n23
McClean, John, 73, 74, 258n17
McClernand, John, 72, 257n11
McCloskey, Robert, 53, 147, 159
McCormick, Ruth, 118
McCulloch, William, 164
McCulloch v. Maryland (1819), 51–52, 224n20, 246–47n8
McKean, Thomas, 34, 36
McKinley, William, 107
McLeod, Clarence, 134
McMillin, Benton, 96
McReynolds, James, 158
Mehrotra, Ajay, 97, 105
Melton, James, 11
Mercer, John Francis, 41
Merriam, Charles Edward, 107
Mettler, Suzanne, 159–60
Michigan: admission to statehood, 251n31; banking law and, 53–54; constitution (1835), 54, 247n13; constitution (1850), 54; constitutional convention (1961–1963), 167; convict slavery and, 267n53; gender equality clauses and, 170; initiative measures and, 180, 275n40; pension laws and, 153; primary elections and, 108; prohibition and, 129, 134, 277n59; slavery and, 76, 78; suffrage and, 115, 117, 253n36, 269n66; tax-cap amendments and, 186; voting age, lowering of, 168

Mid-Atlantic states, slavery in, 39
Mifflin, Thomas, 56
Military Reconstruction Act of 1867, 269n66
Milkis, Sidney, 12
Miller, Frieda, 171
Minnesota, 77, 99, 105, 108, 137, 169, 267n53, 269n66
Minor v. Happersett (1875), 114, 117, 275–76n43
misattribution of national outcomes, 11–14, 192–93
Mississippi: Black citizenship and, 79, 262n33, 268n61; constitution (1832), 252n31; constitutional convention (1890), 139–41; income tax and, 104, 273n24; labor regulation and, 141; legislative apportionment and, 167; poll taxes and, 162–64; primary elections and, 274n32; prohibition and, 127; Reconstruction-era constitutions, 83, 84, 86; secession of, 264n40; slavery and, 57, 65, 252n31, 258n17; suffrage and, 163–65; Thirteenth Amendment ratification and, 266nn51–52; voting age, lowering of, 169
Missouri: citizen initiative and, 275n40; constitution (1820), 247n15; constitutional convention ballot measures rejected (2002), 180; income tax and, 273n24; labor relations and bargaining rights, 152; pension law and, 153; prohibition and, 129, 133, 279n72; in Reconstruction era, 83; slavery and, 58, 251n28, 251n30, 263n34; suffrage and, 269n66; tax-cap amendments and, 186; Thirteenth Amendment ratification and, 84
Missouri Compromise, 57–58, 65, 76, 251n30, 267n53
Monroe, James, 63
Montana, 105, 129, 132–33, 137, 151–52, 169, 173, 269n65, 282n7, 290n55
morality legislation, 15, 17*f*, 136–37
Morrill Anti-Bigamy Act of 1862, 138
Morris, Gouverneur, 40, 43, 241n61, 243n65, 244n71
Morrison, Martin, 129

Morton, Samuel George, 74
Mott, Lucretia, 112
Mugler v. Kansas (1887), 277n61
Munn v. Illinois (1877), 271n14
Murdock, Orrice, 289n47
Murphy, Claudia Quigley, 116
Murray, John (Lord Dunmore), 26, 235n36
Musmanno, Michael, 11, 135

Nash, Gary B., 35
National American Woman Suffrage Association (NAWSA), 116–20, 122, 135–36, 170, 276n43, 276n50
National Archives and Records Administration (NARA) data, 15
National Association for the Advancement of Colored People (NAACP), 147, 148, 160, 162–63, 165, 192
National Bank, 20, 21, 48, 51–53, 246n5, 246–47n8
National Child Labor Committee (NCLC), 142–43
National Committee to Abolish the Poll Tax, 160, 162–63
National Conference on State and Local Taxation, 102
National Congress of Mothers, 152
National Consumers League, 150–51, 170
National Federation of Business, 171, 173
National Governors' Conference, 166
National Grange, 99, 275n39
National Industrial Recovery Act of 1933, 148, 150
National Municipal League, 166
National Organization of Women (NOW), 172–73, 175–76
National Protective Association, 126
National Resources Planning Board, 156
National Tax Association, 102
National Tax Limitation Committee (NTLC), 183–84
National Taxpayers Union (NTU), 183–84
National Woman's Party (NWP), 119, 169–70, 176

National Woman Suffrage Association (NWSA), 22, 113–16
Native Americans: frontier regulation and, 27, 29; Jackson and, 48; slavery and, 230n6, 242n62; suffrage and, 254n40, 267n55
NBER–University of Maryland State Constitutions Project, 228n58, 229n63, 270n1, 282n2
Nebraska: ERA ratification and, 173; income tax and, 103, 105; intangible property tax and, 273n25; prohibition and, 126, 129; senatorial elections and, 108–9, 275n40; state constitutional construction in, 229n60; suffrage and, 115; voting age, lowering of, 169; wage and working-condition protections and, 141–42
Nelson, Adolphus, 121
Nelson, John, 134
Nevada: budget clause and, 185; ERA ratification and, 291n56; income tax and, 273n26; parochial schooling and, 137; pension law and, 152, 156; prohibition and, 132–33; Reconstruction and, 81; senatorial elections and, 108, 274n31, 275n40; slavery and, 84, 264n42; tax-cap provisions and, 186; voting age, lowering of, 169
Nevins, Alan, 37
Newcober, Mabel, 102
New Deal (1932–1939), 7, 22, 145–63, 191; labor regulation, 148, 151–52, 157; pensions and pension law, 151–59; poll tax repeal, 160–61, 192; poor-relief programs, 152, 284n16; state reforms' role in, 146–47; topics of proposed federal amendments during, 15, 16f, 147–48, 149t
New Deal and Great Society era (1932–1979), 22–23, 145–78; gender-equality clauses, 169–77; pension laws and, 151–54; poor-relief programs, 152–54; state constitutionalism in, 146–47, 159, 176–77; suffrage and, 160–69; topics of proposed amendments during, 15–16, 16f, 147–48, 149t; unemployment insurance and, 154

New England: abolition and, 84; banking law and, 51; due process clauses in, 38–39, 250n25; prohibition and, 123; Revolutionary unrest in, 30, 231n14; secession proposal, 245n1; suffrage and, 254n40, 269n65

New Hampshire: bill of rights, state, 244n76; constitutional amendment process in, 232n19; constitution (1784) modeled on Massachusetts, 37, 44, 237n44; first state constitutional convention, 30–32, 236n40, 236–37nn43–44; gender equality clauses and, 290n55; income tax and, 273n24; initiative process to amend constitution in, 222n10; minimum wage law and, 151; parochial school funding and, 137; prohibition and, 124, 133; Revolutionary unrest in, 234n28; slavery and, 39, 78, 79; suffrage and, 240n58, 262n32

New Jersey: constitutional amendment process in, 34–35, 228–29n60, 236n43; ERA ratification and, 175–76; first state constitutional convention, 31, 232n19, 234n30; gender equality clauses and, 290n53; gradual emancipation law in, 39, 241n61; labor relations and bargaining rights, 152; minimum wage law and, 151; no bill of rights, 244n76; prohibition and, 132–35; Revolutionary unrest in, 234n28; slavery and, 241n61; state constitutional convention delegate elections in, 34; suffrage and, 113, 230n8, 254n40, 269n66, 275n41

New Mexico, 69–72, 75, 105, 173, 255n43, 259n22, 290n55

Newsome, State v. (1844), 263n33

New State Ice Co. v. Liebmann (1932), 145

New York: Act for Regulating Slaves (1702), 230n6; bill of rights, state, 244n76; Bill of Rights ratification and, 44; child labor and, 142; constitution (1777), 245n3; constitution (1821), 245n3; constitution (1846), 54; constitutional amendment process in, 236n43; constitutional convention (1776), 39, 234n30, 236n40, 252n35; constitutional convention (1846), 248n17; constitutional conventions rejected (1977 & 2017), 180; election of judicial, administrative, and local officials, 55; Electoral College votes (1850s), 256n8; ERA ratification and, 174–75; federal income tax and, 103; gender equality clauses and, 170; gradual emancipation law in, 39, 241n61; income tax and, 101, 105, 273n24; judicial review in, 38, 41–42; labor relations and, 151, 152, 171, 254n40; literacy tests and, 165; minimum wage law and, 151, 157; personal liberty law and, 250n25; prohibition and, 132–33; Revolutionary unrest in, 231n11, 231n14, 234n31, 235n31; senatorial elections and, 274n34; slavery and, 77, 79, 230n6, 241n61, 250n25, 257n15, 261n27, 263n34; state constitutional convention delegate elections in, 34; state system of governance, 243nn69–70; suffrage and, 38, 113, 118, 254n40, 255n43, 262n32; Trespass Act (1783), 38; veto power of executive in, 41; workers' compensation and, 151

New York Manumission Society, 241n61

Nicholas, John, 56, 252n34

Nicholson, Odas, 173–74

Nimham, Daniel, 29

Nineteenth Amendment, 4, 22, 62, 90–92, 122–23, 144, 193, 277n58

Nixon, Richard, 172, 184

Nonimportation Clause, 251n30

noninterventionism (antebellum era), 56–59, 62

North Carolina: bicameralism in, 37, 239n55; bill of rights, state, 244n76; Bill of Rights ratification and, 44; budget clause and, 185; charter of, 230n5; citizenship and, 262–63n33; constitutional amendment process in, 236n43; constitutional convention (1875), 139; enumeration of rights and, 242n64; equal protection clause and, 268n61; first constitution, 36; income tax and, 97–99, 273n24; judicial review and, 38, 41–42, 240n57; legislative apportionment and, 167; poll taxes and, 162; prohibition and, 127; Reconstruction-era constitutions, 86, 236n43; Revolutionary unrest in, 30, 235n31; secession of, 264n40; slavery and, 39, 73, 230n6, 250n25; state constitutional convention delegate elections in, 34; suffrage and, 162, 165, 254n39, 254n40, 255n43

North Carolina Cession Act, 55–56, 249n21

North Dakota, 109, 116, 124, 133, 137, 153, 170, 173, 273n24

Northwest Ordinance (1787), 55–57, 76, 249n21, 267n53

Northwest Territory, 60, 249n22

Nott, Josiah C., 74

obviation, 3t, 5, 7, 8; suffrage and, 62, 64–65. See also circumvention; preclusion

O'Connor, Sandra Day, 223n20

Ohio: banking and corporate law in, 53–54; child labor and, 142; citizen initiative and, 275n40; convict slavery and, 267n53; Electoral College votes (1850s), 256n8; ERA ratification and, 173; gender equality clauses and, 170; income tax and, 105; labor regulation and, 141–42; minimum wage law and, 151; pension laws and assistance to the blind and, 152–54; prohibition and, 127, 129, 135; slavery and, 56, 57, 65, 78, 250n26, 251n30, 257n15, 261n28; state debt cap and, 185; suffrage and, 113, 117, 253n36, 269n66; Thirteenth Amendment ratification and, 266n51; unemployment insurance and, 154, 158

Oklahoma, 99, 104, 127, 141, 168–70, 186, 273n24, 275n40

Old-Age and Survivors Insurance program, 284n17

Old Age Assistance (OAA) program, 155–56

Oliver, Andrew, 29

Olney, Richard, 96

Omaha National Bank v. Spire (1986), 229n60

Oregon: Black immigration and movement in, 78–79; citizen initiative and, 275n40; gender equality clauses and, 290n53; income tax and, 105; labor regulation, 141; prohibition and, 129, 131, 134; senatorial election and, 107–11; slavery and, 76, 77, 251–52n31, 259–60n23, 262n31; suffrage and, 115, 117, 165, 269n66

Orfield, Lester B., 11

Osborn v. Bank of the U.S. (1824), 51–52

Otis, James, 29

Owen, Robert, 109–10

Oxford Commentaries on the State Constitutions of the United States, 17, 255n43

Paine, Thomas, 34, 36, 48; *Common Sense*, 36, 237n45

Palmer, A. Mitchell, 118

Panic of 1837, 54–55, 97, 246n3, 249n20

Panic of 1893, 96, 98, 99

Panic of 1907, 102

Park, Maud Wood, 170

Parliamentary sovereignty, 25–28, 30

partisan realignment, 7, 7f, 8, 12, 15, 67, 188, 192, 223n17

Patterson, William, 41, 243n68

Paul, Alice, 117–18, 120, 128, 169–70, 288n41

Paxton's Case (1761), 29

Payne, Sereno, 272n20

Pell, Claiborne, 167, 288n39

Pendleton, George, 265n44

Penn, William, 230n5

Pennsylvania: Act for Better Regulating Negroes in the Province (1726), 230n6; banking law and, 51; bicameral legislature in, 35; bill of rights, state, 35–36, 244n76; Bill of Rights ratification and, 44; Black citizenship and, 79; Charter of 1681, 230n5; Constitution (1776), 35, 37, 238nn48–50, 239n56; Constitution (1790), 37, 236n42; Constitution (1873), 115; Council of Censors, 34–35, 236n42; Electoral College votes (1850s), 256n8; enumeration of rights and, 242n64; ERA ratification and, 173–74; Executive Council, 35; frontier regulation and, 27; gender equality clauses and,

Pennsylvania (*continued*)
290n55; gradual emancipation law in, 39, 241n61; legislative apportionment, 35–36, 230–31n9; as model for other state constitutions, 36, 48, 243n70; pension law and, 153; personal liberty law and, 73, 250n25; presidential electors and, 64; prohibition and, 132–33, 135; Provincial Conference (1776), 24–25, 31, 33–35, 236nn40–42, 237n45; Provincial Convention (1775), 35, 237n45; Revolutionary unrest in, 235n31; senatorial elections and, 109, 274n36; slavery and, 77, 230n6, 235n38, 241n61, 250n25, 257n15, 261n27; state constitutional convention delegate elections in, 34; suffrage and, 35, 253n36, 254n40, 255n43; term limits and, 35; unicameral legislature in, 35–36, 237–38n47, 243n67

pensions and pension law, 22, 151–59, 177

People ex rel. See name of party

Pepper, Claude, 162–63

Pepper, George, 143

Perkins, Frances, 154–55, 158, 171

personal liberty laws, 71, 73, 77–80, 250n25, 257n15, 261nn27–29, 263n34, 263n37

Personal Liberty League, 127

Peterson, Esther, 171

Philadelphia Convention (1787). *See* Constitutional Convention

Phillips, Wendell, 66, 112, 140

Pickering, Timothy, 249n23

Pinckney, Charles Cotesworth, 40, 42, 235n36

Platt, Jonas, 61

Plehn, Carl C., 98, 99

Plessy v. Ferguson (1896), 139

Plumb, Preston, 124

polarization: federal constitutional amendment process and, 11, 181; slavery and, 77. *See also* partisan realignment

political question doctrine, 223n20

Pollack, Sheldon, 103

Pollock v. Farmer's Loan and Trust (1895), 96–99, 101–3, 105

poll taxes, use of and repeal of, 9, 10, 23, 27, 139, 147, 148, 160–64, 177, 191, 192, 264n42, 269n66

Pomeroy, Samuel, 113

poor-relief programs, 152–53

popular constitutionalism, 2, 14, 225n32. *See also* initiative and referendum processes

popular vote for senators. *See* Senate, U.S.

populism: in elections of early 1800s, 63; in first state constitutions, 34, 36; in tax-cap initiatives, 186

Populist Party, 94–96, 107, 126

Powell, Lazarus, 82

preclusion: in antebellum era, 49, 61, 62, 65, 258n16; as passive federal response, 5; in Progressive era, 105; providing resolution at state level to national issues, 189, 192

preemption, 2–3, 3*t*, 189, 221n3

Prendergast, William, 29, 231n11

Prentiss, Samuel, 58

pressure buildup and venting, 8, 10, 23, 68, 181

Prigg v. Pennsylvania (1842), 67, 73, 77, 258n18, 261n27

Privileges and Immunities Clause, 4, 73, 74, 79, 85, 262n31, 262n33, 267n57, 275–76n43

Progressive era (1878–1931), 7, 13, 15, 21–22, 90–144, 191; Article V in, 91–93, 115, 118, 143; conflict decentralization in, 91, 92, 94, 112; convergence in, 91–136; female suffrage and, 112–23, 136; income tax and, 94–106; labor relations and, 21–22, 140–43, 151; senatorial elections and, 106–12; state constitutional amendment process in, 92, 228n59; state experimentation in, 101, 108, 115–16, 143; topics of proposed federal amendments during, 15, 16*f*, 68–69, 93–94, 95*t;* workers' compensation and, 151. *See also* prohibition; suffrage

prohibition, 15, 21–22, 90, 92–94, 98, 123–36, 136*f*, 143–44, 191, 278n63

Prohibition Party, 123–26, 278n64

Proxmire, William, 167

public purpose doctrine, 158

Quincy, Josiah, 249n23

Raker, John, 121
Randolph, Edmund, 40–41, 51, 56
Randolph, Jennings, 168–69
Randolph, John, 41–42
Raskob, John, 133
Raushenbush, Paul, 154
Ray, George, 138
Reagan, John H., 125
Reagan era, 7, 173, 179, 183–84, 187, 191
Reconstruction Acts of 1867, 86–87, 89
Reconstruction Amendments, 19, 21, 69, 82, 89, 190. *See also* Fifteenth Amendment; Fourteenth Amendment; Thirteenth Amendment
Reconstruction era (1865–1877), 7, 15, 66–89; abolition of slavery and, 82–83, 266n49, 266n51; citizenship of Blacks and, 68–69, 74, 78–80, 82–87; conflict decentralization in, 69; congressional dictation and convergence in, 10, 81–89, 190; convergence in, 68–69, 81–89; erosion of Black rights after, 88, 139–40; ex-Confederates' disenfranchisement, 81, 86–87; income tax and, 97; Joint Committee on Reconstruction, 85; number of federal amendments proposed during, 82, 256n1; presidential dictation in, 80–81, 88, 190; readmission of Southern states, 82–83; slavery and, 69–75; state constitutional slavery and Reconstruction clauses (1776–1877), 213–19; suffrage of Black voters, 15, 87–89, 269nn65–66; topics of proposed federal amendments during, 15, 16f, 66, 70t; working hours, regulation of, 87. *See also* abolition of slavery; Reconstruction Amendments; suffrage
redistricting. *See* legislative apportionment
Reed v. Reed (1971), 173
Rehnquist, William, 223n20
Republicans: Article V and, 180; in Civil War era, 77, 79–80, 265n44; in contemporary era, 8; ERA ratification and, 171; fiscal-restraint platform (1994), 187; Fourteenth Amendment and, 267–68n59; income tax and, 103; in Kansas (1850s), 260n25; legislative apportionment and, 166–68; in Pennsylvania (1770s), 239n56; poll tax ban and, 160; in Progressive era, 90–91, 96, 107–8, 125–26, 133–34; in Reconstruction era, 85–87, 89, 190, 266n52, 269n66; senatorial elections and, 275n39; tax-cap provisions and, 183–84
Revenue Act of 1894, 96–97
Revolutionary era (1760–1791), 24–46, 190; abolition of slavery, 26–27, 39, 43; colonial period and unrest, 26–30; conflict decentralization in, 25; first state constitutional conventions, 19, 30–32, 33; slavery and, 19, 20, 21, 25, 33–40, 190, 213–19; state constitutions as model for drafting of federal constitution, 40–46; suffrage and, 25, 29, 38–40, 230n8, 231n10, 240n58, 244n71. *See also* Constitutional Convention
Revolutionary War, 31–32
Reynolds v. Simms (1964), 166–67
Reynolds v. United States (1879), 138
Rhode Island: Bill of Rights ratification and, 44; budget clause and, 185; charter of, 236n40, 244n76; federal income tax and, 103; gender equality clauses and, 170, 290n53; income tax and, 105; judicial review in, 38, 41–42; prohibition and, 133–34; Revolutionary unrest in, 29; slavery and, 26–27, 39, 77, 240n58, 241n60; suffrage and, 61–62, 115, 240n58, 255n41, 255n43, 262n32
Rhodes v. Iowa (1898), 127–28, 131
Richardson, Norman E., 127
Roane, Spencer, 246n7
Roberts, Brigham H., 138
Roberts, Owen, 157
Roberts, Willis, 167
Roberts v. City of Boston (1850), 262n32
Robinson, William, 113
Robin v. Hardaway (1772), 242n62
Roe v. Wade (1973), 173

Roosevelt, Eleanor, 171, 289n47
Roosevelt, Franklin Delano, 22, 134, 146, 150–51, 154–57, 159–63. *See also* New Deal
Roosevelt, Theodore, 91, 102–3, 117, 119
Root, Elihu, 106
Rosenberg, Gerald, 161
runaway slaves. *See* Fugitive Slave Acts; fugitive slaves; personal liberty laws
Rush, Benjamin, 26, 237n45
Rutgers v. Waddington (1784), 38, 240n57
Rutledge, Edward, 31
Rutledge, John, 34, 232–33n20, 244nn72–73
Rutledge, John, Jr., 56

same-sex marriages, 174–75, 183, 188
Saulsbury, Willard, 82, 121
Schermerhorn, Richard, 174
Schlafly, Phyllis, 173–76
Schlesinger, Arthur M., 283–84n15
school prayer, 16, 181
Scott, J. W., 116
Scott, Melinda, 170
Scott v. Emerson (1852), 263n34
Scown v. Szarnecki (1914), 276n49
Second Continental Congress. *See* Continental Congress (1776)
Second National Bank. *See* National Bank
Securities Act of 1933, 148
Seligman, Edwin R. A., 94, 100, 102
Senate, U.S.: conservative control in Progressive era, 91; elections, 91–94, 106–12, 110*f*, 143, 191, 273–74n30
Seneca Falls Convention of 1848, 112
Seneca Falls Convention of 1923, 170
Sensenbrenner, James, 176
Sentinels of the Republic, 143, 147
separation of powers, 36–38, 40, 238–39n53
Seventeenth Amendment, 22, 90–92, 94, 107, 111, 130, 140, 144, 150, 275n40
Seward, William, 77, 265n46, 266n52
Shackleford, Dorsey, 138, 280n84
Shafroth-Palmer amendment (1914), 118, 119

Shannon, W. E., 259n23
sharecroppers, 84
Sharkey, William, 266n51
Sharp, Granville, 26
Shaw, Lemuel, 258n16, 262n32
Sheppard, Morris, 129–30, 144
Sheppard-Hobson amendment of 1914, 129
Sherman, Roger, 32, 41–42, 44–45, 244n73
Sherwood, Winfield S., 75–76
Silzer, George, 132
Simon, Paul, 183
Sirovich, William, 283n11
Sixteenth Amendment, 22, 90–91, 94, 96, 102–3, 105–6, 111, 130, 144, 150, 271n15, 272n19
Skowronek, Stephen, 12, 48
slavery: in antebellum era, 4, 20–21, 24, 48–49, 55–59, 65, 68, 72, 74, 88, 190; balancing slave vs. free states, 56, 69, 75; in Civil War era, 68, 69–75, 190; in colonial period, 26, 29, 31, 230nn6–7; Constitutional Convention (1787) and, 42, 244n73; as criminal punishment, 84, 267n53; Declaration of Independence and, 32–33, 235n32; due process clauses and, 38–39, 240n59; first judicial abolition of, 39; freedom suits in state courts, 39, 242n62; proposed federal rights and amendments (1788–2020), 17*f*; in Revolutionary-era state constitutions, 19, 20, 21, 25, 33–40, 190; state constitutional slavery and Reconstruction clauses (1776–1877), 213–19; states' rights and, 58, 235n39; territorial slavery question, 57–58, 65, 69–72, 75–77, 251n30, 257n12, 263n34. *See also* abolition of slavery; Reconstruction era; Thirteenth Amendment
Smith, Abram, 78
Smith, Al, 132–34
Smith, Howard, 172
Smith, William, 110
Smith v. Brown & Cooper (1702), 230n7
Socialist Party, 270n2, 274n36
Social Security Act of 1935, 145, 146, 151, 154–59, 161, 177, 191, 284nn16–17

Soldier Voting Act of 1942, 163
Somerset v. Stewart (1772), 26, 29, 38, 78, 230n7, 258n16
South Carolina: banking law and, 51; Bill of Rights ratification and, 44; charter of, 230n5; constitutional amendment process in, 236n43; constitutional convention (1895), 139; first constitution (1776), 232n19, 234n30; first state constitutional convention, 30–32, 34, 232n19; frontier regulation and, 27; income tax and, 99–100, 104–5, 273n24; legislative apportionment and, 167; no bill of rights, 244n76; poll tax and, 163; prohibition and, 128; Reconstruction-era constitutions, 83, 84; Revolutionary unrest in, 234n28; secession of, 80; senatorial elections and, 109; slavery and, 39, 73, 230n6, 235n36, 250n25; suffrage and, 38, 139, 165, 253n36; Thirteenth Amendment ratification and, 266n52
South Dakota, 99, 105, 115, 124, 129, 137, 168, 273n26, 275n40, 278n63
Southern Conference on Human Welfare, 162–63
Southern Electoral Reform League, 163
Southern states: child labor and, 142; convict slavery and, 84, 267n53; Fifteenth Amendment ratification and, 88; fiscal-reform measures, 184; fugitive slave acts and, 42–43, 57; Great Society and, 146; income tax and, 97, 99, 104, 272n22; literacy and residency requirements for voting, 160–61, 165; New Deal and welfare programs and, 146, 156, 159–60; new territories and states, slavery outcomes in, 71, 79; parochial schools and, 137; poll taxes and, 163–64; primary elections and, 274n32; prohibition and, 126; Reconstruction-era constitutions, 266n51; refusal to educate slaves in, 79; repeal of Fourteenth and Fifteenth Amendments, proposals for, 140; Revolutionary unrest in, 30; secession of, 66–68, 71, 80–81, 264nn40–42, 265n43; sharecroppers in, 84; slavery and, 38–39, 40, 190; suffrage and, 114–15, 117–18, 119–20, 162–63; Thirteenth Amendment ratification and, 84, 265n46. *See also* Confederate states; Jim Crow laws; suffrage *for racial disenfranchisement*
Southwest Ordinance (1790), 57
Spaight, Richard Dobbs, 42, 240n57
Stamp Act, 27–28, 40
Stanley, Robert, 102, 104
Stanmeyer, William, 176
Stanton, Elizabeth Cady, 112–14, 135, 267n58, 276n50
state amicus briefs, 223n20
state constitutional conventions. *See* constitutional conventions, state; *specific states*
state constitutional reform: difficulty of analyzing, 13–15, 18; ease of amending state constitutions, 6, 10, 193; effect on proposed federal amendments and national political development, 9, 9f, 10, 18–20, 20f, 189, 192, 193, 229n64; experimentation of, 5, 10, 14, 22, 24, 33, 64, 101, 108, 115–16, 143, 145, 153–55, 158, 170, 189, 191–92; failure to acknowledge importance of, 1, 10–11, 13–14, 192; failure to specify revision procedure, 256n4; methodology of study, 15–19, 226–27n52, 227–28n56–58, 229n63; modes of, 14, 17, 227n56; prevalence of, 1, 6, 14, 179, 222n10; quantitative vs. qualitative effects of, 18–19, 225n53; revision assemblies, 17, 18t, 195–210, 222n11; without accompanying national reform, 6, 84. *See also* deference; initiative and referendum processes; *specific states, eras, and subjects of amendments*
state constitutions: decreasing veneration, 6; first ones adopted prior to U.S. Constitution, 24, 32, 33, 211–12; flexibility of, 6, 10; length of, 6, 185; as model for drafting of federal constitution, 40–46; modernization initiative, 166–67. *See also specific states and regions*
State Declarations of Rights, 44

states' rights, 16f, 30, 33, 51, 52, 84, 113, 118, 122, 125, 181, 224n20, 233n23, 235n39, 242n64, 244n73, 270n67, 279n71
Stenholm, Charles W., 184
Sterett, Susan, 159, 285n21
Stevens, Lillian M. N., 278n64
Stevens, Thaddeus, 85, 265n43, 267n57
Stevenson, William, 269n66
Steward Mach. Co. v. Davis (1937), 157–59
stock market crash (1929), 144
Stone, Harlan, 157–58
Stone, Lucy, 112–16, 275–76n43
STOP ERA campaign, 173
Story, Joseph, 73, 246n7, 258n18
Stovall, Thelma, 173
Strader v. Graham (1851), 74, 79, 259n20, 263n34
Strauss, David, 15, 180
Struble, Isaac S., 125
suffrage: in antebellum era, 20–21, 49, 59–64, 80, 190, 253–54n38; Black voting rights, 15, 87–89, 112, 114, 190, 262n32, 269nn65–66; Constitutional Convention (1787) and, 42; dictation and, 4; early franchise law, 5, 25, 29, 38–40, 230n8, 231n10, 240n58, 244n71; ex-Confederates' disenfranchisement, 81, 86–87, 112, 139, 265n46, 269n66; first state constitutions and, 25; Fourteenth Amendment and, 267n57; frontiersmen and, 20, 27, 33, 60; immigrants and small farmers, disenfranchisement of, 60, 61; literacy and residency requirements, 23, 139, 160–61, 165, 191; in New Deal and Great Society era, 145, 160–69; political stability and, 255n43; in Progressive era, 15–16, 21; proposed federal rights and amendments (1788–2020), 17f; racial disenfranchisement, 10, 23, 60, 69, 82–84, 85–86, 112, 139, 193, 254n40, 264n42, 266n49, 266n52, 269nn65–66; Revolutionary unrest and, 26; voting age, lowering of, 3t, 4, 148, 168–69, 193; women's voting rights, 3t, 8, 22, 91–94, 112–23, 121f, 130, 143, 191, 193, 254n40, 267n58, 275n41. *See also* poll taxes
Sullivan, John, 231–32n16
Sumner, Charles, 76, 82, 86, 112, 264n42, 267n53, 268n60, 269n65
Sundquist, James, 12
supermajority requirement to amend state constitutions, 133, 222n10
supermajority requirement to amend U.S. Constitution: in antebellum era, 43, 64; as barrier to amendment, 2, 11, 64, 180, 193; in contemporary era, 187; in Jeffersonian era, 20; New Deal and, 142, 146, 150; in Progressive era, 91–93, 97, 106, 133, 137; rare party realignments and, 7, 161, 184, 192, 224n27; in Reconstruction era, 67, 89. *See also* Article V
supersession, 2–3, 3t, 181, 289n46
super-statutory reform, 16, 147, 159, 180, 192
Supremacy Clause, 3, 44, 221n3, 279n78
Supreme Court, U.S.: in antebellum era, 4, 21, 47–48, 49, 53, 62, 64; in Civil War era, 21, 67, 73–75, 79–80, 88; in contemporary era, 180–81, 184, 187–88, 191–92; Court-packing proposal of FDR, 22, 157; dictation of state law, 88; in Great Society era, 145, 147, 161, 164, 173; in New Deal era, 22, 147–51, 157, 159–60, 162, 165, 177; in Progressive era, 8, 22, 91–94, 96, 98, 107, 114, 117, 124–25, 127, 138–43; role of constitutional reinterpretation by, 12. *See also* federal courts; judicial review; *specific case names and justices*
Sutherland, George, 110, 158

Taft, William Howard, 91, 102–3, 117
Taft-Hartley Act of 1947, 285n23
Tallmadge, Eugene, 163
Tallmadge, James, Jr., 57, 250n26, 251n29
Taney, Roger B., 53, 66, 73–74, 78–80, 223n20, 247n12, 258nn17–18, 259n20, 263nn35–36, 264n38
Taney Court, 47–48, 53, 62, 64

Tariff Act of 1833, 52
taxes: corporation tax, 103; first Congress and, 45; inheritance tax, 102, 272n19; property tax, 185, 272n19, 273n26; slavery and, 20; Stamp Act and, 27–28; tax-cap provisions, 16, 181, 183–86, 292n9. *See also* income tax; poll taxes
Taylor, John, 48
Taylor, John W., 57–58, 251n30
Taylor v. United States (1990), 224n21
Tennessee: budget clause and, 185; citizenship and, 262n33; constitutional convention (1870), 139; ERA ratification and, 173; Fifteenth Amendment ratification and, 88; income tax and, 99, 273n24; judicial elections and, 248n18; poll taxes and, 162, 163; privileges and immunities and, 247n13; prohibition and, 127; in Reconstruction era, 81; secession of, 264n40; slavery and, 57, 65; suffrage and, 60, 122, 139, 251n27, 254n40; tax-cap provisions and, 185–86; Thirteenth Amendment ratification and, 84
Tennessee Valley Authority, 148
Tenth Amendment, 3, 45, 51, 56
term limits, 16f, 23, 35, 52, 93, 180, 181, 292n6
Territories Clause, 60, 71, 79, 269n65
Texas: admission to statehood, 251n31; constitution (1845), 251n31; ERA ratification and, 173–74; gender equality clauses and, 290n55; income tax and, 83, 99, 104, 273n26; poll taxes and, 162–65; slavery and, 73; suffrage and, 115, 122, 165, 255n43, 269n66
Texas v. Johnson (1989), 183
Texas v. White (1869), 265n46
Thatcher, George, 56
third parties, 91, 191
Thirteenth Amendment, 4, 66, 82–84, 86, 227n53, 265n46, 266nn51–52, 267n55, 269n65
Thomas, Charles, 122
Thomas, People ex rel. v. Scott (1897), 271n13

Thompson, Smith, 73, 258n17
Three-Fifths Clause, 42, 56, 87
Thurmond, Strom, 184, 286n29
Tichenor, Daniel, 12
Tocqueville, Alexis de, 37, 45, 47
Toombs, Robert, 78
Townsend, John, 171
Train, George Francis, 113
Trevett v. Weeden (1786), 38
tripartite government model, 37, 40–41, 43, 239n53
Truman, Harry, 163
Trumbull, Jonathan, 29
Trumbull, Lyman, 85, 266–67n53
Tucker, St. George, 48, 242n62
Tushnet, Mark, 9
Twelfth Amendment, 47
Twentieth Amendment, 225n53
Twenty-Fifth Amendment, 161
Twenty-First Amendment, 22, 90, 93, 135
Twenty-Fourth Amendment, 4, 9, 10, 23, 62, 147, 161, 164–65, 177, 191–93
Twenty-Seventh Amendment, 179
Twenty-Sixth Amendment, 4, 62, 161, 193
Twenty-Third Amendment, 161
Tydings, Joseph, 167
Tyler, John, 62

Uhler, Lewis, 183, 185–86
Underwood, Oscar, 122, 281n86
unicameral legislative model, 35–36, 41, 190, 237–38n47, 239n55, 243nn66–67
United Auto Workers (UAW), 172
United States' Brewers Association, 125
United States v. See name of opposing party
Urofsky, Melvin, 159
U.S. Constitution: brevity and vagueness of, 12–13; compared to other national constitutions, 1, 11, 13, 221n1; drafting of and reliance on state models, 40–46; gradual court reinterpretation of, 8, 12, 13, 188, 189; inflexibility of, 2, 11–12; preeminence and veneration of, 1, 13, 46, 48, 67, 147,

U.S. Constitution (*continued*)
180, 188–89, 225n33; ratification of, 43–44, 188; signing by framers, 188; stability of, 1–2, 11–13, 16, 47, 188–89, 223n17, 226n50; wholesale replacement of, 226n51. *See also* Article V; federal constitutional amendment; *specific Amendments*

Utah: citizen initiative and, 275n40; gender equality clauses and, 290n55; income tax and, 99, 105; labor relations and, 140, 142; minimum wage and, 151; polygamy and, 138, 290n55; slavery and, 71–72, 75, 259n22; suffrage and, 115–16

Valelly, Richard, 161
Van Buren, Martin, 55, 60, 63, 253–54n38
Vandenburg, Arthur, 168
Vanderbilt, Alva, 170
Van Devanter, Willis, 158
Vardaman, James, 140
Vassall, Anthony, 240n59
Vermont: bill of rights, state, 244n76; constitutional amendment process in, 34–35; constitution modeled on Pennsylvania's, 36; ERA ratification and, 175; first constitutional convention of, 236n40; income tax and, 105; judicial abolition of slavery in, 39; prohibition and, 124, 129, 133; Revolutionary unrest in, 235n31; slavery and, 77–78, 250n25; state system of governance, 243n70; suffrage and, 240n58, 254n40, 262n32
Vesey, Denmark, 73
Vest, George, 114, 117, 125
veto powers: constitutional adoption of, 41, 238–39n53; item-veto provision, 23, 181, 187, 292n9
Vile, John R., 15
Virginia: bicameral model of governance, 20, 35, 37; bill of rights, state, 244n76; Bill of Rights ratification and, 44–45; budget clause and, 185; citizenship and, 262n33; constitution (1776), 38, 211, 234nn27–28, 234n30, 235n35; constitution (1851),

260n26; constitutional amendment process in, 236n43; constitutional convention (1901–1902), 139; Council of Censors, 41; court system in, 232n18; Electoral College votes (1850s), 256n8; equal protection clause and, 268nn61–62; ERA ratification and, 290–91nn55–56, 291n56; first state constitutional convention, 25, 30–32, 232n19, 236n40; freedom suits in, 242n62; frontier regulation and, 27; gender equality clauses and, 173, 290n55; income tax and, 97, 99–100, 272n22, 273n24; judicial review in, 38; as model for federal constitution, 40–41; as model for other state constitutions, 25; poll taxes and, 163–64; preamble to state constitution, 32, 233–34nn26–27; prohibition and, 129, 131; Reconstruction-era constitutions, 81, 83, 86; Revolutionary unrest in, 28, 238–39n53; secession of, 264n40, 264n42; slavery and, 29, 32, 39, 230n6, 235nn35–37, 250n25, 257n14; suffrage and, 38, 163–65, 252n33, 253n35, 254n40, 255n43; Thirteenth Amendment ratification and, 84
Volstead, Andrew, 131
Volstead Act of 1919, 131–33, 279nn71–72
Voluntary Committee of Lawyers, 135
Vorenberg, Michael, 84
Vose, Clement, 11, 282–83n9
voting rights. *See* suffrage
Voting Rights Act of 1965, 23, 145, 147–48, 161, 164–65, 167, 169, 178, 192

Wade-Davis Bill (1864), 82, 265n46, 266n52
Wadsworth, James, 122
Wagner, Robert, 156
Wagner-Peyser Act of 1933, 154
Walker, Joseph, 142
Walpole, Robert, 26
Walsh, Thomas, 143, 144, 170
Warren, Earl, 166
Warren Court, 16, 181
Washington, 107, 115, 117, 129, 133–34, 137, 174, 273n26, 290n55

Washington, D.C. *See* District of Columbia
Washington, George, 56
Webb, Edwin, 129–30
Webb-Kenyon Act of 1913, 128–30
Webster, Daniel, 71
Weeks, John, 121
Weisman, Steven, 105
Wesberry v. Sanders (1964), 166
West Coast Hotel v. Parrish (1937), 151
Western expansion and new states, 52, 61, 67–68, 91, 104, 108, 121, 137–38
West Virginia, 81, 105, 122, 153, 185, 264n42, 269n66
Whately, Thomas, 28
Wheeler, Wayne, 130, 133
Whigs, 33, 36–38, 60–61, 77, 234n29, 237n45, 239n56, 240n58, 243n69, 252n32, 253n36, 254n40, 257n11
White, Sue Shelton, 169
White Citizen Council, 165
White House Conference on the Care of Dependent Children (1909), 152
Whiton, Edward, 261n29
Whittier, John Greenleaf, 261n28
Whittington, Keith, 48, 53, 152
Wickard v. Filburn (1942), 158
Wickersham Report (1931), 134
Wilcox, James, 162
William and Mary (British monarchs), 26, 231n14
Williams, John Sharp, 122
Williams, Robert, 37
Williams, Thomas, 258n16
Williams v. Mississippi (1898), 122, 140
Willis, Edwin, 286n30
Willson v. Black-Bird Creek Marsh Co. (1829), 53, 224n20, 247n11
Wilmot, David, 71
Wilmot Proviso, 257n11
Wilson, James, 25, 40–42, 44–45, 230n4, 233n25, 243n66, 243n68, 243n70, 246n4

Wilson, James Falconer, 125
Wilson, William B., 283n11
Wilson, Woodrow, 1, 23, 91, 107, 109, 118–20, 122
Wilson Act of 1890, 125, 127
Wisconsin: admission to statehood, 251n31; constitutional convention (1846), 248–49n18; convict slavery and, 267n53; ERA ratification and, 176; gender equality clauses and, 288n41; income tax and, 100–101, 273n27; legislative apportionment and, 168; primary elections and, 108; prohibition and, 133; slavery and, 76, 78, 263n34; suffrage and, 117, 253n36, 269n66; unemployment insurance, 151, 154–55, 158
Wisconsin Manufacturers Association, 100
Witte, Edwin E., 154–56, 158
Woman's Christian Temperance Union (WCTU), 124–28, 278n64
women. *See* gender-equality clauses; labor and commerce; suffrage
Women's Organization for National Prohibition Reform, 133–34
Women's Trade Union League, 118, 170
Wood, Fernando, 265n43, 265n46
Woolman, John, 26
Worcester v. Georgia (1832), 52
worker protections. *See* labor and commerce
Workingmen's Party, 61, 99
Works Progress Administration, 284n16
World War I, 130
World War II, 183
Wozencraft, Oliver M., 75
Wyandotte Convention, 260n25
Wyoming, 115–16, 142, 273n26, 290n55
Wythe, George, 30–32, 37, 39, 41, 234n28, 238n53, 242n62

Young, Thomas, 36
Younger, Maud, 119